Sexual Politics in the Enlightenment

SUNY Series,
The Margins of Literature

Mihai I. Spariosu, Editor

Sexual Politics in the Enlightenment

Women Writers Read Rousseau

Mary Seidman Trouille

State University of New York Press

Production by Ruth Fisher
Marketing by Dana E. Yanulavich

Published by
State University of New York Press, Albany

© 1997 State University of New York

For information, address the State University of New York Press,
State University Plaza, Albany, NY 12246

Library of Congress Cataloging-in-Publication Data

Trouille, Mary Seidman, 1951–
    Sexual politics in the Enlightenment : women writers read Rousseau
/ Mary Seidman Trouille.
        p.   cm. — (SUNY series, the margins of literature)
    Includes index.
    ISBN 0-7914-3489-3 (alk. paper). — ISBN 0-7914-3490-7 (pbk.   :
alk. paper)
        1. Rousseau, Jean-Jacques, 1712–1778—Criticism and
interpretation—History—18th century.   2. Rousseau, Jean-Jacques,
1712–1778—Influence.   3. French literature—Women authors—History
and criticism.   4. French literature—18th century—History and
criticism.   5. Feminism and literature—France—History—18th
century.   6. Sex role in literature.   7. Enlightenment.   I. Title.
II. Series.
PQ2053.T74   1997
840.9'9287'09033—dc21   96-44093
                                                                    CIP

Contents

Acknowledgments

This study originally took shape under the direction of Bernadette Fort and Sylvie Romanowski at Northwestern University. I wish to express my deepest gratitude to both for their intellectual guidance and continuing support and encouragement for my project as it has developed over the past few years. I would also like to thank Lawrence Lipking, Christine Froula, and Catharine Stimpson, who read the manuscript in its early stages, for their guidance and support. I am equally grateful to Charlotte Hogsett, Suellen Diaconoff, Julia Douthwaite, and Felicia B. Sturzer for their pertinent comments and expert criticism of the project in its later stages. Finally, I wish to thank Madelyn Gutwirth, Gita May, Nancy Miller, and Janet Altman for their ground-breaking work on eighteenth-century women writers and for the inspiring models of scholarship they provided.

Above all, I wish to thank the members of my family for their unfailing encouragement and support: my mother Virginia Seidman, my husband Bruno, and my children Jennifer, David, and Laura.

Portrait of Rousseau by Maurice-Quentin de La Tour. Courtesy of the Bibliothèque nationale, Paris.

Introduction

Rousseau and His Women Readers

Jean-Jacques Rousseau's views on women have long been the subject of discussion and debate. Nearly all his major works deal, in one way or another, with women's role and education and with the broader issues of sexual politics—the analysis of gender differences and of power relations between the sexes. The view of women that emerges from his writings is complex and contradictory, full of ambivalence and discontinuities. It is not surprising, then, that his views have given rise to widely divergent interpretations among both his contemporaries and our own. With the burgeoning of feminist studies over the past three decades, Rousseau's sexual politics have become the subject of renewed interest and controversy. While some feminist critics regard his writings on women as particularly striking examples of misogyny and paternalism,[1] other Rousseau scholars (feminist and otherwise) have defended him against these charges, arguing that his views on women are considerably more complex and ambiguous than this first interpretation suggests and that, to be understood fully, they must be judged in the context of his life and times.[2] Still others have pointed to what they consider feminist or pro-woman undercurrents in Rousseau's writings (particularly in *Julie* and Book I of *Emile*), which in their view help explain the enthusiastic response of many eighteenth-century female readers to his vision of women's role and education.[3]

However, in all these various studies, relatively little attention has been paid to negative reactions to Rousseau among eighteenth-century women readers. It generally has been assumed that women reacted favorably to his sexual politics, when in fact a number of his female contemporaries wrote pointed critiques of his views, particularly

1

on the subject of women's education. With the exception of Mary Wollstonecraft's criticism of *Emile* in *A Vindication of the Rights of Woman*, these negative appraisals largely have been ignored. At the same time, few studies have explored the reasons behind the positive response to Rousseau's views expressed by other women of the period and, specifically, the impact of class origins and upbringing on their response. Finally, few studies have explored the contradictions in Rousseau's teachings on women and the ambivalent response of women themselves to these contradictions. Although they may have wholeheartedly supported Rousseau's ideal of domesticity, some women found his teachings difficult to follow, either because they were unable to marry (for lack of a dowry, physical appeal, or a suitable husband) or because, once married, they found marriage and motherhood unfulfilling. Despite genuine efforts to conform to Rousseau's feminine ideals of modesty and self-effacement, some women—married and unmarried alike—ultimately found these ideals stifling and felt inwardly torn by the powerful urgings of their talents and aspirations. It is indeed paradoxical that the women writers to whom Rousseau appealed most strongly were often those who, because of their superior gifts and idealistic expectations, were least apt to content themselves with the limited role he prescribed for them.

I have sought to probe these questions and contradictions by comparing how seven women authors of the late eighteenth century responded to Rousseau's writings and sexual politics. The writers include six Frenchwomen (Roland, d'Epinay, Staël, Genlis, Gouges, and an anonymous woman correspondent who called herself Henriette) and the English feminist Wollstonecraft. All seven wrote enthusiastic eulogies or vehement critiques (and, in some cases, both) of Rousseau in the course of their careers. They also responded to each other's reactions to Rousseau, thereby creating a fascinating network of opinions and polemic on the nature, role, and education of women—a curious Enlightenment sequel to the Renaissance Querelle des Femmes, centered around a man who voiced extremely ambivalent views about women.

ﻖﻖﻖﻖ

A comparative study of Rousseau's reception by his female contemporaries raises a number of intriguing questions. How can one explain the puzzling fact that his views on women's nature, role, and education—views that seem reactionary, paternalistic, even blatantly misogynic today—met with such enthusiastic approval among so many women and had such tremendous impact on their ideals, behavior, and family life? Similarly, why is it that Roland, Gouges, and Staël—three of the most progressive and politically active women of their time, whose lives seem incompatible with Rousseau's views on women—became such fervent admirers and defenders of his character and writings? Their enthusiasm for Rousseau forms a curious contrast to the sharp criticism of him voiced by d'Epinay and Genlis, who appear—on the surface at least—more conservative and traditional in their behavior, in their views on women, and in their view of themselves as women writers. Finally, why is it that women of middle-class background seem to have responded with greater enthusiasm to Rousseau's ideals of domesticity and motherhood and to his rhetoric of moral reform, while the women of aristocratic origins appear more ambivalent in their response?

There are a number of possible explanations for Rousseau's paradoxical popularity among his female readers. His appeal may have stemmed in part from a deeply rooted traditionalism conditioned in women by society, from a tacit (albeit self-defeating) support for the status quo. This is the explanation advanced by Condorcet. At the end of his *Lettres d'un bourgeois de Newhaven* (1787), after boldly calling for equal education and civil rights for women and for their full participation in the public sphere, Condorcet adds an ironic note:

> Perhaps you will find this discussion too long; but remember that it concerns the rights of half the human race, rights forgotten by all the legislators. . . . Yet I am afraid of antagonizing women if they ever read this piece. For I speak of their rights to equality, and not of their sway over men; they may suspect me of a secret desire to diminish their power. Ever since Rousseau won their approval by declaring that women are destined only to take care of us and to torment us, I cannot hope to gain their support.[4]

Rousseau's popularity among his women contemporaries might also be attributed to an unconscious distortion, or even to a conscious transformation of his views in accordance with their own needs and values. During the French Revolution, for example, Rousseau's popularizers (male as well as female) appear to have reformulated his sexual politics—indeed, his politics in general—in order to further their own polemical and reformist goals.[5] Rather than seek to understand Rousseau's complex views on women, these readers seem instead to have simplified and distorted them to suit their own personal and political objectives.

Even if their views on women and their political and literary activities seem incompatible with Rousseau's sexual politics (as in the case of Staël, Wollstonecraft, and Roland), his women readers still identified with him and with the characters of his novels because they expressed, on an existential level, their deepest aspirations and longings—for ideal love, self-fulfilling motherhood, and domestic felicity. In an age of loveless marriages and widespread adultery, they saw Rousseau as the champion of a new moral order in which women could play a central role. By nursing their babies themselves (instead of sending them away to wet-nurses, as had long been the custom), by devoting themselves to their husbands and children and to domestic and charitable tasks, they hoped to create stronger affective ties within their families, thereby fostering the moral regeneration of society envisioned by Rousseau and by other moral reformers of the period. Far from being considered a trap, the ideals of motherhood and enlightened domesticity advocated by Rousseau seemed to offer a new dignity to women, regardless of their socio-economic status.

Linked to this rhetoric of moral reform and to the ideals of motherhood and domesticity it fostered was the ideal of romantic sensibility celebrated by Rousseau in *Julie*. This pre-Romantic exaltation of sensibility was widely imitated by writers of both sexes. Rousseau's appeal was particularly strong among women writers in the realms of autobiography and autobiographical fiction. For he not only offered them a new dignity as women and a valorization of *la vie intérieure* (in the double sense of domestic life and affective experience) but, more importantly, he opened up to them exciting new possibilities for self-analysis and self-revelation. Following his bold example, certain women writers dared to transgress social and literary conventions in order to reveal their innermost feelings and experiences in ways that both shocked and thrilled their contemporaries. The writings of Roland, Wollstonecraft, Staël, and Gouges are particularly striking examples of transgressive, innovative women's writing. Their works, like Rousseau's, reflect the increased politicization of discourse during the years directly preceding and following the French Revolution—a development accompanied by a gradual breakdown of boundaries between private and public life, as well as between private and public genres of writing.[6]

A number of women authors seem to have viewed Rousseau as a superior soul, victim of a narrow-minded public incapable of understanding or appreciating him—as a scapegoat who aroused their compassion and symbolized their own frustrations as writers and public figures. For example, both Gouges and Roland identified strongly with Rousseau's persona of persecuted virtue. Guillotined the same month by the Jacobin government, both women viewed Rousseau as a martyr to virtue, misunderstood and maligned by the public. Staël links this martyr image of Rousseau to the popular view of him as a defender of the weak, the unhappy, and the politically disenfranchised— an image that appealed strongly to women readers and that figures prominently in Henriette's correspondence with Rousseau.

Finally, even women who openly criticized Rousseau recognized his eloquence and powers of persuasion over others. This was true of Wollstonecraft and Genlis, as well as the Dutch-born Swiss writer Isabelle de Charrière. Although she strongly disagreed with Rousseau's views on female education, Charrière admired the eloquence of his style: "How is it possible, with such ordinary words often used so ineffectively by others, that he is able to captivate his readers and please them so greatly?"[7] Charrière underlined the seductiveness of Rousseau's writing, which she claimed could have both positive and negative effects on his readers: "To hold people's attention, one must know like Rousseau how to spin a web of illusions and to sing them with a siren's voice."[8] Like Wollstonecraft, Genlis cautioned that it was Rousseau's persuasiveness that explained his popularity and that made his influence so pernicious at times. Yet, like Charrière and Staël, she recognized that Rousseau's eloquence could also have a positive effect on his readers by promoting progressive reforms. For example, after accusing him of plagiarizing Locke, Genlis conceded that Rousseau had been far more persuasive than the English philosopher and consequently more successful in spreading his progressive educational theories and methods than Locke himself. Similarly, both Staël and Roland credited Rousseau with successfully promoting stronger family bonds through his moving depictions of motherhood and domesticity.

⁂

The first chapter examines Rousseau's sexual politics in relation to the gender ideology and social realities of his period. After tracing the traditionalist, feminist (or "pro-woman"), and pseudo-feminist strands interwoven in his writings, I examine how women readers responded to these different strands in Rousseau's thought and how his rhetoric of moral reform and Romantic sensibility influenced the way they viewed their role in society. Chapter 1 concludes with a discussion of the conflicting interpretations to which Rousseau's writings on women and the family gave rise, particularly in the decade following the French Revolution.

The other chapters explore the way seven eighteenth-century women writers responded to Rousseau's sexual politics and his influence on their lives and writings. Chapter 2 examines Rousseau's little-known correspondence with Henriette, a bluestocking and aspiring writer who first wrote to him following the publication of *Emile*. Though timid and respectful in tone, Henriette's response to *Emile* challenges the ideals of domesticity and sensibility advocated by Rousseau, whom she nonetheless greatly admired. Henriette's letters to Rousseau express with eloquence and acuity the plight of the single woman and *femme savante* in eighteenth-century society. Her loneliness and frustrations are echoed in the writings of numerous other women of her period who, like her, were unable to marry for lack of a dowry and who sought to console themselves through intellectual and literary endeavors. The correspondence between Henriette and Rousseau not only throws an interesting light on the image of Jean-Jacques constructed by his women readers according to their own needs and longings, but also presents a unique case history of Rousseau's interaction with an unmarried woman intellectual—his grappling with her dilemma and with the shortcomings of his own teachings on women.

Chapter 3 deals with Louise d'Epinay, Rousseau's one-time friend and benefactress and later his bitter enemy. Of the women included in my study, Mme d'Epinay was the only one to have exerted a strong influence on Rousseau both as a person and as a writer. Although he balked and scoffed at her influence, he found it inescapable, much as she did his. During the last thirty years of her life, she was engaged with him in an intense intellectual and literary rivalry that challenged his narrow vision of women's role and capabilities. After tracing Rousseau's determining influence on d'Epinay's literary career and the challenge to his sexual politics underlying her works, I examine how the rivalry between them served as a key motivating force behind several of Rousseau's major works and how he, in turn, influenced d'Epinay's view of herself as a woman writer and the reception of her works by readers and critics.

In Chapter 4, I look at Rousseau's influence on Manon Phlipon, who later became the wife of Jean-Marie Roland, Minister of the Interior after the Revolution. Her case is a particularly striking illustration of Rousseau's paradoxical appeal; for, of all the women in this study, Roland made the greatest effort to conform her outward behavior to the limited role prescribed by Rousseau. Yet, while seeming to conform to the feminine ideals and norms he advocated, she in fact undermined them by blurring the gender dichotomies and the distinction between public and private spheres that lay at the very core of his discourse on women.

Chapter 5 examines Germaine de Staël's and Mary Wollstonecraft's efforts to transcend traditional gender roles through their literary and political activities. Focusing specifically on Staël's *Lettres sur Rousseau* and Wollstonecraft's critique of them, I compare their very different but equally ambivalent responses to Rousseau. Both were passionate admirers and, at the same time, strong critics of Jean-Jacques; yet both were strangely unaware of—or unwilling to recognize—their own ambivalence. This curious lack of self-insight on the part of two of the most perspicacious women of the period is particularly well demonstrated in Wollstonecraft's scathing critiques of Staël's *Lettres sur Rousseau*, in which she ignores Staël's pointed criticism of his views on women's education and ridicules Staël's admiration for *Julie*—an admiration she nonetheless shared. In the course of Staël's career as a writer and public figure, her views on women and on Rousseau would evolve along parallel lines to those of Wollstonecraft. In a second preface to the *Lettres sur Rousseau* written in 1814 (three years before her death and many years after Wollstonecraft's), Staël in fact outlines a number of the same criticisms of *Emile* that Wollstonecraft developed in the *Rights of Woman*. Moreover, in their mature works, both writers present incisive analyses of the condition of women in society and hold out for future generations a bold new vision of woman—a model each strove to embody in her life and writing.

In Chapter 6, I probe the crucial influence of class and political outlook on Rousseau's reception among women readers by comparing how two women from opposite poles of the social and political spectrum responded to his character and writings: Countess Stéphanie de Genlis, staunch royalist and head tutor to Louis-Philippe, and Olympe de Gouges, a semi-literate woman of working-class origins, whose radical feminist republican manifestoes eventually led her to the guillotine. Although as an outspoken political writer and courtesan turned playwright, Gouges represented everything Rousseau despised, and although she herself rejected the ideal of marriage and domesticity he advocated, she continued to idolize him and to view him as her spiritual father. Like Roland, Gouges identified intensely with Rousseau's egalitarian spirit and with his persona of persecuted virtue, without realizing that it was in large part his narrow views on women and their strong influence on the Jacobin leaders' policies toward women that had led to her persecution. Gouges's enthusiasm for Rousseau forms a curious contrast to the bitter diatribes against him by Genlis, who was far more conservative in her views on women's proper role. For Genlis, who idealized the Classical purity of seventeenth-century literature and the socio-political stability of Louis XIV's reign, Revolution and Romanticism went hand in hand; the moral and political excesses of the Revolution were clearly linked to a disruptive egalitarian spirit and to a dangerous exaltation of sensibility, both of which she traced back to Rousseau. While Genlis was a firm advocate of the Rousseauian ideals of enlightened domesticity and motherhood, she rejected Rousseau's limited view of female capabilities and insisted on the liberating force of a solid education for women.

In the concluding chapter, I compare the seven women's responses to Rousseau and examine the differing degrees and types of influence he had on their work and on their views of themselves as women writers. Specifically, I discuss the extent to which these women adopted, rejected, or transformed Rousseau's feminine ideals; the impact their upbringing and class origins had on their response to Rousseau and on their view of themselves as women writers; and the extent to which his ideal of sensibility and his negative opinion of women writers stimulated or inhibited their self-expression. Finally, I point out gender- and genre-linked differences in the way these authors responded to conflicting motivations and conventions in their writing, particularly in their autobiographical works.

౸ᔕᦗᦀᦣ

The analyses I propose here go beyond current studies of reader response to Rousseau, such as those by Robert Darnton and Claude Labrosse, which generally fail to account for gender differences.[9] Whereas the model of the Rousseauian reader proposed by Darnton and Labrosse is one of unquestioning adoration of—and identification with—Rousseau, the response of the women in my study is considerably more nuanced and ambivalent. To better understand the gender-linked aspects of reader response to Rousseau, I draw on feminist work in reception theory, such as Judith Fetterley's *The Resisting Reader* and the collection of essays titled *Gender and Reading*, edited by Flynn and Schweickart.[10]

I also explore the meaning of these women's contradictory and self-contradictory readings of Rousseau—how these contradictions reflect the ambiguous status of women, and particularly that of women writers, in the late eighteenth century. To what extent are Rousseau's sexual politics and these women's responses to him typical or atypical of the period? Although Rousseau's views on women in many ways reflect the gender ideology of his period and culture, he himself was clearly atypical both as a male writer and as a male. It is in fact his *atypicality*—his deviation from gender and genre-based norms and conventions—that makes him such a fascinating subject for study and comparison. As for these women who responded to him with criticism or ambivalence, are they not atypical of their period by the very fact that they dared to take pen in hand and express their reservations publicly?

Finally, I have examined the obstacles that faced women writers of the period and the themes that recur in eighteenth- and nineteenth-century critiques of their lives and works: the bluestocking, the virago (or *homme-femme*), the unnatural mother, the whore. In order to write, they needed to overcome the traditional prejudices against women writers, as well as the interiorized feelings of inferiority and the fear of censure conditioned in them by society—negative gender stereotypes that Rousseau's writings both reflected and intensified. By exploring the prejudices and material problems confronting these women and the risks they took in pursuing a literary career, we can appreciate more fully what they were able to accomplish.

This is the first book-length feminist study of Rousseau's sexual politics and the reception of his works by women readers. A few studies have examined his reception by individual writers, notably Gita May's work on Roland and Madelyn Gutwirth's work on Staël. However, no single study has yet traced Rousseau's influence on women writers over several generations or traced the impact of class origins and political allegiances on their responses to him. While others have been content to remark (often patronizingly) on the paradox of Rousseau's appeal to women readers, I have sought to provide a framework for understanding the sources, limits, and dilemmas of that appeal by comparing how these seven women responded to Rousseau and by exploring the effects of each woman's conflictual relationship to him on her life and work.

Portrait of Rousseau by Allan Ramsay in 1766, painted during his stay in England with the philosopher David Hume. Rousseau is shown here in his famous Armenian outfit, with fur hat and collar. Courtesy of the Bibliothèque nationale, Paris.

1

Rousseau's Views on Women

Although Rousseau's sexual politics have received considerable attention in recent years from scholars in a variety of fields, much critical discussion of his views is undermined by an inadequate framework of textual and historical reference. There is a tendency to cull anti-feminist remarks from his writings in order to conjure up an ominous, yet entertaining portrait of Rousseau the reactionary misogynist, whom our enlightened twentieth-century minds enjoy ridiculing. There is also a tendency to isolate certain passages from the texts in which they appear and from the general corpus of Rousseau's works, as well as from the socio-historical context in which they were written, thereby ignoring factors that might explain or counterbalance the views expressed.[1] For example, numerous studies have been made of Rousseau's sexual politics based solely on readings of Book V of *Emile* that ignore the more positive views toward women expressed in Book I. Similarly, critics are quick to point to the antifeminist aspects of *La Lettre à d'Alembert*, without taking into account the more favorable view of women presented in *La Nouvelle Héloïse*.

On the other hand, studies that attempt to present a comprehensive, systematic view of Rousseau's sexual politics tend to distort his views on women by ignoring underlying contradictions and ambiguities or by trying to resolve them and make them fit into a coherent system. For example, Stephen Salkever writes: "The problem of Rousseau seems to be that he presents us with two very different ways of life. . . . One is characterized by reason, sociality, and activity, the other by sentiment, nature, solitude, and idleness. The task of much of the critical literature concerning Rousseau has been that of determining how these apparently mutually exclusive patterns can be explained and/or resolved into a single coherent system."[2] Similarly, Colette Piau-Gillot maintains: "Rousseau's fictional heroines can be seen as the concrete representations of a theoretical model of the new woman, mediatress of a new order. . . . This model has a specific function in a coherent philosophical-political system."[3] This tendency toward simplification and systematization also characterizes the two best-known studies of Rousseau's sexual politics by Paul Hoffmann and Joel Schwartz.[4]

It is my contention that Rousseau's sexual politics are too complex to be reduced to a single coherent system. To fully grasp the richness and complexity of his views on women, one must resist the desire to systematize what is not systematic, to simplify what is not simple; more importantly, one must resist the urge to resolve or efface tensions and contradictions that are deeply rooted in, even constitutive of, Rousseau's thought and the thought of his period. Rousseau himself admits the contradictory nature of his thinking. In the Second Preface to *Julie*, feigning irritation with N's persistent questions, "R" retorts: "You want us always to be consistent; I doubt this is humanly possible; but it *is* possible always to be truthful and frank, and that is what I hope to be."[5] Similarly, Julie writes of Saint-Preux (Rousseau's avowed fictional alter-ego): "He is less inclined to search for universal principles now that he has seen so many exceptions; his love for the truth has cured him of rigidly systematic ways of thinking" (II: 427). For Rousseau, it is less important to be consistent with oneself than to engage in the search for truth, a search which (in his view) necessarily involves the recognition of contradictions as a potential source of truth.[6] Hence the bold caveat in *Emile*: "Readers, forgive my paradoxes. Anyone engaged in serious reflection is bound to produce them."[7] This acceptance of contradictions as a constructive, dynamic by-product of reflection is at the very core of Enlightenment thought, and to ignore it is to run the risk of misreading much of the writing of the period.

A second contention underlying my study is that the formal aspects of a work—particularly the conventions and constraints of genre—exert a determining influence on the portrayal of characters and the presentation of ideas. Few studies of Rousseau's sexual politics have sought to analyze the relation between form and content. In this chapter, I examine how seeming discontinuities in Rousseau's writings on women can be traced to differences in genre, voice, and audience. As for women's response to Rousseau, I argue that it was the very ambiguity of his writings on women—the possibility for multiple and even contradictory readings—that contributed in large part to their widespread appeal among female readers of his day.

∂๑๑๑

Let us begin by examining Rousseau's views on women and the contradictions underlying his portrayal of Julie and Sophie, the heroines of his two major fictional works. In the second half of this chapter, I then situate Rousseau's sexual politics in relation to the gender ideology of his period. After tracing the traditionalist, feminist, and pseudo-feminist strands interwoven in his writings, I discuss how women readers responded to these different strands in Rousseau's thought and how his rhetoric of moral reform and pre-Romantic sensibility influenced their values and behavior. The chapter concludes with a look at the conflicting interpretations to which Rousseau's writings on women and the family gave rise, particularly in the decade following the French Revolution.

Rousseau's Views on Women's Nature, Role, and Destiny

For Rousseau, anatomy is destiny. In his view, women's physiology determines their fate, both biologically and socially. From the moment of birth, a girl's life is entirely conditioned and programmed by her sexuality, by her "nature" as a female: "A male is male only at certain moments, whereas a female is female all her life . . . ; she is constantly reminded of her sex," he maintains (IV: 697). By underlining the continuity between woman's procreative function and her social role as wife, mother, and *maîtresse de maison*, Rousseau subtly shifts from the physical to the psychological, from the natural to the social, which he presents as mutually reinforcing and mutually justifying. The anatomy of women serves to distinguish them from men and to define their primary role and destiny, which (in Rousseau's view) is to bear and care for the young in order to assure the survival of the species. He invokes this natural teleology both to restrict the role and education of women and to explain their inequality.

At the core of Rousseau's thought is an idealized concept of nature that serves both as the fundamental guide for human relations and institutions and as the basis for social criticism.[8] He views nature "not just as an external blueprint for human life, but as its inner truth . . . as a model for, and source of, moral regeneration," remarks Genevieve Lloyd. For Rousseau, she maintains, "nature is both a nostalgically remembered mythical past of the human species and a

This engraving by de Launay served as the frontispiece for the 1782 edition of *Emile*. The original caption read: "L'éducation de l'homme commence à sa naissance" ("A man's education begins at birth"). In the foreground, a mother dutifully reads *Emile* as she breastfeeds one baby and changes another. Her daughter looks on, eager to learn from her mother's example. They are seated in a forest clearing at the foot of a pedestal bearing a larger than life bust of Rousseau, who by the 1780s had become a kind of patron saint for nursing mothers. Numerous other children are vying for their mother's attention or are raising garlands toward Jean-Jacques in a gesture of gratitude. In the background are scenes from Emile's childhood. Courtesy of the Bibliothèque nationale, Paris.

16

goal to be reattained."[9] Rousseau's appeal to nature is nowhere more apparent than in his discussion of sex and gender roles: "Do you wish to be well guided in everything?" he asks in *Emile*. "Then always follow nature's instructions. Everything that characterizes the female sex must be respected as nature has dictated" (IV: 700). Throughout his writings, Rousseau invokes nature—his own highly subjective and masculinist conception of it—to define women's role and to justify their subordination. In his view, it is the nature of man (i. e., the male sex) to be free and equal, just as it is the nature of woman to be dependent, unequal, and subordinate:

> Since dependance is a state natural to women, girls feels themselves made to obey; they have, or should have, little freedom. . . . Destined to obey a being as imperfect as man, a woman should learn to suffer—even to suffer injustice—at an early age, and to bear the wrongs of her husband without complaint. You will never reduce boys to the same point; their inner sense of justice rises up and rebels against such injustice, which nature never intended them to tolerate. (*Emile*, IV: 710–11)

It is clear that the egalitarian principles elaborated in the *Contrat Social* apply only to the male sex. In Rousseau's view, women are by nature denied not only the right, but even the desire for freedom, just as they are denied the instinct to resist injustice—an instinct considered "natural" in men.

Elsewhere in *Emile*, Rousseau attempts to sidestep disputes concerning the equality or inequality of the sexes by arguing that men and women are either equal or, insofar as they are different, not comparable. "Everything they have in common is derived from the human species, while their differences are all derived from their sex," he writes. "Through what they have in common, they are equal; through their differences, they are not comparable: the mind of a perfect woman and a perfect man should not resemble each other any more than should their appearance" (IV: 693). However, this principle of different but equal (which Rousseau also expounds in *Julie*) does not obscure the fact that he generally views women as inferior to men physically, intellectually, and morally. Even Julie, whose intellectual and moral superiority sets her above the common horde, recognizes her subordinate position within patriarchal structures: "I am a wife and mother; I know my place and I keep to it" (II: 578).

To justify the subordination of women and their relegation to the domestic sphere, Rousseau advanced an elaborate series of arguments: Since, in his view, the fundamental law of nature was the survival of the species, he maintained that woman's primary destiny was to fulfill her procreative and maternal functions and that activities outside the domestic sphere were basically incompatible with her role as wife and mother. To the law of the survival of the species Rousseau added *le droit du plus fort*—the right to dominance of the strongest.[10] In his view, man was destined by nature to be the master because of his superior intellect and physical force; weaker both in mind and in body, and further weakened by her procreative functions, woman was destined to be dependent upon and subordinate to man. Linked to the maternal role of woman was her role as educator and moral guardian of the family. According to Rousseau, the exclusion of women from public life was necessary to preserve the purity and moral vigor of the home, so that the family could become the basis for the moral regeneration of society.

Not surprisingly, Rousseau also appealed to traditional theological discourse on women. In the *Lettre à d'Alembert*, the First Discourse, and numerous passages of *Emile*, he maintained that women were responsible for the denatured, corrupt state of society. To compensate for the evils they had brought upon the world, these eighteenth-century Eves must be conditioned to sacrifice their own desires to the collective good and to submit unquestioningly to patriarchal authority: "Girls should be taught constraint at an early age. Dissipation, frivolity, and inconstancy are character flaws that easily develop if girls are allowed to yield to their first corrupt inclinations," warns Rousseau in *Emile*. "To avoid such problems, teach them self-control above all else. Because of our insane social practices, the life of a respectable woman is a perpetual struggle against herself; it is fitting that the female sex share the burden of the ills it has brought upon us" (IV: 709).

Finally, Rousseau advocates the segregation of the sexes through the strict maintenance of separate spheres. In his view, excessive familiarity between men and women leads not only to moral corruption and mutual scorn, but also to a progressive effacement of the "natural" differences and roles between them. The segregation of the sexes he called for was designed less as a discipline of love or a precaution against temptation than as a means of preserving the distinctive traits of each sex. It was, as Bernard Guyon observes, "a specific example of the law—never explicitly expressed, but underlying Rousseau's whole anthropological outlook—that difference is inherently corruptive."[11] Subscribing on the whole to traditional gender stereotypes, Rousseau distinguished between masculine and feminine traits, aptitudes, and roles down to the finest detail, even food preferences (sweets and dairy products for women, meat and wine for men).[12] He insisted on the need to preserve these so-called natural differences, arguing that women could not truly love or esteem effeminate men, any more than men could truly love or respect virile women. He was especially critical of Parisian society which, he claimed, "virilized" women and "effeminized" men, making both sexes less willing and less able to fulfill their natural role as parents and, in the case of men, their duty as citizens and soldiers. He warned that women who strove to cultivate the qualities and talents of men and to usurp their prerogatives only worked against their own interests, since (in his view) such behavior deprived them of their feminine charms and hence of their power to subjugate men.

In Rousseau's view, only by conforming to the role nature prescribed for them could women maintain their power over men. Drawing on the old myth of "feminine wiles," he argues that women's intuition and practical intelligence enable them to exert a covert but powerful influence over men that compensates for their physical weakness and material dependence. Since men depend on women for the satisfaction of their sexual desires and for their happiness, an astute woman can easily tip the balance of power in her favor. However, Rousseau insists that women should exercise this power discreetly and not attempt to usurp men's "natural" right to command. After asserting that "it is in the natural order of things that women should obey men," he adds an important explanatory note:

> Recalling that I recognize in women a natural talent for dominating men, many readers—I imagine—will accuse me of contradicting myself; yet they will be mistaken. There is an important difference between usurping the right to command and governing the one who commands. Woman's empire is one of gentle sweetness, artfulness, and an accommodating spirit. Her orders come as caresses, her threats as tears. She should rule her household like a minister his government, by having herself ordered to do what she wishes. . . . But when she fails to heed the voice of the true head of the family and tries to usurp his rights and to

command alone, this disorder leads to nothing but misery, scandal, and dishonor. (IV: 766–67)

The key to this passage is the distinction between woman's covert power and man's overt rule, which Rousseau illustrates by the comparison of the family to the state: A wife serves as her husband's prime minister, implementing the directives which he alone has the authority to establish, but which she has the power to influence.

According to Rousseau, this power hierarchy is grounded in nature and is beneficial to both sexes. He therefore strongly criticizes women who attempt to pervert it by usurping male prerogatives or by adopting traits traditionally ascribed to men. In his view, women's influence on men should be gentle and covert. "If a women is bitter and obstinate, it only increases her troubles and her husband's ill-treatment of her," he warns in *Emile*.

Heaven did not make women ingratiating and persuasive in order for them to be shrewish; nor did it make them weak to be imperious; it did not give them so sweet a voice to speak insults or such delicate features to be contorted by anger. . . . Each person should maintain the tone appropriate to his or her sex. Too gentle a husband can make a woman impertinent; but, unless a man is a monster, a gentle wife will triumph over him sooner or later. (IV: 711)

This passage, like many others in *Emile*, is *prescriptive* rather than *descriptive*. In these passages, Rousseau prescribes guidelines for proper female behavior by distinguishing certain traits as feminine (weakness, delicacy, submissiveness, persuasiveness) and others as unfeminine or otherwise unbecoming to women (shrewishness, anger, impertinence). Like the chapters in *Julie* describing domestic life at Clarens, Books I and V of *Emile* can be read as a fictionalized conduct book and domestic manual for eighteenth-century women. Reader response to *Julie* and *Emile* suggests that they did in fact function in precisely that way for many women—a point I illustrate later in this chapter.

∽◌◌◌∾

In his essays, Rousseau portrays relations between the sexes as a perpetual battle of wills in which each tries to dominate the other. He criticizes what he considers women's corruptive, emasculating influence on men in societies that allow unlimited contact between the sexes. In the *Discours sur l'inégalité*, for example, he denounces the overt rule of society by women as unnatural and describes romantic love as an artificial emotion invented by them to dominate the sex that nature intended them to obey. In his view, women's negative influence on men is nowhere more evident than in literature and the arts. "What kind of mind can one expect to find in a man solely occupied with the important task of amusing women?" he asks in the *Lettre à d'Alembert*. "Our talents and writings reflect our frivolous occupations—pleasant enough, but as petty and cold as our feelings."[13] Hence Rousseau's praise for—and idealized portrait of—the sexual mores and intellectual vigor of Genevan society. In Geneva, unlike Paris, sexually segregated clubs or *cercles* permit men to engage in serious intellectual discussion and debate, while women amuse themselves elsewhere in light, but decent female chitchat.

In his fictional works, Rousseau generally presents a more optimistic and idealized view of the power relations between the sexes. He describes the Wolmars' marriage, like that of the newlywed Sophie and Emile, as a relationship of interdependence, affection, and mutual esteem. Because of the natural differences between the sexes, their bodies and minds complement and complete each other, making of each couple an organic whole. "From this union arises an ethical being whose eyes are provided by the woman and arms by the man, but so entirely interdependent that the woman learns from the man what to see and the man learns from the woman what to do," he explains in *Emile* (IV: 720). Similarly, describing her marriage to Wolmar, Julie writes: "Each of us is exactly what the other needs; he enlightens me and I animate him; we are far better off together. We seem destined to form a single being, of which he is the mind and I the will" (II: 373–74). Yet Rousseau is careful to distinguish between interdependence and equality. In his view, the mutual dependence of men and women does not make them equal; their interdependence, being itself unequal, serves in fact to underline the superiority of men, who are supposedly more self-sufficient. Yet Rousseau is far from unambiguous on this point, since of all his fictional characters, it is Claire who is the most self-sufficient in relation to the opposite sex. She resolutely refuses to remarry, insisting that the institution of marriage is too constraining for her independent spirit.

Aside from Claire, however, Rousseau's women characters generally consider marriage their natural destiny and their greatest hope for happiness. Sophie sees in Emile the Telemachus of her dreams. Similarly, Julie declares that "man and woman are destined for each other;

it is nature's intention that they be united in marriage" (II: 456). She views her own *mariage de raison* with Wolmar as a liberation from the perils of romantic passion. Indeed, in the second preface to *Julie*, Rousseau presents his novel as a defense of companionate marriage:

> I like to imagine a man and his wife reading this book together and drawing from it new strength to persevere in their joint efforts. . . . How could they contemplate its portrayal of a happy companionate marriage, without wishing to emulate it . . . and without their own union being strengthened? (II: 23)

Rousseau views such *mariages d'estime* as the surest path to domestic harmony, social order, and personal happiness. His idealized view of such marriages is presented most forcefully in Julie's account of her wedding ceremony and the dramatic conversion to virtue that it caused in her: "The chaste and sublime duties of marriage, so crucial to the happiness, peace, order, and survival of the human race, the dignity and sanctity of the marriage vow, so forcefully expressed in the Scriptures—all this made such a strong impression on me that I seemed to feel a sudden inward revolution," she later recalls. "Suddenly, an unknown power seemed to correct the disorder of my affections and to set them straight according to the law of duty and nature" (II: 354).

Just as in Rousseau's ideal society the social contract would end the struggle for power among its citizens, so too in the ideal marriage he envisaged, mutual affection and esteem would resolve the war between the sexes and the disruptive, anti-social effects of passion. However, as Burgelin observes in his discussion of Book V of *Emile*, "This sounds good in theory, but in practice it seems as difficult to go from passion to marriage as it is to go from social disorder to the social contract. This is the main problem with Book V."[14] This same attempt to resolve the war between the sexes—that pernicious duel of desire and domination—through the harmony offered by companionate marriage underlies not only Book V of *Emile*, but also the second half of *Julie*.

The Rousseauian Ideals of Motherhood and Enlightened Domesticity

Like many of his contemporaries, Rousseau was alarmed by the high infant mortality rate in France, which exceeded fifty percent in the

This illustration by Jean-Michel Moreau le Jeune from the 1777 edition of *Emile* bears the caption: "Voilà la règle de la nature. Pourquoi la contrariez-vous?" ["This is the rule of nature. Why hinder it?"] This intimate family scene was clearly designed to support Rousseau's claim that a woman's natural role was to bear children, to nurse and raise them herself, and to provide a warm, nurturing environment for her family. Like other leading Enlightenment figures, Rousseau was concerned by his country's slow population growth and high infant mortality rate. He therefore opposed contraceptive practices and abortion and maintained that every married woman should bear at least four children. Courtesy of the Bibliothèque nationale, Paris.

mid-eighteenth century. He was not alone in arguing that each woman should produce at least four children in order to assure a stable population rate.[15] Like Montesquieu and Diderot, he disapproved of parents who, for social and economic reasons, forced their children into unhappy and mismatched marriages; for such matches, in addition to the grief they caused, were less likely to produce children. For the same reason, Rousseau criticized the widespread use of birth control (mainly in the form of coitus interruptus and herbal spermacides) and the frequency of abortions.[16] Rousseau charged that in their frivolous pursuit of pleasure, society women rejected both their procreative and maternal functions: "Not content to have stopped breastfeeding their children, women no longer want them at all," he charges in *Emile*.

> As soon as motherhood becomes burdensome, people find a way to avoid it altogether; they wish to perform a useless act in order to repeat it over and over. In this way, the attraction designed to multiply the human species is turned against it. When added to the other causes of depopulation, this practice foretells the impending doom of Europe. The sciences, arts, philosophy, and morals to which this mentality gives rise will soon turn Europe into a desert. (IV: 256)

Rousseau draws a parallel between the sterility of women and the sterility of the arts and sciences. The link is not simply metaphoric, but causal as well, since in his view intellectual and moral libertinism were closely related, feeding on each other and slowly, perniciously sapping a people's mental and moral vigor.

For Rousseau, the refusal of motherhood was both a symptom and a primary source of the moral corruption and egoism of urban society in eighteenth-century France. "If the force of blood ties is not strengthened by habit and solicitude, it becomes stifled in the first years of life, and the heart dies before ever being born," he warns in *Emile*.

> Because of this corruption of natural ties, the whole moral order deteriorates and the voice of nature is extinguished in everyone's heart; households become less animated, the touching sight of a newly formed family no longer binds husbands . . . . People are no longer fathers, mothers, children, brothers, nor sisters; they are barely acquainted, why would they love each other? People

think only of themselves. When the home is nothing but a place of sadness and solitude, it is only natural to seek to amuse oneself elsewhere. (IV: 257–58)

Rousseau's pessimistic portrayal of family life—or lack of it—in eighteenth-century French society was quite accurate historically, at least for the upper and upper-middle classes. Among the French aristocracy, it was not uncommon for husband and wife to maintain separate residences and to lead completely separate lives. Their children were sent away soon after birth, first to wet-nurses, often living far from their parents, then to boarding schools or convents. As adolescents, they were then brought home to be "polished" and married off as quickly and as advantageously as possible. Given these circumstances, affective ties had little chance to develop among family members. In many upper-class families, children scarcely knew their parents or siblings and grew to adulthood in an emotionally sterile environment. The intimate nuclear family as we know it simply did not exist—or only in rare cases—among the French aristocracy and haute bourgeoisie of the mid-1700s.[17]

   Rousseau maintained that if women conscientiously fulfilled their maternal role and remained at home to nurse and raise their children, family life could be revived, thereby fostering the moral regeneration of society as a whole. "If only mothers would breastfeed their children, then public morals would reform themselves," he affirms in *Emile*.

   The attraction of family life is the best antidote to bad morals . . . . When a family is lively and animated, domestic duties become a woman's fondest occupation and her husband's favorite amusement. The correction of this problem alone would soon lead to a general moral reform; nature would soon have reestablished all its rights. Once women become mothers again, soon men will again become fathers and husbands. (IV: 257–258)

Similarly, in *Julie*, he declares: "Mothers, if you conscientiously fulfill your duties, everyone else will fulfill theirs. . . . If you decide to be wives and mothers again, then the sweetest power on earth will be the most respected as well!" (II: 585).

   Anticipating twentieth-century psychological theory, Rousseau argued that it was not the biological fact of being a mother, but rather the daily physical contact of nursing and childrearing that fostered affective ties between mother and child. To women who were courageous enough to defy social customs and prejudices in order to nurse, Rousseau promised not only a happier domestic life, but also better health for themselves and their children: "I dare to promise these worthy mothers their husbands' solid and constant attachment, a truly filial tenderness from their children, . . . successful deliveries and easy recoveries, a strong and vigorous health, and the pleasure of seeing their daughters imitate them one day" (IV: 258–59). For several decades before the publication of *Emile*, doctors and moralists had urged mothers to nurse their children to help reduce the high mortality rate among infants and postpartum mothers.[18] In his efforts to promote maternal nursing, Rousseau was therefore following the most advanced medical opinion of his period. Thanks to his talents as a polemicist and popularizer, Rousseau's breastfeeding campaign had considerable impact on childrearing practices both in his own period and in succeeding generations.[19]

Commenting on Rousseau's impact on gender ideology in Revolutionary France, Carol Blum writes: "The reabsorption of the sexually active woman into the lactating mother, the substitution of a nutritive for a genital function, was a bold and daring provocation in the eighteenth century, where an egalitarian attitude toward women had become fashionable in enlightened and aristocratic circles."[20] Blum implies here that Rousseau's ideal of motherhood and his rhetoric of moral reform constituted a repressive and reactionary discourse designed to relegate women to a subordinate position after they had succeeded in achieving a certain degree of independence. While his writings on women may well have had a negative influence on the attitudes and policies of the revolutionary leaders, Rousseau and many of his followers considered his ideal of enlightened domesticity an empowering discourse for women—one that could restore their lost dignity, give them a positive influence over their husbands and children, and increase their chances for a happy, productive life.

This interpretation is borne out by Rousseau's advice to Mme de Berthier, a young countess who was expecting her first child and who had written to him of a deep melancholy and inner emptiness for which she could find no source nor remedy: "This inner emptiness of which you complain is only felt by hearts made to be filled. . . . I am offering you a remedy suggested to me by your condition. Breastfeed your child. . . . Don't send your daughter away to a convent. Raise her yourself."[21] He recognizes the unconventional nature of his advice and the class prejudices the young countess would need to defy in order to follow it: "Already I hear objections and a fuss. Out loud, people speak of inconveniences, lack of milk, a husband who is annoyed. Under their breath, they whisper about a woman who feels constrained by the tediousness of domestic life, by duties beneath her station, by the lack of pleasure." Yet Rousseau insists that he is offering her the only sure path to happiness:

> Pleasures? I promise you the kind that will truly fill your heart. It is not by accumulating pleasures that we become happy. The sweetest pleasures that exist are those brought by domestic life. The feelings we acquire in this intimate relationship are the most genuine, durable, and solid that can bind us to mortal beings. They are also the purest feelings, since they are closest both to nature and to social order and, by their sheer strength, steer us away from vice and base inclinations. (*CC*, v. 37: 206–7)

Rousseau concludes his letter by encouraging the young countess to abandon the superficial pleasures of society in order to secure for herself and her husband the simpler but more durable pleasures of domestic life: "Countesses don't ordinarily serve as wet-nurses and governesses; but then they must also learn to do without happiness. If you dislike the life of a bourgeois couple, if you let yourself be controlled by the opinion of others, then you must cure yourself of the thirst for happiness that torments you, for you will never satisfy it" (*CC*, v. 37: 207–8). The class distinctions in this passage suggest that Rousseau's breastfeeding campaign was addressed above all to aristocratic women and that the ideal of domesticity he was proposing was modelled after the lifestyle of the bourgeoisie—particularly the sober Genevan bourgeoisie of his youth recalled through the idealizing lens of memory and the unfulfilled longings of a motherless son.

Rousseau's firm belief in the soundness of his advice is illustrated by the fact that he encouraged his own friends to nurse their children by presenting them with a sash woven by his own hand as a wedding gift, to be worn on condition that they breastfeed their babies. For example, in a letter to Anne-Marie d'Ivernois on the eve of her wedding, Rousseau wrote: "To ensure your good fortune, wear this emblem of the ties of affection and love in which you will entwine your lucky spouse. Remember that by wearing a sash woven by the hand that outlined the duties of mothers, you are promising to fulfill those duties yourself."[22]

∽∞∾

Given the importance of maternal nursing in Rousseau's program of moral reform, it is surprising that no reference is made to it in *Julie*. It may be that Rousseau did not wish to mar his heroine's ethereal image by portraying her engaged in an activity as *terre-à-terre* as breastfeeding. Or perhaps it was only after doing research for *Emile* that Rousseau became convinced of the importance of maternal breast-feeding for the well-being of mothers and children. In any case, Julie's sons are well beyond the nursing stage by the time Saint-Preux returns to admire her in her maternal role. Despite this significant gap, it is *La Nouvelle Héloïse*, more than any other work, that presents Rousseau's most exalted vision of motherhood and domesticity. While Emile's mother is conspicuously absent and Sophie appears singularly ill-equipped for motherhood, given her limited education, Julie clearly represents the ideal mother-educator and the model upon which her educational methods are patterned. Referring to her cousin as "the perfect little mother" ("la petite maman par excellence"), Claire not only designates Julie as the model for her daughter's education, but asks that she raise her in her place: "I relinquish my maternal authority in your hands; and to make my daughter even more precious to me, turn her into another Julie if you can" (II: 439).

In his detailed and enthusiastic descriptions of daily life at Clarens, Rousseau presents his readers with a veritable manual of domestic economy and an eloquent exposition of his ideal of domesticity based on the bourgeois values of simplicity, order, utility, thrift, and virtue. Although Julie and Wolmar are both aristocrats by birth, their modest income and simple tastes lead them to adopt the bourgeois lifestyle of their Protestant compatriots. Both by necessity and by inclination, they have retired to their country estate, which has prospered thanks to their hard work and careful management. The secret of the Wolmars' prosperity lies above all in the successful division of labor and harmonious cooperation between the two spouses in their daily tasks.

∽∞∾

In the ideal world imagined by Rousseau, women would be so immersed in their maternal and domestic responsibilities that they would have neither the time, nor the energy, nor even the desire, to participate in activities outside the home: "Far from being a socialite, a true mother and housewife is no less a recluse in her home than a nun in a cloister," he maintains (IV: 737). The comparison of the home to a cloister recurs in another key passage of *Emile*:

> Will a woman be a nursing mother today and a warrior tomorrow? Will she change her temperament and tastes like a chameleon changes colors? Will she suddenly abandon the shelter of a cloistered life and domestic concerns for the harshness of the elements and for the labors, fatigues, and perils of war? Will she be fearful at some moments and courageous at others; now delicate, now robust? (IV: 699)

Not surprisingly, Rousseau appealed to nature—and specifically to physiology—to justify women's relegation to the domestic sphere. He consistently ignored—or chose to ignore—the extent to which social conditioning determined women's abilities, temperament, and physical condition, that it was society and not nature that made them "fearful" and "delicate," indeed that his very concept of nature was itself an ideological construct designed to naturalize and legitimize male hegemony.

In the ideal society imagined by Rousseau, women were excluded a priori from playing any military or political role, as indeed they were for the most part in reality. War and politics were the business of men, just as love and domestic life were the concern of women. Yet Rousseau did not consider women's exclusion from public life as a privation, but as a privilege. In his view, true happiness and moral decency were possible only in the domestic sphere, while the public sphere was inevitably a locus of corruption, exploitation, and misery. An early formulation of this view is found in Rousseau's unfinished play, *La Mort de Lucrèce*, written in 1754. Responding to a friend's complaint that she has imprisoned herself in her home, Lucrèce asks: "Do you call the pleasure of living peacefully in the bosom of one's family an imprisonment?"

> I will never need any company other than that of my Husband, my Father, and my Children to assure my happiness, nor anyone else's esteem besides theirs to satisfy my ambitions. I have always believed that the woman most worthy of esteem is the one spoken of the least, even to praise her. May the gods protect my

name from ever becoming famous: success of that kind is achieved by our sex only at the expense of happiness and innocence.[23]

In her celebration of the joys of domesticity, Lucrèce appears here as a prototype for the heroine of *La Nouvelle Héloïse*. Her words anticipate a particularly glowing tribute to Julie by Saint-Preux: "Heaven seems to have sent her here to demonstrate the excellence a human soul is capable of attaining, as well as the happiness that one can enjoy in the obscurity of private life" (II: 532).

Women's Education: Rousseau and les femmes savantes

Because women wielded such tremendous power over men for good or for ill, Rousseau underlined the importance of improving female education. Indeed, he saw the improvement of women's education as the key to his program of moral reform; for, in his view, only virtuous, intelligent, and conscientious mothers would be capable of raising children who would later become loving and morally responsible adults. It is Julie who best exemplifies the positive effect women could have on men. Numerous references are made to her powerful influence over friends and family. "My Julie," declares Claire, "you are made to reign. Your empire is the most absolute that I know . . . . Your heart animates everyone around it and gives them a new being" (II: 409).

Like Fénelon and Diderot, Rousseau was highly critical of the convent education traditionally given to girls, since it separated them from their families and, as a result, ill-prepared them for their future role as wives and mothers. He further maintained that convents were to a large extent responsible for the greater coquettishness, affectation, and moral laxity of women in Catholic countries: "Convents are veritable schools of coquetry, not the honest coquetry I spoke of earlier, but the type that leads to all the failings of women" (IV: 739). Rousseau considered the education of girls at home by enlightened, conscientious parents far better than the education available in either convents or boarding schools. He therefore opposed l'abbé de Saint-Pierre's proposal for the establishment of a network of boarding schools for girls.[24]

In Book V of *Emile*, Rousseau offers a detailed plan for women's education. He was especially interested in improving their moral education, which he considered far more important than either academic instruction or domestic training. According to this plan, girls would receive careful moral training to develop the qualities Rousseau considered essential to the fulfillment of their future role as wives and mothers: modesty, chastity, obedience, self-control, and—above all— solid moral judgment. Since, in his view, it was women's destiny to be subjected all their lives to the laws of decorum and to the authority and opinion of others, they should be taught self-discipline at an early age:

> Women should be subjected to constraint from an early age. This misfortune, if it is one at all, is inseparable from their sex. Throughout their lives, they will be subjected to the most constant and severe of restraints: the rules of decorum. They should be accustomed to constraint early, so that it costs them nothing to control their whims and to submit to the will of others. (IV: 709–10)

Rousseau insisted, however, that the moral conditioning of girls should be gentle and reasonable, since excessive constraint might incite rebellion, just as endless sermonizing could lead to boredom and to contempt for their duties.

In his prescriptions for female education, Rousseau aims for a happy medium between what he considers two equally dangerous extremes: leaving a girl in total ignorance (which would make her too dull a companion for her husband and too easy a target for seducers) or turning her into a bluestocking—who, by usurping male prerogatives and by neglecting her domestic duties, would disrupt both the sexual hierarchy and the equilibrium of family life. "Falling into opposite extremes, some would limit a woman's activities to sewing and spinning at home with her servants, making her nothing more than the head servant to her master," he remarks in *Emile*. "Others, not satisfied with guaranteeing her own rights, would have her usurp ours; for, placing her above us in the traits specific to her sex and making her our equal in everything else, doesn't that amount to giving woman the dominance that nature grants her husband?" (IV: 730).

Between the extremes exemplified by Agnès in Molière's *Ecole des Femmes* and Philaminte in his *Femmes Savantes*, Rousseau therefore sought a happy medium. In a simpler, healthier society, women would not need much education, aside from practical domestic training. But in the corrupt social world of eighteenth-century France, argued

Left: Illustration by Maurice Leloir for the *Confessions* bearing the caption "Rousseau enseignant les heures à Thérèse" (Rousseau teaching Thérèse how to tell time). *Right*: Portrait of Louise d'Epinay by Carmontelle. Both pictures courtesy of the Bibliothèque nationale, Paris. Rousseau's satiric portrait of bluestockings in *Emile* may have been aimed at his benefactresses (particularly Mme Dupin and Mme d'Epinay), who criticized him for his choice of the illiterate Thérèse as his companion.

Rousseau, women needed to understand the institutions, customs, and prejudices of society, as well as the seductive wiles of men. In his view, a woman's moral education should prepare her adequately for the social milieu in which she is to live. This is precisely where Sophie's education fails, since her moral education does not adequately protect her against the corruption of the city; moreover, her general culture is so limited that Emile soon tires of her charms and, after their move to Paris, strays from home in search of more stimulating company, thereby compounding her vulnerability to seducers.[25]

Rousseau maintained that a woman's education should also serve to make her an interesting and agreeable companion for her husband. No doubt he was reflecting on his own bitter disappointment with Thérèse's mediocre intelligence and lack of culture when he described the solitude of a cultivated man married to an ignorant woman: "The greatest pleasure of human company is missing when a married man is reduced to thinking alone," he writes in *Emile*. "Only a cultivated mind makes companionship pleasant; it is a sad situation indeed for a family man who likes to stay home to be forced to turn inward and not to have anyone there with whom to share his thoughts" (IV: 767).[26] Nevertheless, Rousseau insists that he would much prefer to share his life with a simple, ignorant woman than with a pretentious bluestocking:

> It does not suit an educated man to take a wife with no education. But I would prefer a simple and uneducated girl a hundred times over to a woman with intellectual and literary pretentions who would turn my home into a court of literature over which she would preside. A bluestocking is the scourge of her husband, of her children, . . . of everyone. From the sublime elevation of her genius, she disdains all her womanly duties and soon transforms herself into a man. She is always ridiculous and is criticized quite justly. (IV: 768)

This satiric portrait of bluestockings may well have been aimed at Rousseau's various benefactresses (particularly Mme Dupin and Mme d'Epinay), who criticized him for his choice of Thérèse and whose wit, talents, and power over him were so threatening to his fragile male ego.

In Rousseau's view, even if a woman possessed true literary or artistic talents, she should not aspire to cultivate them at the expense of her domestic duties or with any ambition beyond that of entertaining her husband and family: "Even if she possesses genuine talent, any pretension on her part would degrade it. Her dignity depends on remaining unknown; her glory lies in her husband's esteem, just as her pleasures lie in her family's happiness," he insists in *Emile* (IV: 768). Literary ambitions and celebrity were clearly incompatible with a woman's dignity and domestic felicity. Rousseau concludes his tirade against women writers with an appeal to his readers' own judgment—and prejudices:

> Reader, I'll let you decide: answer in good faith. Which gives you a better opinion of a woman as you enter her room, which leads you to approach her with greater respect: to see her occupied with household duties, with her children's clothes, and with other tasks appropriate to her sex, or to find her writing poems at her

dressing table, surrounded by all sorts of books and pamphlets and little notes from her friends? (IV: 768)

However, the question is a purely rhetorical one, since Rousseau has already supplied the answer in the preceding sentences and in the emphatic maxim that follows: "If there were only sensible men on earth, bluestockings would forever be old maids" (IV: 768). Rousseau's prefatory admonition to his readers—"answer in good faith"—is ludicrous indeed given Rousseau's own lack of good faith in appealing to his readers' prejudices against women writers and scholars in his effort to ridicule and discredit them.

Even Julie, despite her superior mind and alluring personality, has no desire to become either a bluestocking or a *salonnière*. "She is not one of those indolent housewives, content to study when it's time to work, who waste their time learning about the duties of others instead of fulfilling their own," observes Saint-Preux. "She practices today what she learned before. She no longer reads or studies, she gets things done, . . . and the day never seems long enough for her to accomplish all the tasks she sets her heart on" (II: 556). After her marriage, Julie devotes her full energy to domestic duties, aside from one hour at the end of the day reserved for study and reflection.

໒ເ⊙⊙ເ໐

According to Rousseau, women were generally far inferior to men in intellectual and creative potential and so should not attempt to emulate them in their studies or in their literary and artistic endeavors. Since the roles and intellectual capabilities of the two sexes were in his view so different, he opposed coeducation, as well as the use of the same program of studies for girls and boys. In *Emile*, he argued that the education of girls should be geared toward practical, domestic matters, because such training best prepared them for their future role as housewives and because girls were (in his view) less capable than boys of abstract thought.[27] Although he conceded that "the art of reflection is not totally foreign to women," he insisted that "they should have but a cursory introduction to the analytical sciences" (IV: 791).

In describing Sophie's education, Rousseau maintained that arithmetic was more useful—and less dangerous—than reading or writing. "What pressing need is there for girls to learn to read and write so early?" he asks. "There are few indeed who don't abuse this fatal science instead of benefitting from it; in any case, girls are too curious not to learn how to read and write without being forced" (IV: 708).[28] In Rousseau's view, the "book of the world" was the best reading material for girls: "When they misread it, it's their own fault" (IV: 737). The reading of novels was to be carefully avoided, since they risked corrupting a young girl's morals and giving her romantic illusions that would only frustrate her in dealing with the realities of her everyday life. Yet Sophie was in little danger of becoming corrupt or overly knowledgeable from her reading; for, aside from Fénelon's *Télémaque*, Barrême's *Livre des comptes faits* (a seventeenth-century manual on household management) was the only book that she had read before meeting Emile. At the age of eighteen, she was finally allowed to read a third book—a French translation of Addison's *Spectator*—to prepare her for her future duties as housewife and *honnête femme*.

It could of course be argued that, given the social reality of women's existence in the eighteenth century, Rousseau was merely being realistic in the education he outlined for Sophie. However, in the education of Emile, Rousseau had refused to be limited by custom or prejudice; it was in fact the uninhibited originality of his ideas on male education that made *Emile* such an important landmark in the history of pedagogical theory. Moreover, the education Rousseau proposed for Sophie was in many ways conservative, even reactionary, when compared to the educational practices and proposals of his contemporaries.

ເ໑໖ນ

One cannot compare *Emile* and *La Nouvelle Héloïse* without noticing the sharp contrast between Sophie's education and the education Saint-Preux proposes for Julie. In *Emile*, Rousseau maintains that the education of women should revolve entirely around men.

> To please them and be useful to them, to be loved and honored by them, to raise them when they are young and take care of them when they are grown, to advise and console them, to make life pleasant and pleasurable for them—these are the duties of women throughout the ages, which they should be taught from their earliest childhood. So long as we deviate from this principle, we will miss our mark, and all the lessons we give them will be of no use to their happiness or ours. (IV: 703)

If Emile's tutor improves on Arnolphe by wanting to give Sophie knowledge and skills beyond those necessary for good housekeeping, it is not for her own self-fulfillment, but so that she might be a more charming companion for her future husband: "But does it necessarily follow that a girl should be raised in complete ignorance and limited only to the functions of a housekeeper?" he asks. "Should a man make a servant of his wife and thus deprive himself of the greatest pleasures of human companionship? Should he prevent her from feeling anything or knowing anything, the better to dominate her?" (IV: 702). Appealing to nature once again, Rousseau answers these questions in seeming good faith.

> No, certainly not: this was not the intention of nature, which gave women such a pleasant and nimble mind; quite to the contrary, nature intended women to think, to judge, to love, to know, to cultivate their mind as well as their appearance; these are the weapons given to them by nature to make up for the strength they lack and to govern ours. (IV: 702)

The ambiguity of this answer and the profound ambivalence it reflects toward women's knowledge and power become fully apparent in the paragraph's concluding sentence: "They should learn many things, but only those appropriate for them to know."[29] If Sophie is to cultivate her mind and talents, it is not for her own personal development and pleasure, but in order to please her husband and to entice him into meeting her needs and desires. The main goals of Sophie's education are therefore threefold: to make her a loving mother and efficient housewife; a pleasant, chaste, and obedient companion for her husband; and a successful combatant in the war between the sexes, who knows how to use her feminine wiles to obtain from men what she is incapable of getting for herself.

Sophie has learned her lessons well, for as a result of her education, she has acquired "du goût sans étude, des talents sans art, du jugement sans connaissances" ["natural taste, artless talents, unschooled judgment"] (IV: 769). A model of simplicity and charm, Sophie "gets the gist of everything, but remembers little" (IV: 791). Her mind is pleasant without being brilliant, solid without being profound; it is "an unremarkable mind, not formed by reading, but only by conversations with her mother and father, by her own reflections, and by the observations she has made in the course of her limited experience"

(IV: 749). Yet contrary to the expectations of Emile's tutor, Sophie's limited education and experience are poor preparation for marriage and motherhood and for life in the adult world. Conditioned by her education to be fully dependent upon her husband, to center her life totally around him and their children, she succumbs to grief at the death of her child and to temptation when her husband strays from home in *Les Solitaires*, the sequel to *Emile*.

In contrast to Sophie's stultifying education *à l'Arnolphe*, the education that Saint-Preux proposes for Julie is ambitious and innovative. In a long letter to his pupil, he outlines the method he will use in tutoring her and alludes to a more detailed program of studies he plans to send her later. In interpreting this letter, one cannot ignore its tone (characterized by a curious mixture of pedanticism and seductiveness), nor its function within the context of the novel, nor indeed the motives that seem to underlie it. One could, for example, interpret this letter as yet another step in Saint-Preux's overall plan of seduction. However, taken at face value, the method of education outlined in *La Nouvelle Héloïse* is not inconsistent with the methods and theories of *male* education presented in *Emile*, nor is it inappropriate (even in Rousseau's view) for women of superior intellect such as Julie and Claire. Saint-Preux's plan is designed not to give his pupils a superficial intellectual baggage they can display in public to impress others, but instead to develop their powers of analysis and reflection through attentive readings of a limited number of carefully chosen texts. "For people like us who wish to benefit from our studies, we do not amass knowledge to sell it for profit, but instead to convert it for our own use and enrichment," explains Saint-Preux.

> The best way to digest our readings is to read little, but to reflect a great deal on what we have read or else to discuss these readings often between us (which amounts to the same thing). Once our minds are opened to new ideas by the habit of reflection, it is always better to discover by oneself what one would otherwise find in books; this is the true secret for appropriating new ideas and shaping them to fit one's own way of thinking. (II: 57–58)

In an interesting anticipation of twentieth-century reader-response theory, Saint-Preux describes reading as a creative act of assimilation, appropriation, and transformation in which the reader interacts actively with the text in order to create a new and better text of his or her own. Although he recognizes that most people lack the imagination and insight necessary for this type of reading, he heartily recommends this method to Julie, "who puts back into [her] readings a new and richer meaning, and whose active mind draws from the text a new one, sometimes better than the first" (II: 58).

Given the seemingly ambitious and innovative nature of Saint-Preux's pedagogical method, the actual plan of studies he outlines appears surprisingly limited. Indeed, he seems more concerned with what to omit than with what to include. "We'll stop the study of languages, except for Italian. We'll cut out algebra, geometry, and even physics," he explains. "We'll give up the study of modern history, except for that of Switzerland, our own country, and only because it is a free and simple country" (II: 59). As for the choice of literary texts, Saint-Preux adamantly (and rather hypocritically) opposes the inclusion of romantic novels or love poetry, aside from Petrarch, Tasso, Metastasio, and the masters of the French theater. He attempts to justify the narrow range of Julie's studies by insisting that these restrictions are necessary to preserve her innate moral and aesthetic sense—or what he refers to simply as "the soul" (*l'âme*): "Such readings enervate the mind and soul, leaving them weak and indolent," he explains. "Don't be surprised, then, at what I have omitted from your earlier readings, which must be pared down to make them worthwhile. . . . Anything that fails to speak to your soul is unworthy of your attention" (II: 59–60).

Despite this limited choice of subjects and texts, the program of studies proposed for Julie is still far more ambitious than the education given to Sophie. Whereas Sophie is left in relative ignorance (aside from a purely utilitarian training to prepare her for household management) and is hardly taught to think for herself (except to ward off potential seducers), Julie is encouraged to develop an independent mind and spirit, to sharpen her moral and aesthetic judgment and her critical faculties to their fullest. What is most striking about Julie's education is less its breadth than its depth. In contrast, Sophie's education is rudimentary and superficial—a smattering of *les arts d'agrément* (music, dance, drawing, and embroidery), bolstered by a heavy dose of moral instruction to ensure her obedience and chastity. Sophie is not taught to search for understanding or for self-fulfillment as is Julie, but for what will be most pleasing to men. In fact, Sophie's whole education is designed to make her dependent upon and subservient to men—to their opinion of her, their generosity toward her, their desire for her.

Discontinuities in Rousseau's Portrayal of Women:
The Paradox of Sophie and Julie

How can one explain the coexistence of two such different views of women in the work of the same author? The contrast between Sophie and Julie appears even more striking when one considers that *Emile* and *La Nouvelle Héloïse* were written and published during the same period of Rousseau's life and at times worked on simultaneously.[30] The differences in character between Rousseau's two heroines may be ascribed in part to class differences. Sophie is of modest origins, raised in a simple country cottage by formerly wealthy parents after their financial ruin. Julie, on the other hand, is the only surviving child of a proud and wealthy baron. The contrast in the education they receive reflects in part the very different financial circumstances and social ambitions of their parents.

The contrast between Rousseau's two heroines can also be attributed to the very different purposes underlying the two works—his clearly stated wish to portray an ordinary woman and couple in *Emile*, and an exceptional woman and couple in *Julie*. Unlike Sophie, Julie is portrayed as fully responsible for her destiny, for her failings as well as for her strengths. Because of her exceptional nature, she is able to rise above the opinions and prejudices of others, to live on a higher level than that of common mortals, while still retaining her humanity. In this respect, she is a far more successful product of the type of education Emile's tutor had envisaged for him than Emile himself.

A third explanation for the contrast between the heroines of *Julie* and *Emile* can be found in formal differences between the two works— and specifically differences in genre, voice, and implied reader. *Emile* is not really a novel at all, but a fictionalized treatise on education; its characters lack the depth and vivacity, the poignancy and human dimensions that distinguish the characters in *La Nouvelle Héloïse*. Rousseau's adoption in *Julie* of the epistolary form and frequent use of first-person narrative contribute to the vividness of the characters and to the intensity of the feelings they express. In *Emile*, on the other hand, the style is often dry and impersonal; the use of third-person narrative and pseudo-novelistic form fail to mask the didactic nature of the work. The characters appear superficial and contrived, mere straw figures designed to illustrate Rousseau's educational theories and his sexual politics, puppets dancing on a string manipulated by the omniscient and omnipresent tutor.

Left: Illustration by Moreau le Jeune for the passage in the *Confessions* where Rousseau recalls his sexual initiation by Mme de Warens. The caption reads: "Dreamy and distracted, I was less concerned with what she was saying than with trying to figure out what she was leading up to." *Right*: Illustration by Moreau le Jeune of the scene in *La Nouvelle Héloïse* where Saint-Preux first kisses Julie's hand during a music lesson. The imaginary Julie and the very real Mme de Warens were undoubtedly the two most important female figures in Rousseau's life. Both pictures courtesy of the Bibliothèque nationale, Paris.

As for differences in voice and implied reader, both *Emile* and its sequel are told from a man's point of view, with a male character (Emile or his tutor) serving as the author's *porte-parole* and an implied reader who is also male or who is expected to identify with male interests.[31] *La Nouvelle Héloïse*, on the other hand, is generally told from a woman's perspective, with Julie or Claire as the author's principal mouthpiece and an implied reader who is either female or who is assumed to be sympathetic to the plight of women. Whereas *Emile* is a male-centered novel, in which Sophie is conceived of as the ideal companion for Emile, *La Nouvelle Héloïse* is a feminocentric novel in which Julie is presented not only as the ideal woman, but also as the ideal human being. Sophie permits the full realization of Emile's potential as a human being, just as Wolmar and Saint-Preux permit that of Julie. In *Emile*, Sophie's education is subordinate to that of Emile and her destiny is clearly sacrificed to his in *Les Solitaires*. Her adultery serves as a convenient pretext for Emile to abandon her (along with their son and Sophie's unborn child) in order to become more independent and self-sufficient, so that he can realize his tutor's narcissistic notions of moral perfection. In *La Nouvelle Héloïse*, on the other hand, Saint-Preux's destiny is subordinate to that of Julie, his happiness and independence are sacrificed in an effort (however vain) to ensure hers. Similarly, it is Wolmar who enables Julie—on the surface at least—to free herself from the torments and uncertainties of romantic passion and to find fulfillment in her role as mother and as spiritual head of a seemingly idyllic household.

❧❧❧

The contrast between Julie and Sophie constitutes a central discontinuity in Rousseau's sexual politics. Yet besides the heroines of *Julie* and *Emile*, Rousseau's works contain a rich and dizzying kaleidoscope of *figures féminines*. Some critics have attempted to systematize Rousseau's views on women by grouping the female characters in his writings into categories within some type of classification scheme. For example, in a study titled "La femme selon Jean-Jacques," Jean-Louis Lecercle writes:

> *Sophie* is a creation of Jean-Jacques the philosopher; she illustrates the system of ideas he developed on the nature of women and their place in society. She represents women in general. *Julie* is a creation of the poet, born of Jean-Jacques's imagination. She represents the ideal woman. *Maman* [Mme de Warens] was a real woman, the person who had the deepest, most lasting influence on Jean-Jacques; she was also the poetic image of woman drawn from the real world and elaborated in the *Confessions*.[32]

Lecercle attempts to account for the differences between Sophie, Julie, and Mme de Warens by the different literary genres used to portray them (philosophical treatise, novel, autobiography) and to the different aspects of himself that these women projected (Rousseau the philosopher, Rousseau the poet-novelist, Rousseau the lover/son/protégé). However, his interpretation is artificial in the distinctions he sets up between Sophie as a theoretical, abstract woman, Julie as an ideal woman, and Mme de Warens as a real woman recreated through the poetic lens of autobiography. All of these female figures are in fact idealized by Rousseau in a different manner; yet each in her own way reflects the concrete realities of women's lives in the eighteenth century. Perhaps the best approach to dealing with the discontinuities underlying Rousseau's views on women is simply to accept them as constitutive of his character and of his thought. As Bernard Guyon remarks in his commentary to *Julie*: "Trying to determine Rousseau's personal position is often difficult, since there seem to be as many Rousseaus as there are characters in his works" (*OC*, II: 1449).

It seems appropriate to conclude this overview of Rousseau's sexual politics by sketching a preliminary answer to the vexed question: Rousseau, anti-feminist or feminist, misogynist or champion of women? One could of course choose (as Paul Hoffmann does) to dispute the terms of the question and to dismiss it as an irrelevant line of inquiry.[33] However, in studying Rousseau's reception by eighteenth-century women readers, this question is of crucial importance, since it was continually raised by the women themselves. In the remainder of this chapter, I will seek to demonstrate that the fabric of Rousseau's views on women contains misogynic strands as well as feminist ones, traditionalist strands as well as progressive ones, and that in his works these various threads are interwoven into complex and at times unexpected patterns.

Rousseau's Sexual Politics in the Context of His Period:
Traditionalist Undercurrents in His Works

To fully understand Rousseau's views on women, one must situate his sexual politics in the context of the gender ideology and social realities of his period. How do his views compare with those of his contemporaries on the question of women's role and education? To what extent are his sexual politics a reflection of—or a reaction to—the actual condition of women in eighteenth-century France? Finally, how did the women of the period respond to Rousseau and what influence did his works have on their values and behavior?

In the gender ideology of eighteenth-century France, four main currents of thought can be distinguished: (1) the traditionalist-naturalist view, (2) the rationalist view, (3) the feminist view, and (4) the pseudo-feminist view.[34] The dominant view of women was the traditionalist-naturalist perspective, which was particularly prevalent among jurists, doctors, and moralists, but was also voiced by a number of well-known philosophers and literary figures, including Voltaire, Antoine Thomas, Restif de la Bretonne, and Bernardin de Saint-Pierre.[35] The tone of traditionalist arguments varied considerably, ranging from misogynic diatribes to matter-of-fact exposés of women's inferiority to lyrical idealizations of femininity, motherhood, and domesticity. However, the ideological bases of these writings were essentially the same. Maintaining that women are by nature inferior to and dependent upon men and that their primary function is to serve as wives and mothers, traditionalists argued that women should be excluded from the public sphere and be relegated to—and educated for—a strictly domestic role. They appealed to history, to custom, and above all to nature to justify women's subordination.

The appeal to nature was a particularly important and distinctive trait of the traditionalist view of women. Insisting on the existence of ineradicable physiological and psychological differences between the sexes, the traditionalists invoked these differences both to restrict the role and education of women and to justify their subordination. In the course of the eighteenth century, the ambiguous notion of Nature—"that great beast people talk about all the time without knowing what it is," as Sade once remarked—served as the basis for a new secular morality and empiricism that shook the foundations of the traditional Christian world view. Buttressed by the authority of scientific observation, this new naturalist discourse proved even more oppressive to women than the theological discourse that it challenged. By highlighting the biological specificity of women, the scientific discourse of the Enlightenment tended to perpetuate, rather than to dispel, age-old prejudices against them and to intensify the traditional association of difference with inferiority. In much of the medical literature of the period, women are portrayed as physically and psychologically weak and inferior, as victims to the imperious, uncontrollable urges of their body—particularly the uterus. The popularization of scientific and medical discoveries in the eighteenth century tended to reinforce the already powerful biological determinism underlying traditional views on women. More than ever, woman was reduced to her sexual and procreative functions both in the theoretical and fictional works of the period.

The other three currents of thought were all in a sense reactions to the oppressive aspects of the traditionalist view of women. These three oppositional currents differed not only in the degree to which they challenged the traditionalist view and in the style of their rhetoric, but also, more importantly, in the socio-political implications of their critique of dominant gender structures. For rationalists like Montesquieu, d'Alembert, d'Holbach, and Grimm, the oppression of women was simply one form of injustice among many, a theoretical problem they addressed on isolated occasions.[36] In contrast, for feminists such as Condorcet, Wollstonecraft, and Olympe de Gouges, the cause of women was a central preoccupation of their lives and work.[37] They denounced the inequality of women with greater conviction and vigor; their arguments were generally more detailed and systematic than those offered by the rationalists. Going beyond the limited vision of the rationalists, who restricted their efforts to improvements in women's education, these eighteenth-century feminists claimed for women not only the right to educational and intellectual equality, but political, legal, and professional equality as well. Combining feminist analysis with political action, they proposed concrete reforms that, if instituted, would have radically transformed the legal status of women and the material conditions of their lives. Mobilized into action by the pressure of events, the feminists of the Revolutionary era took public stands and risked their lives in their fight for equal rights for women. Among the writers of eighteenth-century France who addressed the "woman question," there was a fourth group who adopted a rhetoric that was feminist in tone, but whose underlying message was basically traditionalist for lack of concrete proposals and a genuine desire for change. Beneath the surface of their pseudo-feminist rhetoric lies a subtle paternalism and a tacit complicity with the status quo. Particularly striking examples of pseudo-feminist rhetoric can be found in the works of Helvétius, Diderot, and Laclos.[38]

⌒⌒⌒

At first glance, Rousseau's sexual politics seem to place him squarely in the camp of the traditionalists. Echoing the biological determinism and naturalist discourse of De Sèze, Roussel, and other doctors of the period,[39] Rousseau insisted on the existence of ineradicable physiological and psychological differences between the sexes and ascribed the intellectual inferiority of women to their "nature" rather than to their education or social conditioning. Like Joseph Pothier and other legal theorists of the period, Rousseau invoked these so-called "natural" differences, along with history and custom, to justify women's subordinate role and limited education.[40] Like Restif de la Bretonne and other traditionalists, he maintained that women were by nature inferior to men and dependent upon them, that their primary function was to serve as wives and mothers, and that they should therefore be excluded from the public sphere and educated for a strictly domestic role. The tone of Rousseau's writings on women, like Voltaire's and Restif's, ranged from misogynic tirades to matter-of-fact exposés of women's inferiority to lyrical idealizations of femininity, mother-hood, and domesticity. Given these strong parallels, it is hardly sur-prising that Rousseau's views on women have been classified as traditionalist by many twentieth-century scholars and as misogynic by most feminists.

Feminist and Reformist Undercurrents in Julie

Despite the traditionalist-naturalist orientation of many of Rousseau's writings on women, there are feminist or "pro-woman" undercurrents in his works that have not been sufficiently explored and that may help explain why he was seen as a champion of women by many of his female contemporaries.

The most ostensibly feminist passage in all of Rousseau's writings is found in a letter from Julie to Saint-Preux after their separation. Reflecting on the marriage her father has arranged for her with a man she does not love, Julie bitterly laments the constraints imposed on girls of her age. Victims of oppressive rules of decorum and loveless marriages of convenience, they are forced to repress their true feelings and desires and to be forever torn between the irreconcilable demands of love and duty:

> Forced to feign indifference when under the full sway of her passions, . . . constrained by duty to deceive and by modesty to lie: this is the usual situation of any girl of my age. In this way, we spend our youth governed by the tyranny of decorum, which our parents only make worse by forcing us into an ill-assorted marriage. But our inclinations are thwarted in vain, for the heart makes its own laws and escapes bondage by giving itself freely. . . . And so the wretched victim is forced to sin by having to chose between two equally sacred bonds of fidelity. (II: 212)

"Le Premier Baiser"
(Julie and Saint-Preux's first kiss)

Illustrations by Moreau of key scenes from *La Nouvelle Héloïse*.
Courtesy of the Bibliothèque nationale, Paris.

"La Confiance" (Julie and Saint-Preux meet again for the first time after her marriage to Wolmar)

"Le Soufflet" (Julie's father strikes her after discovering her liaison with Saint-Preux)

Illustrations by Moreau of key scenes from *La Nouvelle Héloïse*. Courtesy of the Bibliothèque nationale, Paris.

"L'Amour maternel" (Julie rescues her drowning son from the lake)

Julie's passionate *cri de cœur* is one of the high points of the novel. Reading it, one understands women's intense identification with Rousseau's heroine and their enthusiasm for an author who portrayed their secret miseries with such eloquence and realism. In this passage more than any other, Rousseau stands out as a strong advocate of women and as deeply sympathetic to their plight. In his indictment of oppressive social institutions and customs, he seems to vindicate women's right to dispose freely of their own hearts.

Rousseau's strongest arguments in favor of love matches are found in a letter from Bomston (Saint-Preux's British friend) to Claire. After criticizing Julie's father's selfish, narrow-minded class prejudices, Bomston affirms the right of spouses to choose each other freely. "Let rank be determined by merit and the union of hearts by free choice—that is the true social order," he insists. "Those who would determine rank according to birth or wealth are the real perturbers of that order" (II: 193–94). For Rousseau, the choice of a marriage partner was not strictly a matter of individual or family preference, but part of a much broader political problem that called into question traditional class and family structures and indeed the whole socio-economic hierarchy. His insistence on the right of spouses to choose each other freely constituted a bold challenge to customary power relations between parents and their children and an even bolder challenge to traditional relations between classes.[41]

In the second preface to *Julie*, Rousseau maintains that the moral corruption of women was largely the result of a repressive social order—particularly of their parents' avarice, vanity, and class prejudices, which impelled them to arrange marriages of convenience for their daughters without concern for their feelings:

> Let us be fair to women; the source of their disorder is found less in themselves than in our defective institutions. . . . Their misfortunes and vices stem above all from the despotism of their parents. Victims of their parents' avarice or vanity, young women are forced into ill-matched marriages that leave them vulnerable to seduction. (II: 24)

Rousseau ends this passage with a call for social reform: "If you wish to remedy this problem, then go back to its source. Any attempt to reform public morals must begin with reforms within the family, which depend entirely on mothers and fathers" (II: 24).

Confronted with her father's inflexible opposition to her marriage with Saint-Preux and his determination to marry her to a friend who had saved his life, Julie rebels against the sacrifice of her happiness to the baron's class prejudices and personal commitments: "So my father has sold me, turned his daughter into a piece of merchandise, into a slave? He is paying for his life with my own, for I know I will never survive this marriage!" (II: 94). In her desperation, she tries to become pregnant by Saint-Preux in order to force her father to accept their marriage by making a public *déclaration de grossesse*—a formal attestation of pregnancy to civil authorities. Given her social milieu and her normally obedient nature, Julie's rebellious impulse is startling, particularly her plan to turn oppressive institutions and customs—*les déclarations de grossesse*, public opinion, and shotgun weddings—to her advantage. When this plan fails, she resigns herself to marrying Wolmar, but swears her eternal love to Saint-Preux and resolves to keep him as her lover after her marriage. "My heart will remain yours until my last breath," she writes Saint-Preux.

> I am weary of sacrificing justice to illusory notions of virtue. . . . Nature, o sweet nature, take back your rights! I renounce the barbarous virtues that seek to repress you. . . . Duty, honor, virtue no longer mean anything to me. . . . Let a father enslaved by his word and by an empty title bestow my hand in marriage as he has promised, but let love alone bestow my heart. (II: 334–35)[42]

Commenting on Julie's painful dilemma, Marie-Laure Swiderski remarks: "Reading these lines, how many women readers—and notably Mme d'Houdetot—would have relived thoughts that must have crossed their minds in similar circumstances."[43]

❧

It was above all Julie who captured the enthusiasm of Rousseau's women readers as they read *La Nouvelle Héloïse*. Yet other characters in the novel were also likely to have appealed to the sensibilities of women of the period and to have reflected their hidden longings and frustrations. The character of Claire, although secondary to that of Julie, is the focus of multiple feminist undercurrents in the novel. Her open aversion to marriage, her subtle denial of motherhood (by entrusting her daughter's upbringing to Julie), her criticism of the baron d'Etange's infidelity and tyranny toward his wife, her passionate attachment to Julie above all others, and her outspoken, independent nature—all these traits make Claire one of the most unconventional female figures in eighteenth-century fiction.

Of all Rousseau's fictional characters—male or female—Claire is by far the most independent and self-sufficient in relation to the opposite sex. After her husband's death, she resolutely refuses to remarry, insisting that "the yoke of marriage" is too austere and constraining for her independent, joyful spirit:

> I was not cut out to be a woman. If the decision had been mine, I would never have married. But members of our sex attain freedom only through servitude, and one must start as a servant in order to become one's own mistress later on. . . . Marriage is too solemn a state for me; it ill-suits my temperment and depresses me—not to mention that I find any kind of constraint unbearable. Imagine how I felt about a relationship in which, for seven years, I didn't have a good laugh even once a year. (II: 407–8)

Claire's attitude toward marriage was highly unconventional for the period and appears even more so in a novel ostensibly devoted to promoting the ideal of companionate marriage. Although her husband was, by her own admission, a tolerable enough companion, she describes marriage as servitude and openly rejoices at her new-found freedom. Claire's feelings were readily shared by women of her period, since many of them had been forced into marriages of convenience far unhappier than hers. Just as Julie represented for Rousseau's female readers the ideal of romantic passion and an equally strong (albeit contradictory) desire for the serenity of a companionate marriage, so too Claire represented the unpleasant reality of their daily experience and their unspoken desire to rebel against it.

Claire's independence from men was unusual in the literature of the mid-eighteenth century, as was the strong female bonding between Julie and Claire. Rivalry between women for the affections of men was by far the more common pattern. Even more unconventional was Rousseau's portrayal of homoerotic undercurrents in the friendship between the two cousins. Although fiercely independent toward the opposite sex, Claire is tied to Julie by an all-consuming passion, *une amitié amoureuse* with strong (though not explicit) lesbian overtones. In a letter to Monsieur d'Orbe before their marriage, she recognizes that she is unlike other women: "As a woman, I am a kind of monster. By some quirk of nature, friendship is stronger in me than love. When I tell you that my Julie is dearer to me than you, you only laugh, and yet nothing could be closer to the truth" (II: 179).

When Bomston offers to take Julie and Saint-Preux to England, Claire expresses her readiness to follow them there and to abandon her own marriage plans:

> So I'm abandoning a marriage when the contract is about to be signed? Perhaps it is just as well for Monsieur d'Orbe. Although I hold his character in high esteem, he is nothing to me in comparison to my Julie. Tell me, my child, does the soul have a sex? In all honesty, I hardly think so in my case. . . . A single affection fills my heart, absorbing and eclipsing all my other feelings. . . . It is you alone I truly love. (II: 206–7)

Neither marriage nor motherhood diminishes Claire's passionate attachment to Julie, as she makes clear in a letter to her cousin a few months after Monsieur d'Orbe's death: "I hope now to spend the rest of my life with you," she confides. "You console me for everything; it's impossible to feel grief for anything so long as I have you. Your power over me is the most absolute I've ever felt; you dominate and fascinate me; you fill me with respect and awe" (II: 408–9). This letter could easily be mistaken as that of a lover to his mistress—as indeed it has been by one Rousseau scholar.[44] Finally, the scene where the two women faint when they are reunited after several months' separation can be read as a disguised orgasm, especially when viewed through the complacent, voyeuristic eyes of Monsieur de Wolmar.[45]

Such intense female bonding posed a direct challenge to patriarchal structures, which tended to reinforce male ascendancy over women through a tacit "divide and conquer" strategy by making women rivals for male affections in order to dominate them more effectively. However, unlike other men of the period, Rousseau did not seem to find such intimacy between women personally threatening; it seemed, on the contrary, to arouse in him (as in Wolmar) a peculiar voyeuristic pleasure. The rapture Rousseau experienced during his "idylle des cerises" with Mlles Galley and de Graffenried echoes that of Saint-Preux when he recalls an evening passed alone with Julie and Claire:

What an unforgettable evening! . . . such pure and tranquil enjoyment unequaled among the pleasures of the senses. . . . What
ecstasy to see two such touching Beauties embrace each other
tenderly, the face of one against the breast of the other. . . . No,
nothing, nothing on earth is capable of inspiring such voluptuous emotion as your mutual caresses. Even the sight of two
lovers would have been less appealing to me. (II: 115)[46]

The homoerotic and voyeuristic undercurrents in this passage are unmistakable. Perhaps Rousseau, like Saint-Preux, found love between
women so alluring because his own heterosexual experiences were
generally unsatisfying and, at times, quite threatening to his fragile
male ego.[47]

Claire's question "L'âme a-t-elle un sexe?" ["Does the soul have a
sex?"] merits further discussion. Pierre Fauchery's attempt to trace
this phrase back to Poullain's dictum "l'esprit n'a pas de sexe" ["the
mind has no sex"] is unconvincing. For, as Paul Hoffmann suggests,
"for Rousseau, the soul is not a cognitive faculty, but the organ of
love."[48] However, Hoffmann then adds: "While it is true that Rousseau
sought to liberate the soul in relation to sexuality, it was not from
femininity that he wished to free women, but from desire, which he
considered an inessential relationship between men and women. . . .
What Rousseau proposes to us is the model of a spiritual androgyne."
Although I agree with Hoffmann's critique of Fauchery's interpretation, I would dispute his own interpretation on several grounds. Far
from proposing the effacement of sexuality and sexual desire,
Rousseau's novel underlines the impossibility of their effacement.
Despite all their efforts to sublimate their sexuality, Saint-Preux and
Julie remain prisoners of their desire, irresistibly drawn back to it, as
Julie herself admits. Death is her only escape from an overpowering
libido. Furthermore, the homoerotic undercurrents in the novel between Julie and Claire and to a lesser extent between Bomston and
Saint-Preux—not to mention the incestuous and sadomasochistic overtones of Julie's relationship with her father[49]—express a multiplicity of
desires beyond traditional heterosexual norms. What the novel presents is not a model of spiritual androgyny as Hoffmann claims, but
one of emotional and physical bisexuality, as well as the expression of
a whole range of repressed desires—all of them taboo.

The strong bonds between members of the same sex in *Julie* and
the latent homosexuality underlying them may be considered feminist

in the sense that they challenge traditional heterosexual norms and "normal" power relations between the sexes. That certain readers found this challenge threatening is demonstrated by the fact that Napoleon crossed out a key sentence in Claire's critique of marriage cited earlier: "If the decision had been mine, I would never have married. But members of our sex attain freedom only through servitude, and one must start as a servant in order to become one's own mistress later on" (II: 407). It is not surprising that Claire's independent, feminist spirit should have displeased the father of the *Code civil*.

Laure Pisana, the courtesan redeemed through her love for Bomston, is the focus of another important feminist undercurrent in *La Nouvelle Héloïse*: Rousseau's criticism of prostitution and the hypocrisy of a society that both scorns and condones it. Given Rousseau's aversion for prostitutes (expressed in numerous passages of the *Confessions*), his eloquent denunciation of their oppression is all the more significant. He portrays Laure as the innocent victim of a corrupt society that takes advantage of her youth, sacrifices her happiness to its selfish desires, and then opposes her moral reform through hypocrisy and self-interest.

When Bomston considers marrying Laure and bringing her to live at Clarens, his friends are appalled, with the exception of Julie. Expressing a strong sense of solidarity toward the former courtesan, she insists that there is little difference between Laure and herself: "From the lowest degree of shame she was able to rise to the highest degree of honor. She is sensitive and virtuous, what else does she need to resemble us? If there is no way to make up for the mistakes of youth, what right have I to greater forbearance or forgiveness, what honor can I hope for by refusing to honor her?" (II: 627). In the end, under pressure from Saint-Preux (who makes her feel unworthy of Bomston both socially and morally), Laure renounces her love for him and becomes a nun.

Rousseau not only decries the social prejudices that make a prostitute's return to "respectable" society difficult, if not impossible; he also denounces the double standard and complicity with corruption that foster prostitution as an institution. When Saint-Preux "innocently" allows himself to be taken to a house of ill-repute, where he succumbs to the charms of courtesans, Julie answers his expressions of remorse with a stinging critique of his hypocrisy and of the double standard that requires women to repress their desires, while encouraging men to indulge theirs.[50] Later, when Saint-Preux is about to join her household at Clarens, Julie fears that he may seduce her servants if he lives there unmarried. This leads her to a more general denunciation of the corruption of servants by their masters who, who taking advantage of their wealth and power, seduce servant girls and force them into a life of prostitution, misery, and shame:

> Let him perish, the odious man who pays for women's favors and turns love into a trade! Once a woman lets herself be bought, she will always be for sale. And who is more to blame for her misery and shame: the brute who mistreats her in a house of ill-repute, or the seducer who leads her there by being the first to offer money for her favors? (II: 667–68)

This passage illustrates Rousseau's awareness of the interconnections between class oppression and the oppression of women: the fact— almost as true in the twentieth century as it was in eighteenth—that the sexual vulnerability of women increases as one descends the socio-economic ladder.

Women's Response to Feminist and Reformist Undercurrents in Julie

It is no accident that Rousseau's most vehement critiques of female victimization—through prostitution, forced marriages of convenience, the double standard, and repressive rules of decorum—are generally expressed by Julie. Her own suffering and moral reform make her the ideal *porte-parole* for his condemnation of society's oppression of women. In the eyes of Rousseau's readers, Julie's reformist view of society carried even greater weight because of the enlightened education she had received, which had trained her to think for herself according to her own beliefs. Her independent mind, along with her intense sensibility and love of virtue, made her a heroine capable of appealing to a wide range of readers.

For women in particular, Julie represented an ideal balance between morality and sensibility—a symbol of hope in a period characterized by rigid social decorum, loveless marriages of convenience, sterile family lives, and widespread adultery. The dignity and relative happiness she was able to achieve through motherhood and in a companionate marriage based on mutual esteem and affection constituted a message of hope that went straight to the heart of many women readers. They saw Rousseau as the champion of a new moral order in which women could play a central role. By nursing their babies, by devoting themselves to their husbands and children and to domestic and charitable tasks, these women hoped to create stronger affective ties within their families and thereby foster the moral regeneration of society envisioned by Rousseau and by other social reformers of the period (including feminists such as Condorcet and Wollstonecraft). Far from being considered a trap, the ideals of motherhood and enlightened domesticity represented by Julie seemed to offer a new dignity to women, regardless of their socio-economic status.

Linked to this rhetoric of moral reform and to the ideals of motherhood and domesticity it fostered was the ideal of romantic sensibility celebrated in *La Nouvelle Héloïse*. This ideal is eloquently expressed by Julie on her deathbed:

> Sensibility always brings to the soul a certain contentment with oneself regardless of fortune and circumstances. How miserable I was! How much I cried! Yet, if I had to be reborn into the same conditions, the sin I committed would be the only thing I would change: what I suffered would still be gratifying to me. (II: 725–26)

Rousseau's valorization of *la vie intérieure* (in the double sense of domestic life and affective experience) was enthusiastically adopted by his women readers. For many, *La Nouvelle Héloïse* came as a revelation, opening up hitherto unsuspected possibilities for emotional fulfillment by showing that conjugal fidelity was not incompatible with happiness—indeed that love and virtue could be combined. As their letters to Rousseau suggest, *Julie* seems to have filled an emotional gap for many of his readers by heightening the significance of their existing relationships or by helping them imagine a happier, more fulfilling life, which they might not otherwise have thought possible.

Anna Attridge attributes the unprecedented success of Rousseau's novel to its broad appeal to readers with widely different needs and backgrounds: "The encouragement of sober workaday virtues, the enrichment of family life, support for the type of life one has already chosen, comforting fantasies, consolation in unhappiness, reassurance

about one's own disposition to virtue, a spur to greater effort: different readers found different needs fulfilled by *La Nouvelle Héloïse*, and
what they found depended very much on their individual situations."[51]
Because of the novel's intense emotional appeal, along with the richness and complexity of its "message," indeed because of its very
ambiguity, *Julie* became in a sense all things to all people, in much the
same way as certain religious texts.

The tremendous appeal of Rousseau's novel to women readers
can be attributed above all to his realistic portrayal of their oppressed
condition. As numerous scholars have suggested, *La Nouvelle Héloïse*
was as much a reflection of as it was a reaction to the condition of
women in eighteenth-century French society.[52] However, as in any novel
presenting social criticism and proposing social reform, the mediations between fiction and reality in *Julie* are extremely complex.[53] Since
a detailed exploration of these interconnections would go beyond the
scope of this study, I will limit my discussion to women readers' response to what they *perceived* as a reflection of their experiences and
aspirations in Rousseau's novel and the novel's impact on their values
and behavior.

"Reading your novel, I recognized myself in a thousand places,"
remarked one reader. "It seemed to tell the story of my life."[54]
Rousseau's women readers felt both justified and avenged by his
portrayal and apparent defense of them in *Julie*, and they reacted
with unprecedented enthusiasm to his novel. "Women especially were
wildly enthusiastic about both the book and its author, to the point
that there were few, even of the highest rank, who would have resisted me if I had undertaken to seduce them," recalls Rousseau in
his *Confessions* (I: 546). It is not surprising that *La Nouvelle Héloïse*
would become the greatest bestseller of eighteenth-century France.
In his *Confessions*, Rousseau attributes the success of his novel to his
women readers' strong identification with Julie and to their conviction that the novel was a true story based on his own experiences:
"What made women so partial to me was their conviction that I had
written the story of my own life. . . . Everyone felt that it was impossible to express feelings with such eloquence or to portray the ecstasy of love so vividly without having experienced these feelings
oneself" (I: 547–48). Rousseau's explanation is borne out by the testimony of his readers. For example, in a letter to a friend, Mme de
Polignac confided:

So long as Rousseau seemed nothing more to me than a philosopher and man of wit, I never had the least desire to make his
acquaintance; but Julie's lover, . . . oh! that's not the same thing
at all; and, in my initial enthusiasm, I was on the verge of calling
for my carriage, . . . and to see him at any cost, so that I could tell
him how superior his tenderness made him seem in comparison
with other men. I would ask him to show me Julie's portrait and
then, on bended knee, kiss the image of that divine woman.[55]

As Carol Blum remarks, the reader response to Rousseau differed in
both kind and intensity from that expressed toward other Enlightenment figures: "It was his moral superiority and the moral superiority
one could enjoy by adoring him which were important, not any specific doctrine he had put forth."[56]

Robert Darnton maintains that Rousseau's novel called forth a
new kind of reading, far more intensive than reading habits in the
past, and that it fostered a personal bond between reader and author
unprecedented in literary history: "The flood of tears unloosed by *La
Nouvelle Héloïse* in 1761 should not be considered as just another wave
of preromantic sentimentality. It was a response to a new rhetorical
situation. Reader and writer communed across the printed page, each
of them assuming the ideal form envisioned in the text." Drawing
from the voluminous fan mail that Rousseau received following the
novel's publication, Darnton illustrates the total absorption in his works
that many people experienced, the renewed self-confidence and sense
of moral vigor he instilled in them: "Jean-Jacques opened up his soul
to those who could read him right, and his readers felt their own souls
elevated above the imperfections of their ordinary existence. Having
made contact with 'l'Ami Jean-Jacques,' they then felt capable of re-
possessing their lives as spouses, parents, and citizens."[57] The ability
of readers to identify with the characters depicted in *Julie* was a source
of renewed confidence in their own goodness. Jean Roussel further
documents the intense identification and sense of communion with
Rousseau experienced by many of his readers: "Thanks to this encounter, they felt they had rediscovered themselves. His fans entered
into a unique relationship with him, a new kind of communion, a
personal adventure. . . . There arose, thanks to the emotion and moral
lessons conveyed by his novel, an imaginary world that led the reader
to identify intensely with the author."[58]

The strong identification of women readers with Julie is particularly well illustrated by a letter from a young woman to her husband a few weeks after the novel's publication:

> I did not write to you yesterday, my dear friend, because I read the entire first volume of Rousseau's novel, which I'm crazy about. But you weren't forgotten, because I always saw your face in place of the hero's. Because I found all Julie's feelings mirrored in my own heart, I felt I was writing you as I read their letters. She says all sorts of things I had thought and felt before, but that I could not have found words to express. . . . Everyone is as enthralled as I am. What a wonderful man! Such insight and truth![59]

Even the forbidding Maréchale de Luxembourg was transported by her enthusiasm for *Julie*, as Rousseau himself recalls: "Mme de Luxembourg was crazy about Julie and her creator; she spoke of nothing else and was totally preoccupied by me, constantly paying me compliments and kissing me ten times a day" (I: 522–23). Buffenoir attributes the Maréchale's enthusiasm to her intense identification with Julie: "In Julie d'Etange, she recognized herself—the strong impulses and ardent passions of her youth, then her subsequent reform and useful, orderly life after the stormy days of the past!"[60]

The most famous and extreme case of a reader's identification with Julie was that of Mme Alissan de la Tour, who cast herself in the role of Julie and then enticed Rousseau into playing Saint-Preux and a friend into playing Claire in an intense correspondence that spanned fifteen years. In her initial letter, "Claire" assured Jean-Jacques that "Julie is not dead, she lives in order to love you," since her friend had both the character and soul of Julie: "Julie's soul lives on in her, except for her sin. All who know and appreciate her think so as well." To these ouvertures, Rousseau replied: "so long as there are Julies and Claires, there will also be Saint-Preuxs."[61] Mme de la Tour's identification with Julie became so intense that when Rousseau later tried to break off the correspondence, she accused him of trying to rob her of her identity: "Even if you take Julie's name away from me, you will never rob me of her heart." At one point, Rousseau was so exasperated by her obstinancy that he declared: "No one resembles Saint-Preux less than Jean-Jacques Rousseau, and no one resembles Julie less than Madame de la Tour." He nevertheless sent more than fifty replies to her more than one hundred letters. Commenting on this singular exchange, Claude Labrosse observes: "We find ourselves faced with a reading carried beyond itself . . . an attempt to transport fiction into a realm beyond reading. . . . Like a siren rising from the sea of fictions, it beckons to Jean-Jacques, trying to pull him in, while he hesitates on the shore, both wary and fascinated by this bizarre encounter with this chimera born of his own imagination."[62]

The strong impact that *La Nouvelle Héloïse* had on women's view of themselves as wives and mothers is illustrated by a series of four letters published by the *Mercure de France* in August 1761, under the title *L'Elève de la Nouvelle Héloïse*. Ostensibly written by an anonymous woman who called herself the Marquise de M***, the letters trace the transformation in her attitude toward both herself and Julie as she read Rousseau's novel. At the beginning, the Marquise felt bored by her life, particularly by her children, whom she planned to send away to school, and by her husband, who wanted her to go live with him in the country. Her only source of pleasure and excitement was her love for another man, whom she referred to as "le Chevalier." The first parts of *Julie* alarmed her, for she felt that she would no longer be able to control her adulterous passion for the Chevalier. Despite her misgivings, the Marquise persevered to the end of the book, whereupon, following Julie's example, she underwent a conversion to virtue, renounced her love for the Chevalier, and resolved to devote herself wholly to her husband and children. Her resistance to adultery was no longer prompted by concern for her reputation, but instead by a new appreciation for marriage, motherhood, and family life. Her letters constitute an enthusiastic endorsement of Rousseau's novel, which she claimed had shown her the path to virtue and happiness.

While it is possible that the letters comprising *L'Elève de la Nouvelle Héloïse* were not actually written by a woman, but by a male editor of the *Mercure de France*, they nevertheless reflect the very real impact that Rousseau's novel had on the lives of countless readers, male and female alike, from all walks of life. As Bernardin de Saint-Pierre remarked, "I know libertines who married and young women who publicly attributed their happiness to him. Numerous women aspired to become Heloïses like Julie. Rousseau's maxims made their way all the way to the throne; under his influence, even queens chose to breastfeed their babies."[63] In her *Lettres sur Rousseau*, Mme de Staël also testifies to his strong influence on the attitudes and behavior of his readers, and particularly on women: "It was Rousseau's eloquence that revived maternal feelings in a certain class of society; he helped women understand the duties and joys of motherhood. . . . Is it mothers or their children who owe the greatest debt of gratitude to Rousseau? Ah! surely it is the mothers!"[64] Similarly, in her *Sentiments de reconnaissance d'une mère*, Mme Panckoucke expresses the gratitude that women felt toward Rousseau for showing them the path to happiness and self-fulfillment as wives and mothers: "If families become closer, children more affectionate toward their parents, and marriages more loving at the sight of a mother surrounded by her children, it is to Rousseau that humanity owes all these blessings."[65]

Pseudo-Feminist and Misogynic Aspects of Rousseau's Writings on Women

It is clear from the voluminous and effusive testimonies of Rousseau's women readers that he was widely viewed as a champion of women, even as a kind of feminist. However, a careful reading of his work reveals that Rousseau was in fact a traditionalist who adopted a pseudo-feminist tone and rhetoric to heighten the dramatic effect and popular appeal of his writings. This is particularly true of *Julie*, where he assumed a pseudo-feminist tone to propose what were essentially conservative social reforms based on a traditionalist view of women: abolishing prostitution, fostering companionate marriages, and giving women a more active role in the choice of their husbands and in the upbringing of their children. Indeed, Rousseau's whole campaign for moral reform can be seen as a conscious effort to put women back into what he and other traditionalists considered their rightful place: out of the public eye and back into the domestic sphere.

Although in the course of *La Nouvelle Héloïse* Rousseau writes of the oppression of women with sympathy and at times with considerable eloquence and perspicacity, his impassioned claims are undermined by a profound ambivalence toward women. Like Diderot, Helvétius, and other pseudo-feminist writers, Rousseau oscillates continually between an attitude of sympathy and scorn for women, between images of idealization and vituperation. His writings on women, like theirs, are characterized by recurring expressions of bad faith and by what Pierre Fauchery has referred to as a rhetoric of contradiction.[66] Perhaps the most striking example of Rousseau's rhetoric of contradiction is found in *Julie*, where Saint-Preux exclaims:

Women, women! Beloved and fatal objects that nature has embellished to torture us, whose love and hate are equally pernicious, and whom we can neither seek out nor flee with impunity! . . . Abyss of pleasure and pain! . . . Unhappy is he who yields to your deceptive calm! It is you who produce all the storms tormenting the human race. (II: 676)

Then, responding to Julie's suggestion that he marry Claire, he adds: "Julie! Oh, Claire! . . . Alas, between the two of you, I will never have a moment of peace" (II: 676).

Bernard Guyon finds the theatrical bravura of this passage in bad taste. "This is certainly not the first time that the novelist has transformed himself into an opera composer, but elsewhere the transition was less abrupt," remarks Guyon. "Unable to resist inserting a tirade of which he was no doubt quite proud, the novelist led Saint-Preux to contradict himself."[67] Guyon fails to see, however, that the contradictions in Saint-Preux's attitude toward the two cousins are projections of Rousseau's own ambivalence toward the female sex and that this diatribe arises from a long tradition of misogynic rhetoric. One has only to compare this passage with the misogynic tirades of other eighteenth-century writers such as Diderot or Restif de la Bretonne[68] to realize to what extent Rousseau was influenced by this tradition.

In all Rousseau's writings, the passage that most clearly marks him as a pseudo-feminist is found, not surprisingly, in Book V of *Emile*:

Women never cease to complain that we raise them to be coquettish and vain, that we continually beguile them with trivialities to remain more easily their masters. They blame us for the faults we criticize in them. What madness! And since when do we meddle in the education of girls? . . . Is anyone forcing your daughters to waste their time in foolish chatter or forcing them, against their will, to spend half their time at the dressing table, following your example? Is anyone preventing you from raising and educating them as you wish? Is it our fault if they please us when they are beautiful, if we are charmed by their coy, mincing ways, and attracted by the artfulness they learn from you? (IV: 700)

Although ostensibly addressed to women, this passage can be read as a point-by-point rebuttal of d'Alembert's response to Rousseau's *Lettre à d'Alembert* and as a continuation of the verbal duel between the two ex-friends on the subject of women's role and education.[69] Whereas d'Alembert argues that women are the victims of an oppressive system of education that stultifies their minds and encourages them to be coquettish and frivolous, Rousseau maintains that women are the victims of their own vanity and of their mothers' negligence, ineptitude, and poor example. To d'Alembert's charge that men give women an inferior education and flatter their vanity in order to dominate them more effectively, Rousseau replies that it is not men but women (and particularly mothers) who are responsible for female education, that women are vain and frivolous both by nature and by choice, and that they freely choose to cultivate their bodies rather than their minds in order to please and dominate men.

In Rousseau's view, if women were given the same education as men, they would come to resemble them, which would considerably diminish their femininity and their power over men. "Men would be only too happy if women were raised as men!" he declares. "The more women wish to resemble men, the less women will be able to govern them, and then men will truly be the masters" (IV: 701). Insisting that masculine and feminine traits and roles were basically incompatible and that any effort to combine them was therefore unnatural and ill-advised, Rousseau concludes with a special appeal to mothers: "A conscientious mother must believe me when I urge her not to go against nature by trying to turn her daughter into a gentleman; turn her instead into a respectable woman, and rest assured that this will be far better both for her and for us" (IV: 701). Rousseau's addition of the phrase "and for us" points to the male self-interest underlying his endorsement of traditional gender roles; it suggests that the ideal of femininity he advocated was designed to keep men on top—both literally and figuratively. That Rousseau has men's (and not women's) interest in mind here—indeed, that this whole passage is written from a male-centered point of view—is underlined by the fact that male readers are referred to as "we" or "us" [*on* or *nous*], while women readers are referred to as "you" [*vous*] or "they" [*elles*]. This distinction in pronouns underlines women's alterity, their status as outsiders and inferiors from whom Rousseau wishes to distance himself.

Rousseau's bad faith is apparent throughout this passage. Although elsewhere (notably in the preface to *Julie*), he recognizes the negative effects of women's upbringing and education, here he purposely blurs the nature-culture distinction and attributes women's inferiority to their nature rather than to their social conditioning. By insisting that women, not men, are responsible for female education and that it is therefore the fault of mothers if their daughters are frivolous, empty-headed, and vain, Rousseau hypocritically sidesteps the contradiction inherent in his logic, as well as the real source of the problem: the vicious circle of internalized oppression passed down from mother to daughter generation after generation. If women were continually denied the education necessary to educate their daughters competently, this chain of oppression would never be broken. Rousseau's bad faith is especially apparent in the question: "And since when do we meddle in the education of girls?" since he himself is in the process of doing precisely that, continuing a long tradition of male educators who have prescribed a limited education for women, with the same sexist motives and the same stultifying results. He clearly contradicts himself by first asking "Is anyone forcing your daughters, . . . against their will, to spend half their time at the dressing table, following your example?" and then, soon after, adding: "Is it our fault if they please us when they are beautiful?" (IV: 700).

Rousseau's bad faith—the extent to which he purposefully confuses the social conditioning of women with their natural capabilities and inclinations—is also evident in numerous other passages in *Emile*, particularly the one where he outlines the benefits of doll-play for little girls:

> Look at a little girl playing with her doll all day, constantly changing its clothes: already her natural inclination is clear. She is totally absorbed by her doll, lavishing on it all her coquetry and love of dress. She is waiting for the moment that she can become a doll herself. This natural bent is clear from the start: you need only reinforce and direct it. (IV: 706–7)[70]

At the end of this passage, Rousseau adds: "Nearly all little girls detest learning to read and write, but they are always delighted to learn how to sew. They are pleased at the thought that these talents later will be useful in adorning themselves and enhancing their charms" (IV: 707). Here again, Rousseau ignores the contradiction inherent in his logic; for, encouraged to engage in mindless needlework and frivolous doll-play, girls were conditioned to become precisely what many men desired: empty-headed dolls who thought only of dressing themselves up to attract male attention and who scorned serious intellectual and artistic pursuits because such activities were considered unattractive to men.

Some might argue that the contradictions in these passages stem not from bad faith, but instead from foolish blindness. In my view, however, bad faith clearly underlies Rousseau's statements and rhetorical strategies here—particularly in the way he purposely blurs the nature-culture distinction and, through his use of pronouns, openly appeals to the misogynic prejudices of his male readers.

৵৽৵৵

The two passages from *Emile* cited above are the most openly misogynic and paternalistic statements in the entire Rousseauian corpus. Nowhere does Rousseau express his view of women as sex objects more clearly or portray the power relations between the sexes with greater cynicism. It is a bitter, pessimistic view that contrasts sharply with the seemingly optimistic, idealized portrayal of women in *Julie*. Yet, beneath the idyllic surface of *La Nouvelle Héloïse* lies a deep ambivalence toward women and toward their power over men. Each of the feminist or "pro-woman" currents in the novel discussed earlier is counterbalanced, even negated, by a traditionalist or antifeminist countercurrent. Despite Rousseau's passionate defense of love matches in the first part of *Julie*, not a single character in the novel marries for love—not even Bomston, who hypocritically turns his back on Laure because of class and moral prejudices (prejudices that Rousseau had earlier decried so vehemently). Similarly, despite all Rousseau's arguments against celibacy as unnatural and anti-social, and despite his fine speeches celebrating family life as the foundation for the moral regeneration of society, not a single main character is married when the novel ends. Claire and Saint-Preux resolutely refuse to marry, in spite of their mutual affection and strong attraction to each other, just as Bomston and Laure renounce their love for each other under pressure from their so-called friends.

The other feminist or pro-woman currents in *La Nouvelle Héloïse*—independence from men, female bonding, sympathy for the plight of prostitutes, and the celebration of motherhood and domesticity—are all subtly undermined as well. Claire's carefree independence from men is counterbalanced by her strong dependence on Julie, which is dramatically underlined by her desolation after her cousin's death.

Similarly, Laure's decision to remain in the convent and take the veil is neither an affirmation of independence nor an act of revolt against a society that has reduced her to a sexual object, but a painful sacrifice of her love for Bomston to class prejudices and to the moral prejudices blocking a prostitute's return to "respectable" society.[71] Female solidarity is undermined by Claire's scorn for Laure and even more by the subtle rivalry between Claire and Julie for Saint-Preux's affections. Julie's awkward and premature efforts to wed them nips their nascent passion in the bud, even before it has time to bloom. After her death, the sublime specter of Julie both binds them together and prevents their union.

Finally, the twin ideals of motherhood and domesticity—extolled by Rousseau as the surest path to women's happiness—are undermined by Claire's refusal to remarry and her subtle rejection of motherhood. Those same ideals are undermined even more strikingly by Julie. On the surface, Julie's blissful death can be seen as the triumph of conjugal fidelity and as the apotheosis of maternal love. The heroic sacrifice she makes of her life to save that of her drowning son is lauded by her pastor, who declares: "Madame, your death is as beautiful as your life: Your life has been devoted to charity work; you die a martyr to maternal love" (II: 717). However, as Vartanian and others have suggested, Julie's death is actually a subtle form of suicide and her maternal sacrifice a convenient pretext to escape the tedium of virtuous perfection to which she has devoted her life since her marriage to Wolmar.[72] On her deathbed, Julie is serene, even joyful, not because she has saved her child, but because her death releases her from her marriage vows and gives her hope of being reunited with Saint-Preux. She seems to take a cruel pleasure in showing her joy to Wolmar. "Julie, my dear Julie! You are breaking my heart," he laments. "Yes, I have penetrated your secret thoughts; you are happy to die, happy to leave me. Remember how I have treated you during all the time we have been together; do I deserve such cruel treatment from you?" (II: 719). Despite all her protestations to the contrary, Julie eventually concedes: "It is true that I die content," but then hastens to add: "content to die as I have lived, worthy of being your wife" (II: 720). She then gives her husband a passionate love letter for Saint-Preux, which she asks Wolmar to read after her death and to send to him. In this letter, Julie gives free rein to the passion she has repressed throughout her marriage: "The same virtue that separated us on earth will unite us in heaven. . . . I am only too happy to sacrifice my life for the right to love you forever without crime, and to be able to say it to you freely once again" (II: 743). Wolmar has no choice but to read the letter, and one can well imagine the grief and bitter regrets that such a letter must cause him. By openly expressing her joy to be leaving him and by forcing him to read her letter to Saint-Preux, Julie cruelly punishes Wolmar for having stood between her and the man she loved. The dramatic triumph of extramarital passion at the end of *Julie* presents an overt challenge to the ideals of companionate marriage and conjugal fidelity extolled in the second half of the novel.

The ideal of motherhood is similarly undermined by the novel's dénouement. Far from being a heroic act of self-sacrifice for her children, Julie's death—the fact that she joyfully lets herself die, even *wills* herself to die—is an act of egotistic self-indulgence. This interpretation is borne out by Julie's words concerning her children on her deathbed: "Maternal affection constantly increases, but the affection of children diminishes as they live farther away from their mother. As they grew older, my sons would have been separated from me more and more. They might have neglected me" (II: 726). By dying while her sons are still young, Julie can abandon them before they are able to abandon her—hardly a thought worthy of a martyr to maternal love. One could also argue that the ecstasy Julie feels earlier in the novel as she contemplates her children at play is due less to her feelings of fulfillment as a wife and mother than to the seductive presence of Saint-Preux, himself enraptured by the sight of her. Saint-Preux himself admits that he finds Julie *embellie par la maternité* and even more desirable than before. The phrase describing Julie's children—"one hardly notices their presence" (II: 560)—takes on a new meaning when read in this light. Here, as at the end of the novel, there is a curious subversion of the cult of motherhood. Caught up in a web of desire and self-delusion, Julie's Madonna-like figure is subtly transformed into what Kristeva refers to as *"la mère qui jouit"*—the mother who knows (or desires) sexual pleasure.[73]

Rousseau's characters all reflect his own deep ambivalence toward parenthood, expressed in passages of the *Confessions* where he recalls, at times with remorse and at other times with surprising nonchalance, the abandonment of his five illegitimate children at birth.[74] Despite his insistence in *Julie* and *Emile* that parents should raise and educate their own children, rather than entrust their upbringing to servants and tutors, not a single parent in either work practices what Rousseau preaches, any more than does Rousseau himself. Emile, an orphan (whose parents mysteriously reappear in *Les Solitaires* to scorn Sophie) is raised and educated by a tutor. When Emile in turn becomes a father, he leaves the care of his young son to his wife, who is barely literate, and then abandons them both after he repudiates her for adultery. Similarly, Julie's mother leaves her in the care of a garrulous servant who fills her head with stories of seduction and romance, and then later entrusts her education to a handsome young tutor who seduces her. Although deeply attached to her mother, Julie criticizes her for giving social obligations priority over her maternal duties. As for Wolmar, instead of raising his sons himself, he plans to entrust their education to his wife's former lover. After she is widowed, Claire sends her daughter to be raised by Julie and leaves her at Clarens for months at a time without seeing her. And Julie, the perfect mother, abandons her children by willingly letting herself die in the hope of being reunited with her lover after death.

Conflicting Interpretations of Rousseau during the Revolutionary Era

The ambiguities underlying Rousseau's social and political thought gave rise to widely different and often conflicting interpretations of his views on the family and on women's role in society. This was especially true in the decade following the French Revolution, when the social and political life of France was in a state of flux and turmoil. After 1789, Rousseau's ideal of enlightened domesticity was enthusiastically endorsed by government leaders as a vehicle for their program of social reform. "Rousseauism" became the dominant ideology of the new bourgeois ruling class and had considerable impact on the lives of countless women, particularly in the upper and upper-middle classes.[75] Rousseau's home-and-hearth ethic, along with the bourgeois ideals of simplicity, industry, and frugality extolled in his portrayal of the Wolmar household, were constantly evoked in the public discourse of the period, as well as in private journals and correspondences.

Paradoxically, during the same period, the anti-family undercurrents in Rousseau's writings[76] were drawn upon by some of the more radical leaders—notably Saint-Just and Le Pelletier—to promote the mandatory education of male children in state boarding schools. Their plans for a uniform state education were designed to minimize the supposedly negative, counterrevolutionary influence of the family, which they considered a pernicious source of class prejudices and anti-patriotism. Arguing that children were a financial burden to the poor, Le Pelletier invoked Rousseau's vision of primitive man's sexual freedom and independence as an ideal to be recovered through the rearing of children by the state: "Unhappy citizens," he wrote, "perhaps soon this burden will cease to be one; returned to the financial ease and the delicious impulses of nature, you will be able to give children to the fatherland without regret."[77] Although never carried out, these educational schemes aroused considerable opposition. For example, one man wrote to the revolutionary journal *Bouche de Fer* to angrily protest Le Pelletier's proposal to "relieve" parents of the burden of child-rearing, "You call relief the cruelest sacrifice a tyrant could demand of his victim, the rupture of a bond that holds society together!" he exclaimed. Then, directing his indignation to Rousseau, whom he held responsible for Le Pelletier's anti-family bias, he added: "Oh Rousseau! I cannot pardon you for having forged ahead in a sacrifice to which so many fathers would prefer death. Despite your fame, you are not worth the most common of those fathers."[78]

In the decade following the Revolution, among the most hotly debated aspects of Rousseau's social thought were his views on women.[79] His works were often cited by conservative leaders (notably Mirabeau, Robespierre, and Chaumette) to justify the continued subordination of women, as well as the persecution of feminist militants and the suppression of women's revolutionary clubs. Robespierre, for example, praised women's participation in the October days, but he persistently denied them civil rights on the grounds that they could be manipulated too easily by political factions to work against the general will of the people—a concept he borrowed from Rousseau's *Social Contract*. A leading disciple of Rousseauism, Robespierre heartily endorsed the principle of separate spheres and maintained that women's chief contribution to the Revolution should be to "revolutionize" domestic and public morality. In the course of his successful campaign to suppress women's political clubs, Robespierre launched a bitter attack on the group known as les Femmes républicaines révolutionnaires:

> They feel it is their mission to teach the universe that female modesty and reserve are old-fashioned conventions, that distinctions in the occupations and talents of the two sexes are mere inventions of the aristocracy, that men should relinquish to women

the speaker's platform and seats of the senate, and that all the male political clubs should be under the jurisdiction of the women presidents of the Femmes républicaines révolution-naires. . . . These women are sterile as vice, yet they denounce the founders of the Republic and slander the representatives of the people.[80]

Under Robespierre's Reign of Terror, women who dared to adopt a public role and to meddle in politics were labeled unnatural and counterrevolutionary. Those who persisted were imprisoned and often condemned to death, like Olympe de Gouges and Mme Roland.

It is paradoxical indeed that Rousseau's ideals of motherhood and domesticity were seen as the path to new dignity and self-fulfillment by many women, yet at the same time were effectively exploited by government officials as a pretext for sexist discrimination and repression. On the other hand, although Rousseau's description of Sophie's education at home was occasionally invoked to argue against public education for girls, there was a movement among progressive educators of the period to apply the principles of Emile's education to the upbringing of both sexes, thus contributing to Rousseau's reputation (largely undeserved) as a champion of progressive female education. Some revolutionary women's clubs went so far as to teach the *Social Contract* to their daughters, thereby underlining the feminist implications of Rousseau's egalitarian rhetoric, which both he and the revolutionary leaders chose to ignore, even to deny.

In the decade following the Revolution, these contradictory interpretations of Rousseau's sexual politics led to numerous debates and confrontations on the subject of women's role and proper sphere of activity. Among the most noteworthy was the verbal duel between Mme Blandin-Demoulin, president of the Société des Amies de la République in Dijon, and Louis Prudhomme, editor of *Les Révolutions de Paris* and a chief spokesman for the Jacobin-Rousseauian male oligarchy. In January 1793, Prudhomme launched a vigorous attack against women's participation in political affairs by publishing a diatribe against a recently formed women's club in Lyons:

What do they think they are doing, these women of Lyons, teaching young girl citizens entire chapters of J.-J. Rousseau's *Social Contract*? In the name of the fatherland whose love they carry in their hearts, in the name of nature from which one must never stray, in the name of good domestic morality, of which women's

ITAM IMPENDERE VERO

J. J. ROUSSEAU

ICI REPOSE L'HOMME DE LA NATURE ET DE LA VERITE

A LA NATURE.

LA NOUV.ᵉ HELOISE 1761

CONTRAT SOCIAL

EMILE 1762

LE DEVIN DE VILLAGE 1753

DISCOURS SUR L'INEGALITE DES CONDITIONS 1760

LETTRES ET OEUVRES DIVERS

On disoit un jour à de *Buffon*: *Vous aviez dit et prouvé avant* J.J. Rousseau *que les meres doivent nourrir leurs enfans.* — Oui, répondit cet illustre naturaliste, *nous l'avions tous dit; mais Rousseau seul le commande, et se fait obéir*......

A Paris, chez le Cᵉⁿ Queverdo, rue Poupée, Nº 6. Section de Marat.

Opposite: Engraving by Queverdo celebrating Rousseau's contribution to the campaign to promote maternal breastfeeding. The caption reads: "Someone once said to Buffon: 'You proved the point well before Jean-Jacques Rousseau that mothers should breastfeed their children. —Yes, replied the distinguished naturalist, we all said so; but Rousseau alone commands it and is obeyed.'"

The illustration is divided into three parts. At the top is a medallion-like portrait of Rousseau bearing his Latin motto: "*Vitam impendere vero*" ["I have devoted my life to truth."] In the center is a monument resembling Rousseau's tomb in Ermenonville and bearing the same inscription found there: "Here lies the man of nature and truth." The left side of the central frieze depicts a bee-hive, commonly used in French revolutionary iconography to symbolize equality, cooperation, and the elimination of hierarchy—ideals promoted by Rousseau in his political writings. In the center is a flaming altar honoring nature and tended by a nursing mother and her baby. On the right is a female figure with two pairs of breasts—a symbol borrowed from Classical Antiquity representing fertility and abundance, like the cornucopia below her. In the foreground are more women nursing their babies and surrounded by toddlers bearing garlands and Phrygian caps. The engraving is framed on the far left and right by trees bearing medallions commemorating the publication of Rousseau's major works.

What makes this illustration of particular interest is the juxtaposition of the multi-breasted female figure (symbol of fecundity) with the nursing mothers in the foreground and, more specifically, the appropriation of a symbol from Classical Antiquity and its reinvestment with new, far more literal meaning. There is a certain irony in the fact that one of the female figures wears a Phrygian cap (symbol of liberty and republican citizenship), since by the fall of 1793, women were forbidden to wear such revolutionary garb. Indeed, the same month women were banned from participation in revolutionary clubs and from speaking at public meetings of any kind. Courtesy of the Bibliothèque nationale, Paris.

---

clubs are the scourge, we implore the good citizenesses of Lyons to stay home and to look after their households without claiming to understand the *Social Contract*.[81]

In a spirited reply, Mme Blandin-Demoulin claimed for women the right to play an active role in the political life of their country and described the many activities of her organization on behalf of the Revolution: "We do not limit ourselves, Citizen Prudhomme, to singing the hymn to Liberty, as you advise. We wish to perform acts of patriotism." She denounced Prudhomme's attempt to relegate women to a purely passive, domestic role as a form of class oppression, comparable to the oppression of the common people under the ancien régime: "Give up your system, Citizen Prudhomme, it is as despotic toward women as the aristocracy was toward the people." Invoking

Rousseau's rhetoric of moral reform, as well as his egalitarian rhetoric, she declared: "It is time to operate a revolution in the mores of women; it is time to reestablish them in their natural dignity. What virtue could one expect from a slave?" Blandin-Demoulin then concluded with a quote from Montesquieu: "In Asia from the earliest times we have seen domestic servitude marching in step with arbitrary government."[82]

Rising to the challenge, Prudhomme invoked Rousseau's anti-feminist side in an attempt to put la Présidente in her place: "The sage who repeated endlessly that the most estimable woman is she of whom the least is said would have been pained to read the letter of President Blandin-Demoulin; Rousseau did not like so much wit and such fine reasoning in women." Then, addressing the question at hand, he added:

> We do not deny the good that these societies may have done the Republic, but the citizenesses would serve it better still if they stayed home. . . . Let them not claim to be better than the women of Sparta and of Rome at its finest hour. If Cornelia had belonged to a club we would take back everything we have said according to nature, reason, and J.-J. Rousseau.

Prudhomme took up the debate again from time to time. In an article a few weeks later, he declared that "Julie Wolmar would not have taken her children to the citizenesses' club." It is clear that Prudhomme was trying to replace Blandin-Demoulin's feminist-egalitarian image of Rousseau with an image more in keeping with his own traditionalist view of women's role. Of the two images, Prudhomme's was decidedly closer to the real Rousseau.

Tracing the rise of the Rousseauian ideal of domesticity for which Prudhomme spoke, Elizabeth Fox-Genovese observes that it invested women with authority in the domestic sphere, as if to compensate for depriving them of what little autonomy they had achieved in the public sphere: "Conjugal domesticity and motherhood were gradually seen to offer the perfect molds within which to reconfine female sexuality and female authority. They also had the advantages of offering women a new and flattering image of themselves, control of their own sphere—however marginalized—and a model with which women of different social and economic backgrounds could identify."[83] Celebrated by Rousseau in *Julie*, this dual cult of domesticity and motherhood was to exert a determining influence on the values and social structures of French society for generations to come.

2

The Failings of Rousseau's Ideals of Domesticity and Sensibility:

The Plight of Henriette

Rousseau's eighteenth-century women readers often reacted with tremendous enthusiasm to his writings—and particularly to the ideals of domesticity and sensibility set forth in *Julie* and *Emile*. Yet, for some of his admirers, the limited role he prescribed for women posed a very real dilemma. Although they may have wholeheartedly supported Rousseau's ideal of domesticity, some women found it difficult to follow his teachings, either because they were unable to marry (for lack of a dowry, physical appeal, or a suitable husband) or because, once married, they found marriage and motherhood unfulfilling. Despite genuine efforts to conform to Rousseau's feminine ideals of modesty and self-effacement, some women—married and unmarried alike—ultimately found these ideals stifling and felt inwardly torn by the powerful urgings of their talents and aspirations. It is indeed paradoxical that the women writers to whom Rousseau appealed most strongly were often those who, because of their superior gifts and idealistic expectations, were least able to content themselves with the limited role he prescribed for them.

To explore the contradictions in Rousseau's sexual politics—and, more specifically, the ambivalent response of women themselves to these contradictions—this chapter examines his little-known correspondence with Henriette, a bluestocking and aspiring writer unable to marry for lack of a dowry. Henriette's letters give eloquent expression to the plight of the single woman and *femme savante* in eighteenth-century French society. Through her frustrated attempt to reconcile

73

her life and aspirations with the Rousseauian ideals of domesticity and sensibility, Henriette poignantly illustrates the shortcomings of Rousseau's narrow views on women.

Henriette's First Letter to Rousseau

In the spring of 1764, when Rousseau was living in exile in Switzerland after the banning of *Emile*, he received the first of a series of five letters from an anonymous correspondent who called herself "Henriette." Her true identity is yet to be discovered, which adds an air of mystery to an already intriguing correspondence.[1] From her letters we learn she was a single woman in her mid-thirties, who had been unable to marry for lack of a dowry. Raised in a well-to-do family, she had received the best of educations offered to girls of the period and had looked forward to a happy marriage, only to have her hopes shattered by the financial ruin of her father: "I had been brought up to expect that I would one day marry, have a husband and children to love, a household to run. . . . Each of these prospects seemed to promise happiness, satisfaction, and pleasure. It was not easy to give them up."[2]

Forced to renounce the traditional role of wife and mother prescribed for her by society, Henriette resolved to adopt a gender role generally reserved for men—that of scholar and intellectual. By patterning her thoughts and behavior after those of *un honnête homme*, she attempted to transform herself inwardly into a man: "I resolved to cast myself into a new mold, to reshape my mind into what I imagined would be that of *un honnête homme*,[3] to adopt his tastes, activities, way of thinking, and social behavior. I tried to rid myself of women's problems and petty concerns, and above all of that coquettish air that signals a desire to please."[4]

Henriette also tried to console herself for her inability to marry by pointing to the unhappiness of many married couples in her period—due, as she suggests, to ill-matched marriages of convenience and the widespread infidelity that resulted.[5] Yet, aside from this one isolated comment in her first letter, the rest of Henriette's correspondence with Rousseau presents a highly idealistic view of marriage. This is clearly reflected in her first letter, where in an effort to justify her preference for studying over traditional feminine domestic occupations, she writes:

Perhaps you will tell me that the ordinary tasks of my sex should suffice to keep me occupied and content. In a happier state of mind, embroidery or spinning would be a pleasant activity. . . . Yet when I do work of this kind, my imagination tends to wander, to brood over my sorrows, and even becomes deranged. When a wife and mother engages in domestic tasks, she is sustained by a thousand pleasant thoughts: a husband whose esteem and tenderness she wishes to merit by her efforts, a tenderly loved child whose image cheers her in all she does for him. Do I have a loved one like hers to whom I can dedicate the work of my hands? As I work, can I look into my husband's eyes, . . . and find in the assurance of his love the only true happiness that a woman can enjoy? (*CC*, XIX: 246)

In contrast to the disillusionment with marriage as an institution suggested earlier, this passage expresses Henriette's ardent longing for the conjugal felicity and joys of motherhood described so appealingly by Rousseau in *La Nouvelle Héloïse* and Book I of *Emile*. Yet despite her firm belief in Rousseau's ideal of domesticity, she insists that her status as a single woman exempts her from following his strictures concerning the proper sphere of female activity: "Such are the duties and pleasures that nature prepared for my sex; but they are not for me," she writes. "In place of the tasks that my situation does not prescribe for me, I must substitute an activity stimulating enough to keep me from feeling this lack of affections and responsibilities. By exciting my curiosity, a particular course of study could focus my attention, occupy my thoughts, and little by little restore my peace of mind" (*CC*, XIX: 246–47). If Henriette prefers intellectual activities to domestic tasks, it is because she lacks the family life and emotional ties that would make household tasks meaningful. Indeed, engaging in such traditional "female" duties only makes her more painfully aware of her loneliness, marginality, and lack of purpose.

In her first letter, Henriette considers and then rejects the various roles traditionally reserved for women unable to marry for lack of a dowry: lady companion, kept woman, nun, lay sister, and charity worker. It is curious that she does not refer at all to the occupation of governess, for which she seemed best suited by her character, education, and financial situation. Perhaps class prejudices resulting from her earlier wealth and social prominence prevented Henriette from looking upon such a position without disdain. After a discreet allusion to her refusal to become a kept woman after the loss of her fortune, Henriette recounts her unhappy years as a lay sister in a religious community. She recalls the intense feelings of isolation and melancholy she experienced due to her lack of a religious vocation, to the rigidity of the institution, and to the dullness and narrow-mindedness of her companions, which made any kind of real exchange (intellectual or social) difficult. Then, in terms reminiscent of those used by Julie de l'Espinasse to describe her relationship to the tyrannical Mme Du Deffand, Henriette underlines the humiliation and dependence often experienced by women who served as companion to a wealthy patroness: "It is always understood in the relation between a wealthy woman and a female companion of modest means that all the servilities and sacrifices will be on the side of the latter and that she will be a slave to the other's whims" (*CC*, XIX: 249).

Henriette's criticism of the various roles open to unmarried women reflects a deep disappointment with the members of her own sex, indeed a thinly veiled misogyny. Her general scorn for women is particularly apparent in the following passage concerning her search for lasting friendships as a resource against old age: "There is no winter more bitter for women than that of old age. In this mournful, nebulous time of life, it is too late to make friends. To form genuine, lasting friendships, one must start much earlier. In any case, a woman can hardly expect to find such friends among other women. Their company has so little to offer" (*CC*, XIX: 249). Like the passage recounting her stay in the religious community, this passage reflects Henriette's interiorization of the inferiority and self-hatred conditioned in women by eighteenth-century society. It was therefore toward men, and particularly toward male intellectuals, that Henriette turned in the hope of building lasting friendships capable of satisfying her emotional and intellectual needs: "I decided then to search for friends in the other half of the human race: that is, among men.... I hoped to form a small group of friends with similar tastes and interests who would enjoy meeting together in my home. Their company would suffice, and with them, I would grow old slowly and peacefully" (*CC*, XIX: 249–50). By her own account, Henriette lacked the servility necessary to be mistress to a rich protector or companion to a wealthy patroness, just as she lacked the self-effacement and religious vocation necessary to be a nun, lay sister, or charity worker. Only the role of scholar and hostess to a small circle of enlightened male friends came close to satisfying her emotional and intellectual needs, as well as her quest for dignity and independence.

Despite all her efforts, Henriette was unable to efface her former hopes and innermost longings: "Even with the mind of a man, I still had the heart of a woman, which often rebelled against the will I tried to impose on it. My womanly affections and inclinations had been derived from nature and reinforced by my upbringing. They formed the very core of my being; losing them was a kind of death" (*CC*, XIX: 243). The mind/heart distinction here is crucial: Henriette claims to have successfuly reshaped her mind and will into that of a man, but to have struggled in vain to change her "womanly" heart (her affections, inclinations, the "core of her being") because it was derived from "nature." Her use of the term *nature* here reveals to what extent she had—in spite of herself—internalized the view expounded by Rousseau that gender roles and traits are not imposed by society but derived from nature, and that any effort to deviate from them was therefore *unnatural* and doomed to failure. Torn between her man's mind and her woman's heart, Henriette feels that she has condemned herself to a "kind of death"— to a marginalized existence in a sexual no-man's land: "Alone, isolated, I belong to neither sex," she laments. "I am only a being who thinks and suffers, who remains on the fringe of a society in which I have no place."[6] Painfully aware of her marginal status in a society in which women were expected to marry and have children, Henriette could not rid herself of a nagging sense of isolation and worthlessness. Her social conformism and emotional dependence—traits carefully conditioned in women of her period—made it difficult for her to feel comfortable in the unconventional role she had chosen for herself. Prisoner of a gender ideology in which she had no place, of a dowry system in which she had no future, Henriette nevertheless remained convinced that marriage and motherhood were her natural destiny.

Henriette's Challenge to Emile

These lingering self-doubts reached a crisis level when Henriette, a great admirer of Rousseau, encountered the famous tirade in *Emile* against women writers and intellectuals:

> It does not suit an educated man to take a wife with no education. But I would prefer a simple and uneducated girl a hundred

times over to a woman with intellectual and literary pretensions who would turn my home into a court of literature over which she would preside. A bluestocking is the scourge of her husband, of her children, . . . of everyone. From the sublime elevation of her genius, she disdains all her womanly duties and soon transforms herself into a man. She is always ridiculous and is criticized quite justly. (IV: 768)[7]

Henriette was so shaken by this passage that she wrote to Rousseau to explain her situation and to ask his advice, even his approval, for the life she had chosen. Convinced (like others of Rousseau's many correspondents) that he alone was capable of understanding and helping her, she began her first letter by confiding: "You know the human heart too well not to understand all the emotions that can agitate it. My heart needs complete freedom to express itself. You are the only person in whom I feel enough confidence to confide in completely; for you are the only one whose way of thinking suits me and that I find enlightening and persuasive."[8] Yet this image of Rousseau was quite common among his contemporaries; the unprecedented success of his novel *Julie* had firmly established his reputation as a shrewd analyst of character capable of probing the deepest contradictions of the human heart.[9]

Much of the ensuing correspondence reflects an attempt on Henriette's part to defend herself against Rousseau's criticism by insisting that she was not the type of *femme savante* he had described and that, in any case, her own scholarly pursuits were justified since she had no other worthwhile role to play. She claimed to share Rousseau's scorn for women who displayed their talents and knowledge in public, and she repeatedly underlined her own modesty and lack of pretension. She also agreed with Rousseau that the role of woman scholar ran counter to both the natural and the social order. Yet because of the unusual circumstances of her life, she insisted that her own case was exceptional and hence justifiable: "I am not at all one of those *femmes savantes*; I don't know anything very well, and I seek even less to show off what little I do know," she writes. "I had only planned to engage in scholarly pursuits in an effort to assure my happiness. . . . So, what is unacceptable in general may be reasonable and even necessary in my own case. This is what I ask you to judge."[10]

Later in her first letter, however, Henriette's respectful, apologetic tone shifted to one of defiance and self-assurance: "Society has done nothing for my happiness, so why should I make myself a slave to its opinions?" Bitter but lucid, she pushed her observations to their logical conclusion: "In short, since I exist for no one but myself, it seems to me that I have no obligation to consult anyone besides myself—my own tastes, needs, desires" (CC, XIX: 247). One wonders, then, why Henriette felt impelled to consult Rousseau. Perhaps she sought his approval in order to reassure herself; for, beneath her air of defiance and independence, Henriette seemed to lack the self-confidence and strength of character needed to pursue her unconventional role. She seemed to view Jean-Jacques both as a superior being with a unique ability to guide her and as a kindred spirit, a fellow outsider, who alone could sympathize with her plight. Moreover, Henriette's self-portrayal echoed that of Rousseau himself, as did her repeated attempts to justify her unconventional beliefs and behavior.[11]

At the end of Henriette's first letter, defiance gives way to despair: "I go on living with no clear goal, filled with despair and ennui, painfully aware of the emptiness of my days. Nothing pleases or touches me, everything is dead around me and inside me" (CC, XIX: 247–48). Henriette's sense of worthlessness, isolation, and lack of identity intensified both in feeling and in expression in the course of her correspondence with Rousseau. A year later, she wrote: "Neither daughter, nor mother, nor wife, I have no clear duties that determine my actions, no interests that animate me or that give me a purpose in life. I am utterly useless; no one has any need of me. I could disappear from the face of the earth without anyone even noticing."[12] Echoing Julie's *tedium vitae* at the end of *La Nouvelle Héloïse*, these feelings of ennui and emptiness form an important leitmotif in Henriette's subsequent correspondence with Rousseau and reflect her intense identification with the pre-Romantic ideal of sensibility that he was the first to perceive so keenly and express with such eloquence.

Rousseau's Stern Reply: A Case of Mistaken Identity

Jean-Jacques mistakenly believed that the signature "Henriette" concealed the identity of Suzanne Curchod, a young Swiss *femme savante* of his acquaintance whose life offered certain parallels with that of Henriette.[13] This same Mlle Curchod, governess in the home of Rousseau's close friend Paul Moultou, would that same year marry Jacques Necker and two years later, would give birth to a daughter

Germaine, the future Mme de Staël. It is perhaps thanks to this curious misunderstanding that we owe Rousseau's responses to Henriette's letters, since it is unlikely that he would have devoted so much time and thought to a total stranger. Rousseau's first two responses to Henriette differ dramatically, both in tone and in substance. Convinced in the first letter that Henriette was Mlle Curchod, "une savante et bel esprit en titre," Rousseau chides her for attempting to deceive him as to her true identity and her true motives in writing to him. "I am not fooled by your letter," he declares. "You are less interested in receiving my advice for the path you should follow, than in gaining my approval for the one you have already chosen. Between the lines of your letter I see these words written big and clear: 'Let's see if you will dare condemn to mental idleness someone who thinks and writes as I do.' "[14] Rousseau then launches into a diatribe against *les femmes savantes* and *les femmes bel-esprit* reminiscent of those in *Emile* and the *Lettre à d'Alembert*, which he concludes with the stinging remark: "It would have been far better to look like a girl in search of a husband than a philosopher in search of praise."[15]

Rousseau accuses Henriette of trying to turn herself into a man in order to usurp male prerogatives to knowledge and power; through her studies, it is not independence and self-sufficiency that she has tried to gain, so much as the admiration of others and the ability to dominate them. Invoking traditional gender roles, he argues that a woman who adopts male manners and occupations not only violates her "natural" role as a woman and "normal" power relations between the sexes, but also jeopardizes her chances for happiness—which, in his view, could only fully be realized through heterosexual love and, more specifically, through marriage. According to Rousseau, knowledge in women and other "masculine" traits make them unappealing, even threatening, to men.[16] Echoing traditional prejudices against women scholars, he insists that love and learning—"l'empire des charmes" and "l'empire du savoir"—are incompatible and mutually exclusive domains. By trying to compete in both, Henriette has, he maintains, failed in both. His harsh criticisms of Henriette's supposedly "masculine" qualities and aspirations reflect the fear widespread in his period (and pervading Rousseau's own work) of the hermaphrodite or "man-woman" (*homme-femme*).[17]

The rest of Rousseau's first letter to Henriette is somewhat more conciliatory and constructive in tone, yet he insists that it is too late for her to change her character and style of life, for in his view, she is already too dependent upon her studies to renounce them: "It is too late to go back to sewing and embroidery. . . . You cannot change your head as easily as you can your bonnet."[18] As in the *Discours sur l'inégalité*, Rousseau expresses nostalgia for a simpler life—for the lost innocence and benign ignorance of a mythic state of nature to which it is impossible to return.[19] He concludes that for Henriette, study is a necessary evil, but one that can nevertheless be turned to positive use: "Henceforth, you should look upon study as a kind of Achilles' sword, which healed the wound that it had made earlier. You only wish to calm the pain, but I want to cure the problem at its root. Through your study of philosophy, you only wish to take your mind off your sorrows; I want it to detach you from everything so you can be at peace with yourself" (*CC*, XX: 19). Like Saint-Preux in the plan of education he proposes for Julie, Rousseau distinguishes between knowledge that embellishes the mind and that which nourishes the soul, and he encourages Henriette to cultivate the latter above all. Then, like a priest giving absolution to a penitent confesser, he concludes: "If you are still able to cry over your situation, then it is not yet hopeless" (*CC*, XX: 22).

Henriette's Contradictory Protest

In her response, Henriette insists that her motives and character are quite different from those Rousseau has ascribed to her. She assures him that she is shy, modest, and soft-spoken, as befits a woman of her station. If she has pursued a life of study, it was not in order to display her talents in public, but rather to give herself a worthwhile occupation and to console herself for her lack of a family. To Rousseau's charge that she has tried to turn herself into a man in order to usurp the knowledge and power traditionally reserved for males, Henriette replies: "I have not tried to turn myself into a man. Belonging to one sex or the other seems of no importance to me, so long as one is happy." Since, in her view, an unjust dowry system has prevented her from fulfilling what she considers her "natural" role as wife and mother, Henriette feels justified in ignoring the other gender roles and distinctions imposed by society in order to secure the happiness she feels is her due:

> Since society has prevented me from fulfilling my natural function and has given me no other role to play, it should let me

choose my own way of life. With no specific role to fill, I felt I could ignore such roles and distinctions altogether. Without worrying about the traits and activities assigned to each sex, I have adopted those that would contribute most to my own well-being, ignoring customs and prejudices that are of no use to me.[20]

Startling in its perspicacity and modernity, this passage anticipates recent theories concerning the cultural construction of gender roles. Like contemporary feminist theorists, Henriette challenges the dominant gender system, ascribing it to custom and prejudice. Like them, she affirms her right to choose her own manner of being. By transcending the constraints of traditional gender distinctions and roles, she hopes to build a happier, more fulfilling life for herself. This passage constitutes a bold declaration of independence from traditional gender norms, as well as a protest against the social oppression underlying them. However, it is a double and indeed *contradictory* protest in that Henriette criticizes the oppression inherent in the dominant gender system yet, at the same time, decries the injustices (class prejudices, the dowry system, etc.) that prevented women like herself from fulfilling the limited (and in many ways oppressive) role society prescribed for them. This is especially clear in a later letter, where she describes herself as "torn between the desire to preserve my independence and despair caused by the knowledge that this freedom will never be of any use to me or bring me happiness."[21] In a sense, Henriette is a feminist who lacks the courage of her convictions. She wants to have her cake and eat it too—and winds up starving either way.

Henriette's attempt to find happiness by rising above traditional gender distinctions has failed because of the tension between her desire for independence (both emotional and economic) and the conformism and fear of isolation conditioned in her by society. Her conformism is reflected in the caveat with which she concludes her protest: "I have never rebelled openly against any of the prejudices I'm criticizing. I have always kept these thoughts to myself."[22] However, her use of the loaded term *préjugés* [prejudices, prejudgments] to denote traditional gender roles and distinctions constitutes another form of protest against them and belies her seeming deference to them.

In her correspondence with Rousseau, Henriette repeatedly makes the claim that "society" is the cause of her unhappiness. "Society has done nothing for my happiness, so why should I make myself a slave

to its opinions?" she asks. "Since society has prevented me from fulfilling my natural function and has given me no other role to play, it
should let me choose my own way of life," she later declares.[23] What
exactly does she mean by the term *society*? In the context of her letters,
the term has multiple resonances. The nuance varies depending on the
specific context in question, but in general Henriette uses the term to
refer to social structures and institutions and specifically to (1) the
dowry system that made it difficult for women of modest means to
marry, (2) the gender structures that marginalized single women, and
(3) traditional prejudices that prevented women (married or single)
from participating actively in the public sphere and cultural activities
without being stigmatized. She also uses the term more loosely to
mean "people in general," and no doubt specific people—friends, relatives, former suitors—who had disappointed her. In each case, Henriette
sees "society" in an oppositional manner, as a collective body of people
and practices that has prevented her from finding happiness and self-
fulfillment.

One could argue that Henriette was more a victim of her own
psychological state: the depression, excessive sensibility, and feelings
of worthlessness and alienation to which she so frequently alludes in
her letters. But the fact remains that she *viewed herself* above all as a
victim of the inequities and prejudices of "society." Like Rousseau,
Henriette failed to see that the two main sources of her unhappiness—
her marginalized social status and her feelings of loneliness and alienation—were in fact two sides of the same coin, that these two problems
fed on each other and could not be resolved separately. Only by transcending the traditional gender norms and prejudices supported so
vigorously by Rousseau, only by pursuing the literary and scholarly
vocation he condemned, could Henriette have found the inner serenity and sense of purpose she so ardently desired.

Rousseau's Blindness to Henriette's Dilemma

In his second response to Henriette, Rousseau excuses the harsh tone
of his first letter, which he attributes to the misunderstanding concerning her identity, rather than to its true source—his deep hostility toward women scholars. Confronted with Henriette's dilemma, Rousseau
expresses perplexity and a feeling of helplessness: "How can I find a
solution to your problem, when your situation is impossible for me to

imagine? You are a distressing, humiliating enigma for me. I thought
I knew the human heart, but yours is a mystery to me." He is clearly
moved by the eloquence and poignancy of her plea for help: "I fear I
can do nothing to relieve your suffering. . . . Yet you interest me too
much to leave you without an answer. Your last letter, filled with such
deep feelings and insights, affects me even more than the first one."[24]

Henriette's faith in Rousseau's ability to probe and heal the sufferings of the human heart was tragically misguided, given the nature of
her problem. Prisoner of his own limited views on women, he was
unable to comprehend her situation or to grasp its social implications.
In describing the ideal wife and mother in *Julie* and *Emile*, it apparently had not occurred to Rousseau that some women would be unable to fulfill the role and duties he had outlined for them, not for lack
of interest or desire (as in the case of certain society women), but for
lack of opportunity—for lack of a dowry, physical attractiveness, or
fertility that prevented them from marrying and from having children.
Although, in Book V of *Emile*, Rousseau briefly considers the plight of
the ugly woman whose appearance repels potential suitors,[25] nowhere
does he consider the dilemma of a woman unable to marry for lack of
a dowry. Nor does he realize that some women may have turned to
study and writing for reasons similar to his own—both to fulfill their
creative impulses and to compensate for a lack of satisfying human
relationships. Blinded by traditional prejudices against women writers
and scholars, Rousseau could not imagine that a woman might be
drawn to intellectual and literary pursuits for reasons other than vanity, that her love of learning and desire for self-expression could be
genuine and salutary, even necessary for her happiness. Henriette
represented a painful and humiliating enigma for Rousseau precisely
because she did not fit into any of the narrow roles he had prescribed
for women, because within his naturalist vision of woman's destiny
there seemed to be no solution to her dilemma, no remedy for her
suffering.

Rousseau's only suggestion to Henriette was that she learn to turn
her sensibility to her advantage—to find consolation in it rather than
affliction: "This same sensibility that makes you unhappy with yourself, should you not withdraw into it and let it console you with a
sublime feeling of *self-love*? . . . I know how much the need for affection is painful for sensitive hearts who are unable to satisfy it. Yet this
melancholy has a certain sweetness, it makes us shed delicious streams
of tears."[26] Perhaps he recalled the period of bitter disenchantment in

his own life that, impelling him to seek solace in an ideal world spawned by his imagination, had led to the creation of *Julie*.

In Rousseau's own experience, the sublimation of his unfulfilled desires through the exaltation of sensibility and of the self had a liberating effect and served as the creative impulse for his greatest fiction. The ideal of sensibility was also to have a potentially liberating effect on women authors of the period, provided they had the self-confidence and strength of character needed to rise above traditional gender barriers. By transcending the traditional conventions of female modesty and silence, women such as Graffigny, Riccoboni, Roland, and Staël were able to express their unfulfilled aspirations and desires through their writing, to transform their personal suffering into works of art. Yet for women like Henriette, who lacked the strength of character and self-confidence necessary to rise above traditional prejudices and to express their longings in writing, this cult of sensibility constituted a source not of liberation but of further oppression. For it impelled them to turn back upon themselves, to indulge masochistically in their own suffering. Henriette in fact evoked this image in her effort to explain to Rousseau that, far from relieving her problems, the narcissism and exaltation of sensibility he had recommended to her would only serve to exacerbate them: "The more I think about it, the less I understand how we can find real happiness by withdrawing into ourselves. It seems unnatural to me. For even if we find pleasure in ourselves, we are not made to feed on our own substance. The heart is communicative and needs to connect with others."[27] Henriette was acutely aware of the dangers of excessive sensibility—of its antisocial, emotionally destabilizing force. She clearly recognized the threat it posed to her efforts to achieve inner peace: "My intense sensibility causes me great distress because it makes me so hard to please. As a result, nothing I find seems to suit me, or else what would please me is beyond my reach."[28] Moreover, the exaltation of sensibility, which in Henriette's case would amount to a masochistic idealization of suffering and self-sacrifice, was poor consolation for what was as much a personal problem as it was the result of social injustices—the inequities of the dowry system, the marginalization of unmarried women, and the prejudices against women writers and scholars. Yet Rousseau was as incapable of grasping the limits of his ideal of sensibility as he was the failings of his vision of domesticity, nor did he seem aware of the subtle links between them. For both ideals were based on the principle of separate spheres that circumscribed women within *la vie*

intérieure (in the double sense of domestic life and affective experience), while encouraging men to express themselves freely and publicly in speech and in writing.

The most ironic—and tragic—aspect of Henriette's situation was
that she firmly believed in the naturalist-traditionalist discourse on
women advocated by Rousseau: that a woman's natural destiny was
to be a wife and mother and that any departure from this pattern was
both unnatural and anti-social. Furthermore, she accepted the prejudices against women scholars and writers as a logical extension of this
same discourse—which indeed it was. As much as Rousseau himself,
Henriette was prisoner of a gender ideology that, viewing the unmarried woman and woman scholar as aberrations of the natural and
social order, regarded them with pity and scorn.

Rousseau's Repression of Henriette's Vocation as a Writer

What Rousseau seemed unable or unwilling to recognize was that
Henriette represented the shortcomings of his narrow views on
women—of the ideals of domesticity and sensibility he had so confi-
dently elaborated in his novels and various other writings. Had he
been less blinded by his own limited view of women, he might have
advised Henriette to express her sensibility in a more constructive
manner than in "streams of tears." He might have encouraged her to
pursue a career as a writer—a vocation for which she exhibited undeniable flair and to which she seemed drawn both by disposition and
by circumstances.

"It seems to me," she writes, "that there is a need to give expression to one's ideas, impulses, and feelings, to air them freely and to
share them with others."[29] At the end of her first letter to Rousseau,
Henriette openly expresses the pleasure that she had experienced in
writing to him, the consolation and sense of purpose it had given her:
"Writing to you . . . has clearly proven to me that a serious, stimulating occupation is necessary to my well-being. Ever since I took up the
pen which is so foreign to me and I yielded to the desire to write you,
I have found that time passed more peacefully. . . . Writing has given
me a mental activity absorbing and stimulating enough to help me
forget my unhappiness."[30] Expressing her thoughts and feelings to
another in writing had provided an escape from her inner brooding
and sense of isolation, as well as an occupation rewarding in itself: "I

was so absorbed by the desire to express my thoughts to you that this activity dissipated the pain and sadness that usually arise when I reflect on my situation alone."[31]

Conscious of literary and social *bienséances* that equated women's self-revelation with immodesty and fearing that Rousseau might find her letters indiscreet, Henriette strove to justify herself in the face of his possible disapproval: "I must speak to you again of myself to clear up any misunderstanding concerning what I have already written you," she writes in her second letter. "When I write to you, it is not a man of the world, but a philosopher that I am addressing. Moreover, the confidence you inspire in me and my need for your advice free me from the general rule of silence that decorum dictates concerning the expression of one's own feelings" (*CC,* XXI: 123). Adopting Jean-Jacques's persona as an *être à part,* as well as his confessional style and self-justifying tone,[32] Henriette maintains that in her correspondence with him she is dispensed from the traditional rule of female modesty because of their exceptional nature as individuals (they are both *êtres à part*) and because of the exceptional nature of their relationship (her conviction that only he can save her from her despair). Casting Rousseau into the role of *philosophe* (or secular father confessor), Henriette attempts to justify her indiscretion by underlining her need to clarify what she has already revealed about herself and her confidence in Rousseau's ability to guide her. In her efforts to express herself, Henriette feels both intimidated and encouraged by Rousseau's invisible presence as interlocutor—by the conflicting images she constructs of him and of his reactions to her:

> Preoccupied by what I wish to write you, wanting to say enough yet afraid to say too much; . . . torn between the fear of appearing ridiculous to you and the hope of finding a dependable and indulgent guide; alternately bold and timid; . . . my writing varies according to how I imagine you to be; when my imagination only lets me see the philosopher, I become afraid and I tear up my letters and burn them; but when I imagine you endowed with all the traits of goodness and humanity, I regain my confidence and begin to write again with ease.[33]

This passage eloquently expresses the timorous coming to writing of a woman faced not only with all the stigmas against women writers in the eighteenth century, but also with her own personal anxiety of

influence stemming from her unfortunate choice of Rousseau as mentor. Knowing Rousseau's disapproval of women writers, how could
she help but feel intimidated by him? Yet convinced that he somehow
held the key to the happiness that had eluded her, she overcame her
self-consciousness and bared her heart to him: "Teach me how to live;
if you are not able to help me, then who else can? The confidence I feel
in your ability to guide me sustains me; no one has the gift of persuad-
ing me as you do."[34] Henriette's faith in Rousseau's ability to save her
from her despair, to guide and console her, was almost of a religious
nature; her entreaties to him resemble prayers: "Despite my impatience and no matter how long it takes you to respond, I will always
receive your advice with gratitude, as if it were a gift from heaven."[35]
She looked upon Rousseau as a spiritual guide, with the insight and
healing powers of a psychoanalyst: "Teach me how to rid myself of a
feeling so oppressive and overwhelming that it spreads its poison
everywhere. . . . Take drastic steps if necessary, tell me blunt truths if
I need to hear them, take away all the gangrene and heal me. I have
faith that with your help I will succeed in achieving the serenity that
I have yearned for so long."[36] Henriette's correspondence with Rousseau
strikingly illustrates how, even in his lifetime, Jean-Jacques had become a cult figure for certain of his readers.

In his second letter to Henriette, Rousseau had written: "I promise
you that I will think carefully about your situation and try to help
you. Whatever happens, I will never forget you as long as I live."[37]
However, tormented by serious problems of his own in 1765, Rousseau
never responded to Henriette's last three letters. In her letter to
Rousseau of December 1765, Henriette expressed her deep disappointment and concern at his silence. Afraid of having displeased him, she
respectfully assured him that she had abandoned her former course of
studies: "While I await your response, Monsieur, I have followed your
teachings concerning women scholars and your disapproval of them."[38]
Recalling this decision, she later wrote: "I abandoned my studies in
order to become a better person. . . . I retired to the country, where I
divided my time between domestic tasks and charity work."[39] Perhaps
it was Henriette's secret hope that by conforming to Rousseau's ideals
of female modesty, domesticity, and self-sacrifice, she would be more
likely to win his approval and sympathy—and, more important, that
he might reward her obedience by sending her the response for which
she had waited in vain for over a year. This hypothesis is supported

by the timid, almost obsequious tone of her last letter and by the curious shifting back and forth from the first- to third-person pronoun in referring to herself:

> I have just reread the last letter you wrote to Henriette a little more than a year ago. The kindness with which you promised never to forget her encourages me to be so bold as to remind you of her and to hope that you will not be irritated if I try to recall her to your memory. She has spent the whole summer hoping to receive a letter from you and fearing that she had perhaps annoyed you. . . . I dare to flatter myself with the hope that your silence is perhaps due to other causes: your private affairs, your infirmities, and your travels.[40]

This pronominal instability, this constant shifting back and forth from *I* to *she* and from *me* to *her*, not only underlines Henriette's lack of self-confidence, but also suggests a splitting or dissolution of her identity under the pressure of multiple griefs and disappointments.

Learning of Rousseau's return to Paris in 1770, Henriette sent a short note asking if she might call on him.[41] Rousseau's response was brusque and unencouraging: "The storms that have battered me for so many years have effaced a multitude of memories from my mind. I vaguely recall the name of Henriette and her letters, but this is not enough to desire to see her without knowing exactly who she is and what she wants of me." He then asks her to furnish a full account of herself and her motives in wishing to see him, and concludes with the warning: "If despite this letter, Henriette insists on coming to see me to suit herself, without worrying about whether her visit suits me as well, I will refuse to see her."[42] Rousseau's reluctance to see Henriette was in keeping with his general withdrawal from society, but she was nevertheless bitterly disappointed by it. "Reading this response, I felt my heart ache and my body grow cold: I was stunned," she recalls. "To avoid irritating him, I decided not to write back."[43]

Despite Rousseau's lack of encouragement for her scholarly and literary endeavors, despite her sense of having been forsaken by him, Henriette continued to find consolation and inspiration in his writings. In her last letter to him in 1765, she had written: "I have just read your *Lettres de la Montagne*, and I found them as fascinating as all your other works. There is no one but you, Monsieur, who writes like that and who knows how to speak to both the heart and to the mind."[44] It is interesting to note that the work in which Henriette found the greatest inspiration was neither *Julie* nor *Emile*, but Rousseau's lesser-known *Pensées*:

> Reading and reflecting on Rousseau's works, I felt as though I were conversing with him. I almost always had opened before me his *Pensées*, a collection which presents everything that he had ever thought or written on the subjects most interesting to humanity. For many years, the chapter on happiness served as my favorite text for daily meditation. When I felt agitated, troubled, or discouraged, I would immediately resume my conversation with Jean-Jacques, and I would not leave him until I felt at peace again.[45]

This passage illustrates the religious nature of Henriette's devotion to Rousseau and the strong impact he had on her daily life. As for many of her female contemporaries, Rousseau exerted a determining influence on Henriette's view of herself as a woman—an influence that seems tragically limiting to us, but that was in her view a source both of inspiration and consolation.

Due to the unfortunate choice of Rousseau as her idol and mentor, not only did Henriette renounce her plan of studies, but she also abandoned her activities as a writer. Her relationship with Rousseau provides a striking illustration of the adage that "the man who made her also broke her." For had it not been for the ideal of domesticity extolled in his writings, perhaps she would not have been so idealistic in her expectations or so painfully aware of her marginal status in society. Yet, at the same time, without Rousseau's ideal of sensibility and his bold literary style (which she strove to emulate), Henriette would undoubtedly have been less conscious of her own creative gifts and felt less compelled to analyze or justify her own life in writing. Finally, had it not been for his disapproval of women writers and scholars, perhaps she would have pursued her intellectual and literary activities, which until then had been the greatest source of consolation and pleasure in her life. Given her literary talents and strong motivation, both so evident in her letters, Henriette might well have become a writer of note. One wonders how many other literary vocations and works of art by women were stifled in this way by men like Rousseau.

Going Public: Henriette's Ironic Tribute to Her Mentor

The end of Henriette's story presents an unexpected twist. After Rousseau's death, she decided to publish their correspondence.[46] If he had been alive at the time, one wonders what his reaction might have been. Given his negative opinion of women writers—indeed of any woman who dared to assume a public role—he no doubt would have disapproved. Henriette's decision to publish the correspondence can even be viewed as an act of defiance and self-assertion—an unconscious rebellion against an overbearing mentor and against the oppressive gender system he represented, in which cultural productions were a jealously guarded male preserve. However, in the preface to the letters, Henriette claimed that their publication was a means of repaying her debt to Rousseau: "By publishing these letters, I am paying tribute to all I owe Rousseau, the serenity he brought me. . . . For it is he who taught me how to live."[47] This of course does not exclude the possibility of double motives behind the decision—that her desire to publish the letters may have reflected both a conscious expression of gratitude and an unconscious act of revolt.

Henriette's correspondence with Rousseau has elicited surprisingly little critical commentary, aside from a brief discussion by Paul Hoffmann in *La Femme dans la pensée des lumières* and a book by Anna Jaubert titled *Etude Stylistique de la Correspondance entre Henriette*** et J.-J. Rousseau. La Subjectivité dans le Discours.*[48] Jaubert's study is a detailed and highly technical analysis of Rousseau's and Henriette's respective styles (and the similarities between them), using the methods formulated by John Austin and other speech-act theorists. She does not discuss the sociohistoric context of the letters or the gender issues they raise. And, for reasons that are not explained, Jaubert excludes from her discussion Henriette's crucial last letter to Rousseau (dated December 12, 1765), in which she announces her decision to abandon both her studies and her writing. Neither Jaubert nor Hoffmann even mentions the preface that Henriette prepared for her own edition of the correspondence, which provides valuable insight into the evolution of her thinking about Rousseau and her decision to publish their letters.

Hoffmann's discussion focuses on Rousseau's inability to comprehend Henriette's situation or to grasp its social implications in terms of his own teachings on women. However, he evades the question of Henriette's vocation as a writer and her abandonment of it through Rousseau's influence; nor does he discuss the mimetic quality of her style—the way she patterned her writing and her self-portrayal after his. Moreover, Hoffmann's analysis of Henriette's dilemma reflects a distinctly sexist bias, since he ascribes her unhappiness to her inability to conform to Rousseau's limited view of women, rather than to the limits of the vision itself. According to Hoffmann, "Henriette illustrates the dilemma of a woman who needs to be bound by chains in order to feel alive; of a woman who, in the absence of precise and constraining duties, feels her personality dissolve."[49] Furthermore, Hoffmann implicitly adopts Rousseau's prejudices against women writers, for like Jean-Jacques, he fails to recognize Henriette's talents as a writer and the social constraints that oppose their development. "Henriette's solitude stems from her dependence upon others, . . . from a radical inability to transform her outer poverty into an inner richness," affirms Hoffmann. "Rousseau, on the other hand, is a prisoner of his own genius, which makes him deaf to the lament of those who lack such genius and who even lack his other forms of self-consolation" (or "suppléments de soi-même," as Hoffmann calls them).[50] If Henriette was lacking in "suppléments de soi-même" that could console her and fill her solitude, it was not because she lacked talents or inner resources, but because society in general, and Rousseau in particular, had deprived her of the freedom and self-confidence necessary to develop them. Although Henriette may not have been a genius, her letters reflect exceptional intellectual and literary gifts that were tragically stifled.

Given the richness and socio-historical significance of Henriette's letters, it is curious that she is virtually ignored in all the major studies of reader response to Rousseau. For example, in his study of the reception of *La Nouvelle Héloïse*, Labrosse does not include Henriette, perhaps because her letters to Rousseau deal more explicitly with *Emile* than with *Julie*. Nor is Henriette mentioned in Darnton's study of the Rousseauian reader, which is not surprising, since she does not fit his model of unquestioning adoration of and identification with Rousseau. Unlike Ransom and the other Rousseau enthusiasts studied by Darnton and Labrosse, Henriette dared to question Jean-Jacques's ideals of sensibility and domesticity, as well as his views on women, although she did acquiesce to them in the end. Moreover, Darnton's analysis of reader response to Rousseau does not deal at all with the issue of gender—whether men and women responded differently to his writings and sexual politics. In my reading of Henriette's little-known correspondence with Rousseau, as in the other chapters of my book, I have focused specifically on the issue of gender in order to give a more accurate picture of how his contemporaries responded to his views on women.

What makes Henriette's letters to Rousseau so valuable as sociohistorical documents is that they express with eloquence and acuity the plight of the single woman and woman scholar in eighteenth-century society. Her loneliness and frustrations are echoed in the writings of numerous other women of her period who, like her, were unable to marry for lack of a dowry and who sought to console themselves through scholarly and literary endeavors.[51]

Though timid and respectful in tone, Henriette's response to *Emile* challenges the dominant gender structures of the period and undermines the ideals of domesticity and sensibility extolled by Rousseau, whom she nonetheless greatly admired. The correspondence between Henriette and Rousseau not only throws an interesting light on the image of Jean-Jacques constructed by his women readers according to their own needs and longings, but also presents a unique case history of Rousseau's interaction with an unmarried woman scholar—his grappling with her dilemma and with the shortcomings of his own teachings on women.

3

La Femme Mal Mariée:

Madame d'Epinay's Challenge to *Julie* and *Emile*

Louise d'Epinay is best remembered today as the wealthy patroness of Rousseau who lent him l'Ermitage, where he wrote much of *Julie*. Among her contemporaries d'Epinay was best known as a friend of the Encyclopédistes, whose home attracted some of the most brilliant minds of her time, including Diderot, Duclos, d'Holbach, Grimm, Galiani, d'Alembert, and of course Rousseau. Voltaire, whose close friend she became during a prolonged stay in Geneva, referred to her affectionately as *"ma philosophe"* and described her as "an eagle in a gauze cage."[1] However, d'Epinay was not merely *l'amie des philosophes*; she was a gifted and prolific writer as well. Author of a remarkable 1800-page autobiographical novel, *Histoire de Madame de Montbrillant* (not published until long after her death), she also wrote *Les Conversations d'Emilie*, a series of lively conversations between a mother and child, first published in 1773. Shortly before her death in 1783, an expanded version of this second work was awarded the Montyon Prix d'Utilité by the Académie Française for its contributions to the field of education. D'Epinay was also an important, albeit anonymous, contributor to the *Correspondance littéraire*, directed by Frédéric Melchior Grimm, her long-time friend and lover. During Grimm's frequent absences abroad, she wrote many of the articles and, on several occasions, served as unofficial director of the journal, with nominal help from Diderot. Her talents as an editor were highly valued by her friends, who often submitted their work to her for critical appraisal. For example, Rousseau entrusted the first version of *Julie* to her, Diderot several of his plays, Galiani his controversial *Dialogues sur les Blés*, and

Grimm frequently sought her advice concerning articles to be published in the *Correspondance littéraire*.[2] In addition to these literary and
journalistic endeavors, d'Epinay maintained a lively correspondence
with some of the most celebrated figures of her time, including Voltaire,
Diderot, Galiani, and Catherine of Russia.

In studying Rousseau's reception by eighteenth-century women
writers, I have found d'Epinay's reponse to him to be particularly
important and complex. For not only was she his close personal friend
(and later his bitter enemy); but, during the last thirty years of her life,
she was engaged with him in an intense intellectual and literary rivalry that challenged his narrow vision of women's role and capabilities. Over the years, they became rival figures of authority on the issue
of women's education and their proper role in society. In this chapter,
I examine Rousseau's determining influence on d'Epinay's literary
career, the challenge to his sexual politics underlying her works, and

Portrait of Louise d'Epinay by the Swiss painter Jean Etienne Liotard.
Courtesy of the Bibliothèque nationale, Paris.

his response to that challenge. I then look at how Rousseau influenced d'Epinay's view of herself as a woman writer and trace the emergence of a feminine voice in her writing.

The Life behind the Works

Since much of this chapter deals with d'Epinay's autobiographical novel, it seems appropriate to begin by briefly tracing the main events of her life. Born in 1726, Louise d'Esclavelles was the only child of an impecunious nobleman, the last male descendant of a distinguished family from Normandy. At the age of fifty-nine, after a long military career, her father had married the daughter of a prominent bourgeois of Valenciennes. When Louise was ten, her parents moved to Paris to complete their daughter's education and to begin making the social connections necessary for an advantageous marriage. These hopes were shattered, however, by the sudden death of M. d'Esclavelles soon after their arrival. Left practically destitute, Louise and her mother were taken in by Mme d'Esclavelles's sister, Mme de Bellegarde, wife of a rich *fermier général*. Although dazzled by the luxury of her new surroundings, young Louise was made painfully aware of her position as a poor relation by the humiliating remarks of her aunt, who constantly reminded her of all they owed to her generosity. Louise's keen intelligence and aptitude for learning only aggravated her strained relations with her aunt, who mocked her scholarly inclinations and threatened to fire their governess for supposedly neglecting the education of her daughter (the future Mme d'Houdetot) in order to tutor her niece. The governess was forbidden to give Louise further instruction. D'Epinay would spend much of her adult life trying to compensate for the inadequacy of her education.

Mme d'Esclavelles soon tired of her sister's tyranny and moved to a small apartment with her daughter before sending her to a nearby convent for two years. There Louise received the convent education typical of the period: a smattering of academic instruction, lessons in *les arts d'agrément* (music, drawing, embroidery, and dance) to enhance her value on the marriage market, and a heavy dose of religious training. D'Epinay gives few details concerning her stay in the convent, except that she left it at the age of thirteen, very pious and barely literate.

When Louise was sixteen, negotiations were undertaken for her marriage to a duke, but the plans fell through for lack of a sufficient

dowry, which her uncle refused to provide. Louise was secretly relieved at this setback, since she had for several years harbored a secret
passion for her cousin, Denis-Joseph de la Live d'Epinay, son of M. de
Bellegarde. Their affection was mutual, but the Bellegardes vehemently
opposed the match because of Louise's meager dowry. After his wife's
sudden death in 1743 and after considerable pressure from his son, M.
de Bellegarde finally consented to the marriage. Louise soon discovered, however, that she had been only a passing fancy for her cousin;
the marriage had been a convenient way for him to gain access to part
of his inheritance and appointment as adjunct *fermier général* to his
father. Within three months of their wedding, shortly after Louise
learned she was pregnant with their first child, M. d'Epinay was
publicly pursuing a pretty actress—the first in a long series of mistresses who, by exploiting his penchant for debauchery and ostentation, were to dilapidate his large fortune and lead him into bankruptcy
and disgrace.

     Through her husband's negligence, Mme d'Epinay often found
herself unable to meet basic household expenses. To protect her limited dowry and the inheritance of her children, she was able, with the
help of her father-in-law, to obtain a legal *séparation de biens* in 1749.
Her predicament is a striking illustration of the legal and financial
dependence of married women even among the upper classes; her
autobiographical novel demonstrates how easily a woman could fall
victim to an irresponsible and egotistic husband. Without her father-
in-law's legal and financial support, Louise would have been practically penniless and would have had little recourse even in a court of
law.

     After trying in vain to revive her husband's affections, Mme
d'Epinay finally separated from him after he carelessly infected her
with venereal disease. Lonely and vulnerable, she succumbed to the
charms of Claude Dupin de Francueil.[3] D'Epinay's affair with Francueil
lasted several years (from mid-1749 until late 1752) and resulted in the
birth of at least one and probably two children.[4] Early in the relationship, she discovered to her horror that she had infected him with the
venereal disease caught from her husband. Her happiness was further
clouded by Francueil's attraction to other women and his growing
indifference to her. As with her husband, Louise underwent the torments of doubt and jealousy, rendered more painful by her own sense
of remorse and humiliation. After a period of emotional desolation,
she fell in love again at the age of twenty-eight with Frédéric Melchior

Grimm, who was to remain her companion until her death thirty years later.

c∞∞

In examining d'Epinay's life, one inevitably confronts the problems of fictional autobiography posed by her novel. These problems are compounded by the fact that most of her editors and biographers—with the exception of Georges Roth and Ruth Weinreb—tend to take her novel at face value as authentic memoirs. One must distinguish carefully between the events of d'Epinay's life and the fictionalized presentation of those events in her novel, which is not an authentic memoir, but a fictionalized autobiography presented as a *roman à cléf*.[5] As Roth and Weinreb point out, the mediations between fiction and reality in *Histoire de Madame de Montbrillant* are complex and problematic and are often further complicated by d'Epinay's underlying aims, both personal and polemical.[6] For example, in her novel, d'Epinay describes in detail—and no doubt exaggerates—the various ploys and deceptions used by her cousin to persuade his father (and Louise herself) to consent to their marriage. According to Roth, d'Epinay's purpose was to defend herself against accusations that she had encouraged her cousin's affections in order to usurp the family fortune. The episodes leading up to her wedding also serve to illustrate her cousin's unscrupulous, impulsive character and her own naiveté for the dual purpose of foreshadowing the failure of their marriage and blaming her husband for it, while exculpating herself. These episodes—like the chapters describing Louise's unhappy marriage, her affairs with Francueil and Grimm, and her stormy friendship with Rousseau—exemplify the complex mediations between fiction and reality in d'Epinay's writing and must be read with a certain critical distance.

Madame d'Epinay and Rousseau: Les Affaires de l'Ermitage

It was through Francueil that Mme d'Epinay became acquainted with Rousseau. Their first meeting probably took place in the summer of 1749, when Rousseau was invited to the d'Epinay's country estate to help organize a performance of his play *L'Engagement téméraire*.[7] He was then thirty-eight and still unknown; not until the following year would he attract attention in literary circles by winning the Académie de Dijon's first prize with his *Discours sur les sciences et les arts*. However, like

Francueil, Mme d'Epinay quickly recognized that this moody clockmaker's son from Geneva was a man of superior intelligence and remarkable talent. In the hope of providing Rousseau with the security and peace of mind needed to develop his creative potential, d'Epinay would later offer him l'Ermitage, a small but comfortable house on the grounds of la Chevrette, her country estate north of Paris.

The six years leading up to this invitation were marked by significant changes in the lives of both d'Epinay and Rousseau. The latter would achieve celebrity with the success of his opera *Le Devin du*

Illustration by Maurice Leloir for the 1889 edition of the *Confessions.* Here Rousseau thanks Mme d'Epinay for offering him the house and garden of l'Ermitage, pictured in the background. Courtesy of the Bibliothèque nationale, Paris.

village and with the publication of his two discourses and his article in the *Encyclopédie* titled "Economie politique." During the same period, Mme d'Epinay would also become well known as a salonnière. Through Francueil, she became friends with the novelist Duclos, who introduced her to the lively circle of literati hosted by Mlle Quinault. Later, through Grimm, she became friends with the Encyclopédistes and was admitted to the distinguished d'Holbach coterie.[8] Thanks to these connections, d'Epinay's home gradually became the meeting place for some of the most important figures in Parisian literary and diplomatic circles, rivaling even the prestigious salons of Mmes Necker, Geoffrin, and Du Deffand.[9]

It was both as a patroness of the arts and letters and as a personal friend to Rousseau that d'Epinay offered him l'Ermitage in 1756. It may well be, as Rousseau later charged, that her offer was motivated in part by vanity and self-interest—by the desire to have a literary celebrity as a permanent fixture in her constellation of stars. In the *Confessions*, he describes how his initial joy and gratitude gradually turned to resentment and even rage at the dependent role he was forced (or felt obligated) to play with her:

> Until then, I had filled this role without thinking of it as an obligation. But now I realized that I had hung a chain round my neck, and that only friendship had so far prevented me from feeling its weight, which I had made even heavier by my dislike for large gatherings. Madame d'Epinay took advantage of this to make me a proposal that seemed in my favor but that was even more favorable to her: to send me a message whenever she was alone or nearly so. . . . As a result, I no longer called on her at my convenience but at hers, and I could never count on having any time to myself.

Rousseau clearly felt that d'Epinay had invited him to live on her estate not so much for his benefit as for her own amusement: "In this way she filled up as best she could the voids that the absence of her usual circle of friends left in her amusements," he claimed. "My company was at best a poor substitute, but it was better than downright loneliness, which she could not bear."[10]

Not surprisingly, d'Epinay presents quite a different view of the story. Like Diderot,[11] she underlines Rousseau's difficult personality— his moodiness, hypersensitivity, unsociability, and tendency to paranoia. In *Montbrillant*, d'Epinay recalls a visit to Rousseau (whom she refers to as "René") a few months after his move to l'Ermitage: "His solitude has already caused him to get all worked up. He complains about every one" (III: 24–25). After their first quarrel, she complains bitterly of what she considers his duplicity and ingratitude. She accuses him of picking fights with her and with her friends so that he could later claim that she had forced him to leave. A key source of friction between them was Rousseau's passion for her sister-in-law Mme d'Houdetot, which d'Epinay viewed as hypocritical and deceitful. "In my eyes, René is nothing but a moral dwarf perched on stilts," she declares in her novel (III: 151). To which Roth responds: "This is indeed the conclusion to which the author wishes to lead her readers" (III: 151, n. 3).

The truth of the story no doubt lies somewhere in between the versions given by d'Epinay and Rousseau and by various witnesses to the events who sought to corroborate or to contest the veracity of their accounts. It is not my purpose here to reiterate the tensions and misunderstandings that punctuated his two-year stay at l'Ermitage or to compare the rival versions of their successive quarrels and final falling-out presented by Jean-Jacques in his *Confessions* and by d'Epinay in *Histoire de Madame de Montbrillant*. This has been done quite amply by other scholars.[12] Of greater interest to me is an aspect of their relationship that largely has been neglected by Rousseau and d'Epinay specialists alike: how the personal and literary rivalry between them served as a key motivating force and creative impetus behind some of their most important works.

Histoire de Madame de Montbrillant *as a* Literary Response and Challenge *to* Julie

It was in the summer of 1756, during his solitary walks and reveries in the forest surrounding l'Ermitage, that Rousseau first imagined the characters of Julie, Saint-Preux, and Claire and began composing the letters between them that gradually developed into *La Nouvelle Héloïse*. When d'Epinay returned to la Chevrette in the spring of 1757, Rousseau gave her the first two *cahiers* (probably Books I and II) of his novel to read. She recalls her first impressions of *Julie* in *Montbrillant*:

> After lunch, we read René's notebooks together. I don't know why exactly, but I was disappointed. The manuscript is beauti-

Top: Illustration by Maurice Leloir for the 1889 edition of the *Confessions* showing Grimm and Rousseau with Mme d'Epinay in her drawing room at la Chevrette. Courtesy of the Bibliothèque nationale, Paris.

Bottom: Illustration by Alfred Johannot for the 1837 edition of the *Confessions* showing Sophie d'Houdetot's first visit to Rousseau at l'Ermitage, after he began writing *Julie*. This unexpected visit sparked his passion for her, "the first and only love in all [his] life" and which would become a bitter source of contention between Rousseau and d'Epinay's circle. The caption reads: "She came; I saw her; I was drunk with love that lacked an object. . . . I saw my Julie in Mme d'Houdetot." Courtesy of the Bibliothèque nationale, Paris.

fully written, but it seems overdone to me and rather artificial. The characters don't speak naturally; it's always the author who speaks for them. . . . I don't want to lie to René, but I don't want to hurt his feelings either. (III: 100)

D'Epinay's negative comments regarding the first two books of Rousseau's novel parallel those made by a number of her contemporaries, including Mme du Deffand, Mme de Choiseul, Grimm, and Diderot. Diderot, for example, found the manuscript *"feuillu,* . . . that is to say wordy and redundant," as Rousseau himself later reported.[13] We have no way of knowing whether d'Epinay expressed her opinion of *Julie* to Rousseau in as frank a manner as Diderot. In *Montbrillant,* she does not report her conversation with him, but simply alludes to it in passing: "I conveyed my opinion to him as gently as I could. He didn't seem offended by it, but instead of staying four days as planned, he left at the end of lunch, greatly exaggerating the regret he felt at having to leave us" (III: 108).

Although disappointed by Rousseau's novel, d'Epinay seems to have found it sufficiently inspiring to try writing a novel of her own. In a letter to her lover Volx (Grimm's alter-ego in *Montbrillant*), Emilie confides: "I just began writing a piece, and I'm quite satisfied with the beginning. It was René's novel that gave me the idea of writing it. When I have a few notebooks finished, I'll send them to you to find out if they are worth continuing" (III: 131). Grimm was away on military duty for six months, and Roth contends that d'Epinay's primary motive for composing the novel was to amuse herself and her lover during his absence. The desire to fill the emotional void caused by Grimm's absence may also have been an important motivating factor, as Elisabeth Badinter has suggested.[14] However, both these explanations trivialize the ambitiousness of d'Epinay's project. In my view, it was above all her literary rivalry with Rousseau—the desire to measure her creative talents against his—that prompted d'Epinay to write her novel.

That *Madame de Montbrillant* was conceived as a response to *Julie* is made clear in the novel itself. In a letter to Volx, Emilie explains: "René's work gives me the urge to write a novel in letter form. It seems to me that one needs only a natural style and good taste in order to write well in this genre" (III: 118). The claim that Rousseau's style lacked naturalness and taste—and that d'Epinay herself could do better—is made more explicit in a subsequent letter from Emilie to Volx: "All his letters are so flowery, so overdone, that the style strikes me as cold and tiresome" (III: 131). D'Epinay's literary rivalry with Rousseau is expressed most clearly in a letter from Volx to Emilie, in which he conveys his initial reaction to her novel: "It's a true masterpiece," he declares.

> If you take my advice, you won't show this work to anyone until it is finished; for your writing might become constrained, your style less natural if you worried about your readers. Look upon your work as a monument reserved for yourself alone, and you will produce a work worthy of a woman of genius. . . . As for René, if you have shown him any of this work, I predict trouble ahead. His judgment is too keen for him not to sense the huge difference between your Sophie and his boring, pedantic heroine. (III: 171–72)[15]

In this passage, d'Epinay makes it clear that she created her heroine as a rival to Julie and wrote her novel as a challenge to *La Nouvelle Héloïse*. She was, moreover, fully confident that she would emerge victorious in her literary rivalry with Rousseau. Using Volx as her *porte-parole*, d'Epinay insists on the superiority of her character portrayals in comparison to Rousseau's. "The author makes no show of false modesty," notes Roth. "She ascribes to Grimm's pen the same enthusiastic praise for her writing later expressed by Sainte-Beuve and the Goncourts" (III: 172, n. 2).

Here, too, d'Epinay's criticisms of Rousseau's novel parallel those made by other literary critics, who found Julie's long letters redundant, didactic, and often boring. For example, in a devastating review of *Julie*—"a work in which the author so arrogantly puts himself above the rules both of language and of decorum"—Voltaire was especially critical of the work's moralizing tone. "All these grand adventures are embellished with wonderful commonplaces on virtue. Never was there a wench who preached so finely, nor a girl-seducing valet who philosophized so grandly. In his long novel, Jean-Jacques has managed to write three or four pages worth reading and about a thousand pages of moralizing speeches."[16] And, in another review of Rousseau's novel, Grimm declared: "Oh, you can have that priggish Julie and her pedantic tutor; you know that I can't stand them."[17] Similarly, d'Epinay's charge that Rousseau's style lacked naturalness and taste echoes Fréron's review of *Julie* in *L'Année littéraire*: "The style is often emphatic, incorrect, enigmatic, obscure, affected, and vulgar," he charged. "The novel is filled with gibberish, false wit, and artificial images."[18]

Casting Volx in the role of omniscient literary critic, d'Epinay re-
iterates these criticisms of *Julie* and claims that she has avoided all
these problems in her own novel. Volx is especially impressed by the
naturalness, realism, and spontaneity of her style. He is amazed that
her first drafts require so few corrections: "So far, I haven't found the
need for a single correction. It's really hard to believe that this is only
the first draft you're sending me" (III: 196). Contrary to Rousseau,
who complained that writing was often a laborious and painful effort
for him, requiring constant revisions, d'Epinay underlined the ease,
rapidity, and pleasure with which she wrote.

Finally, in contrast to Rousseau's "cold and tiresome style," Volx
praises Emilie's ability to hold her reader's interest. Despite his fatigue
when he began her novel, Volx soon found himself totally absorbed by
it: "I couldn't put it down. At two in the morning, I was still reading"
(III: 171). Volx's reaction to Emilie's novel parallels Mme de Talmont's
experience reading *Julie*, which Rousseau relates in the *Confessions* (I:
547). Like Rousseau, d'Epinay invokes her ability to keep a reader awake
all night as proof of her skill as a writer. Volx especially praises the
vividness of her character portrayals and the liveliness of her dialogue:
"Your portrait of Beauval is a masterpiece. Nothing could be truer to
life, nor more delicate and refined" (III: 124). And later: "Your work is
truly a masterpiece and deserves to be published" (III: 163).

This passage, like the panegyrics that precede it, is clearly designed to elicit a positive response to d'Epinay's own novel. Not only
does it express her self-confidence as a writer; it also suggests her
intention to publish her work and her faith that the public will appreciate its value. Given d'Epinay's observations in her novel concerning
the strong prejudices against women writers—"Few people are willing to acknowledge their talent, and many are apt to accuse them of
literary pretensions" (III: 141)—this unabashed expression of self-
confidence constitutes a bold challenge to the literary and social conventions of the period.

What is most striking about d'Epinay's self-appraisals as a writer
is the recurrence of the label *chef-d'œuvre*, which she applies to her
work more frequently than the conventions of modesty would seem to
permit, with such frequency that the repetition has an almost incantatory effect—as if by repeating the claim she could make it come true.
And indeed, the enthusiastic praise of d'Epinay's novel by nineteenth-
century critics such as Sainte-Beuve and the Goncourts vindicates her
faith in her literary talents. "No other work provides such a vivid and

accurate description of eighteenth-century society and *mœurs*," affirms Sainte-Beuve. "The memoirs of Mme d'Epinay are not simply a work, they are an epoch."[19] The Goncourts were even more enthusiastic in their praise. Evoking d'Epinay's literary rivalry with Rousseau, they unequivocally proclaim her superiority as an autobiographer: "There is a man in Rousseau's *Confessions*, but a whole society in Mme d'Epinay's memoirs," they declare.

> Marriage, love, family life, adultery, social institutions, and scandals come to life. The female characters seem to rise up from the page, and Rousseau is frighteningly true to life. D'Epinay's confessions are unparalleled, for the portrayal of her family and milieu always leads back to her probing study of herself, revealing her secret failings and her deepest desires. . . . Self-knowledge and knowledge of others have perhaps never advanced so far in the writings of any man and certainly will not go any farther in the writings of any woman.[20]

Their praise for d'Epinay's novel is all the more impressive when one considers that the text published is in fact an unfinished first draft.

Since d'Epinay's correspondence with Grimm appears to have been lost,[21] there is no way to know for certain whether the letters exchanged between Emilie and Volx in *Montbrillant* were actually exchanged in real life between d'Epinay and Grimm. Roth claims that the letters are largely fictional, while Schlobach suggests that some may be authentic.[22] Whether they were drawn from real life or not, these letters provide valuable insight into d'Epinay's view of herself as a young woman writer embarking on a doubly ambitious project: writing her first novel and attempting to rival the work of a well-known male author.

Histoire de Madame de Montbrillant
as an Ideological Challenge to Julie

Thus far, we have considered how *Histoire de Madame de Montbrillant* responds to *Julie* on a stylistic level. Let us now turn to the more complex issue of how d'Epinay's novel responds to Rousseau's on an ideological level—that is, on the level of norms, conventions, ideals, and their representation. For not only is *Montbrillant* an eloquent response to the repression of female desire underlying Rousseau's novel.

It also represents the strivings of a woman writer to create within the confines of male-dominated novelistic genres—*le roman aristocratique et mondain* (the aristocratic, worldly novel best represented by Duclos's works)[23] and *le roman bourgeois* epitomized by *Julie*—*un roman de femme* in which the experiences and dilemmas of women might be presented in a more authentic manner, in which their grievances and longings could be expressed from within, rather than viewed from the outside through the refractive lens of male desire and self-interest.

Through its detailed description of d'Epinay's unhappy marriage, *Montbrillant* illustrates the painful dilemma of *la femme mal mariée* in eighteenth-century French society. Because of her upbringing, and especially her mother's influence, d'Epinay fervently believed in the Christian ideal of conjugal fidelity and the newly evolving bourgeois ideal of domesticity that together were to find their most powerful expression in *La Nouvelle Héloïse*. Her husband, on the other hand, belonged to the generation of financiers of the *haute bourgeoisie* who attempted to rival the lifestyle of the French Court through ostentatious spending and by publicly flaunting their relations with richly kept courtesans. Along with other aristocratic values, he had adopted the conception of marriage prevailing among the court nobility, who accepted and even expected infidelity on the part of both spouses. The incompatibility of the young couple's views on marriage and family life soon became evident through her husband's flagrant love affairs, his virtual abandonment of her and their children, his financial irresponsibility, and his thwarting of her desire to breastfeed their children and to educate them at home. All these obstacles to domestic happiness, painstakingly described in her novel, challenge the idealized view of marriage presented in *Julie*.

In an effort to fill the emotional void created by the failure of her marriage, d'Epinay explored the various outlets available to married women of her age and class. She carefully explored each of these options, with illuminating and sometimes painful results. In *Montbrillant*, she records her experiences at length, providing an inside view of the everyday lives of upper-class women of her period and valuable insight into the problems and frustrations they faced. Nearly all the options explored by d'Epinay in her life and later in her novel are also presented in *La Nouvelle Héloïse*, either as acceptable or unacceptable outlets for female energies. However, the options Rousseau considers most appropriate for respectable married women— dedication to children and husband, close friendships with women, and religious devotion—are precisely the ones toward which d'Epinay expresses the most ambivalence. On the other hand, the options criticized most strongly by Rousseau—extra-marital affairs and participation in literary and intellectual activities—are the very ones d'Epinay comes to view as the most fulfilling. In this way, *Montbrillant* challenges the feminine ideals of self-effacement and self-sacrifice advocated in *Julie*. By refusing to deny her ambitions and desires in her self-portrayal, d'Epinay provides a far more realistic view of the problems and tensions experienced by her female contemporaries and, in so doing, points to the distortions and blind spots in Rousseau's male-centered view of women. In many ways, *Montbrillant* can be read as a survival manual for eighteenth-century women in their struggle to find happiness and self-fulfillment despite woefully inadequate educations, repressive social conventions, unhappy and indissoluble marriages, and all the traps and contradictions of the double standard.

During the early years of her marriage, Emilie de Montbrillant feels continually torn between the *morale chrétienne* and *esprit bourgeois* of her mother on the one hand and, on the other, the *morale mondaine* and *esprit aristocratique* of her husband and many of their friends. Her mother had raised her to believe that a married woman's principal duty was to devote herself to her husband and children and to maintain a reputation beyond reproach through strict observance of traditional Christian morality. The ideals of domesticity, chastity, and maternal devotion she preached were virtually identical to those advocated by Rousseau in *Julie*. Emilie's husband, on the other hand, encourages her to engage in the activities and pleasures of *la vie mondaine*, like other women of her age and class. For a year or so she tries desperately to sustain her husband's affection by accompanying him to the opera, the theater, balls, and soirées, despite her mother's disapproval. Her husband's growing indifference causes her to become increasingly dependent on the whirl of social events to fill the emotional void within her.

After the birth of her son, Emilie becomes increasingly disenchanted with the frivolity of society life. She asks her husband to let her withdraw to their country home in order to take a more active role in the raising of her child, who was living thirty miles away with a wet nurse. However, her husband only ridicules her plan. Emilie's hope that the birth of their child might revive their marriage are shattered by his indifference, which he makes no effort to conceal. When she expresses her hope that the presence of their son might rekindle his affection for her, he coldly replies: "I'm not about to come back to you. You are a child lost in your dreams. . . . The conventions of society and good taste simply don't allow me to pay more attention to you or to show more affection" (I: 395).

This statement may appear exaggerated or even facetious to twentieth-century readers. Yet the extent to which it reflects prevailing attitudes toward marriage in mid-eighteenth-century France is illustrated by the fact that even thirty years later (in the 1780s), Condorcet was mocked by his friends for showing too much affection toward his wife in public and for appearing too frequently in her company. More than any other single passage in d'Epinay's novel, this remark by M. de Montbrillant presents the strongest challenge to the ideal of companionate marriage advocated in *Julie*; for it illustrates the force of social attitudes and prejudices that prevented women like d'Epinay from realizing the domestic happiness that Rousseau seemed to offer devoted wives and mothers. Without the participation of both spouses, there clearly could be no companionate marriage or any hope for the kind of family life portrayed in Rousseau's novel.

Dismayed by her husband's slavish imitation of aristocratic mores, Emilie exclaims: "What madness not to dare to love one's own wife and to prefer one's own torment to the effort it would take to rise above this barbaric way of thinking!" (I: 396). In a lame effort to excuse his own infidelities, Emilie's husband reminds her of the freedom he has given her, hinting that he would not mind an occasional infidelity on her part: "Haven't I always encouraged you to amuse yourself as you liked? Haven't I given you complete freedom?" he asks. But Emilie is not duped by his efforts to placate her or to belittle her feelings: "You speak of my amusements, when it's my happiness I'm talking about. . . . There can be no happiness for me without your love. What could ever make up for your absence and console me for the loss of your heart?" (I: 395). Much of the rest of the novel is an attempt by d'Epinay to answer this crucial question: How indeed could a woman like Emilie fill the emotional void created by an unhappy marriage?

ﮯﮯﮯ

Abandoned by her husband, separated from her child, and no longer finding consolation in the religious devotion of her childhood, Emilie tries for a time to fill her emotional needs through friendships with other women. When she becomes close friends with a young single woman named Darcy, Emilie is too naïve to recognize the strong homoerotic overtones of their relationship. After Mlle Darcy's first visit to the Montbrillant's country estate, Emilie confides to her: "If you were a man, I would be frightened by the emptiness I've felt since you left" (I: 453). And in her journal she confesses: "I'm feeling sad and restless. I haven't seen Mlle Darcy today; I can't get along without her. I feel a strange emptiness and languor inside me. . . . I must be more attached to her than I realize, for I can think only of her" (I: 456). Yet Mlle Darcy has a lover who occupies much of her time and affection, as does Emilie's other closest friend, her cousin Mme de Sally. In her diary Emilie sadly writes:

> I can't get used to the emptiness in my heart, which searches in vain for something to hold on to. When I try to explain my feelings to Mme de Sally, she only laughs and answers that I'm all mixed up in my desires and that she is not so foolish as to take me at my word, since one fine morning she would find that she is only the shadow of what my heart is seeking. Mlle Darcy gives me whatever spare time is left over from her liaison. As for my children, taking care of them is still only a duty for me and does not yet fill my heart. (I: 468)

Prisoner within the dominant heterosexual ideology, Emilie gradually comes to the conclusion that close friendships with other women and even motherhood are but poor substitutes for what everyone around her considers the ultimate object of female desire: the love and companionship of a man.

This also seems to be the conclusion that Julie ultimately reaches at the end of *La Nouvelle Héloïse*. After painfully repressing her passion for Saint-Preux throughout her marriage—by sublimating it through religious pietism, devotion to her husband and children, and love for Claire—Julie finally recognizes its invincible power over her. The parallels between Julie's relationship with Claire and Emilie's friendships with Mlle Darcy and Mme de Sally are quite striking in this respect. However, what gradually emerges in *Montbrillant* is a pointed critique of the idealized view of female friendship presented in *Julie*. In the course of her novel, d'Epinay implicitly challenges this view by drawing attention to the homoeroticism underlying such friendships (which she considers a poor substitute for heterosexual relations) and to the rivalry and self-interest that makes genuine friendship and solidarity between women difficult, if not impossible, in the socio-economic context of the period. Through her realistic portrayal of the intense jealousy Emilie feels toward her rivals and her bitter disenchantment when she discovers the self-interested perfidy of her two closest friends (Darcy and Sally), d'Epinay points to the blind spots in Rousseau's idealized view of female friendship.

While female rivalry is systematically suppressed in *La Nouvelle Héloïse*, along with all other disruptive forms of female desire, its constant recurrence in *Montbrillant* underlines the fact that, in eighteenth-century French society, rivalry among women was a fact of life. The intense competition for husbands on the marriage market, the widespread adultery and ostentatiously frivolous lifestyle prevalent among the upper classes, and, above all, the lack of serious outlets for female energies—all these factors fostered bitter rivalry among women. D'Epinay probes this situation in a series of conversations between Emilie and her sister-in-law, Mme de Ménil. Worldly and pragmatic, Mme de Ménil insists that women should recognize female rivalry for what it is: a role they are forced to play by society and which they should not allow to destroy their friendship or their sense of compassion for each other. "Nothing can excuse lack of solidarity between women," she declares. "You're indicting a good number of women!" replies Emilie.

[Ménil] Not so many as you think. I don't believe women are naturally capricious, and when they quarrel, it's almost always the fault of a third person. [Emilie] That's because this third person often creates a rivalry between them. [Ménil] No, that's not what I mean. . . . Each woman has only to make the best use of her advantages, and the one who misses her mark can then scorn the fool who prefers her rival. But as for *la pauvre préférée*, the poor woman he prefers, . . . she eventually finds herself abandoned in turn. [Emilie] But what if *la pauvre préférée* taunts the other woman with her triumph? [Ménil] Oh! she's an idiot who doesn't deserve to be envied, because one should never take too seriously a role one is forced to play. (II: 253)

Despite the difficulties and dangers posed by genuine friendship between women, d'Epinay underscores the importance of female solidarity as a source of strength and consolation: "Since friendship is the best consolation for the pains of love, one should always seek out a close woman friend when one has a lover," declares Mme de Ménil.

"Men aren't interested in friendship; they find its obligations too difficult to fulfill. . . . When they've slept with us on a regular basis, they think they've satisfied all our needs" (II: 327).

When Emilie expresses surprise to learn of her sister-in-law's affair with an opera singer, Mme de Ménil openly mocks the conventions of discretion and prudishness that traditionally create barriers between women: "Just because you married the older brother, you think you alone have the right to make a cuckold in the family. . . . Drop your prudishness. We're alone here and trust each other, so why shouldn't we talk freely?" (II: 328). It is ironic that Emilie's most courageous act of solidarity toward another woman—honoring her dying sister-in-law's request to burn her personal papers to hide an adulterous liaison—is misinterpreted as an act of self-interest and causes her to be publicly ostracized until the misunderstanding is finally resolved.

Since Emilie finds female friendships, society life, and even motherhood incapable of fulfilling the emotional void created by the failure of her marriage, it seems almost inevitable that she would eventually yield to the temptations and pressures of *la morale mondaine*, which her husband openly advocates and to which the majority of her friends tacitly subscribe.[24] When Emilie finally resolves to break off all intimate relations with her husband after he carelessly infects her with venereal disease, he nonchalantly replies:

> Very well, Madame, just as you like. . . . Let's go peacefully our separate ways. For my part, I promise that I'll approve anything you do, and I expect the same indulgence from you. From now on, whenever we see each other, we'll always be happy and content. Anxiety and suspicion will give way to cheerfulness and trust. Such mutual tolerance makes for happy couples! (I: 466)

D'Epinay carefully reconstructs her husband's complacent apology for marital infidelity to illustrate the obstacles that lay in the way of realizing the Rousseauian ideal of conjugal felicity and also, no doubt, to excuse her own well-publicized liaisons with Francueil and Grimm.

Through Emilie, d'Epinay portrays herself both as sexually attractive and as a virtuous heroine in distress. (Both aspects of this self-portrait contradict Rousseau's portrayal of d'Epinay in the *Confessions* as sexually unattractive and morally corrupt, unashamedly embracing Diderot's "secret doctrine" of sexual libertinism.) After resisting efforts to seduce her by various men in her circle of acquaintances—including an attempted rape by a friend of her husband (in Montbrillant's presence)—Emilie finally succumbs to the charms of Formeuse (Francueil).

In her novel, d'Epinay attempts to justify her liaison by evoking her husband's repeated infidelities, her earnest attempts to save their marriage, the impossibility of divorce, and above all the genuineness and superior nature of her love. Formeuse's claim that love is man's (and presumably woman's) "noblest and most precious prerogative" is ardently adopted by Emilie as her new credo. The belief that adultery is justified in a case like hers, that a woman has the right to search for love outside an unhappy marriage, gradually becomes the core of a personal morality distinct from both the *morale mondaine* of her husband and the Christian morality of her mother. This credo sustains Emilie through the pain and humiliation caused by Formeuse's gradual abandonment of her for other women. She senses that happiness would still be possible for her if only she could find some worthier object for her affection—a faithful lover, with whom she could realize her ideal of monogamous heterosexual love.

Before Volx appears on the scene to console her for her first lover's betrayal, Emilie undergoes a long period of emotional desolation similar to what she experienced with her husband, but rendered more painful by her own sense of remorse and humiliation. Under her mother's guidance, Emilie seems to undergo a religious conversion (not unlike Julie's) and resolves to lead a pious, retired life. In a meeting with her mother's confessor, she even expresses the desire to enter a convent. However, the priest senses that Emilie's sudden wish to renounce the world is neither genuine nor healthy. When he learns that her resolution has been prompted by an unhappy love affair, he wisely observes: "You are in the same situation as any unhappily married but respectable woman who still feels a need for love. God becomes the focus for a restless sensibility that is difficult to restrain. Are you prepared to lead a life of hypocrisy that can never satisfy your needs?" (II: 371–72). The priest's criticism of false conversions and of religious hypocrisy can be read as a critique of Julie's conversion experience and of her efforts to sublimate her desire for Saint-Preux through religious pietism and through her role as spiritual guide to the community at Clarens. Emilie's realization that it is not God she desires, but a lover, poses a direct challenge to the ideals of self-sacrifice and religious exaltation advocated in Rousseau's novel. Although she admires and envies her mother's genuine religious faith, she recognizes her inability to follow her example. Rejecting the masochistic martyrdom that Julie embraces, Emilie resolves to seek the fulfillment of her desires not in heaven, but on earth.

This credo is later expressed more explicitly by Emilie on her deathbed. "Do you believe that death really ends our ability to think, to feel, and to love?" she asks her friend Garnier. His confusion confirms her own doubts: "I see that everything ends when we die. . . . Oh, how I regret not to be a believer, for then at least I could hope to see my dear Volx again in some other, happier life in which our souls would never be separated again!" (III: 546). Firm in her convictions, Emilie refuses to see a priest and dies with Volx's portrait clutched to her breast. Her sister-in-law, Mme de Ménil, is even more emphatic in her rejection of the Christian faith and in her affirmation of earthly love. On her deathbed she declares: "If I believed in all that nonsense, I would freely confess my sins; but I don't believe in anything, and I refuse to let the last act of my life be one of hypocrisy. . . . Now kindly leave me alone, so that I can try to forget everything I'm losing and all the pain I've caused" (II: 468–69). Both these deathbed scenes in *Montbrillant* can be read as a critique of Julie's ostentatiously pious death and as a challenge to the Christian ideal celebrated in Rousseau's novel of self-denial in exchange for happiness after death.

In *Montbrillant*, as in *Julie*, the expression of female desire through adulterous passion constitutes a central leitmotif and mainspring of the plot. However, the ideological implications of the two novels are quite different. Although Julie ultimately acknowledges the invincible nature of her passion for Saint-Preux, she steadfastly resists it in order to remain true to the ideals of conjugal fidelity, maternal devotion, and self-sacrifice to which she has devoted herself since her marriage. In *Montbrillant*, on the other hand, these ideals are thrown into question early in the novel, giving the heroine ample time to explore other outlets for her ambitions and desires—including the options criticized most strongly by Rousseau: extra-marital affairs, creation of a literary salon, and active participation in the social and intellectual life of her period.

Emilie's earthly prayers are finally answered when she falls in love with Volx. Although in real life, d'Epinay complained of Grimm's tyrannical and egotistic character and of his increasingly frequent (and

often unnecessary) trips abroad, in her novel she presents an idealized, almost godlike portrait of him. Reincarnated as Volx, he is the
perfect lover Emilie has dreamed of through all her trials and tribulations—morally and intellectually superior, strong and protective, and
above all, faithfully devoted to her.[25] Combining Wolmar's sagacity
and maturity with Saint-Preux's romantic appeal, Volx is (as his name
suggests) actually more of a Wolmar-type, rather austere and autocratic, and clearly a father figure, once their initial passion has sub-
sided.[26] With Volx's encouragement, Emilie gradually overcomes her
inferiority complex and gains confidence in her intellectual and literary gifts. Through him, she gains admittance into distinguished literary circles, where she finds the type of friends and intellectual
stimulation she had so long craved. Thanks to these new connections,
Emilie is gradually able to fulfill her ambitions as a patroness of the
arts, as a salonnière, and eventually as a writer.

Most important, Volx helps Emilie resolve the tensions arising from
her conflicting roles and desires as a woman. In addition to the tension between the Christian morality of her youth and the *morale
mondaine* of her milieu, Emilie had long felt torn between her inclination for a quiet, domestic life devoted to her family and an irresistible
attraction to the wider social and cultural sphere beyond the home.
Volx helps relieve these tensions by restoring her self-confidence as a
mother:

> One of the traits I cherish most in you is the strict self-control you
> show, especially in the presence of your children. When we are
> with them, we sometimes have no choice but to voice disapproval
> for what brings our greatest happiness; for everything has been
> corrupted by society and its foolish institutions. Since we aren't
> able to change society, we must submit to its conventions and
> make up for this necessary failing through a thousand acts of
> goodness and charity. . . . One must have solid virtues to earn the
> right to scorn moral priggishness. Continue to do good deeds as
> you are accustomed, and don't worry anymore about that devil of
> a sophist who sees things only in a negative light. (III: 150)[27]

The sophist in question is of course Rousseau, whom Grimm, Diderot,
and others in the d'Holbach circle jokingly referred to as *"le sophiste."*
This passage serves to reinforce, through the greater authority of Volx,
the arguments made earlier by Formeuse in favor of extra-conjugal

affairs. Volx raises the argument to a higher level by presenting Emilie's adultery less as a reaction to a personal problem than as the result of an unjust, corrupt society. He argues that in a society where divorce is prohibited, adultery is a necessary evil for which morally superior individuals like themselves can compensate through otherwise exemplary behavior. Volx then concludes by scoffing at *la pédanterie de la morale,* the priggish morality expounded by Rousseau. This is by far the most explicit attack by d'Epinay on what she considered the narrow-minded and hypocritical condemnations of adultery by Rousseau in *Julie* and in his conversations with Mme d'Houdetot (whom he supposedly tried to "reform" in order to satisfy his own ulterior motives). In contrast to Julie's masochistic and ultimately self-destructive fidelity, d'Epinay considered "monogamous" liaisons (such as her long relationship with Grimm) as the only feasible and dignified solution to unhappy, indissoluble marriages.

D'Epinay's Response to Rousseau's View of the Ideal Mother

D'Epinay's strongest challenge to Rousseau in *Montbrillant* lies in her realistic portrayal of pregnancy, motherhood, and family life—a view that contrasts sharply with the idealized vision of domesticity presented in *Julie* and in Book I of *Emile.* Throughout her novel, d'Epinay expresses considerable ambivalence toward motherhood; yet, at the same time, she is highly critical of the social conventions and prejudices of her period that prevented the formation of strong family bonds.

When she becomes pregnant after three months of marriage, Emilie's first reaction is irritation that her pregnancy will prevent her from accompanying her husband on his first six-month round of inspections as *fermier général.* She complains of nausea, depression, and general lassitude—banal symptoms from everyday life that never seem to enter Julie's ethereal realm of existence: "For several days now, I have felt terribly depressed, and I can't seem to enjoy anything. It's no doubt due to my condition," she confides. "This pregnancy is off to a bad start; every morning, I have painful vomiting fits and violent headaches every night" (I, 351, 387). After she learns of her husband's infidelity, she comes to resent the "creature" within her that forces her to go on living. Yet as the term of her pregnancy draws near, she is obsessed with the fear that she will die in childbirth or of childbed fever, as had a number of her friends.[28] Even the joy of feeling the baby move within her for the first time serves only to reinforce her sense of doom.

To calm her fears, M. de Lisieux (Emilie's trusted friend and former guardian) encourages her to nurse her child, insisting that breastfeeding would help protect her from childbed fever and strengthen the baby's health as well. Emilie eagerly seizes upon this plan, but her mother opposes it, fearing both for her daughter's health and for her reputation. "This plan raised all kinds of fears in her mind: fear that her daughter might appear peculiar in the eyes of others, fear of ridicule if the plan failed, fears that her health might suffer. A new objection surfaced with every word" (I: 288). Her mother finally agrees to the plan, as does her father-in-law, providing that Emilie's doctor and husband consent to it. Encouraged by her doctor's support, Emilie dutifully writes to her husband in the hope of gaining his approval. However, his callous response shatters her hopes and illustrates the total incompatibility of their views of parenthood. "Here's another one of the crazy ideas that sometimes pass through my poor little wife's head!" he exclaims.

> You, nurse your child? I thought I'd die laughing. Even if you were strong enough to do it, do you think I'd ever consent to such a ridiculous idea? Certainly not. So, my dear, whatever the advice of the midwives and doctors may be, this plan is completely out of the question. It simply doesn't make any sense. What satisfaction can one possibly get from breastfeeding a child? Who are the ninnies who gave you that idea? (I: 295)

The arguments presented against maternal nursing by Emilie's husband and mother provide a realistic picture of the often insurmontable prejudices and obstacles faced by middle- and upper-class mothers who wished to breastfeed their children. Her experience demonstrates what little voice women had even in the most important—and most personal—decisions affecting their lives. The eloquent arguments presented by d'Epinay in favor of maternal nursing constitute a vigorous attack on the tyranny of prejudices and social conventions, on the pernicious influence they exerted on family relations and especially on the health and happiness of women.

D'Epinay's strongest attack on the prejudices opposing maternal breastfeeding is found in a letter from Emilie's uncle to her father-in-law after the birth of her son. "I don't understand why they prevented her from nursing him, when she had her heart set on it," he declares.

> To me it would have made perfect sense both for her and for her child. Forcing the milk out of a woman in twenty-four hours plays havoc on her system, and for what purpose? To make her physically unable to do what nature intended her to do? What nonsense! How strange men are the way they torment themselves, attaching importance to this, shame or ridicule to that. . . . I don't understand how they can constrain nature like that, as if in a vise! (I: 332)

This is one of d'Epinay's most vigorous indictments of the oppressive influence of social conventions on the lives of women. One wonders why she chose a male character here as her mouthpiece. Perhaps she felt that her opinions carried more weight when expressed by a male voice.

Commenting on this exchange for and against maternal breast-feeding, her editor Paul Boiteau writes: "Perhaps Mme d'Epinay expresses her wish to nurse her children here only because of her later friendship with the author of *Emile*."[29] Given the fact that the events described here took place in 1746 (sixteen years before the publication of *Emile*) and that this portion of d'Epinay's novel was, according to Roth and Badinter, probably written in 1757 or early 1758 (before Rousseau began writing *Emile*),[30] it is more likely that d'Epinay influenced Rousseau on this subject than the reverse—if indeed they discussed the question of nursing at all. In any case, the arguments made in *Montbrillant* in favor of maternal breastfeeding and against the tyranny of social conventions are far more eloquent than those made in *Emile*, precisely because d'Epinay describes in realistic detail her own painful experiences. The rather glib advice Rousseau offered to Countess Berthier in his correspondence with her and to women in general in *Emile*[31] seems highly unrealistic and impractical in light of the attitudes described so vividly in *Montbrillant*. Moreover, the long debate concerning maternal breastfeeding in d'Epinay's novel contrasts sharply with the total lack of reference to the subject in *Julie*.

Emilie's fears of dying from childbed fever are painfully revived by her husband's refusal to let her nurse their child. The callousness of his reply and his flagrant infidelities throw her into a deep depression. She begins to fantasize about death in childbirth as a means of escape from suffering and of revenge against her husband. As in *Julie*, death—and, more specifically, martyrdom for one's child—is envisioned as an escape from an otherwise inescapable marriage. Contrary to Emilie's expectations, however, her delivery and recovery go well. Yet her joy is clouded by her mother's choice of a wet-nurse who lives almost thirty miles away. Not only is Emilie prevented from nursing her son, but even from seeing him more than once or twice a week, which hardly makes for strong family bonds.

Later in her novel, d'Epinay recalls how her husband constantly thwarted her plans and desires concerning the upbringing and education of their children. When M. de Montbrillant proposes sending their children away to live with his mother-in-law, insisting that "that will take care of them for us, amuse her, and save us the expense of paying room and board," Emilie firmly opposes the plan. "No, sir; I insist on having my children with me, and I won't give up the plan I have long cherished to raise them myself," she declares. "It's a duty which I consider my greatest source of satisfaction and happiness. That won't prevent me from also considering it my duty to manage your household and to entertain any guests you may wish to invite" (II: 267). "All you ever talk about anymore is duty!" replies her husband. "How ridiculously pedantic and dull you've become!" (II: 267).

Emilie succeeds in keeping her children with her, but her plans for their education are continually overruled by her husband. He ignores her objections to the mediocre tutor he chooses for their son, mocks the ambitiousness of the studies she proposes, and objects to the low priority she gives to *les talents agréables* (music, drawing, dance, and parlor games). His response to the plan of studies proposed by Emilie for their son reflects the prevailing attitudes and prejudices of the period: "What can a child possibly learn if all you do is chat with him all day?" he asks.

> Those walks you make him take for his health will bore him to death if you try to use them for his instruction. . . . It's Latin he should be learning; he doesn't need to understand the authors he reads very well, since people never read them again once they finish school. . . . I also don't agree with your plan to interrupt his study of music and other *talents agréables* for two or three years. I want him to spend two hours a day practicing violin and two more learning cards and other parlor games. He needs to know how to defend his money." (III: 333)

"My plan of education seemed to him peculiar and far too serious," she sadly reports to Volx. "Fate has ill served me; I had hoped to find happiness in my maternal duties and in domestic life; but I needed my husband's support" (III: 333). M. de Montbrillant's irresponsibility as a parent and his refusal to adopt his wife's progressive plan for their children's education contrasts sharply with the Wolmars' affectionate cooperation in such matters. By illustrating the difficulties faced by women married to men whose views they do not share or respect, d'Epinay's novel challenges the idyllic view of marriage and parenthood presented in *La Nouvelle Héloïse*.

⋅⊙⊙⋅

In *Montbrillant*, d'Epinay not only describes her frustrations and tribulations as a mother, but is surprisingly candid in expressing the ambivalence she feels toward her children. Despite her efforts to devote herself to her young son and daughter following her mother's advice, she openly admits that they cannot console her for the loss of her husband's affections. Emilie's candid recognition of her ambivalence toward motherhood contrasts with the suppression of maternal ambivalence in *La Nouvelle Héloïse*. Whereas Julie pretends to fill the emotional void within her by playing the perfect mother, refusing to admit until her death that Saint-Preux had always been the first object of her affections, Emilie openly recognizes that children cannot fully satisfy a woman's need for love and companionship.

In a clever subversion of the Rousseauian ideal of domesticity, Emilie uses her children's education as a pretext to invite her lover to take up residence at her country estate. Later, he shares these tutorial duties with Volx (her second lover) in an amusing *ménage à trois,* from which Emilie's husband is significantly absent. The parallels are of course striking with Julie's plan to keep Saint-Preux at Clarens as her sons' tutor. Through her heroine, d'Epinay both mimics and mocks Julie's exemplary motherhood.

Challemel-Lacour, editor of the 1869 edition of d'Epinay's works, is quick to point out the ambiguities in her attitude toward motherhood reflected in *Montbrillant*. Commenting on Volx's apology for adultery and his efforts to assuage Emilie's feelings of guilt as a mother, he quips:

> Forced to divide her affection between her lover and her children and to hide her weaknesses from them, Mme d'Epinay manages

remarkably well. . . . Although she falters more than once, she never fails to display the austere rules of conduct that win her lover's praise. She is indeed grateful to M. Grimm for the severity of his principles, for it gives them the double pleasure of sinning together and of chastizing themselves for it later in a most philosophical and stoic manner.[32]

Challemel-Lacour's comments are singularly ungenerous toward d'Epinay, particularly on the part of an editor introducing certain of her works to the public for the first time. Yet, despite the exaggerations and distortions in his remarks, he points to a central tension in her life reflected in her novel. The guilt she felt as a mother for not devoting more time to the upbringing and education of her children— for being distracted from her maternal duties by her social and literary activities and especially by her love affairs—is repeatedly expressed and never satisfactorily resolved, despite all her efforts at rationalization and self-justification. "Madame d'Epinay is so preoccupied by the education of her children that she devotes forty-five minutes or even an hour to their instruction each day," writes Challemel-Lacour, in his customary mocking tone. "This duty, ever present in her mind and so faithfully carried out, is her greatest source of pride; her maternal devotion would be more convincing if there were less affectation in it" (xviii). In his comments on d'Epinay's novel, Auguste Rey echoes Challemel-Lacour's skepticism concerning the genuineness of her maternal feelings: "The maternal feelings d'Epinay expresses seem artificial. Preoccupation with her lovers prevents her from being a real mother."[33] Like Rousseau, Challemel-Lacour and Rey clearly disapproved of women who dared to have ambitions and desires outside the domestic sphere. However, they failed to recognize that d'Epinay herself was painfully conscious of her shortcomings as a mother and that, in her novel, she deals quite explicitly with the tensions and contradictions underlying her relations with her children.

In *Montbrillant*, d'Epinay repeatedly expresses guilt and frustration for not having lived up to the ideals of motherhood and domesticity she herself espoused. These guilt feelings are especially apparent in a conversation between Emilie and her mother, who chides her for neglecting her maternal duties. Alluding indirectly to Emilie's budding affair with Formeuse (of which she disapproves), Mme de Gondrecourt urges Emilie to abandon frivolous amusements and to devote herself to the upbringing of her children:

Now is the time to sow the seeds of a good upbringing in their
hearts. To do so, you must study their inclinations and their
characters, which reveal themselves even in the cradle. Be with
them all the time. . . . It is not by playing music, acting in comedies, and wasting your time on other frivolous activities that
you will prepare yourself for your new responsibilities or inspire
your children with love for their own duties. When one is destined to serve as an example, one must be very scrupulous in all
aspects of one's behavior. (I: 547–48)

This idealized view of the mother's crucial role as educator and moral
exemplar for her children closely parallels the view presented by
Rousseau in *Julie* and *Emile*. It is an ideal that d'Epinay had earnestly
tried to follow after the birth of her son and which she articulated in
a series of letters to her son when he was nine. Privately printed in
1759 and excerpted in *Montbrillant*, d'Epinay's *Lettres à mon fils* constitute her first attempt to outline principles and methods of education
for parents who, like herself, wished to educate their children at home.
The problems women of the period faced in trying to emulate this
exalted model of the mother-educator are described far more realistically by d'Epinay than by Rousseau, who largely ignores or dismisses
such difficulties. What distinguishes d'Epinay's novel from both *Julie*
and *Emile* is her effort to articulate the complexities of important issues such as maternal breastfeeding, the choice between home-schooling and boarding-school education, and women's participation in the
broader cultural sphere beyond the home. By presenting opposing
viewpoints on these issues and insights drawn from her own experience, d'Epinay offers a much richer and more nuanced view of the
obstacles encountered by mothers who sought to follow Rousseau's
teachings yet, at the same time, to fulfill their own needs and desires
as women.

D'Epinay's ambivalence toward motherhood was heightened by
her husband's financial irresponsibility and his negative influence on
their son. She openly expresses these conflicting feelings in her novel.
As her children grow older, Mme de Montbrillant begins to find great
pleasure in their company; yet her joy as a mother is clouded by the
financial uncertainty of their situation: "As for my children, they would
be my greatest source of happiness if I were completely in control of

their fate and mine; but since this is not the case, the happier I am with them, the more I worry about their future" (III: 133). Her husband's indifference and irresponsibility toward them alarms her, as does his negative influence on their son. She is delighted by her daughter's intelligence, sensibility, and marked resemblance to herself, but is increasingly alarmed by her son's equally marked resemblance to his father: "My son is lackadaisical and spineless; he'll bring me nothing but sorrow," she sadly predicts (III: 285). In a letter to her husband, reproving him for his reckless extravagance, she warns: "Your son is now thirteen years old. Despite all my efforts, I will perhaps soon experience the grief of seeing him try to justify his own youthful failings by pointing to the daily example of his father. His frivolity and lack of ambition already worry me greatly" (III: 411–12).

Madame d'Epinay's forebodings concerning her son turned out to be only too well justified, for at the age of twenty-three Louis d'Epinay had accumulated so many gambling debts that his parents had him imprisoned. "This was the only time that Louise and her husband ever made a decision together concerning the upbringing of their son," remarks Badinter, who is careful to point out that it was not uncommon in eighteenth-century France for parents to have their children imprisoned even for less serious offenses.[34] Her friend Galiani tried to console her by pointing to the inexorable influence of heredity: "What folly it was for you to have children with M. d'Epinay! Didn't you know that children always take after their father?" he asked. "You realized that M. d'Epinay was an incorrigible spendthrift, so you should have had children instead with the Italian ambassador who was in Paris at the time of your son's conception, and he would have set the family's affairs back on course." Galiani then pointed an accusing finger at Rousseau, whose theories on education had strongly influenced Mme d'Epinay in the upbringing of her children: "Were you ever crazy enough to take Rousseau and his Emile seriously? Did you ever really believe that education . . . can change the way people act and think? If you think so, then take a wolf and turn it into a dog if you can."[35]

A year later, in a letter to Diderot, d'Epinay again evoked Rousseau's theories of education as she bitterly reflected on her son's imprisonment and on her feelings of failure as a mother:

> The claim that education can somehow be perfected reminds me of a conversation I had fifteen years ago with Jean-Jacques. . . . He

maintained that, by nature, parents are ill-suited to raise their children. I lacked experience in those days and was filled with illusions. I found his opinion revolting. But the illusions are shattered and I admit now that he was right.[36]

This passage presents an indirect rebuttal of Galiani's position and his reductive view of Rousseau's pedagogical theories. Rather than find fault with Rousseau's theories for the failure of her son's education, d'Epinay blamed her own naïveté in believing she could overcome her son's heredity and the negative influence of her husband's example. In her discouragement, she even began to agree with Rousseau's claim that parents are ill-equipped to raise children and would do better to send them away to state boarding schools. Yet this claim—which Rousseau made no doubt in part to defend the abandonment of his own children, and which he later developed in his *Considérations sur le gouvernement de Pologne*—is in complete contradiction with the pedagogical theories and the ideal of enlightened motherhood he presents in *Julie* and *Emile*. At first, d'Epinay failed to recognize this contradiction and found herself trapped within it. However, in her *Conversations d'Emilie*, as we shall see, she works through the contradictions in Rousseau's views on education, as well as the ambivalence they shared toward parenthood.

Emilie vs. Emile: d'Epinay's Views on Women's Education

Both d'Epinay's autobiographical writings and her pedagogical works can be read as a response to Rousseau's views on female education—particularly to the narrow views set forth in Book V of *Emile*. In her autobiographical writings, d'Epinay carefully retraces and criticizes the upbringing she received as a child, which was not unlike the education outlined by Rousseau for Sophie. "I'm very ignorant. My entire education was limited to the cultivation of female accomplishments and to becoming adept in the art of sophistry," she confides in her self-portrait.[37] In *Montbrillant*, she laments the inadequacy of her education, the spirit of dependence and submission inculcated in her by her mother and, above all, the lack of self-confidence that resulted from her upbringing. That her novel was intended as a critique of the traditional upbringing and education of women is made clear in the preface:

These memoirs are intended to serve as a lesson for mothers of young children. They illustrate the dangers of an upbringing that lacks coherence and direction, as well as the need to study the character of a child in order to formulate a consistent plan of education. Madame de Montbrillant's education had weakened or effaced her natural aptitudes so completely that it took a number of years spent in misfortune for her to recover the firmness of her character. (I: 4)

Despite her affection for her mother, d'Epinay realized quite early that Mme d'Esclavelles, like many women of her generation and milieu, was a prisoner of traditionalist views on women and of the strict rules of decorum that had dominated her own upbringing. In her novel, d'Epinay describes her mother's rigid conformism and traces the stifling effect it had on her own development. It was not until her son-in-law's disgrace that Mme d'Esclavelles would succeed in rising above her blind subservience to decorum and public opinion: "It is curious indeed," remarks d'Epinay, "that a woman who has spent her entire life subjugated by the childish conventions of society and enslaved by prejudices and by public opinion should show such rare firmness and courage near the the end of her life" (III: 490). As an adolescent and young adult, Louise bitterly regretted the lack of confidence between them. Recalling her mother's efforts to help her after her unhappy love affair with Francueil, she writes: "If only she had given me such sensible advice earlier, she could have spared me so much grief, and so much foolishness as well perhaps! Until now, I never had more than four real conversations with her. Despite my confiding nature, I have always been so afraid she would scold me that I never dared to confide in her" (I: 549). Only after Louise had achieved a sense of inner worth and independence from public opinion would she at last grow close to her mother.

After her marriage, d'Epinay tried to compensate for the serious gaps in her education by reading and studying as much as possible on her own. In *Montbrillant*, she recalls her excitement when she was given the keys to her husband's and father-in-law's well-stocked libraries. There she spent countless hours discovering books and subjects she never knew existed. Her intellectual horizons were also greatly broadened by her friendships with Duclos, Francueil, and Grimm, and even more so by the literary salons to which they introduced her, particularly the distinguished gatherings in the homes of Mlle Quinault and Baron d'Holbach (referred to as "Mme Médéric" and "Milord Wils" in her novel). "They were the first true intellectuals she had met," remarks her guardian Lisieux. "Her own largely uncultivated mind was irresistibly attracted to this circle" (II: 83). In *Montbrillant*, d'Epinay reconstructs several of the lively discussions in which she took part at Mlle Quinault's famous "Société du Bout-du-Banc,"[38] and she underlines the tremendous impact these gatherings had on her intellectual development:

> An hour of conversation in that house stimulates my mind more— and gives me greater satisfaction—than almost all the books I have read until now put together. . . . After listening to the discussions between Mme Médéric and her guests, my mind is more enlightened, my imagination livelier, my feelings more intense. (II: 91, 103)

D'Epinay's experience is a striking illustration of Evelyn Bodek's claim that literary salons served as informal universities for women.[39] Yet it was only when d'Epinay began to express her thoughts and feelings in writing that she would truly develop a mind and voice of her own.

In the early years of her marriage, d'Epinay claims to have been primarily motivated in her studies by the desire to be better prepared to raise and educate her children. Adopting a method of instruction similar to that proposed by Rousseau in *Julie*, she kept a notebook of reflections on her readings which she planned to read and discuss later with her children. Soon, however, she begins to view study not simply as a way to become a better mother, but as an end in itself capable of yielding multiple benefits and satisfactions. She discovers that intellectual pursuits provide a woman with a means of becoming more self-sufficient and of protecting her interests (financial and otherwise); they also constitute a source of consolation and pleasure, a stimulating and worthwhile occupation, a resource against boredom, and a means of gaining the esteem of others. These arguments, made repeatedly in *Montbrillant*, are best summed up in a letter to Galiani:

> A woman is completely justified in acquiring as much knowledge as she can. Once her duties as a mother, daughter, and wife

are fulfilled, she is right to engage in scholarly work because it is a way to become independent and self-sufficient and to console herself for the unfairness of men and fate. Moreover, we are never respected and cherished more by others than when we have no need of their esteem.[40]

D'Epinay's view of women scholars is not without ambivalence, however. In the same letter to Galiani, she stressed the risks and obstacles that women scholars faced: the danger of being justly criticized and ridiculed for displaying any pretension to wit or learning, of neglecting their primary duties as wives and mothers, and of trying to pursue studies that were too complex or otherwise inappropriate for their sex and that they were unable to apply in any useful manner (347). D'Epinay seems to be trapped here within the traditionalist (and Rousseauian) gender ideology she appeared to challenge earlier. Yet in the discussion that follows, she made it clear that the gender hierarchy she was describing stemmed not from natural differences between the sexes, but from differences in social conditioning and inequalities in education. In a detailed argument that is worth quoting at length, she pointed to the complex network of social and educational constraints that hindered women from fully developing their intellectual and artistic potential:

So many fields of study are barred to women: business administration, politics, commerce . . . . Only literature, philosophy, and the arts are open to them. Yet, even in the field of literature, their occupations, duties, and their weakness prevent them from serious study of Classical Greek and Latin. . . . As for philosophy, their knowledge is limited because they are denied access to Classical texts, which they know only through bad translations. When they try to reason or hypothesize, their ignorance stops them at every turn. . . . In the arts, they are forced to renounce sculpture and even painting. Their inability to travel and to study the works of masters abroad, the laws of decorum which forbid them from studying nudes, indeed everything in our culture seems to oppose their progress. So they find themselves limited to music, dance, and light verse—poor resources, to be sure. (348–49)

By underlining the complex network of social and educational constraints that prevented women from developing their full potential, d'Epinay implicitly challenged the naturalist-traditionalist view of women epitomized in Rousseau's *Emile*.

Ever conscious of the pressures of social conventions and public opinion, d'Epinay concludes this letter to Galiani with a mixed message of inner liberation and outward conformism: "A woman of intelligence, wit, and character who possesses only a superficial knowledge of these fields which she cannot study in greater depth—such a woman would still be a very rare object, much loved and admired, so long as she remains free of literary and intellectual pretensions." In her view, an accomplished, cultivated woman was worthy of admiration and respect, providing she maintain an outward appearance of modesty and decorum.

To help women provide a sounder education for themselves and their daughters, d'Epinay composed and published *Les Conversations d'Emilie,* a series of twenty dialogues between a mother and child. Spanning a five-year period beginning when the child was five, the dialogues provide detailed practical advice concerning the methods and materials to be used in the upbringing and instruction of girls by their mothers at home. The dialogues were patterned after conversations between d'Epinay and her granddaughter Emilie, who lived with her from 1769 until d'Epinay's death in 1782.

In her biography of d'Epinay, Badinter maintains that she wrote *Les Conversations d'Emilie* to alleviate her feelings of guilt as a mother and to fill the loneliness caused by Grimm's increasingly frequent absences. She further argues that "only the field of childcare and education seemed worthy of her attention. It was a fresh new topic about which other women knew very little."[41] I would dispute Badinter's claims on several grounds. First, the subjects of pedagogy and homeschooling were both very much in vogue when d'Epinay began writing her *Conversations* around 1770, as d'Epinay herself remarks in her preface.[42] Second, Badinter implies that d'Epinay lacked ambition and talent outside the field of education, a contention amply disproved by her autobiographical writings, her correspondence, and her activities as an editor, journalist, and salonnière. Finally, I would dispute the narrowness of Badinter's view of *Les Conversations d'Emilie* as primarily a "grandmother's revenge." In my opinion, d'Epinay composed this work not merely as a means of reconciling her aspirations (and

guilt) as a mother with her ambitions as writer and pedagogical theo-
rist, but also—and above all—as a response and challenge to *Emile*.

In *Les Conversations d'Emilie*, d'Epinay points to four major shortcomings in *Emile*, which she strove to overcome in her own work. In
her preface, she questions the practical value of abstract theoretical
formulations and pedagogical systems in works such as Rousseau's.
"In the field of education, as in most other fields, general precepts are
of little use," she asserts. "By nature, they are too vague to indicate
any precise course of action; in fact it's not unusual to see people who
preach the same maxims following entirely opposite paths" (vii). Second, d'Epinay underlines the fact that her own approach to education
was drawn from her daily experience as the mother and educator of
real children, which enabled her to join theory with practice and to
gear her methods and goals to the real world. D'Epinay's own experience as a mother and grandmother made her wary of pedagogical
treatises written by men like Rousseau who never raised children of
their own.

A third shortcoming of *Emile* that d'Epinay strove to avoid was
Rousseau's preachy tone, "that imperative, didactic tone which people
who are . . . in a position of authority tend to adopt, without even
realizing it" (vi). Instead of an abstract pedagogical treatise thinly
disguised as a novel, she offered her readers lively conversations drawn
from real life, in which theory and practice, as well as style and content, were perfectly fused. Moreover, her conversations with her granddaughter had shown her "the advantages of confidence, innocent irony,
and playful allusions over dry precepts and stern reprimands" (v–vi).

It was above all the stultifying education traditionally given to
women—and epitomized in the education prescribed for Sophie in
Emile—that d'Epinay challenged in *Les Conversations d'Emilie*. "I would
not venture to set limits for what our sex can or cannot learn," she
declared.

> When I was a child, girls usually were not taught much of any-
> thing. We were given rather haphazard religious instruction. . .
> and then a very good dance teacher, a very poor music teacher,
> and at best a mediocre drawing instructor. Along with that, a bit
> of history and geography, but with little substance; all we did
> was memorize names and dates, which we forgot as soon as the
> instructor was let go. That's all there was to a polished education
> in those days. People never took our minds seriously and care-

fully avoided any kind of real instruction, since serious scholarship was considered totally inappropriate for our sex. (Conv. 12,
I: 442–43)

In reaction to the limited education she herself was given and the
spirit of dependence it engendered in her, d'Epinay resolved to give
her granddaughter the kind of upbringing she would have liked to
receive. She announced her plan in a letter to Galiani:

To console myself for my misfortunes, I am transforming myself
into a schoolteacher or, more precisely, a nursemaid. My two-
year-old granddaughter has just arrived, and she's quite an exceptional little girl. . . . I wager she'll have a strong character, and
to make sure she keeps it, I'd like to raise her myself. . . . Tomor-
row, I'll take her from her mother and take charge of her, and, for
once, we'll see what becomes of a child who is neither constrained
nor repressed. She'll be the first such example in Paris.[43]

Like Emile, Emilie was to serve as the model of an ideal education
provided by an enlightened educator. And like Rousseau's *Emile, Les
Conversations d'Emilie* was purportedly written to share the methods
of this model education with parents who wished to raise their own
children at home. While Rousseau's perspective was undeniably
male-centered in the education he proposed for both Sophie and
Emile, the view of education presented in *Les Conversations d'Emilie*
is strikingly feminocentric. Written by a woman for women,
d'Epinay's book deals exclusively with the education of girls by their
mothers. "She knows that her female readers, especially mothers,
will identify more with her than with Rousseau," remarks Badinter,
perhaps over-optimistically.[44] D'Epinay was not interested in raising
a Sophie, whose main purpose in life was to please her husband and
submit to his whims, but rather an intelligent, autonomous woman
capable of finding happiness and fulfillment in herself. While the
education of Sophie was designed to produce the ideal female companion for Rousseau's ideal male, d'Epinay's goal was to raise her
granddaughter (and other girls like her) to lead a happy, productive
life in the real world.

Unlike Rousseau's Sophie, Emilie was taught to read and write
before the age of five and, by the age of ten, had been introduced to

a broad range of subjects (including geography, history, mathematics, and the natural sciences) following a plan of studies quite ambitious for the period. However, the true originality of *Les Conversations d'Emilie* lies less in the plan or method of studies it proposed (which in fact resembled the more enlightened educations given to boys of the period) than in the distinctly feminocentric goals it sought to achieve. Whereas Sophie's upbringing was designed to reinforce traditional female dependence, submission, and inferiority, Emilie's education fostered a sense of self-esteem and an inner source of strength and independence. "When you take care to cultivate your mind and to enrich it with useful, solid knowledge, you give yourself new sources of pleasure and satisfaction, as well as valuable resources against boredom and consolations against adversity," explains d'Epinay to her granddaughter.

> These are treasures that no one can take away from you and that free you from dependence on others, since you will be able to occupy your mind and to be happy without them. In fact, such resources make others dependent on you; for the more talents and intelligence one possesses, the more useful and necessary one becomes to society. Moreover, study is the best remedy against idleness, which is the greatest obstacle to happiness and virtue. (Conv. 12, I: 466–67)

Contrary to Rousseau's assertions in Book V of *Emile*, d'Epinay affirms the intellectual equality of women and their right to an equal education. She insists that the intellectual development of women is essential to their happiness and well-being. In contrast to the blind submission to authority instilled in Rousseau's Sophie, d'Epinay encourages her granddaughter to think for herself. Yet ever conscious of the outer constraints placed on women by the society of her period, d'Epinay seeks to give Emilie an education that balances this sense of inner freedom and critical judgment with respect for social roles and conventions. Since her primary goal is to ensure her granddaughter's happiness, she also teaches her the social and housekeeping skills she will later need in her daily life. "By learning various types of handiwork suitable to our sex, you give yourself another valuable weapon against idleness and help free yourself further from dependence on others. If you add to these occupations those of the mind that lend strength and resiliency to one's character, you will then take an important step forward toward perfection" (Conv. 12, I: 468–69).

Given her commitment to a serious education for girls, d'Epinay is faced with the problem of explaining the prejudice against women intellectuals to her granddaughter, who is puzzled by satirical remarks she overhears concerning a woman in their circle of acquaintances. "Do you remember how much people made fun of that lady? The one who is such a bluestocking?" asks Emilie.

> Count Vieuxpont said that all she needs is a professor's hat, since no one can utter a word in her presence without her quoting a Greek or Latin author. . . . She's always showing off what she knows, although she doesn't even know the price of a chicken. The Count said that, instead of wasting her time lecturing us, she would do better to teach her daughter how to speak properly and how to read. . . . But, if it's so shameful to be ignorant, why do people make fun of knowledge? (Conv. 12, I: 457–59, 461)

D'Epinay explains that it was not the woman's knowledge in itself but her scholarly pretensions and neglect of her domestic responsibilities that had led people to mock her. True scholars do not feel the need to display their knowledge in public; their knowledge and intelligence are reflected in their conversation and behavior. As in *Montbrillant*, d'Epinay makes it clear that she fully supports women who engage in intellectual pursuits, providing they do not neglect their domestic duties or pedantically display their knowledge in public.

In *Les Conversations d'Emilie*, d'Epinay insists on the need to complete a girl's academic education with the other kinds of activities necessary for her development into a happy, healthy, well-rounded woman. These include moral instruction, training in domestic tasks and social etiquette, and a healthy dose of recreation and physical exercise. Although the first two were standard elements of traditional female education, d'Epinay's insistence on the need for physical exercise for girls was quite innovative for the period. Madame d'Epinay herself had suffered all her life from bad health and bouts of depression or "vapeurs," which she attributed to her lack of exercise and fresh air as a child: "I'd like to see you develop an iron constitution," she tells Emilie. "No doubt my own constitution would have been much stronger if my mother's ill-guided affection had not kept me away from everything that might have strengthened it" (Conv. 20, II:

456).[45] To maintain Emilie's good health, her grandmother takes long walks with her every afternoon and encourages her to engage in lively games.

In the case of girls more high-strung than Emilie, d'Epinay even recommends activities traditionally reserved for males (such as horseback riding, hunting, farming, and fencing) as a means of restoring their mental and physical health. In *La Fille Amazone*, one of several didactic tales told to Emilie for her edification, d'Epinay tells the story of a high-strung girl whose violent fits of anger and depression are cured through vigorous physical exercise:

> Adélaïde's father believed that his daughter's illness stemmed from her sedentary life. . . . He took her with him to his country house, gave her men's clothing to wear, . . . and had her work with him in his gardens, where he kept her engaged in continual and sometimes arduous labor. He taught her how to ride a horse, how to handle a gun, and took her hunting with him. If he could give her a vigorous constitution through activities seemingly ill-suited to her sex, he was convinced that this would put an end to her fits of anger. He also hoped that the strength and agility she gained from this exercise would enhance her beauty and grace. All his hopes were realized. Never again did Adélaïde show the slightest trace of anger or ill-temper.[46]

Although d'Epinay makes it clear that the measures employed by Adélaïde's father were "extraordinary remedies" called for by an unusual case, *La Fille Amazone* nevertheless presents a bold challenge to eighteenth-century gender norms and stereotypes. In contrast to the traditional "feminine" ideals of delicacy and passivity and to the customary relegation of women to a narrow sphere of "female" activities, this tale presents an androgynous model—a balance of male and female activities and traits quite innovative for the period. Through its critique of the constrained, sedentary lifestyle imposed on upper- and middle-class women in eighteenth-century society, this tale illustrates d'Epinay's conviction that the physical, mental, and emotional weakness of her female contemporaries was culturally conditioned.

In the case of her granddaughter, d'Epinay preferred to take a more conservative and pragmatic course. Instead of teaching her to openly defy a society in which so many forms of activity and expression were closed to women, d'Epinay preferred to give Emilie a sense of inner freedom and self-fulfillment, an inward path to happiness. It is not surprising, therefore, that the central discussion of happiness in *Les Conversations d'Emilie* should conclude with a message of inner liberation rather than one of outward emancipation: "The most important ingredient for happiness is to have done one's duty and to be content with oneself," she explains. "A person can enjoy every possible material advantage, great wealth, and good health, without being happy. Yet without money and with only a feeble constitution like my own, we can be perfectly happy: for true happiness comes from within ourselves" (Conv. 5, I: 140–41). Like Mme de Lambert and Mme de Genlis, two other influential pedagogical writers of the period, d'Epinay stressed public glory for boys, but inner happiness for girls.[47]

In the final paragraphs of *Les Conversations d'Emilie*, d'Epinay addresses the crucial question left unresolved by Rousseau concerning the relative merits of public education (or boarding-school educations) as opposed to the education of children by their parents at home. She alludes to Rousseau repeatedly as "*mon censeur*," who favors certain pedagogical views and methods that young Emilie in turn criticizes and ridicules: "It seems to me, Maman, that your censor approves or disapproves of a lot of things" (Conv. 20, II: 457). After poking fun at Rousseau's views concerning the dangers of "*une culture trop hative*"— an education he claims is botched by introducing subjects too early— d'Epinay returns to the choice between public education and home-schooling: "My censor claims that a gardener who has only a single plant to take care of would run the risk of hampering its growth by too much attention; whereas if he were obliged to divide his time among a certain number of different plants, this danger would be avoided." To which Emilie replies: "Goodness, Maman, your censor is starting to annoy me with all his talk about gardeners! He seems to take me for a head of lettuce whose only purpose in life is to vegetate!" (Conv. 20, II: 462). After further explanations of his views by her grandmother, Emilie impatiently exclaims: "Maman, your censor is an old chatterbox who will spoil our conversation if we let him go on preaching at us" (Conv. 20, II: 462).

Yet d'Epinay then surprises her granddaughter (and her readers) by offering a series of forceful arguments in favor of public education:

> One of the key advantages of a republican form of government
> is the opportunity it gives to directly influence the character of
> its people and to show them their individual worth, which they

might not have realized otherwise. At the same time, it offers the possibility of shaping the public spirit in order to promote the general welfare. Good public schools follow the republican model and offer the same advantages to their students. The instruction they provide is designed to enhance each student's abilities and talents. . . . In such schools, the students' individual efforts and talents determine their success and rank. (Conv. 20, II: 460–61)

This glowing tribute to public education seems strangely out of place at the end of a work ostensibly devoted to promoting progressive home-schooling for girls. However, d'Epinay fully recognized the dis- advantages of educating children at home, particularly the danger of spoiling them with too much attention, the lack of social interaction and healthy competition with other students, and the risk of inferior meth- ods and materials due to parental inexperience or ineptitude. It was only because the boarding schools and convent educations then avail- able for girls posed even greater problems that d'Epinay chose to edu- cate her granddaughter at home: "After considerable uncertainty, I opted for the disadvantages of a private education, despite all its faults, to those of a public education which I could neither approve nor correct" (Conv. 20, II: 464). She insisted that as soon as good public schools were established for girls, she would be the first to support them. Referring again to her *"censeur,"* she maintains: "As soon as he establishes a pub- lic school that follows his own principles, I will be relieved of a great burden and Emilie will be the first to prove the innumerable advantages of so desirable an institution" (Conv. 20, II: 458).

In this open-ended conclusion, d'Epinay may have been respond- ing to the national education plan proposed by Rousseau to the gov- ernment of Poland in his *Considérations sur le gouvernement de Pologne.* According to this plan, public education would be exclusively reserved for males, while girls would be relegated to the home for a strictly utilitarian education to prepare them for their limited role as house- wives and mothers.[48] In her conditional support for public education, d'Epinay points to the contradictions inherent in Rousseau's so-called republican ideal, which despite its egalitarian rhetoric, served only to reinforce male domination by continuing to exclude women from the public sphere. In her critique of Rousseau's views on public education, d'Epinay anticipated the protests later made against the revolutionary government in France by Condorcet, Gouges, and Wollstonecraft for its failure to provide equal education for women.

Rousseau's Response to d'Epinay

After his falling-out with d'Epinay and her entourage, Rousseau retreated to the Maréchal de Luxembourg's estate in Montmorency, where he completed *Julie* and wrote both the *Lettre à d'Alembert* and *Emile*. The marked difference in tone between the first work and the latter two—particularly in the attitude expressed toward women—can be attributed in part to Rousseau's anger toward d'Epinay and all she represented to him. While *Julie* generally conveys a positive and even progressive view of women, the *Lettre à d'Alembert* and *Emile* present a reactionary and highly negative view, particularly of society women and salonnières.

In the *Confessions*, Rousseau recalls his state of mind when he composed his famous response to d'Alembert, particularly his anger at Mme d'Epinay and her circle: "I was so preoccupied with all that had just happened to me and still shaken by so much violent emotion that my troubled feelings mingled with the thoughts inspired by my subject. My work reflects the circumstances of its composition. Without realizing it, I described my situation of the moment; I portrayed Grimm, Mme d'Epinay, Mme d'Houdetot, Saint-Lambert, myself" (I: 495–96). Taking Molière's *Misanthrope* as a paradigm both for his own situation and for that of society, Rousseau compared himself to Alceste, Grimm to Philinte, and Mme d'Epinay to Célimène—coquette, duplicitous, and insincere, the epitome of all that was wrong with French society.[49] When the *Lettre à d'Alembert* is read with this in mind, passages like the following take on an unmistakably autobiographical ring: "Cravenly serving the will of the sex that we should protect, not serve, we have learned to scorn women while obeying them; and every woman of Parisian high society gathers in her home a harem of men more womanly than herself" (136).

In the *Lettre à d'Alembert*, Rousseau launches a bitter attack on what he considers the pernicious, emasculating influence of bluestockings and salonnières like d'Epinay, who—by invading public discourse, literature, and the arts—threatened to corrupt the integrity of these jealously guarded male domains and of the male sex itself. Looking back nostalgically to the sexually segregated societies of Ancient Greece and Rome, where "the most respectable woman was the one people talked about the least," he laments the moral degeneracy of eighteenth-century France:

In our society, the most esteemed woman is the one who causes the greatest stir, who is talked about the most, and who is seen the most often in society; . . . [the one] who most imperiously sets the tone, who judges, resolves, decides, pronounces, and determines the relative merits, virtues, and talents of others, and whose favor is most sought after by groveling male intellectuals.

This leads Rousseau to an impassioned defense of the principle of separate spheres and the segregation of the sexes: "To this I'll add that it is not possible for a woman to remain virtuous outside a quiet domestic life, that taking care of her family and household is her lot, that the dignity of her sex lies in modesty, . . . and that a woman who calls attention to herself in any way brings dishonor to her name" (110).

In Book V of *Emile*, Rousseau continues his campaign to put women back in what he considers their proper place—out of the public eye and back into the domestic sphere. His bitter diatribe against *les femmes savantes* and *les femmes bel-esprit* can be read as an attack on d'Epinay's activities as a writer and salonnière.[50] Rousseau's insistence that he would rather share his life with a simple, ignorant woman than with a witty, learned lady with literary pretensions seems clearly aimed at his two benefactresses—Mme Dupin and Mme d'Epinay—who criticized him for choosing Thérèse as his companion and whose wit, talents, and power over him seem to have been so threatening to his fragile male ego. This hypothesis is supported by the conclusion of this paragraph, where he declares: "All those women with great talents never impress anyone but fools. We always know who is the male artist or friend who holds the pen or brush for them, . . . the discreet *homme de lettres* who dictates their oracles for them in secret" (IV: 768). Rousseau may be alluding here to his work as Mme Dupin's secretary and researcher when she was writing a feminist history of women. However, given the context in which it was written, this statement is more likely a sarcastic reference to Diderot and Grimm's alleged collaboration on the revisions of *Montbrillant*—particularly the passages in d'Epinay's novel attacking Rousseau.[51]

In any case, Rousseau's claim that women are incapable of truly original, creative work without the help of a man reflects the uneasiness that gifted women aroused in him and his attempt to deny their talent by attributing it to male mentors. This passage in *Emile* also reflects Rousseau's strong disapproval of women with ambitions and desires outside the domestic sphere. In his view, even if a woman possessed true intellectual, literary, or artistic talents, she should not aspire to cultivate those gifts at the expense of her domestic duties or with any ambition beyond that of entertaining her husband and family. "Even if she possessed genuine talent, any pretension on her part would degrade it. Her dignity depends on remaining unknown; her glory lies in her husband's esteem, just as her pleasures lie in her family's happiness" (IV: 768). Indeed, one of the central messages that emerges from Book V of *Emile* is that literary ambitions and celebrity are incompatible with a woman's dignity and domestic happiness. This was a traditional prejudice that women authors of the period were all forced to confront and that caused many of them, including d'Epinay, to feel considerable ambivalence toward themselves as writers.

ಆⓈⓈಾ

Rousseau's most explicit attacks on d'Epinay are found in Book IX of the *Confessions*, which in many ways can be read as a response to her portrayal of him in her novel. René's glowing praise for Emilie's writing in *Montbrillant* contrasts sharply with Rousseau's satiric account of d'Epinay's literary efforts in the *Confessions*: "She decided to try her hand at literature and dabbled at writing novels, letters, comedies, short stories, and other such rubbish," quips Rousseau. "But what amused her most was not so much to write them as to read them; and if she managed to scribble out two or three pages at a time, she insisted on finding at least two or three indulgent listeners with whom to share this huge production" (I: 411). This passage reflects a deliberate attempt to ridicule d'Epinay as an author and to trivialize her work. By accusing her of laziness, dilettantism, and above all of vanity, Rousseau was both expressing and appealing to traditional misogynistic prejudices and stereotypes concerning women writers. His choice of the pejorative terms "dabble," "scribble," and "rubbish" to describe her literary efforts, his ironic use of the phrase "huge production" to refer to her supposedly meager output, his insistence on the indulgence of her audience—all this was intended to deny the seriousness and value of d'Epinay's writing.

On a deeper level, Rousseau's satiric portrait of d'Epinay in the *Confessions* reflects the anxiety and rage generated by his financial dependence on her and by the threat she posed to him both as a woman and as a writer. This interpretation is borne out by his complaints later in this passage that his feelings and talents were constantly belittled by d'Epinay and her friends and by his vigorous denial that he ever felt any physical attraction to her. "I was generally considered a complete nonentity in all respects, not only in Mme d'Epinay's circle, but in M. d'Holbach's too, and wherever Grimm set the tone," he explains.

> This insignificance suited me perfectly except when I was alone with her; then I did not know what posture to assume. I dared not talk of literature since I was not a competent judge of it, nor of gallantry since I was too timid and feared, more than death itself, to be laughed at as a ladies' man. Besides, the idea never occurred to me in Mme d'Epinay's company.... She was very thin and pale, with a chest as flat as my hand. That defect alone would have been enough to dampen my desires; for neither my heart nor my senses have ever been able to view someone without breasts as a woman; and other reasons which there is no need to mention always caused me to forget her sex when I was with her. (I: 411–12)[52]

Rousseau's insistence that he never felt any sexual attraction to d'Epinay is perhaps intended to corroborate a later passage in the *Confessions* where he seeks to counter rumors that he had been her lover: "My surprise upon learning from Saint-Lambert that no one doubted that I had had the same type of relations with Mme d'Epinay as Grimm now had with her was equal only to his own surprise upon learning that this rumor was completely false," writes Rousseau. "Everything I learned from this conversation effaced any regrets I might still have felt to have definitively broken with her" (I: 497).

Rousseau's detailed, defensive account of "les affaires de l'Ermitage" in the *Confessions*—his falling-out with d'Epinay and her entourage, his conviction that his former friends were in league against him, and above all his fear of the distorted portrait d'Epinay might present of him in her autobiographical novel—all these factors point to the crucial role that *Montbrillant* played in motivating Rousseau to write his *Confessions*. The threat that d'Epinay's pseudo-memoirs represented to Rousseau is reflected in a letter he wrote to Duclos in 1764: "In Geneva, there has just appeared a frightful piece of slander in which Mme d'Epinay has supplied her own dubious version of events."

The conclusion of the letter makes it clear that Rousseau was already thinking of responding to d'Epinay in an autobiography of his own: "Heaven forbid that I should imitate her, even to defend myself! Yet without revealing the secrets she confided to me, I still have enough information from other sources to show her true character," he writes. "She doesn't know that I'm so well informed; but, since she is forcing me to it, she will one day learn how discreet I've been."[53] That d'Epinay's revisions of *Montbrillant* were in turn motivated by fear of what Rousseau wrote about her and her friends in the *Confessions* has been amply demonstrated by other scholars. Suffice it to say that, following Rousseau's private readings from the *Confessions* in various Parisian salons in early 1771, d'Epinay was so alarmed by the negative impression his account of her might produce that she used her influence to have future readings banned by the police.

An Eagle in a Cage of Gauze: D'Epinay's View of Herself as a Writer

In her early literary efforts, d'Epinay was very dependent on the approval and encouragement of others. This lack of self-confidence is reflected in her novel. When Volx finally responds to Emilie's manuscript with enthusiastic praise, she expresses pleasure and relief: "I'm delighted that you are pleased by my novel. . . . Since I received your letter, I no longer doubt the value of my work. Sometimes all we need is encouragement to develop our talent. . . . Nothing stifles it so much as a lack of self-confidence" (III: 173).

The detailed advice Volx gives Emilie on how best to proceed with her novel amounts to a profession of faith by d'Epinay in her approach to writing. In order to preserve the naturalness and spontaneity of her style, Volx advises Emilie to value truth and realism over imagination and elegance, to write for herself alone, not to show her work to others, and—above all—to forget she is writing a book: "Make a point of forgetting that you are writing a book. It will be easy enough to tie it all together later on; but it's difficult to achieve a feeling of truth and naturalness when it's not there from the start" (III: 171).

Ignoring Volx's instructions, Emilie does show her novel to "René" and to another friend, "M. de Beauval" (Margency), who express quite different reactions to her work:

René gave me many compliments. However, M. de Beauval said that . . . the style was too familiar and the overall structure very weak. I felt that what I had written was better than he thought, yet that it didn't deserve all the praise René had given it. I was even tempted to interpret René's admiration simply as surprise that my work wasn't as bad as he expected. (III: 174)

René's praise for Emilie's writing—praise she suspects to be ambivalent and insincere—presents an ironic contrast to Rousseau's satiric and entirely negative judgment of d'Epinay's literary efforts in the *Confessions*. On the other hand, Beauval's remark that Emilie's novel was structurally weak and her style too familiar recalls criticisms made not of d'Epinay's novel, but of Rousseau's. Emilie is perplexed by these contradictory appraisals of her work, but Volx quickly reassures her in his next letter: "What you tell me about the various appraisals of your work is quite amusing. Have confidence in my good opinion of it and in your own, and I promise you that the public will agree with us in time" (III: 196).

The comments about d'Epinay's novel embedded in the text itself constitute a kind of self-reflexive allegory of reading that illustrates the dilemma of the eighteenth-century woman writer. Faced with such conflicting appraisals of her work, Emilie finally resolves to trust her own judgment and that of Volx, who serves as a mirror for her self-image as a writer. However, in real life, d'Epinay's relationship to her male mentors—particularly Grimm—was not without ambivalence. Her heavy dependence on male approval, particularly marked at the beginning of her literary career, would seem to undermine her authority and autonomy as a woman writer. If her ultimate goal was to present an authentic portrayal of the female condition to counter inaccurate depictions by male authors such as Rousseau, her constant appeals for male approval of her writing seem oddly self-defeating.

D'Epinay's feelings of ambivalence toward her mentors is expressed in her novel. Volx's problematic stance as a male authority figure is reflected in the dual semantic resonances of his name, which signifies "voice" and "opinion" [*vox*] in Latin and "public" or "people" [*volk*] in German. By casting Volx in the role of omniscient literary critic and then choosing this name for him, d'Epinay no doubt wished to establish him as a spokesman for public opinion, or "voice of the people," in order to give added weight to his approval and praise of her writing. Yet the very fact that he advises Emilie not to show her work to anyone and to look upon it as a "monument reserved for [herself] alone" suggests his complicity (and d'Epinay's as well) with the social and literary conventions of female modesty and silence and with the traditional exclusion of women from public discourse. Volx functions therefore both as mentor and critic, muse and censor. His is at once a nurturing, private voice that echoes and amplifies Emilie's own and a repressive, public voice that expresses society's disapproval of women writers. Volx's role as Emilie's mentor is further complicated by the fact that he is a literary projection and idealization of Grimm, who as d'Epinay's mentor was far less supportive of her writing than his fictional counterpart, often judging her work condescendingly, while at the same time appropriating her contributions to the *Correspondance littéraire* as his own.[54] However, as we shall see, Emilie did not adhere slavishly to Volx's opinions any more than d'Epinay did to Grimm's. Like her fictional alter-ego, d'Epinay gradually learned to speak for herself in her own voice; her novel traces this coming to speech and to writing.

છાજી

Emilie's first serious literary endeavor (like d'Epinay's) is a series of letters on education addressed to her nine-year-old son—an appropriate enough genre for a novice female writer. She gives the first draft of the letters to René and to M. de Lisieux (her former guardian) for their critical appraisal. To her surprise and disappointment, their comments are almost entirely negative. In their view, the letters are too pedantic and abstract to be comprehensible to a nine-year-old; yet, at the same time, they are too personal and limited in scope to be of much interest to adult readers outside the family circle. Emilie's self-confidence and enthusiasm for the project are at first dampened by these criticisms, and she responds with exaggerated self-deprecation. She resolves nevertheless to continue writing and revising until she is satisfied with her work. In real life, d'Epinay in fact had the complete series of these *Lettres à mon fils* privately printed by a friend in a village near Geneva called Montbrillant. The fact that she chose to call her heroine by this name illustrates the importance this work represented to her. Madame de Montbrillant, the new self that d'Epinay created in her novel, was in a sense born through the experience of printing her first book.[55]

By recalling in such detail the frustrations of her first literary efforts, d'Epinay underscored the dilemma experienced by women writers of her period. It was not so much from a lack of talent or inspiration that she suffered as from a lack of faith in herself and of encouragement from others. Her repeated appeals for male approval and marked deference to male standards and judgment reflect both a lack of self-confidence and a desire to justify her literary endeavors in the eyes of her readers. When she was completing the first edition of her *Conversations d'Emilie*, for example, she belittled her work and avoided discussing it in her weekly letters to Galiani. "I'm not talking to you about my book because I know you will tease me about it. Since I still have work to do on it, that might discourage me from finishing it," she explained. "When it's done, I'll let you say anything you like and I'll be the first to laugh about it with you."[56] D'Epinay's ambivalence toward herself as a writer continued even after she had become a successful author. Despite public acclaim for her *Conversations*, she still feared that her closest friends might not approve of her work. In another letter to Galiani, she confided:

> You haven't yet received my Dialogues. They have started circulating here, despite the precautions I thought I had taken to keep them from the public. The book is a huge success, which is really hilarious, since it wasn't written to attract attention from people who don't have children. . . . I hear all this from my sickbed, and it makes me laugh. . . . And yet, what if my book doesn't please you?[57]

Like Emilie anxiously awaiting Volx's judgment of her novel, d'Epinay was greatly relieved when Galiani finally responded with glowing tributes to her talents and originality.

Although Rousseau also suffered from an inferiority complex and from hypersensitivity to the judgment of others,[58] these problems were compounded in d'Epinay's case by her interiorization of the prejudices against women writers, along with all the feelings of inferiority traditionally conditioned in women by society. Like other women writers of her period, d'Epinay was haunted by what Mary Poovey refers to as the specter of the "Proper Lady"—the ideal of femininity according to which female self-assertion and activity outside the domestic sphere were considered improper and unladylike. As Poovey points out, "the very act of a woman writing during a period in which self-assertion was considered 'unladylike' exposes the contradictions inherent in [this model of] propriety."[59] The tensions and contradictions generated by the "Proper Lady" model are played out in d'Epinay's life and works in a striking manner. In conformity with the ideals of modesty and self-effacement ingrained in her by her mother, d'Epinay long believed and even taught her granddaughter "that the ideal woman is one about whom nothing is ever heard, either good or bad . . . . Boldness or outspokenness of any kind is unbecoming to our sex."[60] Similarly, in her novel, she insists: "I have no desire to win praise or fame, no ambition for success." (III: 85) When Sedaine, to whom she had given her novel to read, encouraged her to publish it, she firmly replied: "No praise could flatter me more than yours. . . . But I am quite firm in my resolve never to publish this work. Even if I were certain of its success, I still would refrain from publication, since I fear celebrity of any kind."[61] In these passages, d'Epinay seems to echo similar pronouncements by Rousseau in *Julie, Emile*, and the *Lettre à d'Alembert* concerning women's proper sphere of activity.

D'Epinay's reluctance to publish her writings is mirrored in the novel itself. When incorrect and unauthorized copies of Emilie's *Lettres à mon fils* begin to circulate in Geneva, her Genevan friends urge her to publish a corrected version to dispel the negative effect that these mutilated versions might have on her reputation. However, Emilie firmly refuses to follow their advice. Underlining the importance that she attaches, "not to the work itself, but to keeping it from the public," she replies: "I'm only interested in stopping the public attention the letters have attracted and in putting an end to this indiscretion." She then enumerates all the reasons why she feels the letters should not be published:

> You have seen my letters, and you certainly must agree with me that they were not written to be published. I intended them for the instruction and benefit of my children. . . . If the letters are good, they will create enemies for me; if they are worthless, people will simply laugh at me. And, to be perfectly blunt, the claim an author makes that he is publishing a work merely to justify himself nearly always seems to me a specious argument dictated by vanity and pride. (III: 447–49)

Reflecting on the dilemma of the woman writer, Mme Roland astutely observed: "If her writing is bad, people make fun of her; if her works are good, people deny that she wrote them . . . [or] they attack her character, morals, behavior, and talents to such an extent that they destroy her reputation as an author through the notoriety they give her."[62] D'Epinay's insistence that publication of the letters would hurt her reputation regardless of the quality of her writing echoes Mme Roland's analysis. Indeed, this passage from *Montbrillant* parallels Mme Roland's expressions of dismay when she learned that her travel journal *Un Voyage en Suisse* had been published without her knowledge.

This letter in *Montbrillant* may be entirely fictitious and may have been included simply to justify the private printing and distribution of d'Epinay's *Lettres à mon fils*. In any case, to counter the charge of vanity she feared might be leveled against her, d'Epinay takes care to emphasize her lack of ambition and the disinterested motives that had led her to write in the first place: love for her children and affection for her friends. Yet, in a marginal note in *Montbrillant*, d'Epinay offers quite a different motive for printing and distributing the *Lettres à mon fils*. In answer to the question "Why print them, then, if you don't intend to show them to anyone?" she replies: "Why? We don't live forever, and memories fade. It is comforting to leave behind clear principles and a sense of what really matters that will keep our memory alive after we are gone" (III: 448, n. 2).

This frankly expressed desire for immortality through her writing seems to contradict the ideal of self-effacement and the fear of celebrity d'Epinay repeatedly expressed elsewhere, especially in her letters to Galiani. When he reminded her half seriously, half mockingly, that their correspondence would no doubt be published after their death, she replied: "It's terrible of you to remind me that our correspondence will be published when we are gone. I've known it all along, but had forgotten. . . . Immortality frightens me."[63] In another letter to Galiani, d'Epinay complained that one of her correspondents had read her letters in public and asked l'abbé to keep her letters to himself:

> Ah! you say then that I wrote you a charming letter? To tell the truth, I suspected that it was a good one, but I hope nevertheless that you will keep your reflections to yourself and that you will not behave like our friend the intendant of Auverge, who stupidly read one of my charming letters to a house full of guests in Riom. Doesn't he realize that I now have a reputation to maintain there? I'll no longer be able to write him without thinking about what I say. I find that unbearable; I like to chat with my friends in complete confidence, and I don't want to feel obliged to play a role. Is it a question of pride? Of modesty? Perhaps a bit of both.[64]

One finds similar protests in Mme Roland's letters. "I do not wish to write for anyone but myself," she insists. "The idea of writing for an audience would irritate my pride, constrain my thoughts, . . . and spoil the charm of expressing myself freely."[65] As with Roland and Henriette, one suspects that "the lady doth protest too much," that d'Epinay's repeated insistence on her lack of ambition, her modesty, and her fear of celebrity masked a strong pride in her talents and a secret desire for recognition—both of which she denied out of fear of being censured or ridiculed. This same tension between pride and modesty, between desire for recognition and fear of ridicule, is also apparent in the letter to Galiani cited earlier, where the prospect of publication elicits both pleasure and apprehension in d'Epinay, which she disguises beneath exaggerated protestations of modesty. One senses that d'Epinay's constant denials of her literary ambitions (like Henriette's and Roland's) were above all token gestures of conformity to literary and social conventions of female propriety—conventions that these women were subverting by the very act of writing.

D'Epinay's desire for recognition as a writer is clearly reflected in her novel by Emilie's refusal to follow Volx's injunction to consider her work as a "monument reserved for [her] alone" (III: 171). Commenting on this passage, Alice Parker claims that d'Epinay "accepts the advice of her lover not to show her work to anyone and . . . only dimly realizes the extent to which this injunction represents the repressive intervention of the Logos."[66] I would argue, quite to the contrary, that d'Epinay was fully aware of the strictures of female modesty that repressed women's writing and that she not only consciously challenged these strictures, but defiantly recorded her challenge to them in the text itself. Disregarding Volx's instructions not to show her novel to anyone, Emilie eagerly shared it with her circle of friends, as did d'Epinay in real life. Moreover, d'Epinay's constant literary activity—her 1800-page autobiographical novel (which she fully expected would be published after her death), her 1200-page *Conversations d'Emilie* (which she spent ten years expanding for a second edition), as well as her important contributions to the *Correspondance littéraire* and her voluminous correspondence with important figures of her time—all this intense literary activity clearly belies her insistence that she had no ambitions as a writer. Her denial of ambition is contradicted by the lavish praise for her writing voiced by the characters in her novel, by the pleasure she experienced in seeing the success of her *Conversations d'Emilie* and in receiving the Prix Montyon for this work, and by her expectations concerning the publication of her novel and of her correspondence with Galiani.[67]

Without overtly defying the moral and literary conventions of female pudeur, d'Epinay subverted these conventions from within. In both her autobiographical and pedagogical writings, she used the Rousseauian ideals of motherhood and sensibility as vehicles for—rather than as obstacles to—the realization of her ambitions outside the domestic sphere. Love for her children and concern for their education became a source not of self-effacement and self-denial, but instead an impetus for self-expression and self-affirmation. In the *Conversations d'Emilie*, as in *Montbrillant*, d'Epinay simultaneously fulfilled and downplayed her ambitions as a writer by underlining the didactic purpose of these works and by presenting them as manuals to help women in the upbringing and education of their children. For example, in the preface to the *Conversations*, d'Epinay insists that this work was not originally written for publication:

> A mother whose deplorable state of health left her no other consolation than the education of a much beloved daughter realized that the child took a special interest in conversation and that it would be easy to take advantage of this to develop her mind. . . . Since she had no desire to draw public attention to her works and lacked the necessary talents to warrant such an ambition, she was wary of the encouragement of her friends, who felt that these essays might be of use for the education of other girls. After much uncertainty, she decided to send her manuscript [for publication], . . . and the public, naturally disposed to encourage such projects, graciously confirmed the judgment of her friends.[68]

To justify the publication of this work, d'Epinay stresses her desire to serve the public welfare and the approval of this motive by her friends and the public. She also underlines her granddaughter's unwillingness to take the *Conversations* seriously unless they were published: "Children her age assume that only what is printed is worthy of being read and preserved" (ii). This statement represents a subtle challenge to the Rousseauian ideal of motherhood, since it is not the mother who wishes to have her work published, but her child. D'Epinay's feigned self-effacement both as author and mother is further emphasized by her claim that it was her granddaughter who provided the

ideas and even the text for her book. Yet the awkward syntax of
d'Epinay's French in the passage cited above suggests a certain embarrassment at her attempts to justify the publication of this work—particularly the double negative at the end of the second sentence: "elle dut
se défier de l'indulgence de quelques amis, qui pensèrent que ces essais
pouvaient n'être pas sans utilité pour l'éducation des filles." Or perhaps
this is simply another example of the *modestie de circonstance* I spoke of
earlier; perhaps d'Epinay is merely feigning embarrassment in order to
quell potential criticism of her literary ambitions.

To justify the publication of a revised, augmented edition of her
Conversations, d'Epinay again invokes the welfare of the public and of
her granddaughter, to whom she claims to have sacrificed her own
need for rest and tranquillity during her illness. "Only the benefits
that the child drew from these conversations and the public's indulgent support were able to sustain the mother's courage through the
cruellest sufferings and allow her to continue her work," she explains.
"Maternal love is stronger than the fear of dying; for, even when the
author was close to death several times, her suffering could not make
her abandon her project" (iv–v). D'Epinay's subversion of the
Rousseauian ideals of motherhood and the public good is pushed to
its logical conclusion at the end of her preface, where she insists that
the public would benefit even more if every devoted mother were to
write and publish her experiences as she herself had done:

> It would no doubt be desirable if all conscientious mothers shared
> the fruits of their experience with the public, especially at a time
> when maternal love seems to penetrate all hearts with greater
> conviction and when all interests and inclinations have given
> way to this imperious and touching passion in the minds of most
> young mothers. It would be a sure means of establishing solid
> foundations for a well-designed general education. (viii–ix)

This rather inflated tribute to the importance of the maternal role in
educational reform reflects the growing importance attached to motherhood in the 1770s and 1780s. As in the writings of other educators
and moralists of the period (ranging from Rousseau to Genlis to
Wollstonecraft), such statements tend to be more *prescriptive* than *descriptive*, reflecting a shift in ideals rather than in actual practice. What
makes this passage subversive is that d'Epinay invokes the twin cults
of motherhood and the public good (both drawn from Rousseau) as

pretexts to encourage other women to write and publish. This "call for papers" presents a clever challenge to the ideal of female silence and to the authority of male educators. Not only does d'Epinay urge women to defy the prejudices against women writers; she also encourages them to share their experiences as mothers with each other in order to supplement (indeed to supplant) the abstract and, in her view, often useless writings of pedagogical theorists like Rousseau.

Breaking out of the Cage: The Emergence of a Feminine Voice in Histoire de Madame de Montbrillant

By reconstructing her life as fiction, d'Epinay was able to distance herself from what she saw as the social and linguistic oppression of women, to create a self of her own choosing from the raw materials of her experience. There is no reason to suggest, as Georges Roth and Pierre Fauchery have done, that d'Epinay turned to autobiographical writing for lack of imagination or that her life was less suitable for narrative manipulation than the experiences of an imaginary heroine.[69] In her autobiographical venture, she had virtually limitless possibilities to "sound her own consciousness," as Philip Stewart put it in his discussion of the memoir form.[70]

In her desire to lead a productive life according to the norms of her class and gender, Emilie de Montbrillant finds herself continually foiled. As she listens to the chorus of voices around her, the only authentic sound is the one she must strain the hardest to hear: that of her own voice. As an adolescent, she is taught to repress her own feelings and desires: "No matter how others may treat you, you should respond only with patience and gratitude," her great-aunt advises her. "Above all, never allow yourself to be distressed by the injustice of others; so long as you have a clear conscience, you will be in a position of strength" (I: 31, 33). Later, as a young bride, she is expected to submit without a murmur of protest to the double standard, to repress her pain and indignation at being betrayed and virtually abandoned by her husband. "Is it possible," she asks, "that women have no re-course or consolation other than tears? If not, why have authority and power been placed in the hands of men who are least in need of such help?" (I, 367). Silence and tears become her habitual refuge: "Over-whelmed by all I felt the need to say, I simply retreated into silence," she explains (I: 297). Where this leads is articulated many years later by the mature Emilie: "Having a will of my own seemed like a crime to me. . . . I've thought about it carefully since then and I've finally begun to dare to be myself" (III: 209). What she begins to dare to look at is the life she has led; the way that she becomes herself is by retelling her story.

Emilie's "coming to writing" is traced in the course of her narrative. Her efforts to express buried grievances and repressed desires are at first hesitant and awkward. Unable to find the words to express what she feels and sensing that her feelings are at odds with what is expected of her, she finds herself continually retreating into silence. This is particularly true in her dealings with her husband, who is incapable of understanding her point of view. When he finds her in tears one day and asks her to explain the cause of her distress, she finds she lacks the self-confidence and even the vocabulary needed to express herself. "Even when he urged me to tell him what was troubling me, I was reluctant to speak to him openly, fearing that I lacked the necessary firmness and resolve," she later explains.

> Besides, my situation is so difficult to explain: grievances that affect me so strongly when I am alone often seem so petty and childish when I try to explain them that I feel ashamed even to mention them. That is why, even with my closest friends, I keep silent about the problems in my marriage. But I would never have the courage to remain silent if I knew how to express my grievances in a way that did not seem laughable. (I: 361–62)

A few weeks later, she does in fact try to explain her feelings to her husband, but in vain: "When you ask what grieves me, I don't know how to put it into words. It's simply that I feel you have changed, but I can't say exactly how. It's up to you to examine yourself and figure it out" (I: 362). Yet, as she had feared, her husband only mocks her and belittles her feelings: "I don't know what you mean by grievances that you feel but that you can't express," he declares. "At least that shows they aren't very serious. I'm sorry to see what a state you've put yourself in over silly fantasies." Then, alluding to her second pregnancy, he adds: "I'm afraid it's your condition that has brought on these vapors" (I: 395–96). His statement reflects the belief—widespread even in medical circles of the period—that the uterus was the source of a wide range of psychosomatic disturbances (generally referred to collectively as *hystérie* or *vapeurs*).[71]

Emilie wonders if keeping a diary might help her learn to distance herself from her emotions: "Let's see if by writing down what troubles me today, I will judge my current situation the same way later when I consider myself happier" (I: 362). It is significant that the idea of keeping a diary comes not from Emilie herself but from her former guardian M. de Lisieux, who insists on the therapeutic benefits of writing in combatting her excessive sensibility and emotional vulnerability:

> I'd like you to be able to see yourself as you have been in the past, as you are today, and as you may be in a few months. This ongoing record of your life . . . could serve as a valuable guide for you. It could help you see yourself as you really are, to have a clearer view of your relations with others, and to make wiser decisions based on your past experience. Through your diary, you will find within yourself a stern but unfailing friend. (I: 334–35)

Writing in general, and diary-keeping in particular, are presented as means of self-analysis and self-discipline, a way of distancing herself from her emotions and channeling them in a positive way. This is precisely the advice that Rousseau fails to give Henriette, but that Emilie receives from Lisieux and Volx. Through Emilie's male mentors—the two most important voices of authority in the novel—d'Epinay underscores the value of writing as an acceptable, even salutary, activity for women. In response to Lisieux's suggestion, Emilie confides: "You can't imagine how pleased I am at your suggestion to keep a diary, since the idea had often occurred to me before. However, I would never have dared to follow through on it without your encouragement, for fear of being considered crazy for writing to myself" (I: 336). She especially values the freedom to express her innermost thoughts and feelings without feeling constrained by the rules of decorum governing social relations and literary productions or by the artificial requirements of conventional literary genres (chronology, diction, etc.): "I'd like to be able to talk freely about myself," she explains to Lisieux. "But besides the fact that I don't know where to begin, there are certain things that I'd like you to know without having to tell them to you face to face" (I: 335).

Lisieux and Volx both stress the importance of channeling her emotions into constructive outlets through study and writing. When Volx leaves for a six-month tour of military duty, he warns Emilie of the dangers of excessive sensibility and of overdependence on others for her happiness: "Sensibility has positive effects that we should cherish. The feelings you express toward me are very precious, but we should not lose control of our sensibility and exaggerate our unhappiness to the point that we are unable to fulfill our responsibilities. . . . It is not in tears that you will find the energy you need to fulfill your obligations to others and to yourself" (III: 88). He urges her to find increased satisfaction in her maternal role, yet also to take advantage of the intellectual stimulation offered by her new friendships in the d'Holbach circle. At the same time, Volx encourages her vocation as a writer and points to creative work as a key path to self-sufficiency: "You mustn't miss your calling. You could be the happiest woman on earth, if only you learned to be self-sufficient and to draw on your inner strengths and talents. Each new look within yourself, recorded in your writing, will enrich your life" (III: 119).

Volx's insistence on the need to balance domestic duties with social and literary activities and to control emotions through constructive activity challenged the models of sensibility and domesticity advocated by Rousseau. In contrast to Jean-Jacques, who encouraged the dependence of women on male authority and on the opinion of others, Volx stressed the importance of female independence and self-sufficiency. Whereas Rousseau tried to circumscribe women within the domestic sphere, Volx encouraged Emilie to seek constructive outlets for her creative energies beyond the domestic sphere. In her fiction, as in her life, d'Epinay challenged the principle of separate spheres and the narrow female role advocated by Rousseau.

In the course of d'Epinay's autobiographical venture, the main narrative voice shifts back and forth from male to female, from Emilie to the various figures of authority in her life, particularly her various male mentors. However, unity is maintained by the focus on Emilie's search for her own voice. At the beginning, her voice is always accompanied by that of a male double who dominates and directs it from outside. "You have tried so hard to hide your worth from others that you have almost succeeded in hiding it from yourself," Volx cautions her. "You don't know the value of your mind, nor the strength of your character and talents. Take my word for it: you can't short-change yourself this way without paying a heavy price" (II: 562–63). As Emilie gains confidence in her own judgment and feelings, this male voice functions less as a voice of authority to which she must acquiesce than as an echo and reinforcement of her own voice. Like M. de Lisieux,

Volx begins to serve less as a mentor than as a mirror and mouthpiece for d'Epinay's view of herself as a woman and as a writer. Gradually, Emilie learns to speak in her own voice, to express her desires and ambitions directly, rather than through a male *porte-parole*. For example, in response to a conservative family friend who—in Rousseau-like fashion—reproaches her for having "multiplied her interests and talents" and for supposedly neglecting her family duties, she replies:

> I've begun to dare to be myself and no longer worry about what others think of me. I do only what pleases me and it suits me just fine. . . . Why should anyone reproach me for trying to cultivate my talents, especially when there is nothing immoral or pretentious in what I'm doing, when I am writing only for myself and my own pleasure? . . . If I'm happy with myself, why shouldn't others be satisfied with me as well? (III: 209)

This passage represents a turning point in d'Epinay's novel, for it is the first time she defends her activities as a writer in her own voice, that of Emilie. In this way, Emilie's diary—and the autobiographical novel in which it is framed—comes to serve as her inner guide and conscience, the "stern but unfailing friend" her guardian hoped it would become.

The novel that results is a complex mixture of fact and fiction, male and female voices, "public" and "private" writings, presented in a variety of narrative styles and genres. Fragments from Emilie's journal, letters exchanged among a dozen or more correspondents, theatric *scènes dialoguées*, stylized portraits, and brief summaries of events narrated by her guardian are artfully alternated and intertwined in an ever-changing sequence. The overall effect is to create the literary equivalent of a patchwork quilt: a rich array of colors, designs, and moods, in which the seams between the pieces are as important to the pattern as the pieces themselves. This constant shifting from one genre to another and from one speaker to another allows d'Epinay to present the same or successive episodes from different points of view as from within a kaleidoscope. But the main focus is always on Emilie and on her inner journey toward self-understanding and self-expression.

తుంలు

The mutilations to which *Histoire de Madame de Montbrillant* was subjected by its male editors can be ascribed in part to their uncertainty as to its true genre, purpose, and intended audience. Memoirs, autobiographical novel, *roman à clef*, sentimental novel, or *bildungs-roman*—which genre best describes it? Was it written for a public or private audience, for a male or female readership? Finally, in writing the novel, what was d'Epinay's primary motive: to tell her own story for purposes of self-analysis and self-therapy, or to defend herself and her friends against Rousseau's charges? Or, as she herself claims in her preface, was her primary aim to take a probing look at the condition of women for purposes of social criticism and to provide a survival manual for her female contemporaries?

Most of d'Epinay's editors have viewed her novel primarily as a response to Rousseau's *Confessions* and have therefore felt justified in cutting out long sections that preceded or digressed from the d'Epinay-Rousseau story. Similarly, on the assumption that *Montbrillant* was an autobiography disguised as a *roman à clef*, d'Epinay's early editors deleted all passages that strayed from what they arbitrarily determined to be the truth, including the entire fictional dénouement.[72] In his 1951 edition, Roth was the first to publish the original ending. He claimed, nevertheless, that d'Epinay would have done better to omit it:

> After her husband lost his post as *fermier général* in 1762, Mme d'Epinay finally had time to complete her novel. Her inspiration and verve failed her, however, and she succumbed to an awkward and dull imitation of Jean-Jacques's style. The final chapters, which focus on the dying heroine and her devoted lover, are turgid, sentimental, and purely romanesque . . . a tedious effort to rival *Julie* and to surpass Rousseau in his own domain. (I: xviii)

Although Roth was not altogether unjustified in his criticism, he failed to recognize that d'Epinay used the conventional death-for-love ending of the sentimental novel as a means of protest against the condition of women in general and the conditions of her own life in particular. Whereas in real life, Grimm abandoned her for frequent and often unnecessary trips abroad, in *Montbrillant*, his fictional alter-ego Volx is forced to leave Emilie against his will and then goes blind and tries to commit suicide when he learns of her death. Like the intense jealousy and nearly fatal grief that Emilie unwittingly provokes in her first lover Formeuse, Volx's sudden blindness represents a kind of poetic justice and revenge wrought by a woman novelist upon lovers who abandoned her in real life and who belittled her talents. Moreover, what Roth claims is an awkward, second-rate imitation of the ending to *Julie* is in fact an innovative challenge to it, since Emilie refuses the sacraments on her deathbed and rejects the Christian ideal of happiness after death, just as she had the Christian ideal of conjugal fidelity, in a bold affirmation of earthly love and female desire.

ఛ౧౧౧౬

In this chapter, we have examined how *Histoire de Madame de Montbrillant* challenges *La Nouvelle Héloïse* on both a literary and ideological level and how this dual challenge is in turn reflected in the style and structure of d'Epinay's novel. I have suggested that her novel represents the strivings of a woman writer to create within the confines of male-dominated novelistic genres a *roman de femme*—a feminocentric novel in which the experiences and dilemmas of women might be expressed in a more authentic manner. There were few models for d'Epinay to follow in elaborating what was essentially a woman's story.[73] Her originality lay in her efforts to develop a language that would allow her to break through the strictures of female silence and to articulate her feelings and perceptions from a distinctly feminine point of view.

In reaction to the prescriptive tendencies of male writings on women, d'Epinay drew on her own experience to present a more authentic picture of women's lives. In contrast to Rousseau's prescriptive, moralistic pronouncements in favor of maternal breastfeeding, she describes in realistic detail the practical problems (both social and physical) that women encountered when they tried to nurse their babies themselves. The physical realities of the female condition (pregnancy, childbirth, motherhood, aging) are recurring themes in her novel—details from daily life glossed over or ignored in male-authored texts of the period. Finally, in contrast to the idealized, male-centered view of domesticity presented by Rousseau, d'Epinay describes the realities of married life from a woman's point of view: financial and legal dependence upon irresponsible husbands, the injustices of the double standard, the frustrations of motherhood, and the daily misery of being wedded for life to a man one neither loves nor respects. By rewriting her life as fiction, d'Epinay was able to distance herself from the problems and tensions inherent in the female condition of her period and to begin to resolve them, at least at the level of fiction. If her heroine continues to be oppressed by what she calls the "miserable bondage of [her] life" (II: 338), the author, through the act of writing, was on her way to becoming what Margaret Atwood refers to as a "creative non-victim."[74]

∽◦◉◦∽

In an article comparing d'Epinay's and Diderot's responses to Antoine Thomas's *Essai sur le caractère, les mœurs et l'esprit des femmes dans les différents siècles*,[75] Michèle Duchet argues that Diderot's critique of Thomas's essay is more original and more "feminist" than d'Epinay's. "In her own way, d'Epinay is just as trapped as Thomas within conventional ways of thinking. Her text is merely the flip side of the coin in relation to the dominant ideology," asserts Duchet.

> This explains the failure of her writing , which lacks teeth and nails, as well as a clear stake and purpose. Her central argument concerning the equality of women completely skirts the issue of the difference between the sexes as the locus of conflict and of textual difference. By tracing these differences, Diderot—unlike d'Epinay— gives himself the freedom to engage in a new discourse on women, with the boldness of the philosopher going beyond conventional ways of seeing things in order to probe their true nature.

Duchet then concludes: "The insignificance of Mme d'Epinay's letter, which fails to go beyond philosophical commonplaces and which remains neutral, clearly shows that it would be difficult to find eighteenth-century texts in which the feminine voice seeks to express itself authentically."[76]

I would argue, quite to the contrary, that d'Epinay's writings are exemplary "textes au féminin"—texts drawn from a woman's experience and expressing a woman's point of view in a distinctly feminine style. In contrast to Diderot's and Thomas's prescriptive, stereotypical pronouncements concerning women, d'Epinay's views and style are grounded in her experience as a woman and evoke with vivid realism the condition and aspirations of her female contemporaries. In contrast to their backward-looking view of women's destiny, d'Epinay presents a forward-looking view that seeks to transcend the narrow gender roles and distinctions imposed by eighteenth-century society. She dares to challenge the status quo and the male self-interest that Thomas and Diderot only seek to perpetuate. By underlining the fundamental similarity of character between men and women, d'Epinay calls into question the traditional gender distinctions and hierarchies underlying Thomas's view of women.

Above all, d'Epinay contests Thomas's argument that the physical and intellectual inferiority of her female contemporaries resulted from nature. She maintains that, by nature, women are as strong as men both mentally and physically and become weaker only through their education and upbringing. "Men and women possess the same constitution and nature," she declares.

> The proof of this is that primitive women are as robust and agile as primitive men; the weakness of women's minds and bodies is therefore due to their education and to the role assigned to them by society. Since men and women possess the same constitution and nature, they are capable of possessing the same failings, the same virtues, and the same vices. The virtues generally ascribed to women by society almost all run counter to nature and lead only to artificial, petty virtues and to very real vices.[77]

This last sentence constitutes an implicit attack on the ideals of "feminine" delicacy, modesty, and self-effacement advocated so strongly by Rousseau in *Emile*. In d'Epinay's view, these ideals compelled women to repress their ambitions and talents and to seek frivolous and sometimes pernicious outlets for their energies. She maintained that the natural equality between the sexes could not be restored until these artificial and often oppressive models were rejected. However, she recognized that changing such deeply rooted attitudes would be difficult, particularly since the whole gender hierarchy was, in her view, founded on male self-interest: "It would no doubt take several generations to restore our natural condition. We would perhaps benefit from it, but men stand too much to lose," she explains. "They are lucky indeed that we haven't turned out any worse, after all they have done to denature us with their fine institutions" (254).

Like d'Alembert in his famous response to Rousseau,[78] d'Epinay denounced male complicity with the status quo as the single greatest obstacle to equality between the sexes, and she insisted on the need to alter deeply rooted patterns of thought before any real progress could be made: "We need new heads to help us imagine things from a different point of view" (255). Like d'Alembert, d'Epinay saw improved education as the key to future equality for women and as the surest means for her female contemporaries to achieve a certain degree of inner freedom despite the persistence of external inequalities.

D'Epinay's writings—and her novel in particular—constitute *textes au féminin* not simply because of the woman-centered perspective they offer, but also because of their distinctly feminine style. Rejecting or subverting the traditional conventions of female modesty and silence advocated by Rousseau, d'Epinay strove to convey repressed female desires, thoughts, and emotions—to go beyond existing possibilities of expression by defying literary and social *bienséances* of what was considered "proper" for a woman to articulate. She attempted to develop a style in which her grievances and longings could be expressed from within rather than viewed from outside through the distorting lens of male desire and self-interest. Her use of gaps, silence, gestures, and a highly original mixture of styles, genres, and voices anticipates the *écriture féminine* called for by Hélène Cixous in her 1975 essay *Le Rire de la Méduse*.[79] There is, for example, a striking passage in *Montbrillant* where Emilie tries desperately to penetrate the meaning of Volx's mournful silence after he has received word of his political disgrace and impending exile:

> Quelles peines! Comment décrire? . . . Je cherchais à le pénétrer, et son air me remplissait de terreur. . . . Je croyais que le sang glacé dans les veines était une façon de parler; mais je vous assure que je l'ai senti quand je le regardais, ou que ma main me retraçait son regard.

> Such sorrow! How can I describe it? . . . I tried to penetrate the meaning of his silence, and the look on his face filled me with terror. . . . I thought that when people said "the blood froze in my veins," it was only a manner of speaking; but that's how I felt when I later recalled his expression. (III: 519)

This is a particularly vivid example of d'Epinay's use of an elliptical style and "body language" to convey repressed female desires, thoughts, and emotions that go beyond existing possibilities of expression. Other efforts to "express the inexpressible" are found in Emilie's two conversations with her husband cited earlier (I: 361–62, 395–96).

Perhaps the most striking example in *Montbrillant* of what Duchet calls "*un texte au féminin*" in which the feminine voice seeks to express itself is found in the scene where Emilie urges her rival, Mme de

Versel, to confide in her in an effort to discover if Formeuse has betrayed her:

> Not knowing what I was saying, nor what I should say, I asked her: "Are you in love with someone?"—"Alas! yes," she replied with a sigh.—"With whom?... Well?... Why don't you answer?"—"Oh! I can't tell you; don't ask me to tell...."—"Why not?"—"It's because... I'm afraid.... I'm afraid of not being loved in return, and I'm just as afraid of being loved."—"Oh! Then surely you are loved!" I cried...—"What?" she replied, quite startled. "You know who it is then?... Don't tell me, don't tell me! Perhaps you won't respect me anymore," she cried, putting her hands over her eyes. "Let's talk about something else."—"I don't understand you," I said, believing I understood her only too well, "Is it possible?"... She covered my mouth with her hand.—"Quiet!" she bid me. We remained silent for a while.—"Well," I told her, "don't say a word, but let me guess." (II: 357–58)[80]

After repeated hesitations and lapses into silence, Emilie and her rival begin a long guessing game that finally leads Mme de Versel to confess that Formeuse does indeed love her, but that she is uncertain of her own feelings toward him: "I no longer know myself if I have anything to say or to hide." No longer able to contain her impatience and anxiety, Emilie cries: "Decorum can be so cruelly exasperating! Let me assure you, Madame, that I am strong enough and certainly open-minded enough to handle the most painful truth." To which Mme de Versel replies, with a curious mixture of solidarity and sadism: "Forgive me, dear friend. You can count on me now to tell you the whole truth" (II: 360). These repeated hesitations and lapses into silence reflect the barriers created between women by competition for male affections and by the conventions of female modesty and discretion. Through her persistent, often painful efforts, Emilie is able to break through these barriers of silence, not only with Mme de Versel, but with the other women to whom she is closest (especially her mother and sister-in-law) to form a network of female solidarity.

    It is above all through her writing that Emilie is able to break out of the cage of silence in which society has imprisoned her. By bestowing unchanged on her heroine the flattering epithet that Voltaire devised for her—*"un aigle dans une cage de gaze"*—d'Epinay expresses most clearly her view of herself as a woman writer. This image no doubt appealed to her because of the flattering connotations of the word *aigle* (eagle), which in French is used to refer to a person of superior intellect and talents, and (as in English) to someone with unusually keen, perceptive vision. Similarly, the term *gaze*—with its multiple connotations of wire, gauze, and veil—must have seemed particularly apt to describe the cage in which d'Epinay felt herself to be trapped. The metaphor suggests a cage that appears almost transparent from the outside but that, seen from within, is almost as confining as iron bars. By describing the cage from the inside, d'Epinay was slowly able to deconstruct it and to escape—or at least to achieve a significant measure of inner freedom.

With the passage of time, d'Epinay gradually changed from an enthusiastic admirer of Rousseau into a resisting reader and protesting writer. Drawing on her experiences as a wife and mother, daughter and lover, and responding to the powerful impulse of her talents and ambitions, she came to view his limited vision of female destiny with increasing ambivalence. By engaging in an overt literary rivalry with the author of *Julie* and *Emile*, who epitomized all the traditional prejudices against women authors, d'Epinay both proclaimed and concretized her challenge to the male-dominated literary establishment.

4

Revolution in the Boudoir:

Madame Roland's Subversion of Rousseau's Feminine Ideals

Among the women of the prerevolutionary era, Mme d'Epinay was one of the few to question Rousseau's sexual politics. Her female contemporaries generally responded to his writings and to his feminine ideals with uncritical fervor. The enthusiastic response to Rousseau increased among women of the succeeding generation, particularly after the events of 1789 seemed to confirm his political theories, thereby giving added prestige to his views in other areas as well. Rousseau's ideals of motherhood and domesticity were vigorously advocated by many revolutionary leaders as a vehicle for their program of social reform. "Rousseauism" became in a sense the dominant ideology of the new bourgeois ruling class and had considerable impact on the lives of countless women, particularly in the middle and upper classes. Rousseau's home-and-hearth ethic, along with the ideals of simplicity, efficiency, and frugality extolled in his portrayal of the Wolmar household, were constantly evoked in the public discourse of the period, as well as in private journals and correspondences.

To probe Rousseau's paradoxical appeal to women of the revolutionary era, this chapter examines how one woman of the period—Marie-Jeanne Phlipon, who later became Mme Roland—responded to his views on women and, specifically, how she interpreted his cult of domesticity as an empowering discourse. Her case is a particularly striking illustration of Jean-Jacques's influence, since of all the women examined in this study, Mme Roland is the one who made the greatest effort to conform her outward behavior to the limited role prescribed by Rousseau. Yet, while seeming to conform to these feminine ideals

and norms, she in fact undermined them by blurring the gender dichotomies and the distinction between public and private spheres that
lay at the very core of Rousseau's discourse on women. Her subtle
transgression of traditional gender barriers did not go unperceived and
was capitalized on by the Rolands' political enemies in the campaign of
slander and persecution that eventually led her to the guillotine.

A Passionate Disciple of Rousseau

Born in 1754, Marie-Jeanne (or Manon as she was affectionately called)
was the only child of a Parisian engraver. M. Phlipon's small but
thriving trade permitted him to provide his gifted daughter with an
education far above that customary for her sex and social rank, as well
as excellent marriage prospects. However, M. Phlipon's reckless business speculations after the death of his wife considerably dimmed
Manon's hopes for the future. It was at this critical juncture in her life,
at the age of twenty-one, that she first read *La Nouvelle Héloïse*. By
then, Manon had perused the works of an impressive number of authors, in virtually every period, field, and genre, including all the
major *philosophes*—except for Rousseau, conspicuous by his absence.
Mme Phlipon, who in general had given her daughter complete freedom in the choice of her readings, seems to have taken special care to
prevent her contact with Rousseau, apparently fearing the negative
influence he might have on her daughter's passionate, sensitive nature.[1] Madame Roland seems to have approved her mother's pru-
dence, for recalling Rousseau's impact on her, she writes: "I read him
late, which is just as well; he would have driven me wild; I would
have wanted to read no one else. Even as it is, he has perhaps only
served to strengthen my weakness."[2]

It was only after her mother's death in 1776 that Manon read *Julie*,
which a friend gave her to help calm her grief. The novel made a
profound impact on her and was to have a determining influence on
the course of her life. In her *Mémoires*, she recalls: "It seemed to me
that I then found my true substance, that Rousseau became the interpreter of feelings and ideas I had had before him, but that he alone
could explain to my satisfaction. He showed me the domestic happiness to which I had a right to aspire and the ineffable delights I was
capable of enjoying" (302). At a time of stress and crisis in her own
life, when she had practically given up hope of finding a suitable

Nineteenth-century engraving by Nérandan of an anonymous portrait of Marie-Jeanne Roland, generally considered the best likeness of her. The picture is thought to have been done by a fellow prisoner at the Conciergerie, where Roland was imprisoned before her execution. Courtesy of the Bibliothèque nationale, Paris.

husband because of her modest personal circumstances and idealistic expectations, Rousseau renewed her faith in the future through his appealing picture of the domestic felicity to which a virtuous woman could aspire. Far from being considered a trap, his ideals of motherhood and enlightened domesticity seemed to offer a new power and dignity to women, regardless of their socio-economic status.

After reading *La Nouvelle Héloïse*, Manon devoured Rousseau's works one after the other. Her correspondence of the period expresses the enthusiasm he inspired in her. "I find it strange that you are surprised by my enthusiasm for Rousseau," she wrote to a friend. "Who else portrays virtue in a more noble and touching manner? Who makes it more appealing? His works inspire love for truth, simplicity, and goodness. I truly believe that I owe him the best part of myself. His genius has inspired me; I feel myself elevated and ennobled by him."[3] Ignoring Rousseau's stern warning that the book should not be read by young girls lest it inflame their imaginations and corrupt their morals, Manon firmly defended the novel's moral and didactic value.[4] In the course of this same letter, each of Rousseau's works is praised in turn, including *Emile*: "I don't deny that there are some paradoxes in his *Emile*, and certain recommendations that are impractical in this day and age. But such profound insights! Such useful and healthy ideas! So many treasures atone for a few small flaws!"[5] Nowhere in her writings does Roland explicitly criticize the ultra-conservative, repressive view of women set forth in Book V of *Emile*. However, when raising her daughter Eudora, she would conscientiously apply the principles outlined for the education of Emile, while ignoring the far more limited education prescribed for Sophie.[6] Like Rousseau, Roland felt that a woman's place was in the domestic sphere; however, contrary to Rousseau, she did not feel that a woman's activities should be limited to purely domestic tasks. In this respect, she was not unlike other Rousseau fans of the period, who did not hesitate to adapt and even distort his views according to their own needs and values.

Until the end of her life, Rousseau was to remain her favorite author and *Julie* her favorite work: "Of all our writers, Rousseau is my favorite because he makes me content with my lot and always inspires me with the desire to become better and with the hope of succeeding. . . . I re-read *Julie* every year."[7] Her admiration for Rousseau became so intense that when her friend Sophie dared to criticize her idol, Manon took it as a personal affront. "I am vexed that you do not care for Rousseau, for I adore him beyond all expression, and I will not tolerate any vague charges against him." Like many of her contemporaries, Manon clearly viewed Rousseau as a martyr of persecuted virtue: "No one was ever more consistent and steadfast in his conduct. And yet he has been the victim of violent prejudice, stupidity, envy, and cruelty unleashed upon him in an unprecedented manner. Indeed, they came close to dragging to the scaffold a man to whom future generations will perhaps erect altars!"[8]

Mme Roland's response to *La Nouvelle Héloïse* has generally been described by her biographers as a revelation or even as a conversion experience.[9] However, as she herself observes in her *Mémoires*, she was predisposed by both her character and her upbringing to embrace Rousseau's cult of domesticity, as well as his pre-Romantic, pre–revolutionary spirit. Rousseau simply confirmed—and gave eloquent expression to—her deepest convictions and aspirations: "When I read Rousseau or Diderot, but especially the first, I felt transported by a tremendous enthusiasm; they seemed to have captured my deepest convictions, expressing them in ways I myself would no doubt have been incapable of matching, but that I could fully appreciate because they were feelings I shared."[10] That Manon was a firm believer in the ideal of enlightened domesticity long before she read Rousseau is borne out by the following passage of her memoirs, where she recalls Sunday walks with her parents as an adolescent and her growing aversion for the crowded public promenades of the capital:

> After these walks, I felt a terrible emptiness. . . . Is it merely to attract attention and to receive vain compliments that the members of my sex acquire talents and are schooled in virtue? . . . Do I exist only to waste my time with frivolous concerns and tumultuous feelings? — Oh, surely I have a higher destiny! . . . The sacred duties of wife and mother will one day be mine: my youth should be spent preparing me for these roles; I must study their importance and learn to control my inclinations, so that I can direct those of my children. Above all, I must become worthy of the man who will one day win my heart and be able to assure his happiness.[11]

Although Manon's domestic ideals may seem self-limiting to modern readers, her refusal to be reduced to a *femme-objet* and to engage in the frivolous games of vanity and ostentation so prevalent at that time constituted a conscious act of revolt on her part against what she considered an oppressive gender system. Above all, this passage reflects an independent mind and a strong desire for dignity and for a useful, meaningful life.

Manon's faith in Rousseau's program of moral reform and the crucial contribution that women could make to it is reflected in an essay she wrote on women's education in 1777. There she expressed her hope "that the sublime transports of virtue would inspire in women's hearts the noble ambition to reign over public morals, so that domestic happiness would assure that of the State."[12] Like Rousseau, she viewed the family as a microcosm of the State and women as the guardians of public morals. Through their positive influence in the domestic sphere, wives and mothers could contribute directly to the moral regeneration of society.

In her quest for happiness through companionate marriage and motherhood, Manon seemed to take Julie as her model by accepting as her husband an erudite and austere man twenty years her senior. During their six-year stay at Le Clos, Roland's modest country estate, she took great pleasure in emulating the sober domestic virtues embodied in Julie's life at Clarens. Like the Wolmars, she viewed rural life as the privileged locus of happiness and virtue. During her peaceful retreat at Le Clos, which she affectionately referred to as "mon Ermitage," she conscientiously fulfilled her role as wife and mother—educating her daughter (whom she had dutifully nursed in infancy), running her household, serving as doctor and benefactress to the local peasants, and overseeing the farm work when her husband was away on his frequent tours as regional inspector of manufactures.

Roland's Early Writings:
The Specter of Emile *and the Proper Lady*

In addition to these domestic activities, Roland actively collaborated with her husband on numerous technical and scholarly works, including his three-volume *Dictionnaire des Manufactures, Arts et Métiers* for the revised edition of Diderot's Encyclopedia. She had a direct hand in the research, writing, and proofreading of every article. Yet, far from satisfying any personal ambition on her part, this work was in her eyes merely an extension of her devotion to her husband. "It was almost as natural for me to write with him as it was to eat with him," she insists in her *Mémoires*. "Existing only for his happiness, I devoted myself to what brought him the greatest pleasure. If he wrote about industrial arts, I wrote about them too, although they bored me. Since he liked scholarship, I helped him in his research. If it amused him to send a literary piece to an academic society, we worked on it together" (154).

Although well aware of her intellectual and literary talents, Roland consistently refused to publish anything (even works entirely her own) under her name, preferring to remain anonymous or to hide behind her husband's signature. She seems to have subscribed wholeheartedly to Rousseau's ideals of female modesty and self-effacement and to his views of the "natural" superiority and domination of the male sex. Her interiorization of female inferiority and of traditional prejudices against women writers and scholars is particularly apparent in a letter written to a male family friend in the early years of her marriage:

> I believe in the superiority of your sex in every respect. . . . You have strength, and everything that goes with it: courage, perseverance, wide horizons, and superior talents. It is up to you to make the laws in politics and discoveries in the sciences. Govern the world, change the face of the globe, be proud, terrible, clever, and learned. You are all that without our help, and because of it you are destined to be our masters. But without us, you would not be virtuous, loving, loved, nor happy. So keep your glory and authority. For our part, we have and wish no other power than over your morals, no other throne than in your hearts. I will never claim anything beyond that. It irks me to see women claiming privileges which suit them so poorly. Even the name of author strikes me as ridiculous when applied to them. However gifted they may be, women should never show their learning or talents in public.

She concluded her Rousseauian credo by declaring: "I can imagine no destiny more rewarding than that of assuring the happiness of one man alone."[13]

Roland firmly believed that women who pursued ambitions and desires outside the domestic sphere jeopardized not only their happiness, but their reputation as well. She was, moreover, acutely aware of the double standard and prejudices affecting women writers. "I never had the slightest temptation to become an author," she insists in her *Mémoires.*

> It became clear to me very early that a woman who earned this title for herself lost much more than she gained. She is disliked by men, and criticized by her own sex. If her writing is bad, people make fun of her, and rightly so; if her works are good, people deny that she wrote them . . . [or] they attack her character, morals, behavior, and talents to such an extent that they destroy her reputation as an author through the notoriety they give her. (304)

Although Roland recognized that the prejudices against women writers were at times unjust and that they were often criticized for faults shared by male authors,[14] she did not hesitate to portray mediocre *femmes de lettres* in a negative, even satirical manner. Her portrait of Mme de Puisieux reflects her scorn for women with literary pretensions whose talents are not equal to their ambitions.[15]

Yet, conscious of her own talents, Manon was not insensitive to praise. When M. de Boismorel, a scholar and much-respected friend of the family, expressed enthusiasm for a collection of her writings entrusted to him by her father (without her permission), she was secretly flattered. She was even more flattered when a moralistic letter she sent anonymously to M. de Boismorel's wayward son (at Boismorel's bidding) was mistaken by the boy and his family for the work of Jean-Jacques himself. She nevertheless hastened to add: "My only fear is that he might publish it in some newspaper; for I dislike anything that might disturb my privacy and tranquility."[16]

When a friend predicted that she would one day write a book, Roland retorted: "Then it will be under someone else's name; for I would eat my fingers before I ever became an author."[17] She was in fact quite indignant when friends published long sections of her travel journal, *Un Voyage en Suisse*, without her knowledge or permission. At the beginning of that same work, Roland had written: "I do not wish to write for anyone but myself; the idea of being read would irritate my pride, constrain my thoughts, . . . and no doubt destroy the charm of expressing myself freely." As if to justify this somewhat curious blend of modesty and narcissism, she hastens to add: "Women are not supposed to express their ideas or learning publicly. What could they say that others don't already know better than they? Their sex as well as their duties require them to stay out of the public eye, as if behind a veil, where they are more certain to find happiness than in the glitter of society life."[18] This passage has a definite Rousseauesque ring to it and could easily be mistaken for a passage from Book V of *Emile*. Indeed, Roland seems to invoke Rousseau's negative view of women authors in order to underline her own modesty and deference to literary and social conventions.

The importance Manon ascribed to female modesty and disinterestedness may also have been designed to hide a secret lack of self-confidence and fear of failure. She seems to have interiorized the traditional view of women's inferiority so thoroughly that she felt that she could not successfully compete with male authors. At age twenty-one, she wrote: "Great talents are beyond the reach of women. I have no ambition for success or fame, nor any hope for it, since I cannot aspire to excellence in any new or important field. Unable to do much for others, I'll study for myself and strive to perfect my mind."[19] This passage clearly reflects Manon's interiorization of traditional prejudices against women writers and scholars. However, her reiterated denials of her literary ambitions—like Henriette's and d'Epinay's—may be seen as a form of protest against a gender system in which cultural productions were a jealously guarded male preserve.

Convinced that a woman's place was out of the public eye, Manon voluntarily relegated herself to the domestic sphere both before and after her marriage: "I like the shadows, and twilight is enough for my happiness. As Montaigne says, one is only at ease in the backshop."[20] Despite her passion for learning and the intense pleasure she experienced as a writer, she carefully avoided calling attention to her scholarly and literary activities, fearing the ridicule and censure generally encountered by *les femmes de lettres*: "I am not interested in becoming a scholar, nor is it my goal to earn a reputation for wit or talent or the pleasure of being published; I study because I need to just as much as I do to eat. . . . My work brings me happiness and much pleasure, or at least some consolation for my troubles."[21]

The six years spent at Le Clos unquestionably represent the most serene period in Roland's life. With peaceful resignation, she looked forward to finishing out her days in tranquil domesticity, enlivened by readings from her favorite authors: "Yes, I feel that I will spend my whole life in the country, in peace and contentment," she wrote her husband, "all I need are the works of Jean-Jacques; reading them will make us shed delicious tears and rekindle feelings that will bring us happiness whatever our fate may be."[22] Her formerly keen interest in political events waned under the influence of domestic preoccupations. To a Parisian friend who kept her informed of the latest news, she quipped: "I no longer dabble in politics."[23] Yet her political apathy was not destined to last, for the events of 1789 jolted her out of this comfortable routine and brought to the surface unfulfilled aspirations and talents that had lain dormant during her nine-year retreat into domesticity.

The Revolution's Impact: Breaking out of the Domestic Mold ✓

Fervent disciples of Rousseau's political and social thought, the Rolands greeted the Revolution with immediate and unbounded enthusiasm:

"The Revolution took hold of all our ideas and subjugated all our plans; we devoted ourselves entirely to our passionate desire to serve the public welfare."[24] All personal feelings and private activities were relegated to the background in favor of the national events that were making history. The *aurea mediocritas*—the notion that happiness can be found only in a simple, tranquil life—by which she had lived for so many years, now seemed totally forgotten in the flurry of excitement and exhilaration. In her memoirs, Roland recalls: "I was seduced by the Revolution, ... penetrated by the desire to see my country prosper, and seized by a feverish and continual preoccupation with public affairs" (154). Her repeated use here and elsewhere of amorous terms and images to describe her revolutionary zeal underlines the extent to which her libidinal urges were sublimated in her political fervor. More than once in the course of her memoirs, the Revolution is personified as a seductive, but ultimately faithless lover.

Under the pressure of events, Mme Roland's life and writings underwent a radical politicization. Her character and tone grew more energetic and direct, even brusque at times, as a result of her revolutionary zeal. In her letters from Le Clos to friends in Paris, her charming vignettes à la Sévigné gave way to urgent exhortations and warnings expressed in a trenchant, sometimes violent style: "It is true that I no longer write of our personal affairs: where is the traitor who today has other affairs than those of the nation?"[25] When some of her letters disappeared in the mail, censured perhaps because of their radical anti-monarchism, she angrily warned the culprits: "If this letter does not reach you, let the cowards who read it blush with shame upon learning that these words were written by a woman, and let them tremble to think that she can inspire a hundred men who will in turn inspire a million others."[26]

Increasingly conscious of the power of words and of her own ability to use them to further the revolutionary cause, Mme Roland became a regular, albeit anonymous contributor to republican journals. In 1790, her husband was sent to represent Lyon in the Constitutional Convention in Paris, where he became an active member of the Jacobin Society. When he was appointed secretary of the club's correspondence committee, Mme Roland eagerly shared his work. She was convinced that shaping public opinion could play a vital role in the success of the Revolution, and she put all her literary skill into answering the many letters from provincial correspondents. After her husband's unexpected appointment as Minister of the Interior, Mme

Roland's collaboration became even more crucial to the success of his career. She was not only the moving force behind his propaganda bureau, the famous "Bureau d'Esprit Public," but also served as his secret political advisor and ghost writer.[27] She composed many of the key documents of his ministry, including his protest to the Pope concerning French prisoners in Rome, as well as his famous letter of protest to Louis XVI. Published by the Assembly (at Mme Roland's urging), Roland's letter to the King led to the dissolution of the first Cabinet and played a significant role in turning the tide of public opinion against the monarchy.

As in her earlier journalistic endeavors, Mme Roland remained resolutely anonymous. "It was with intense pleasure that I wrote these pieces, because I felt they could be useful," she explains in her memoirs. "I found greater satisfaction in doing it anonymously. . . . I have no need of glory" (155). As before, she claimed that her work was simply an extension of her devotion to her husband. In response to charges that she had secretly run her husband's ministry, she loyally defended his probity and capabilities. She insisted that she merely served as his secretary and had always refrained from influencing his decisions: "I never meddled in administrative affairs. . . . Why should it detract from a man's professional reputation or merit if his wife serves as his secretary?" (305) However, from Mme Roland's own testimony elsewhere in her *Mémoires*, it is abundantly clear that she was much more than a mere scribe and that charges that she was the hidden power behind her husband's ministry were not unfounded.

It is also clear from her memoirs that Mme Roland derived a secret pleasure and amusement from the important role she played behind the scenes: "A letter to the Pope, written in the name of the Executive Council of France, secretly composed by a woman in the austere office that Marat liked to call a boudoir—the situation struck me as so amusing that I laughed about it quite a while afterward. It was the secrecy of my participation that made these contrasts so amusing" (305). At one point in her memoirs, she could not resist discreetly poking fun at Roland's tendency to take her talents and efforts for granted and to appropriate them as his own: "If one of his pieces was singled out and praised for its graceful style, . . . I took pleasure in his satisfaction without remarking that I had written it, and he often ended up convinced that he had truly been inspired when he had written a passage that I myself had composed" (304). Although on the surface this passage suggests that Manon was being exploited by an ungrateful and egotistic husband, her ironic tone conveys quite a different impression—that if Roland became the powerful political figure that he was, it was due less to his exploitation of her than to her clever manipulation of him. He became in a sense her mouthpiece, just as she was his hidden voice.

In the early years of their marriage, Manon had been somewhat intimidated by her husband's greater age, knowledge, and experience. Eventually however, she gained enough confidence in her abilities and judgment to voice her own opinions.[28] She began to resent Roland's autocratic, self-centered manner and the fact that she had always sacrificed her happiness for his; but she carefully repressed any resentment behind a mask of submission and devotion to him and his work. "After considering only my partner's happiness for so long, I finally realized that there was something missing in my own," she confides her in *Mémoires*.

> I often felt that our relationship was unequal, due to Roland's dominating character and the twenty-year age gap between us. If we lived alone together, I sometimes had a difficult time with him; if we went out into society, I was admired by people, some of whom I sensed might attract me. I plunged myself into my husband's work—another excess which had its disadvantage, for he became too dependent upon my help, . . . and I wore myself out. (332–33)

This passage suggests that Manon plunged herself into her husband's work not simply to prove her devotion and worth to him, but also to fill emotional and intellectual needs that her marriage had not satisfied, as well as to protect herself from the attractions of younger men. Her collaboration on her husband's work may also have helped compensate for the disappointments of motherhood. For despite all her efforts, her daughter remained a rebellious and indolent child of mediocre intelligence, utterly lacking in intellectual curiosity and artistic gifts.[29]

The Revolution gave Roland a unique opportunity for self-fulfillment outside the domestic sphere—the chance she had secretly longed for to play an active role in shaping the ideal republic she had dreamed of ever since she first read Plutarch. As a young woman, she had lamented the powerlessness and obscurity to which she seemed condemned by her sex and inferior social status:

I am truly vexed to be a woman: I should have been born with a different soul or a different sex or in another century. I should have been born a woman in Rome or Sparta, or else a man in France. At least then I could have chosen the Republic of Letters as my country, or another of those republics where as a man, one only needs to obey the law. . . . I feel imprisoned in a class and an existence that is not at all mine. . . . Everywhere I turn, my mind and heart run up against the constraints of opinion and prejudice, and all my strength is consumed in vainly struggling against my chains. . . . My enthusiasm for the welfare of society seems utterly wasted, since I am unable to contribute anything to it![30]

Conscious of her rich inner gifts, Manon felt stifled and out of place in the petit bourgeois world of her father. For lack of proper training and a stimulating environment, she felt that her intelligence and imagination were being wasted.[31] Ardently she aspired to a higher level of existence, to a place in the "Republic of Letters" where her intellectual and literary endeavors would be appreciated and encouraged. She bitterly resented the socio-economic and gender barriers that prevented her from traveling abroad and from participating actively in the cultural life of her period. In several letters to Sophie Cannet, she fantasized about dressing like a man to gain greater freedom to study and travel.[32]

Parallel to Manon's frustrated intellectual and artistic ambitions as a young woman of the petite bourgeoisie were her frustrated political aspirations—her desire to participate in the political life of her country, to contribute actively to the public good in accordance with her republican convictions. At the age of twenty, she had written to Sophie: "It seems to me that man's vocation is to be useful to his fellow creatures, that the first and most admirable virtue lies in working for the public good. . . . You can imagine how frustrated I feel to be confined to the narrow circle of my private life, living only for myself and totally useless to others."[33]

Madame Roland's Revolutionary Salon: The Fusion of Public and Private Spheres

Manon's important contribution to her husband's work during his two terms as Minister of the Interior enabled her to participate covertly in the public sphere and to help shape the future of the new French republic without having to sacrifice her outward conformity to Rousseau's ideals of female modesty and domesticity. When Roland first became active in the Jacobin Club in early 1792, their home served as an informal gathering place for Brissot, Robespierre, and other deputies who at the time constituted the radical Left. After he became minister, they had dinner gatherings twice a week for his political associates.

As a hostess, Mme Roland maintained a simple, almost Spartan style of entertaining. There were generally no more than fifteen guests at a time. Moreover, women were strictly excluded from the gatherings in her home. "When my husband served as minister, I made it a rule to never visit other women or to invite them into my home," she explains in her memoirs.

> This required no great sacrifice on my part, since I had never participated in society life before and since I cherish a quiet, studious life as much as I detest gambling and foolishness. Accustomed to spending my days in the tranquility of my home, I shared Roland's work and cultivated my own interests. By keeping this sober, austere lifestyle, I was able to preserve my usual way of life and to avoid the problems encountered by high-placed officials who allow themselves to be surrounded by a crowd of self-interested people. (72)

Roland attempts to justify her exclusion of women as a means of maintaining an atmosphere suitable for serious political discussion, free from frivolity and intrigue (both amorous and political). In this she was conforming to Rousseau's dictum concerning the segregation of the sexes and his notion of separate spheres. She also viewed the exclusion of women from her home as a means of preserving her independence and privacy. For the same reason, she refrained from participating in the social life of the capital. In maintaining this austere lifestyle, she claims to have merely been following the positive example set by Mme Pétion, wife of the mayor of Paris. Yet her exclusion of women from her home and refusal of their invitations suggests that she had interiorized her male contemporaries' distrust and scorn for women. The passage cited above reflects a thinly veiled misogyny.

During the discussions that followed dinner, Mme Roland officiated with simplicity and tact and—what was even more appreciated—

in silence. In her *Mémoires*, she insists that she never allowed herself to utter a word until the meetings were over, although occasionally she had to bite her lip to keep from disagreeing with what was being said. Deliberately seating herself outside the circle of men, she quietly did needlework or wrote letters while the debates went on. Yet despite her voluntary self-effacement, she does not deny that she listened attentively to all that was said; nor did she hesitate to offer her opinion when it was asked for. Moreover, since Roland's associates tended to call on him at home rather than at his office, political matters were frequently discussed in his wife's presence. Under the pretext of leaving messages for the absent Roland, they got in the habit of calling on Manon and presenting their case to her, for they were well aware that she would be consulted anyway. In her *Mémoires*, Mme Roland tries to repudiate accusations that she was running her husband's ministry by insisting that since she was nearly always at home and enjoyed her husband's fullest confidence, she found herself quite naturally "in the midst of things without intrigue or vain curiosity" (72). But she hardly needed to resort to intrigue or subterfuge to impose her views, for in the intimacy of the Girondist circle her opinions carried increasing weight.

The Virtuous Martyr: Reliving Julie's Passion

Madame Roland's "secret" collaboration in the political affairs of the Girondists seemed to offer the ideal opportunity to satisfy her unfulfilled political ambitions. However, by putting her in contact with dynamic young men, her role as Egeria of the Girondist party exacerbated the equally painful dilemma of her unfulfilled desire for romantic love and sensual pleasure—desires that she recognizes quite openly in her *Mémoires*.[34]

In the fall of 1792, when the Girondists were under constant attack from the Montagnards, Manon fell passionately in love with the Girondist deputy François Buzot. Young, handsome, eloquent, and dynamic, he was everything Roland was not: a worthy Saint-Preux-like foil to the aging, Wolmarian Roland. Despite her disenchantment with marriage and motherhood, as well as her growing disillusionment with the Revolution, Mme Roland stoically resisted yielding to her passion, which was shared by Buzot with equal ardor. Like Julie's death, Manon's imprisonment and execution resolved her moral impasse. By allowing herself to be imprisoned in place of her husband, she was able to free herself from conjugal duties and to give full expression to her love for Buzot, without restraint or remorse. In a letter to Buzot from prison, she expressed her secret joy:

> I was not greatly distressed to be arrested. They will be less angry and vindictive toward Roland. . . . If they put him on trial, I will be able to defend him in a manner that will enhance his reputation. In this way I can pay the debt I owe him for his sorrows. Don't you see that by being alone, it is with you that I remain? Through imprisonment I can sacrifice myself for my husband and keep myself for my friend, and it is to my persecutors that I owe this reconciliation of love and duty. Don't pity me! Others may admire my courage, but they don't know my joys.[35]

She firmly rejected all plans for her escape, for she was convinced that freedom would not bring her happiness, "but only replace [her] chains with others that no one can see."[36] In a final message to Buzot (embedded in her "Dernières Pensées") she wrote: "And you whom I dare not name! . . . who respected the barriers of virtue in spite of the most overwhelming passion, will you grieve to see me go before you to a place where we will be free to love each other without crime, where nothing will prevent us from being united? . . . There I will await you. . . . Adieu. No, in leaving the earth, I am not leaving you, but bringing us closer together."[37] The parallels with the dénouement of *La Nouvelle Héloïse* are of course striking, for on her deathbed, Julie had expressed herself in almost identical terms in a letter to Saint-Preux.[38]

Dorinda Outram convincingly argues that through her intense identification with Julie, Mme Roland was able to turn her erotically charged relationship with Buzot into a verbal performance and thereby overcome the contradiction between the unchastity of her desires and the self-portrait she cherished as chaste wife and stoic revolutionary heroine.[39]

Roland's Subversion of Rousseau's Feminine Ideals

In her final farewell to the man she loved, as throughout her adult life, Mme Roland had followed the inspiring example of Rousseau's heroine. Like Julie, Manon had conscientiously devoted herself to an idealized view of marriage and motherhood, and, like her—rather than accept moral defeat or disenchantment—had heroically sacrificed her life in order to preserve the precarious balance between duty and passion, virtue and sensibility. However, while seeming to conform to the feminine ideals and norms advocated by Rousseau in his novels, she in fact subverted those models by undermining the gender dichotomies (public/private, self-assertion/self-effacement, reason/sensibility) that lay at the very core of his discourse on women. While appearing to relegate herself to a role of silence and self-effacement in the domestic sphere, she in fact transformed her home into a public forum, her tiny office into the unofficial center of Roland's ministry, and her devotion to her husband into a dynamic political partnership—thereby giving herself the power to influence public affairs in a very direct and dramatic manner. Furthermore, through her ability to combine qualities traditionally reserved for men (reason, authority, energy, superior intelligence, and strength of character) with traits traditionally ascribed to women (sensitivity, intuition, persuasiveness, and charm), she was able to command the respect of her husband and colleagues and to make herself valuable, indeed indispensable, to their political cause. As she herself remarks in her *Mémoires*:

> Roland would have been no less a fine administrator without me; his capabilities, diligence, and probity are entirely his own. With my help, he caused more of a sensation because I infused his writings with that special mixture of strength and gentle persuasiveness, that blend of reason and authority with the charms of sentiment, which perhaps only a sensitive woman with a sound mind is capable of achieving. (155)

Her elevated opinion of her husband's capabilities is disputed somewhat by biographers and historians. They generally agree that Roland was a dedicated, hard-working administrator, but that without his wife's conviction, boldness, literary talents, and shrewd judgment of character "he could be rated barely higher than a superior clerk," as Gita May remarks.[40]

Madame Roland's exceptional talents and her distinctly androgynous character and style are confirmed by numerous contemporary accounts, including a review of her *Mémoires* in the *Analytical Review* of 1795: "She possessed a mind uncommonly vigorous and masculine, and her situation as wife of the minister Roland in a moment of great peril called forth all her energy [to display] talents which will not fail to rank her among the distinguished ornaments of her sex."[41] As for

MARIE ~ JEANNE ~ PHÉLIPPON

FEMME DE ROLAND MINISTRE DE L'INTÉRIEUR EN 1792,

et jugée à mort le 19 Brumaire l'an 2.

Parmi toutes les femmes dont les noms seront inscrits dans les fastes de la révolution française, aucune n'a joué un rôle plus noble, plus intéressant que Madame Roland. C'était une femme de 30 à 40 ans, d'une figure spirituelle; l'héroïsme qu'elle montra à sa mort l'a élevée bien au dessus de presque tout son sexe. Nourrie dès l'âge de douze ans de la lecture de Plutarque, elle ne démentit jamais ses premiers principes, ses grands sentimens d'une vraie philosophie.

Ce fut au mois de Septembre 1775 que M. Roland de la Platière s'unit avec elle. Il avoit été nommé pour la seconde fois ministre de l'intérieur, après la journée mémorable du 10 Août 1792. Il fut persécuté, parcequ'il avoit eu le courage de ne pas faire l'apologie des massacres des 2 et 3 7bre; c'est à cette conduite ferme et généreuse qu'il a dû tous ses malheurs, et qu'on doit attribuer la fin tragique de sa femme. Les ennemis de son mari, qui étoient les siens, la firent arrêter. Des correspondances qu'elle avoit eues avec les députés proscrits au 31 mai, servirent de prétexte pour l'immoler. Lorsque le président eut prononcé son arrêt de mort, elle dit aux juges du tribunal révolutionnaire: « Vous me jugez digne de partager le sort des grands hommes que vous avez assassinés; je tâcherai de porter à l'échaffaud le courage qu'ils y ont montré ».

Lorsqu'elle fut arrivée sur la place de la révolution elle s'inclina devant la statue de la Liberté, et dit ces mots bien remarquables: « O Liberté, que de crimes on commet en ton nom! ». Étant aux pieds de l'échaffaud, elle adressa ces paroles au nommé Lamarche, son compagnon d'infortune: « Allez, que vous é-pargne au moins la douleur de voir couler mon sang ». Elle monta ensuite sur l'échaffaud d'un pas ferme, et reçut le coup fatal avec courage.

Ainsi périt une femme qui fut un modèle de philosophie, de fermeté, et de vertu. Elle a fait revivre parmi nous les Arrie, les Cornélie, toutes ces héroïnes dont l'histoire romaine a conservé les noms à l'immortalité.

Opposite: Pro-Girondist broadside honoring the memory of Mme Roland and recalling important events in her life: her role during the Revolution, her devotion to Republican ideals, her trial and execution. Below the medallion-like portrait is a scene from her trial, in which she is shown pleading her case before the revolutionary tribunal. The text below cites, among other phrases attributed to her, the famous line she is said to have uttered as she passed the Statue of Liberty on the way to her execution: "O Liberté, que de crimes on commet en ton nom!" ["O, Liberty, what crimes are committed in your name!"] Courtesy of the Bibliothèque nationale, Paris.

the "virile" quality of her writing, even Rousseau had been struck by it. After an unsuccessful effort to meet her idol during his last stay in Paris, Manon's disappointment had been somewhat allayed by the fact that Rousseau had mistaken her letter of introduction for that of a man: "Surely it was not you who wrote a letter like that," reported Thérèse, as she blocked the door. "Even the handwriting looks like that of a man."[42]

Contrary to traditional eighteenth-century views of women as victims of their imagination, emotions, and sexual desires (views clearly reflected in Rousseau's portrayal of Sophie), Manon underlines her belief in the primacy of reason and consistently portrays herself as in control. "I kept my imagination in check and followed lines of reasoning," she declares in her memoirs. "I channeled my imagination through studying" (303, 346). Her "masculine" firmness, self-possession, and strength of character inspired even her strongest critics with a grudging sort of admiration, mixed with deep ambivalence and distrust.

Gita May maintains that Mme Roland's transgression of traditional gender restrictions was involuntary and largely due to the unusual circumstances in which she found herself. If Roland contradicted her own convictions regarding the proper role of women, argues May, it was not through any personal ambition or will to power on her part, but through a disinterested, self-sacrificing devotion to the revolutionary cause.[43] She goes on to defend Roland against the criticism of pro-Jacobin historians who, in May's view, unjustly question her intentions and motives. While there is little doubt that these historians were unduly harsh and misogynic in their judgment of the Girondists' Egeria,[44] May seems to give too much credence to the mask of modesty and self-effacement that Mme Roland assumed in an effort to defend herself against similiar attacks by her contemporaries. She tends to take her self-justification at face value and to ignore or minimize the importance of passages in her memoirs and correspondence where she momentarily lets her mask fall, revealing a woman of intense personal and political ambitions. The passages expressing her desire to develop her talents to the fullest, her secret pleasure at manipulating power relations behind the scenes, and above all her deep satisfaction at fulfilling her adolescent dream to escape the confines of her sex and class in order to help shape the future of the new French republic—all these passages reveal the woman behind the mask who consciously subverted the limited gender role imposed upon her by society.[45]

On Trial: Misogynic Attacks by the Press and Revolutionary Leaders

Mme Roland's subtle transgression of traditional gender barriers did not go unperceived and was capitalized on by her political enemies in the campaign of slander and persecution that eventually led her to the guillotine. As the Girondists' popularity declined, Jacobin politicians and journalists multiplied their attacks against the Rolands. Joan Landes underlines the extent to which the schism between Jacobins and Girondists was fought out in gendered terms, with Mme Roland as a key figure.[46] As a woman, Manon was particularly vulnerable to denunciations and satire. No insult or innuendo, no matter how far-fetched or obscene, was spared to destroy her influence and to belittle her party by picturing the Girondists as wholly dominated by a scheming female— a form of ridicule particularly withering to the Gallic ego. For example, in an issue of his highly popular *Ami du peuple*, Marat inserted "Un mot à la femme Roland" which read: "Roland is only a ninny whose wife leads him by the nose; it's she who is Minister of the Interior."[47]

Ten days later (in late September 1792) Roland went before the Assembly to resign as Minister in order to become a simple deputy; however, upon the urging of a majority of the deputies, he agreed to retain his post. Hearing this, Danton rose from his seat and launched his famous sarcasm: "No one does justice to Roland more than I, but if you invite him to be Minister, you should also extend the invitation to Mme Roland; for everyone knows that he was not alone in his department! As for me, I was alone in mine." He then added: "We need ministers who see through other eyes than those of their wives." The following spring, Danton would again make Mme Roland the butt of his sarcasm in an effort to save the Girondists from an assassination plot hatched by Varlet: "Those glib talkers are not worth such a fuss," quipped Danton, "they are as enthusiastic and flighty as the woman who inspires them. Why don't they choose a *man* as their leader? That woman will lead them to their destruction. She's the Circe of the Republic!"[48]

Following Danton's lead, the Jacobin press tirelessly harped on the theme that it was not Monsieur Roland but Madame Roland who actually ran the Ministry of the Interior. Day after day, the popular press echoed with outrageous reports of the "orgies" over which Manon had presided and of the sexual and political favors she had distributed in order to maintain her influence. In his popular *Père Duchesne*, Hébert artfully exploited both the antifeminist and anti-aristocratic sentiments of Mme Roland's enemies by comparing her to Marie-Antoinette and to various royal mistresses—minus their beauty, for he later describes her as a toothless, balding old hag:

> The tender wife of virtuous Roland is ruling France just like the Pompadours and the du Barrys. Brissot is the grand squire of this new queen, Louvet is her chamberlain, Buzot her chancellor. . . . [Barbaroux, Vergniaud, Guadet, Lanthenas are then each assigned a role.] This is the new court that is running things today. Like our former queen, madame Coco, stretched out on a sofa, surrounded by all those *beaux esprits*, talks on endlessly about war, politics, supplies. It is from this den of corruption that daily proclamations issue forth to the public.[49]

In the midst of Hébert's grotesque slander, one recognizes a man who is perceptive and well-informed and who does not strike at random. All the politicians who were among Mme Roland's circle of close friends are named. Moreover, Hébert rightly guesses that several of them (and Buzot in particular) might be enamored of her and that she might not be insensitive to their admiration. In the following issue of *Père Duchesne*, Brissot is "overheard" saying to Buzot:

> Admit that you are fortunate to serve as the right-hand man of someone like me. I got you in with the *beaux esprits* that are governing France. If it weren't for me, you wouldn't be the favorite among the admirers of the virtuous wife of the virtuous Roland. What a pleasure it must be to rehearse at her feet the role you will play at the Convention the following day, to hear

her applaud you when you recite a fiery tirade against
Robespierre, to see her swoon in your arms when you have passed
some fine decree banishing loyal revolutionaries or encouraging
civil war.[50]

In general, Mme Roland chose to maintain a dignified silence in
response to such slander. Referring to Marat's repeated attacks, she
told her husband: "He is foolish enough to imagine that I would be
sensitive to such nonsense, that I would answer him in writing, and
that he would have the pleasure of dragging a woman into the public
forum in order to ridicule her husband." And defiantly, she declared:
"Let them slander me as much as they like; I won't complain or even
concern myself with them."[51] In prison, however, she felt physically
threatened by the danger of mob violence that might result from the
increasingly inflammatory articles published by Hébert. When an angry
mob began to shout insults and threats outside the window of her cell,
she dashed off a fierce letter of protest to Garat, who was then Minister of Justice.

The viciousness and frequency of the attacks against Mme Roland
reflect the degree of power and influence that were attributed to her.[52]
Like her subsequent imprisonment, trial, and execution, they constitute a paradoxical tribute to her importance as a political figure. The
misogynic nature of the charges made against her by both the periodi-
cal press and the revolutionary government—the fact that she was
condemned more for alleged moral transgressions and for overstepping traditional gender barriers than for any specific political act—
illustrates how women's political and intellectual activities were
associated with moral and social deviance. It is interesting, moreover,
to note how in their allusions to Roland's writing her enemies make
use of *double entendres* to equate literary self-revelation with sexual
promiscuity. For example, in one of his articles in *Père Duchesne*, Hébert
recounts how she "unbuttoned herself/spoke frankly to" Père
Duchesne, and "lui a découvert le pot aux roses"—that is, revealed
her secret plots/private parts.[53] Similarly, in the bill of indictment
against the Girondists, Amar refers to the "prodigieuse facilité" with
which Mme Roland provided the Bureau d'Esprit Public with propaganda pamphlets in order to corrupt the public. Once again, ease of
writing in a woman is associated with easy virtue, and both are directly linked to corruption of the public mind and morals. The connec-
tion between women's writing and female sexuality (and sexual

promiscuity) is illustrated most graphically—and grotesquely—in another issue of *Père Duchesne* in which Hébert reports an alleged visit to the Rolands on New Year's Eve:

> It was around midnight and, in the arms of her lackey Lanthenas, the virtuous Mme Roland was diverting herself from the moral pleasures provided by her feeble old husband. Pregnant with a discourse that the billboarders would deliver in the morning, she was right in the midst of her labor when little Louvet rushed in and interrupted their love-making.[54]

In this passage, Hébert evokes the hackneyed comparison of writing to childbirth in order to mock Mme Roland's literary and political activities more effectively. By appealing to misogynic prejudices and stereotypes (women writers and politicians as witches, whores, and monsters), he and his colleagues added highly effective ammunition to their campaign of verbal terrorism against the Girondists and their ill-fated Egeria.

Well aware of the misogynic tenor of the charges against her, Roland strove to counterbalance them by underlining her strict conformity to traditional gender roles. "I took a keen interest in the public welfare and in the progress of the Revolution, but I never went beyond the limits prescribed for my sex," she maintained in the speech prepared for her trial. "It was no doubt my talents, knowledge, and courage that turned people against me. . . . Only odious tyrants would sacrifice a woman whose sole crime was to possess a few merits about which she never boasted."[55] Much to her chagrin, Manon was never permitted to deliver her speech or indeed to utter more than a few words at her trial. However, during the two interrogations that preceded it, she cleverly turned the antifeminism of her examiners against them. When questioned about her husband's political activities, she replied that as a woman it was not her role to meddle in public affairs and that her only knowledge of events had been through the newspapers. This, of course, was hardly the case; but when her examiners insisted that she must have had more information than the average citizen, she coolly observed that a woman was not expected to make special inquiries into matters that did not concern her sex.[56] When asked about various pamphlets distributed by Roland's propaganda bureau, she maintained that they were available for anyone to read and that it was up to the public and not to her, a mere woman, to pass judgment on them. She also firmly denied accusations that she had directed the propaganda bureau or any other of her husband's political operations.[57] Finally, when her interrogators demanded to know Roland's whereabouts, she responded that no human law could force her to betray her loyalty to her husband—another dictum of the Rousseauian code. She then attempted to defend her husband's probity as an administrator and his loyalty to the Revolution, but was rudely interrupted, accused of being a chatterbox, and ordered to respond to all further questions with a simple yes or no. Resisting the prosecutor's efforts to intimidate and silence her, and rejecting the self-incriminating script he tried to impose on her, Manon appealed to higher principles of justice and reason to affirm her innocence.[58] She even tried to seize control of the proceedings by ordering the court clerk to write under her dictation. But this open defiance of the prosecutor's authority only served to infuriate him so much that he abruptly ended the interrogation, thereby silencing her definitively.

That Mme Roland was imprisoned and condemned to death more for overstepping traditional gender barriers than for any specific political act is clearly underlined by newspaper accounts of her execution. For example, *Le Moniteur Universel* wrote: "In a short period of time, the revolutionary tribunal has given women several valuable examples that will not be lost for them." After unflattering epitaphs to Marie-Antoinette and to the feminist Olympe de Gouges (both executed the same month as Mme Roland, along with Mme du Barry), Roland's memory was then evoked in blatantly misogynic terms:

> That woman Roland, who fancied herself a great mind with great plans, a philosopher, was in every way a monster. Her disdainful attitude, her proudly opinionated replies, her ironic gaiety, and the firmness she displayed on the way to her execution prove that she was devoid of any grief. She was a mother, but she sacrificed nature. . . . The desire to be learned led her to forget the virtues of her sex. Such negligence is always dangerous and caused her to perish on the scaffold.[59]

In other accounts of her execution, Mme Roland's courage was invariably construed as proof of her insensitivity and baseness: a truly virtuous woman, a truly loving wife and mother, would have shown regrets, weakness, tears.[60]

It is clear from all these commentaries that Mme Roland's execution, like that of Gouges and other "public" women, was being used as a warning to women activists: If they did not give up their political activities and conform to the passive domestic role prescribed for them by the revolutionary government, they, too, would risk imprisonment and death. After pointing to Mme Roland's example, the article in *Le Moniteur Universel* ended with the following exhortation:

> Women, do you wish to be true republicans? Then love, follow, and teach the laws that guide your husbands and sons in the exercise of their rights. Be diligent in your housework; never attend political meetings with the intention of speaking there; but let your presence serve as an example for your children. The fatherland will then bless you, for you will truly have given what it expects from you.[61]

Similarly, in the ruling banning women's participation in political clubs and meetings, Chaumette, head counsel of the Paris Commune, pointed to the examples of Roland and Gouges as justification for the ban: "Remember *la Roland*, that haughty wife of a stupid, perfidious husband, who thought herself fit to govern the republic and who rushed to her downfall. Remember the impudent Olympe de Gouges, who was the first to set up women's societies, who abandoned the duties of her household to meddle in politics, and whose head fell beneath the avenging knife of the law."[62]

It is indeed ironic that Mme Roland—who had so painstakingly conformed her outward behavior to Rousseau's ideal of domesticity—should be frequently cited along with the militant feminist Gouges as a pernicious example for women by revolutionary leaders and journalists.[63] The charges against them were surprisingly similar, despite the striking differences in their lives and characters. Both were accused of neglecting their duties as wives and mothers in order to meddle in politics, of attempting to usurp male powers and prerogatives and, graver still, of forgetting their proper place as women. Both were victims of the revolutionary government's increasingly repressive policies toward women—policies strongly influenced by Rousseau's writings.[64] Given the concerted effort to represent these women as dangerous deviants from the prescribed norms of domestic life, it is quite striking, as Simon Schama has observed, that both Roland and Gouges—like numerous other female victims of the Terror—presented themselves as tender and conscientious mothers following the Rousseauian model in their parting letters to their children.[65]

Roland's Memoirs: The Influence of Rousseau's Confessions

Above all, Mme Roland was a victim of long-standing tensions within herself between the Rousseauian ideals of domestic happiness and female self-effacement and an irrepressible urge to develop her talents to the fullest—an urge that impelled her, almost in spite of herself, to take an active part in the intellectual and political life of her period. As the attacks against her in the press became increasingly frequent and violent, she bitterly lamented the loss of her anonymity. "Those who have lifted the veil under which I wished to remain have done me an ill turn indeed! . . . If they had judged the facts as they really were, they would have spared me the kind of celebrity for which I had no desire," she confides in her memoirs. "Instead of having to write my confessions to defend myself against their slander, I could brighten the solitude of my imprisonment by reading the essays of Montaigne" (304–5).

Despite all her protestations to the contrary, Manon was secretly grateful to her persecutors for giving her the ideal pretext to write her autobiography. For it was an opportunity not only to justify herself in the eyes of posterity, but also to fulfill her talents and ambitions as a writer and her secret desire for celebrity and immortality through her writings: "I only aspired to keep my soul pure and my husband's glory intact," she declares in her memoirs. "My wish is fulfilled. Though persecuted and outlawed, Roland will not die for posterity; . . . and I too will live on for future generations" (277). This passage reveals the secret desire for celebrity and recognition of her talents that lay behind Roland's mask of modesty and self-effacement. Recounting her life's story and the political personages and events she had witnessed proved to be a richly rewarding experience. Despite the gloom of prison and the specter of impending death, Roland ended her memoirs with a proud affirmation of her powers as a writer, mixed with the regret of being unable to develop her talents more fully: "If I had been allowed to live," she declares, "I would have had only one ambition: to record the annals of my century and to be the Macaulay of my country; I was going to say the Tacitus of France, but that would be immodest, and . . . some might say that I am not quite up to his level" (338–39). Overtly mocking the conventions of modesty and inferiority imposed upon women—conventions to which she had always previously deferred—she then expressed her confidence that with time and practice, and on a subject of equal richness, she might well have rivaled the writings of Tacitus. By composing her memoirs and correspondence, Roland was in fact able to fulfill her ambitions at least partially, for together they provide a vivid chronicle of her period and a rich sampling of what she might have accomplished as a writer had she lived longer and pursued a literary career.[66]

Despite her special fondness for Tacitus and Plutarch, it is Rousseau who is most often evoked by Roland as her literary and spiritual father. From her prison cell, she wrote to a friend: "These memoirs will be my *Confessions*, for I will not conceal anything. . . . I've thought about it carefully and made up my mind. I will tell all, absolutely everything. That is the only way to be useful."[67] Following Rousseau's example in his *Confessions*, Roland gave free rein to her thoughts and feelings in her memoirs and, like Rousseau, attempted to justify herself in the eyes of posterity by presenting an authentic self-portrait and self-analysis to counter what she perceived as misrepresentations of her character and motives by her contemporaries.

Elissa Gelfand has convincingly argued that in her memoirs, Roland strove to counter the charges of promiscuity and defeminization brought against her by her enemies by highlighting crucial moments in her psychosexual development. She analyzes how Roland underscored her modesty and chastity, as well as her carefully controlled sexual desires and desirability, in response to charges that she had become defeminized or debauched through her lust for knowledge and power.[68] The events recounted include the onset of puberty and the anxiety and shame her nascent sexual desires produced in her; her wedding night and the unpleasant shock (and disappointment) it proved to be; and two incidents at age eleven involving her father's apprentice, who forced her to feel his genitals, and her subsequent desire to enter a convent.[69]

Since Roland's inclusion of these last two incidents in her memoirs elicited considerable controversy (particularly among nineteenth-century critics), these passages merit further discussion. Sensing that her account of her experience with the apprentice might shock or offend some of her readers, she begins the episode by confiding à la Rousseau: "I am a bit embarrassed by this next episode, for I want my memoirs to be as chaste as I myself have always been, and yet what I must now reveal is a bit risqué" (207). After recounting the episode in detail, she confides: "The memory of this incident remained so strong and painful for me that I never spoke of it even to my closest friend or to my husband. To write of it here has required as much courage as Rousseau needed to reveal his story of the stolen ribbon, which is hardly comparable to my own experience" (221). She tries to justify the inclusion of this incident by stressing its importance in her moral development, the courage required to reveal it, and the valuable lesson it offered parents on the dangers threatening their daughters. As a precedent to strengthen her argument, she cites the episode of the stolen ribbon in the *Confessions*, but minimizes the boldness of Rousseau's revelation compared with her own.

Critical Response to Roland's Memoirs: Sainte-Beuve's Ambivalence

The arguments Roland invoked to justify inclusion of this episode were apparently unconvincing, for it was censored along with a number of other passages from all editions of her memoirs until 1864. Even then, a number of critics found it offensive. Commenting on this episode, Sainte-Beuve writes: "Imitating Rousseau's example, she revealed certain particularities that it behooves a woman to conceal and, with stoic aplomb and disdain for decorum, indulged in unchaste allusions degrading for a woman who was chastity itself."[70] His criticism of this episode was harsher and more detailed in a later essay:

> I regret that Mme Roland did not respect the instinctive feeling of repulsion that had led her to bury this sad incident deep within herself. To excuse her, to explain this frankness that no one in the world asked of her to this degree, one must recall the powerful influence that Rousseau had on her and on others of her generation. But *she* was a woman and should not have forgotten it.[71]

According to Sainte-Beuve, Roland's inclusion of this episode was *"un acte immortel d'impudeur."* In his opinion, traditional gender restrictions—particularly the conventions of female modesty and discretion—outweighed the need for sincerity, indeed its very desirability. "She could have discreetly hinted at what had happened; but this cold-blooded account, written by a woman of high moral character, who nevertheless dwells on a sordid image, is extremely unpleasant," he maintained. "It is not only a serious flaw, but a tactlessness on the part of woman who otherwise was very tactful. But in this instance, the ambiance of the Revolution and Jean-Jacques's example led her astray.

This vile episode is a bad imitation of Rousseau, and of the worst kind."[72] Curiously, Sainte-Beuve concludes the same essay with a glowing tribute to Roland's emulation of Rousseau's character and style: "Because of her plebeian spontaneity and the rich blend of warmth and reason, enthusiasm and clarity that distinguish her writings, Mme Roland can truly be called the Jean-Jacques Rousseau of women."[73]

Sainte-Beuve's comments on Roland's writings strikingly illustrate the strong gender bias underlying the critical appraisal of literary works by women. Unlike male-authored works, women's writings were judged as much—if not more—by their moral and social propriety (and that of their authors) than by their intrinsic literary value. In his extensive—and often enthusiastic—commentaries on Roland, Sainte-Beuve frequently has recourse to traditional class and gender stereotypes in judging her character, as well as the moral and literary value of her work. He insists that she is most original when she no longer attempts to imitate male models and is content to be herself—that is, when she is most *feminine*. He especially praises the letters in which she extols the twin virtues of domesticity and country life: "In these letters, she is natural and spontaneous; she is what she should be . . . a Sévigné of the bourgeoisie, a Sévigné George Sand."[74] Yet he is quick to point out the less desirable aspects of her character and writings— her "plebeian" and "virile" traits: "Mixed in with these healthy bourgeois qualities, one finds a certain plebeian cockiness, a brazenness and disdain for decorum due no doubt to the influence of the *philosophes* and the *révolutionnaires*. I find these traits quite shocking in a woman otherwise so chaste, so feminine and refined," he writes. "However, these influences could never seriously tarnish her perfect feminine polish and grace."[75]

Sainte-Beuve is nevertheless concerned that Manon's life and writings might have a pernicious influence on other women. In a passage strangely reminiscent of *Le Moniteur Universel*'s scathing epitaph, he warns her readers from misinterpreting her example: "Mme Roland is sometimes pointed to as a model for future generations: a strong, republican woman, equal or superior to her husband, who serves as his inspiration and who substitutes a noble, clairvoyant audacity for Christian modesty and submission. This is an outrageous misconception."[76] As in his reviews of other eighteenth-century women writers (including d'Epinay), Sainte-Beuve carefully reshaped Roland's image so that it conformed to nineteenth-century ideals of femininity: "Let us not make the mistake of remembering Mme Roland as a stoic philosopher and inflexible citizen like her husband—in short, as anything but a woman," he urged. "She was in no way pedantic or pretentious. . . . Despite the virile qualities she demonstrated, she never lost her womanly grace."[77] In this way, Sainte-Beuve sought to efface tensions and subversive elements in Mme Roland's memoirs that might undermine the Rousseauian model of female modesty, domesticity, and submission he espoused. Paradoxically, this was the same repressive model from which Roland had to distance herself in order to write her life story in her own name. It is only in the past two decades, with the reexamining of Roland's texts by feminist critics, that the full force of her challenge to traditional gender roles has been brought to light, unburied from beneath the muted images constructed of her by critics like Sainte-Beuve.

Rousseau's Paradoxical Influence on Roland's Life and Writings

In the course of her autobiographical venture, Roland emerged from anonymity as her husband's secret political advisor and ghost writer to become a writer and public figure in her own right, as well as a woman with passions and ambitions outside the domestic sphere to which she had voluntarily—on the surface at least—confined herself until then. Yet without the Revolution and the Terror, without the creative impulse provided by the constant threat of death and the desire to justify herself in the eyes of future generations, would she have felt impelled to write her memoirs? Given her earlier reluctance to pursue a literary career and to publish under her own name, this appears doubtful.

Rousseau's influence on Roland's life and writing is therefore crucial, yet paradoxical. For although on the surface she appeared to conform to the Rousseauian cult of domesticity and sensibility, her superior intelligence and education, coupled with her political and literary activities, made her a very different woman indeed from the feminine ideal advocated in *Julie* and *Emile*. In fact, because of her involvement in politics, she was the very kind of woman Rousseau would have been inclined to criticize. Perhaps the most paradoxical aspect of Rousseau's influence on Roland is that, following his bold example in the *Confessions*, she dared to transgress social and literary conventions of female modesty and silence to reveal her most intimate thoughts, feelings, and experiences in ways that both shocked and thrilled her readers.

5

Toward a Bold New Vision of Womanhood:

Staël and Wollstonecraft Respond to Rousseau

In the flourish of female literary activity in the late eighteenth century, Mary Wollstonecraft and Germaine de Staël stand out as iconoclasts both as women and as writers. In the works of no other women of the period do we sense the impact of two such powerful personalities. Their power as writers resides above all in their incisive analyses of women's condition in society and in the bold new vision of womanhood they hold out for future generations—a vision each strove to embody in her life and later works. Although Wollstonecraft and Staël were products of very different backgrounds, their lives reveal a number of striking—and unexpected—parallels. Both were highly successful, often controversial, women of letters who eagerly entered into the political debates of their period. Yet they longed for a domestic felicity and security that seemed incompatible with their independent temperaments and with their political and literary activities. Neither was afraid to brave public censure for her unconventional lifestyle; nor did they hesitate to take on male figures of authority—no less formidable than Edmund Burke and Napoleon—in genres traditionally reserved for male writers. Yet they were at times surprisingly timid and traditionalist in their writings on women, particularly in their early works.

Perhaps the most striking parallel between Staël and Wollstonecraft is that both were strongly influenced by Rousseau and responded repeatedly to his writings in their own. The ideals of domesticity and sensibility set forth in *Julie* had a profound impact on their development as women and as writers. Both were passionate admirers yet, at the same time, strong critics of Rousseau and strangely unaware of (or unwilling to recognize) their own ambivalence. This curious lack of self-insight on the part of two of the most perspicacious women of the period is particularly well demonstrated in Wollstonecraft's scathing critiques of Staël's *Lettres sur Rousseau*, in which she totally ignored Staël's pointed criticism of his views on women's education, as well as the admiration for *Julie* she herself shared with Staël. It is not known whether Staël ever met or responded to her English critic.[1] However, in 1814, three years before her death (and many years after Wollstone-craft's), she wrote a second preface to her *Lettres sur Rousseau*, in which she indirectly challenged his traditionalist views on women and, as in *Corinne*, proudly affirmed her identity as a woman artist.

The question of woman's role and destiny is central to the lives and works of both Wollstonecraft and Staël and to their reputations among succeeding generations of readers and critics. By examining their ambivalent responses to Rousseau and their lifelong ambivalence toward themselves as women authors, we can gain greater insight into the complex sexual politics of the late eighteenth century.

Staël's Lettres sur Rousseau*:* *A Self-Serving Encomium to Genius?*

Madame de Staël made her literary début in 1788 at the age of twenty-two with the publication of her *Lettres sur les écrits et le caractère de J. J. Rousseau*. In the opening paragraph of the preface, she makes it clear that her *Lettres* are intended as an encomium to a genius whose talents had not been sufficiently appreciated by his contemporaries or her own: "No panegyric of Rousseau yet exists: I felt the need to see my admiration for him expressed. I would no doubt have wished that another had depicted what I feel; but I felt a certain pleasure in recall-ing the memory and the impression of my own enthusiasm."[2] The preface anticipates the tone of the *Lettres sur Rousseau* as a whole, and indeed, of much of Staël's future writings. She approached her subject as a disciple, eager to convince her readers of the worthiness of her idol.

Rousseau's influence on Staël's development as a thinker and a writer was crucial, second perhaps only to that of her parents, and her *Lettres sur Rousseau* attest eloquently to this fact. Her *éloge* is an am-bivalent one, however; for despite its tone of passionate admiration, the arguments themselves—as we shall see—clearly reflect Staël's reservations concerning Rousseau's ideas, and particularly his views on women.

What was Staël trying to accomplish in this first published work, and why did she choose Rousseau as her subject? Madelyn Gutwirth points to multiple personal motives underlying the letters: Staël's desire to establish herself as a public figure, to impress her readers with her literary talents and moral seriousness, and above all to win her parents' forgiveness for her failure to conform to the Rousseauian model of womanhood they believed in so strongly.[3] To those who viewed her as an immoral virago, she evokes, in thinly disguised terms, the unhappy arranged marriage with the rakish baron de Staël two years earlier that had left her vulnerable to the charms of Louis de Narbonne.[4]

Staël's parents condemned her liaison with Narbonne as strongly as they did her literary ambitions. Her *Lettres sur Rousseau* may well have been an effort to win back their approval by praising Rousseau's conservative vision of woman's proper role. Madame Necker had personally known the author of *Emile* and had been strongly influenced by his views on marriage, motherhood, and education.[5] Although she hosted a brillant salon, she was totally, even ostentatiously, devoted to her husband. She provided her gifted daughter with a superior education and access to some of the best minds of the period in her salon; but much emphasis was laid on religious and moral instruction in an effort to temper Germaine's high-strung, exuberant character.

Staël's father was even more conservative in his views. He disapproved of women scholars and writers, indeed of women who engaged in any independent form of self-expression. To make his point, he called Germaine "Monsieur de Sainte-Ecritoire" or "Sir Saint Writing-Desk." Despite her father's gentle chiding, she refused to give up her writing, but would continue to feel guilty about her literary ambitions long after his death. "My father is right to insist that women are ill-suited to follow the same path as men, to battle against them and excite in them a jealousy so different from that which love inspires!" she wrote in her diary at age nineteen. "A woman should have nothing of her own and find all her pleasure in the one she loves."[6] As Madelyn Gutwirth points out, this is the first overt statement of the very problem that lay at the core of her creative life and that would be illustrated so strikingly in *Corinne*.[7] To avoid drawing attention to her writing, Staël learned to write quickly and covertly, often standing up, and never had a real desk until after Necker's

Portrait of Germaine de Staël painted by Bouvier in 1816 at the Château de Coppet in Switzerland. Courtesy of the Bibliothèque nationale, Paris.

death. The fact that even a woman as wealthy and successful as Staël felt compelled to downplay her writing and had no real "room of her own" in which to work illustrates the perceptiveness of Virginia Woolf's analysis of the woman writer's dilemma.

In her first published work, Staël evidently tried to placate her parents by choosing a subject likely to please them (an *éloge* of Rousseau) and by inserting a long panegyric to Necker's career as a statesman and to his book *De l'Importance des opinions religieuses* at the end of her discussion of Rousseau's "Profession de foi du vicaire savoyard": "This work [Rousseau's] was only the forerunner of the book [Necker's] that mankind will one day present to the Supreme Being as the greatest step that they have ever taken toward Him," she declares. "Its author is the greatest genius, the finest, most equitable administrator of the century" (I: 15).[8] As Gutwirth observes, Staël's pompous tribute to her father, like her *éloge* of Rousseau, constitutes a "propitiatory gesture" of deference to masculine authority, while in the very act of defying it by daring to write and to publish.[9]

Throughout the *Lettres*, and particularly in the preface, Staël's praise of Rousseau is highly personal, self-reflexive, even narcissistic in tone: "I felt the need to see my admiration for him expressed . . . I felt a certain pleasure in recalling the memory and the impression of my own enthusiasm" (I: 1). The pleasure she experiences in writing about Rousseau stems as much from the act of expressing her own thoughts and feelings as from praising those of her idol. Although she adopts a posture of humility and even apologizes for the presumption of attempting such an ambitious task when still so inexperienced a writer,[10] Staël makes it clear that she has enjoyed the challenge and is not dissatisfied with the results. In the preface, she maintains that only superior minds are capable of understanding and judging the character and works of a genius like Rousseau, and in her conclusion she clearly identifies herself as one of the chosen few: "Ah! Rousseau! . . . you are indeed worthy of inspiring that feeling of compassion that your heart knew so well how to feel and to express; may a voice worthy of your memory rise up to defend you!" (I: 24). Georges Poulet aptly remarks that "Madame de Staël's literary criticism is . . . nothing other than the participation by the critic in the genius of others." He formulates her narcissistic persona as a critic as follows: "I admire, therefore I am; that is, I discover myself in the feeling of admiration that I experience."[11] While celebrating Rousseau's creative genius, Staël is clearly seeking to develop and demonstrate her own—in clear defiance of Rousseau's narrow view of women, expressed so bluntly in *Emile*: "All the thoughts of women not directly pertaining to their domestic duties should be directed toward the study of men or the attainment of female accomplishments," declares Rousseau. "As for works of genius, they are beyond women's reach."[12] By "female accomplishments" [*connaissances agréables*], Rousseau is referring here not to serious artistic endeavors, but to *les arts d'agrément* that presumably made women more desirable to men.

One wonders what Rousseau would have thought of this brilliant young salonnière who was attempting to establish herself as a writer through her perceptive reading of *him*, whose works of genius she felt were by no means beyond her reach? No doubt he would have found her literary ambitions presumptuous, particularly at the conclusion of the *Lettres*, where she boldly claims a place for herself in what she refers to as "the league of genius" as Rousseau's defender and interpreter:

> It is time that the gratitude of the men he enlightened at last find an interpreter. . . . Who is the great man who could disdain assuring the glory of a great man? How wonderful it would be to see this league of genius united through the ages against envy! What a sublime example for their successors would be given by superior men who took up the defense of the superior men who preceded them! The monuments that they raised would one day serve as a pedestal for their own statue. (I: 24)

This view of literary history, with male authors passing the torch of genius from one generation to the next, erecting monuments one on top of the other, is a curiously patriarchal one, in which women authors are excluded both semantically and metaphorically. Staël's almost incantatory repetition of the word *man* (*great man, superior man*) underlines to what extent she was—at that point in her career—a male-identified author. One senses that in raising this "monument" (her *Lettres*) to Rousseau's genius, Staël is preparing a pedestal for her own. Indeed, this passage prefigures her persona as a woman of genius in *Corinne*.

Conflicting Images of Rousseau in Staël's Lettres

Staël's *Lettres* provide valuable insight into the response of eighteenth-century women readers to Rousseau and the various images they constructed of him according to their own needs and values. In the course of these letters, Staël presents multiple and at times conflicting images of Jean-Jacques that reflect her ambivalent response to his views on women. Like many of her contemporaries, Staël hailed Rousseau as a champion of domesticity, motherhood, and moral reform—indeed as a champion of women. In her view, he was a writer for and about women, especially in *Julie*: "This work was written for women; it is above all women that this work can either help or harm" (I: 6). His mission, she claimed, was to teach women the path to happiness through a virtuous life in the domestic sphere, fulfilling their natural role as wives and mothers. According to Staël, this program of moral reform formed the basis of *Julie*, and any charge of immorality should be dismissed in light of the novel's positive moral effect: "Let us pardon Rousseau if, after reading this work, we attach greater importance to our duties and feel greater love for virtue, for acts of kindness, and for a simple, solitary way of life" (I: 5).

Staël also hailed Rousseau as a champion of love and of *les mariages d'amour*. Staël agreed with Rousseau's view that marriage was a woman's natural destiny, but like him, she was critical of forced marriages of convenience: "Through the example of Julie's sufferings and her father's inflexible pride, he wanted to attack social institutions and class prejudices. But how he reveres the ties of marriage to which nature destines us!" (I: 7).[13] The happiness offered by an enduring, exclusive, all-consuming love was an ideal that Staël would search for in vain with each of her lovers. As Gutwirth observes, it was the uncontested primacy of love in her own scale of values that allowed Staël to endorse Rousseau's views on women so enthusiastically, and at times so uncritically.[14] Indeed, so enchanted was she by the idealized view of love in his works that she was willing to overlook the limitations of his narrow views on women: "He believes in love; his forgiveness is secured" (I: 4).

A third image that emerges is that of Jean-Jacques, champion of the weak, the suffering, and the politically disenfranchised: "Ah! Rousseau! Defender of the weak, friend to the unhappy, . . . [who] was moved by all types of misfortunes, you are indeed worthy of inspiring that feeling of compassion that your heart knew so well how to feel and to express . . . ." (I: 24). Yet in her discussion of the *Contrat social* and Rousseau's other political works, Staël fails to point out his exclusion of women from the political and social rights he claimed for males. This is, as we shall see, one of Wollstonecraft's main criticisms of Rousseau and of the revolutionary leaders he influenced so strongly.

The most striking image in Staël's *Lettres*, and the one that recurs most often, is that of Rousseau the inspired genius, whose life and works embodied her twin ideals of sensibility and enthusiasm. She describes him as "the most astonishing genius combined with the purest heart and strongest soul" (I: 16). In her eyes, he was a man whose feelings and imagination were so intense that they often precluded reason and will, a genius who acted and wrote involuntarily—in a state of enthusiasm, taken in its etymological sense of being possessed by a divine spirit.[15] "I believe that his imagination was his primary faculty, even to the point that it absorbed all his other faculties. Instead of living, he dreamed" (I: 19). Describing Rousseau as "the one

who was exalted by the transports of his imagination and of his soul,"
she exclaims: "Ah! that exaltation was the delirium of genius" (I: 20).[16]
In Staël's view, Rousseau's intense imagination and introverted character made him incapable of truly understanding or relating to the
people around him. For this reason, she contested the image—common
among her contemporaries—of Rousseau as *un connaisseur du cœur
humain*: "Rousseau was even more lacking than most people in the
divine power to read into the hearts of others," she affirms (I: 19–20).
Moreover, despite her claim that Rousseau was above all a writer for
and about women, she questioned his ability as a male author to comprehend women's feelings and to portray them in a realistic manner.

According to Staël, Rousseau was the victim of his own talents
and excessive sensibility, which proved to be more of a curse to him
than a blessing: "He had too strong a dose of all these qualities; because of his superiority, he bordered on madness" (I: 19). She portrays
him as a superior soul, victim of narrow-minded, ungrateful public
incapable of understanding or appreciating him, and as the scapegoat
of literary rivals envious of his talents and success. She saw him, as he
saw himself, as *un être à part*—a separate, solitary, unique individual—
whom only superior souls (like herself) could fully understand and
appreciate. Misunderstood and maligned, Rousseau aroused Staël's
compassion and seemed to symbolize her own frustrations as a woman
writer. She identified intensely with Rousseau and with his heroines,
with their unfulfilled and contradictory longings for romantic love
and domestic felicity.

In Staël's eyes, Rousseau's companion Thérèse Levasseur was
totally unworthy of his confidence and affection. She held her responsible not only for his alleged suicide, but also for the abandonment of
their children and for his growing paranoia.[17] By blaming Thérèse for
Rousseau's greatest failings, Staël was clearly trying to rehabilitate his
memory. Although Staël presents herself to her readers as a male-
identified author, she responds to Rousseau above all as a woman,
indeed as *une amante manquée*—the woman who might have been the
ideal companion for him. Her identification with Rousseau is so intense that she casts herself into the role of his would-be lover and
consoler: "How sad it is that he did not meet a tender soul entirely
devoted to loving him, to reassuring him, and to bolstering his shattered spirits; he would have put his trust in her and found peace at
last," she muses.

Ah! Rousseau, how sweet it would have been to restore your faith in life, to accompany you on your solitary walks and bring your thoughts back to happier prospects for the future! . . . Rousseau was tormented by remorse; he needed to feel loved so as not to feel detestable. So many fears are calmed when one no longer faces the world alone! (I: 23)

Convinced that Rousseau committed suicide out of loneliness and despair heightened by Thérèse's infidelities,[18] Staël bitterly regrets that she could not have been at his side to love and console him as he deserved: "What! The author of *Julie* died for lack of love!" (I: 23). Just as Staël felt that she alone was capable as a writer of doing full justice to Rousseau's talents, so too as a woman she felt that she alone could have fulfilled his needs for love, companionship, and consolation. Like her passion for her father, her love for Rousseau was rendered all the more poignant by its very hopelessness, by the impossibility of union with her beloved.[19]

Staël's Response to the Two Discourses and the Lettre à d'Alembert

Despite the intrusion of autobiographical elements into the *Lettres sur Rousseau*—digressions that are in some ways more revealing than her treatment of the "official" subject—Staël does discuss Rousseau's writings at length. In the course of the six letters, each of his major works is commented on in turn and particular attention is given to his views on women.

The first letter deals with the two *Discours* and the *Lettre à d'Alembert*. Although she praises the eloquence of Rousseau's style, the richness of his ideas, and his love of virtue, Staël does not hesitate to criticize several of the main arguments presented in these works, and notably Rousseau's claim that knowledge and love for the arts and sciences constitute a source of corruption and an obstacle to happiness: "It is remarkable that one of the most sensitive and learned men of his time wished to reduce the human heart and mind to a state almost akin to brutishness," she remarks. "He should have recognized that this ardent desire for knowledge and understanding is a natural feeling, a gift from heaven, and a means to happiness when it is exercised, just as it is a torment when it is condemned to inaction" (I: 3). But neither here nor in her discussion of *Emile* V does Staël apply this criticism to the question of women's education. It is only much later, in her second preface to the *Lettres sur Rousseau*, that Staël develops the feminist implications of this argument.

Staël begins her discussion of the *Lettre à d'Alembert* by expressing an almost slavish approval for the sexual politics outlined by Rousseau in that work:

> Although Rousseau tried to stop women from meddling in pub-
> lic affairs, . . . and to curb their sway over the deliberations of
> men, how he revered their influence over men's happiness! He
> urged them to give up the throne they had usurped, but he put
> them back in the throne for which nature truly destined them!
> And though he was outraged when women tried to resemble
> men, how he adored them when they came before him with all
> the charms, weaknesses, virtues, and errors of their sex! Yet his
> pardon is granted, for he believed in love! (I: 4)

Rousseau could not have hoped for a more eloquent endorsement of his reactionary vision of woman's role and destiny. After perusing this text, it is difficult to imagine that its author would later create so independent and undomestic a heroine as Corinne, who takes such delight in her power over men and in the public display of her talents. Considering Staël's own conspicuously public, undomestic existence as hostess of one of the most important salons of Paris, as well as the political and literary influence she wielded with such gusto, this apology for Rousseau's traditionalist view of women appears hypocritical and insincere.

However, at the end of this passage, Staël adds an important condition to the *voluntary* (and hence not necessarily "natural") submission of woman to man's alleged superiority and her relegation to the domestic sphere: that the object of her affections would love her and her alone. "No, it is sweeter for a woman . . . to submit voluntarily, to humble herself at the feet of the man she loves, and not to ask for anything in return except the heart for which she has rendered herself worthy through her love" (I: 4–5). This call for mutual fidelity between spouses echoes that of many moralists of the period, including Wollstonecraft and Rousseau. However, Staël (like Wollstonecraft) gives a strongly feminist cast to her argument. Although in principle, Rousseau also disapproved of the double standard, he maintained that the infidelity of wives was far more reprehensible than that of husbands. Given the prevalence of the double standard in eighteenth-century France, Staël's call for male fidelity is of crucial importance. It is an argument she would develop with greater force twenty-two years later in *De l'Allemagne*.[20]

Staël then undermines her initial endorsement of the principle of separate spheres by exempting women in non-republican governments (and notably prerevolutionary France) from conforming to it. Since, according to Rousseau, women are above all subordinate to their husbands, Staël maintains that they are not corrupted by the tyranny of monarchs as are men. In monarchies, therefore, the moral superiority of women makes it desirable for them to preserve their public role and influence.[21] This argument can be seen in part as an indirect defense of Staël's increasingly active participation in the public sphere, both in politics and in the intellectual and cultural life of the capital.

Finally, Staël contests Rousseau's claim in the *Lettre à d'Alembert* that women are unable to portray passion "with truth or emotion." She begins her argument by feigning to accept the traditional stereotypes underlying his view of women writers: that their "weak organs" and "natural" preoccupation with love and domestic concerns make them incapable of originality and genius and that female literary pretensions alienate potential lovers:

> Let him, if he wishes, refuse to grant women those vain literary talents which, far from making them loved by men, pit women against them; let him refuse to grant women the strength of mind and deep power of concentration that distinguish great geniuses: women's weak organs are ill-suited to such endeavors and their heart, too often preoccupied with other matters, continually runs away with their thoughts, refusing to let them focus on anything beyond its dominant concern—love. (I: 5)

Yet Staël again turns Rousseau's arguments against him, insisting that by their very nature (as he himself has defined it), women are better able than men to probe the inner workings of the human heart and to portray the passions that animate it:

> But never let him accuse women of writing without passion, of not knowing how to describe love. . . . Ah! Women surely know how to express what they feel; and this sublime abandon, this

melancholy suffering, these all-powerful feelings by which they live and die, might have a greater impact on the hearts of readers than the transports born of the exalted imagination of poets. (I: 5)

Confined within *la vie intérieure*, destined to center their lives around the men they love, and having no other occupations to distract them from the object of their affections or from the source of their grief, women are, claims Staël, better able than men to understand and express the longings of their own hearts. Affirming the authority of female experience and the superiority of female sensibility over male knowledge and imagination, she maintains that writing by women often possesses greater eloquence and realism than found in the works of even the most gifted male authors.

One senses that in her first published work, Staël is consciously staking out territory for future literary conquests. Although she pays lip service to Rousseau's hierarchy of genders and genres (by feigning to accept men's superior powers of analytic reasoning and by insisting that women should not attempt to rival them), this would not prevent her from venturing into genres and spheres of activity traditionally reserved for men: politics, political treatises, literary criticism, lyric poetry, and drama. Indeed, the very act of writing the *Lettres sur Rousseau* defies Jean-Jacques's claim that women are incapable of abstract thought and independent judgment. As for his claim that women are incapable of originality and genius, Staël's whole literary career can be seen as an effort to disprove him. Her heroine, Corinne, like Staël herself, is a self-styled woman of genius fully conscious of her talents, who delights in rivalry with men both in love and in art. Thus, hidden beneath her seeming acceptance of Rousseau's sexual politics in the *Lettre à d'Alembert* are several subtle challenges to his views. In each case, Staël turns Rousseau's arguments against him by following them to their logical conclusion, thereby revealing contradictions at the core of his thinking on women.

Staël's Response to Julie

Staël's claim that women are better able than men to portray female experiences and feelings is amplified in her discussion of *La Nouvelle Héloïse*. Like countless other women readers, Staël identified strongly with Julie and her plight: "Ah! How sad it is to come to the end of a work that affects us as strongly as would an event in our own lives and that . . . animates all our feelings and all our thoughts!" (I: 10). Yet, drawing on her own experience as a woman, she finds the portrayal of Julie's passion too tame:

> I cannot bear the methodical way Julie at times manipulates her passion, the way her letters so clearly suggest that she is still in full control of herself and that she makes the conscious decision beforehand to yield to her passion. . . . Rousseau was mistaken if he believed that Julie would seem more modest by appearing less passionate; quite to the contrary, the extreme nature of her passion should have served as her excuse. (I: 9)

The autobiographical echoes of this passage are clear, as is the effort at self-justification underlying it. Carrying Rousseau's ideal of sensibility to its logical conclusion, Staël insists that a woman of intense sensibility who was passionately in love would no longer be mistress of herself, and that the very force of her passion would excuse her adultery. If Rousseau's portrayal of Julie lacked verisimilitude, it was because her character and feelings were drawn not from the experiences of a woman, but from the imagination of a man.

The claim that Julie is an unconvincing fantasy spawned by a male imagination, indeed a projection of Rousseau himself, is made more pointedly in another passage: "Rousseau was wrong . . . to always have Julie speak as he himself would have spoken," declares Staël. "I do not like to see traces of Rousseau in Julie; I would like to find a man's ideas in her, but not a man's character. Several of her letters lack the modesty and propriety one would expect to find in a woman—especially in a woman guilty of moral transgressions" (I: 9). Staël is irritated by Julie's didactic, moralistic tone, by her self-proclaimed vocation as a *prêcheuse*; for she finds it contrary to both literary and social *bienséances*, indeed hypocritical, for a "fallen woman" to preach to her seducer in such a superior tone.

Staël's discussion of the sexual morality in *La Nouvelle Héloïse* is, like the novel itself, filled with contradictions. While in the passage cited earlier she finds the portrayal of Julie's passion too tame, elsewhere she objects to her adultery: "I would have preferred if Rousseau had portrayed Julie guilty only of the passion in her heart" (I: 5). And later, she adds: "Saint-Preux struggled against his passion: that is the virtue of men; the virtue of women is to triumph over their passion.

Saint-Preux's example is not immoral; but Julie's might be" (I: 7). Portraying such a heroine—one who is passionately in love, but who remains chaste—is the difficult task Staël sets for herself in *Delphine*. In this respect, as in others, Staël's first novel can be read as a response to *Julie*. In *Delphine*, Staël imitates Rousseau's epistolary style, his *ménage à trois* scénario, and his critique of *la vie mondaine*, yet she challenges the ideals of domesticity and female friendship presented in *Julie*. Above all, *Delphine* can be seen as an affirmation of the moral superiority of women over men, and hence as a challenge to the notion of inherent female weakness that underlies Rousseau's novel.

According to Staël, Julie should have shown greater moral strength (as would Delphine); or, if she did yield to her passion, she should have done so completely and unhypocritically (as would Corinne). It was not Julie's adultery that disturbs Staël so much as her suspicion that this adultery was premeditated. In Staël's view, true passion was impulsive, overwhelming, indeed *involuntary*, and hence worthy of forgiveness and redemption.

Despite these reservations, Staël disagrees with the charge often made by her contemporaries that Rousseau's novel was immoral and that Julie's adultery set a dangerous example: "The depiction of Julie's errors could set a dangerous example if her remorse and the rest of her life had not reversed its effect, if virtue were not portrayed in this novel in traits as indelible as love itself" (I: 7). Like Rousseau, Staël maintains that Julie is more convincing as a heroine precisely because she is *not* perfect, because she has erred and then redeemed herself through her exemplary life as a wife and mother. In her view, far from corrupting public morals, *La Nouvelle Héloïse* could serve an important didactic function in society; for by the eloquent picture it painted of genuine passion, as much as by the noble vision it presented of conjugal fidelity, Rousseau's novel would encourage women— married and unmarried alike—to spurn the advances of frivolous seducers.

Staël then launches into a long tribute to Julie's sober yet serene life at Clarens and the Rousseauian ideals of virtue, domesticity, sensibility, and country life that it embodies.

> He portrayed a woman married against her will, feeling only esteem for her husband and, deep in her heart, . . . continuing to feel love for another man; a woman who spent her entire life far from the whirl and bustle of society, . . . alone with M. de Wolmar

in the country.... The novel depicts a different kind of happiness from that which one finds in a love match; it is more melancholy; one can enjoy it, yet still shed tears from time to time. It is a happiness better suited to people who are not long for this world; one can enjoy such happiness without regretting it when it is lost. (I: 8)

Yet the melancholy tone of this passage undermines Staël's endorsement of Rousseau's feminine ideals and reflects her ambivalence toward their repressive effects on women. Although she praises Julie's conjugal fidelity, she suggests that the success of a companionate marriage such as the Wolmars' depends on the woman's self-sacrifice, on the repression of her needs and desires.

The discussion of *Julie* concludes with a critique of Rousseau's portrayal of Claire, the heroine's cousin. By far the wittiest and most independent of Rousseau's female characters, Claire is precisely the one whom Staël criticizes most severely. It is not so much her independence that she reproves as her lack of taste and *savoir faire*. "In my opinion, Claire's banter is almost always lacking in good taste as well as charm. In order to attain perfection in this type of conversation, one must have acquired in Paris the refined sense that rejects . . . everything which closer examination would condemn," Staël observes. In her disapproval of Claire's manners, Staël expresses her disdain for provincial women, as well as her class prejudices against rural gentry like the d'Orbe family and petty bourgeois like Rousseau. "Moreover, Rousseau was the least likely of any man to write gaily," she remarks. "He would have done better to renounce this type of banter so unworthy of admiration!" (I: 9). Once again, Staël chides Rousseau for trying to describe feelings and situations of which he has little experience. By his temperament, social class, and upbringing, he lacked what Staël herself possessed to a supreme degree: social poise, exquisite taste, and above all brilliant wit and repartee as a conversationalist. These are qualities that Staël would impart to her fictional counterparts, Delphine and Corinne.

Staël's Response to Emile and Les Solitaires

Not surprisingly, Staël expresses the most ambivalence toward Rousseau's views on women in her comments on *Emile* and its sequel

Les Solitaires. Although she expresses enthusiasm for the ideals of motherhood and domesticity advocated in Book I of *Emile*, she is highly critical of the limited education given to Sophie in Book V and the problems resulting from it in *Les Solitaires*.

In her comments on Book I of *Emile*, Staël credits Rousseau with having strengthened the maternal bond and family ties in general by encouraging mothers to breastfeed their children and to take a more active role in their upbringing:

> It was Rousseau's eloquence that revived maternal feelings in a certain class of society; he helped women understand the duties and joys of motherhood. . . . Is it mothers or their children who owe the greatest debt of gratitude to Rousseau? Ah! surely it is the mothers: did he not teach them (as wrote one woman whose mind and soul are a delight to all who know her) "to find in their child a second childhood, whose promise begins anew for them when their own youth is fading"? (I: 12)

She draws attention to the fact that it was above all upper-class women whose lives had been enriched by Rousseau's message, since traditionally they were the ones least involved in child-rearing. Yet, aside from her life-long attachment to her daughter Albertine, Staël seems to have taken relatively little interest in her own children.[22] She was often separated from them due to her active social and political life, turbulent love affairs, and frequent travels. Unlike her mother, and in contradiction to her own pronouncements cited above, Staël refused to nurse her children and considered breastfeeding a health hazard, as well as a nuisance.[23]

Staël's bombastic tribute to the cult of motherhood in the *Lettres sur Rousseau* may have been designed to placate her mother, who was highly critical of her seeming indifference to maternal and domestic matters. Indeed, the quote at the end of the passage cited above from an unnamed woman is probably drawn from the writings of Staël's mother. The style and content of the quote parallel that of other statements by Mme Necker in support of Rousseau's exalted view of motherhood. If this is in fact a quote from her, it is an ironic one indeed, given the long-standing frictions between mother and daughter. Consciously or not, Staël may have been trying to placate her mother, while at the same time mocking her ostentatious displays of maternal devotion when Germaine was a child—a devotion which in fact veiled a deep ambivalence toward motherhood. Whatever its

Portrait of Mme de Staël painted by Gérard in 1818. Courtesy of the Bibliothèque nationale, Paris.

source, the quote embedded in the passage contradicts, almost word for word, a declaration by Mme de Ternan in *Delphine*: "When our youth is drawing to a close, that of our children is only beginning, and all the attractions of their new existence rob them from us at the very moment when we have the greatest need of their affection."[24]

In her comments on Book V of *Emile*, Staël gives high marks to Rousseau's depiction of the happiness enjoyed by a couple united in a love match. She finds this description of conjugal love more satisfying, from both an artistic and moral standpoint, than the portrayal of adulterous passion in *Julie*. However, she vehemently criticizes Rousseau's decision to portray Sophie as unfaithful to Emile in *Les Solitaires*; for her adultery shatters the vision of conjugal felicity presented at the conclusion of *Emile*. "Ah! Why does he tarnish our image of Sophie and Emile with such a sad ending to their story? Why give weight to the opinion of those who, denying that feelings can last, think that it makes little difference whether one begins or ends by being unfaithful?" she asks (I: 13). Why present such a hopeful and morally useful picture of *le mariage d'amour* only to destroy it? Staël feared that the failure of Emile's marriage might lead to cynicism among Rousseau's readers and might negate whatever positive moral effects his work might have had. Above all, Staël objects to the degrading—and, in her opinion, *false*—view of woman's nature conveyed by Sophie's betrayal of Emile: "Why turn Sophie into a woman incapable of preserving even the happiest situation in the world?" she asks. "How could he present her to us as so unworthy, as unfaithful to the man she loves?" (I: 13). Staël feels personally betrayed by *Les Solitaires*, both as a woman and as an ardent believer in the happiness offered by love matches. Although she recognizes the work's artistic power (calling it "a sublime work"), this sequel to *Emile* arouses her indignation. In her view, Rousseau's portrayal of Sophie in *Les Solitaires* lacks verisimilitude, since a happily married woman would not betray a husband she cherished or risk the happiness of a marriage she valued above all else. Again Staël suggests that, as a man, Rousseau lacks the insight and experience needed to understand women fully and to portray them realistically.

Staël is willing to accept Rousseau's depiction of women as physically weak, and even finds a certain charm in his descriptions of Sophie's delicate body. Recalling the scene where Emile races with Sophie and carries her over the finish line in his arms, she remarks: "Conscious of his strength, Emile cannot run this unfair race. He adores Sophie's weakness and, carrying her to the finish line in his arms, he falls to the ground at her feet and declares himself vanquished. This enchanting image has often passed through my mind" (I: 14). Staël is so enchanted by Emile's chauvinistic gesture of adoration that she seems to overlook the debilitating gender stereotypes underlying it, as well as the fact that the physical weakness of women was not natural, but culturally conditioned—a point underlined by Wollstonecraft.

Although Staël seems to accept Rousseau's view of woman as "naturally" inferior to men—physically, morally, and intellectually— she criticizes the education he prescribes for women as *reinforcing* their weakness, thereby making them less satisfying companions for their husbands, less capable of fulfilling their maternal duties, and more vulnerable to seducers:

Rousseau wanted women, like men, to be raised according to nature, . . . but I don't know whether nature should be followed to the point that women's weaknesses are merely reinforced. I see a far greater need to teach them virtues that men lack than the need to encourage their inferiority in other respects. Women would perhaps contribute as much to their husband's happiness if they limited themselves to their destiny by choice rather than by an inability to do anything else, and if they obeyed the object of their affections out of love rather than out of a need for guidance and support. (I: 13)

Like Wollstonecraft, Staël suggests that improved instruction for women would make them better wives and mothers and that greater intellectual parity between spouses would lead to happier marriages. After praising the education outlined for Emile, Staël points to the benefits such an education could yield for women: "If women were to raise themselves above their lot and dared to take part in the education of men, what a noble destiny would await them!" (I: 11).

In Staël's view, Sophie's adultery and the failure of her marriage reveal the weakness and inadequacy of the education she has received. Had Sophie received an education equal to that of Emile, she would have been a more interesting companion for him and better able to sustain their marriage. She would also have been less dependent on Emile's moral guidance, and hence less vulnerable to seducers. Staël recognizes that Sophie's adultery had been dictated by Rousseau's narrative strategy, that her moral weakness was above all a means of testing and illustrating Emile's moral strength. Underlining the pernicious implications of this narrative strategy, she decries the fact that Sophie's education and destiny were sacrificed to Emile's: "He himself condemned the education she received; he sacrificed it in order to demonstrate the strength of Emile's education by showing his courage when confronted with the most difficult of all emotional situations" (I: 13). That Rousseau would purposely degrade his heroine in order to embellish his hero arouses Staël's indignation and impels her to vigorously defend the honor and dignity of her sex: "Why debase all women by degrading the one who should have served as their model? Ah! Rousseau, how little you know them!" she exclaims. "No woman, even as weak as you wish women to be, would have banished herself from such an earthly paradise by breaking the vows of a marriage based on love" (I: 13). In this passage, Staël is on the brink of a crucial insight: it is not nature, but male self-interest that is the real cause of women's weakness. Through the debilitating education they are given (by men like Rousseau), women are more easily subjugated and seduced. Furthermore, Staël suggests in this passage that the *representation* of women as weak in works such as *Emile* and *Les Solitaires* serves to reinforce their socially conditioned inferiority. In her sarcastic aside to Rousseau ("even as weak as you *wish* women to be"), Staël points to the pernicious role of literature in perpetuating negative stereotypes of women—an argument developed with much greater force by Wollstonecraft.

Staël's Ambivalence toward Rousseau

In the course of Staël's *Lettres*, Rousseau emerges as a highly respected figure of authority, indeed as a kind of spiritual father and mentor. However, despite her enthusiasm for Rousseau, Staël's attitude toward him remains deeply ambivalent. She appears torn between a respectful admiration, an almost filial piety for him, and a sense of the fundamental incompatibility of his views on women with her own—indeed with her very identity as a woman writer. Her criticisms tend to be couched in timid, almost apologetic terms, as if she were ashamed of daring to speak out against so formidable a figure of authority, whom she genuinely respected and even idolized. For example, in her comments on *Les Confessions*, Staël admits that "this work no doubt lacks the elevated character that one would wish in a man speaking of himself" and that, as a result, it is "perhaps justly criticized" (I: 18). Yet she chooses to overlook Rousseau's character flaws, as well as his lack of taste in displaying them so openly in his autobiography; for, as she explains, "I cannot reconcile admiration and scorn" (I: 18). She therefore chooses simply to ignore what she cannot praise.

Staël's reluctance to criticize Rousseau is further illustrated by the apologetic preamble to her discussion of Claire: "There remains one last criticism for me to make: I will hurry to do so, for such criticisms trouble me" (I: 9). After underscoring Rousseau's lack of taste and decorum in his portrayal of Julie's cousin, Staël abruptly shifts to effusive praise for the eloquence and dramatic power of his style, as if to efface whatever impression of disrespect her criticisms may have conveyed. Her negative comments regarding Claire cited earlier are immediately—and quite incongruously—followed by the enthusiastic exclamation: "Such eloquence! What talent Rousseau had to communicate the strongest feelings of the soul" (I: 9). Similarly, after decrying the degrading portrayal of Sophie in *Les Solitaires*, Staël abruptly launches into another panegyric of Rousseau's talents as a writer: "What charm in all the scenes of this work! Such refinement, such breadth in his ideas! . . . What originality we find in this writer who views ordinary things in a new and true light!" (I: 13). In each case, the disjunction in her rhetoric reflects the ambivalence she feels at daring to criticize a figure of authority she respects so highly.

Commenting on Staël's *Lettres*, Mme Necker de Saussure (Staël's cousin and first biographer) observes: "However much enthusiasm Rousseau inspires in her, [Mme de Staël] maintains the independance of her mind and spirit; she expresses her own thoughts freely and abundantly, although she seems a bit embarrassed as a young woman to show such strength."[25] This points to a basic tension in Staël's attitude toward Rousseau, and indeed toward male figures of authority in general. As Gutwirth remarks, "Rousseau engendered in her from the very beginning the same qualms she felt in arguing against her father. Toward both, and in fact toward men in general, she would always feel an underlying need to atone for being a woman and yet speaking so loudly and with so much authority."[26] As with her father, Staël seems to have sublimated her contradictory feelings of love and anger toward Rousseau by elevating him to the status of a cult figure, whose ideals she adopted through sheer faith in his wisdom and virtue: "I believe, instead of thinking; I adopt, instead of reflecting; . . . I have yielded to faith to spare myself the effort of formulating a reasoning that would justify my conviction nonetheless" (I: 16). She seems to find a certain serenity in this suspension of critical judgment and abdication of will, not unlike that experienced by religious converts.

Exalting in "this blind faith which had become [her] guiding light"—an oxymoron that clearly reflects the ambivalence of her stance—Staël calls upon her readers to join in her devotion to Rousseau and his political ideals in order to assure the successful outcome of the historic meeting of les Etats Généraux the following year. She regrets that Rousseau could not himself witness and take part in this glorious event: "Ah! Rousseau, what happiness it would bring if your eloquence could be heard in this august assembly!" She then invokes Rousseau's spiritual guidance for her father, whom she in turn hails as the "guardian angel" of France:

> O, Rousseau! Come back to life! . . . and let your ardent words encourage the career of . . . the man whom France has named its guardian angel, . . . whom all should support, as if they were

coming to the rescue of the public's welfare; in short, the man who deserves a judge, an admirer, a citizen like you. (I: 17)[27]

Like the passage cited earlier where Staël interrupts her discussion of the "Profession de foi du vicaire savoyard" to praise Necker's book and career, this passage presents a curious fusion of her cults for her father and Rousseau. Yet her devotion to Jean-Jacques, her spiritual father, is clearly secondary to what she feels for her natural father. Unabashedly, she calls upon Rousseau's spirit and all of France to join with her in doing hommage to *le grand homme* Necker.

The religious nature of Staël's cult for Rousseau is especially clear at the conclusion of her *Lettres*, where she recalls, in sombre elegiac tones, her pilgrimage to his tomb: "How well his lovely final resting place reflects the feelings his memory inspires! . . . The religious devotion that impels visitors to cross the lake surrounding his island tomb shows that they are indeed worthy of bringing their offerings there. I did not lay flowers on that sad tomb; instead, I contemplated it for a long time, my eyes overflowing with tears" (I: 24).

The Second Preface of 1814

In 1814, 26 years after the original publication of her *Lettres sur Rousseau*, Staël wrote a second preface to this work that had marked her literary debut. She was then forty-eight years old and at the height of her success as a writer and *salonnière*, after a triumphant return to Paris following Napoleon's abdication. For Staël, 1814 marked the end of a painful decade of exile and the beginning of what was certainly the most serene period of her life. Although suffering from chronic ailments that would lead to her death only three years later, she felt more in control of her destiny and surer of herself than ever before, having achieved a certain detachment from the turbulent love affairs and political turmoil that had clouded her life until then. Reflecting the self-confidence and self-insight she had attained both as a woman and as a writer in the intervening years, this second preface offers a striking contrast to the view of Rousseau and of herself presented in the original preface and in the *Lettres* as a whole. It is, as David Larg remarks, "one of the last documents that Madame de Staël wrote, . . . and, in a sense, constitutes her last testament and the supreme expression of her mind."[28]

Staël begins the second preface on a modest note, declaring that her *Lettres* were first published *"sans son aveu"*—without her knowledge or consent—and that this "chance occurrence" (*hasard*) had launched her literary career almost in spite of herself.[29] According to Gutwirth, Staël is in bad faith when she claims that the letters were published without her knowledge; for, while it is true that the letters appeared anonymously, "everyone was calculatedly informed of the author's identity." Yet, as Gutwirth suggests, "this heightens our sense that there is something about them she would like to disavow."[30] Indeed, the second preface can be read as a disavowal of much of what Staël wrote in the original preface and in the *Lettres* themselves, particularly concerning Rousseau's views on women. It is, however, an indirect disavowal, since Rousseau is referred to by name only once and only in the opening sentence. Staël carefully avoids criticizing Rousseau and his views directly, and instead does so obliquely by addressing her criticisms to public opinion (referred to as *la société*), or by using the pronoun *vous* (the formal "you") or the more impersonal *on* (which means "one" or "people in general"). This curious absence of direct reference to Rousseau is at first disconcerting, particularly in the preface to a work originally presented as a tribute to him. It proves, however, to be an astute strategy that allows Staël to reassess and challenge Rousseau's views on women, without having to disavow the enthusiastic tribute of her youth to his important influence on her development as a thinker and writer. In this way, Staël was able to leave her *Lettres sur Rousseau* intact for posterity without betraying the critical spirit and more feminist point of view she had acquired through experience and reflection in the intervening years.[31]

The discussion centers around two related themes: women's education and women writers. Both are crucial points of contention in Rousseau's sexual politics, which Staël had hesitated to challenge with much force in her *Lettres*. In the second preface, however, she vigorously affirms the multiple benefits for women of a serious education, as well as the deep satisfactions offered by the cultivation of their literary talents. She begins by recalling her literary debut with the *Lettres sur Rousseau*, which had launched a career that had, in her view, "brought her more pleasure than pain." As if to vindicate herself in the eyes of her critics (past and future), she adds: "Only the most passionately proud and self-centered person would derive more pain from criticism than pleasure from praise" (I: 1). Staël challenges

Rousseau's view that no man in his right mind would ever love a woman writer or scholar and that, by attempting to rival men, such women are doomed to unhappiness. Drawing on her own experiences, she contests these misogynic views by underlining the lasting pleasures that intellectual and artistic pursuits offer to women: "There is in the development and progress of one's mind a continual activity and a constantly renewed hope for the future which the ordinary course of life cannot possibly offer. Everything in a woman's life presses onward toward decline, except for the life of the mind, whose immortal nature continues to thrive" (I: 1). In all her writings, this is Staël's strongest affirmation of a woman's right to the full development of her mind and talents. No longer dominated, as she had been at twenty-two, by the Rousseauian notion that love is woman's *raison d'être*, Staël at forty-eight viewed the development of a woman's intellectual and creative gifts as a means of transcending the limits of age and gender, indeed as a path to immortality.[32]

Staël then advances a series of arguments to support women's right to a better education and to participation in the broader cultural sphere beyond the home. She begins by observing that "people have seldom denied that literary tastes and endeavors are a great advantage for men, but they don't agree about the influence such activities may have on the destiny of women" ["On n'a presque jamais nié que les goûts et les études littéraires ne fussent un grand avantage pour les hommes, mais on n'est pas d'accord sur l'influence que ces mêmes études peuvent avoir sur la destinée des femmes"] (I: 1). While the first *on* here clearly refers to public opinion, the second seems to refer to the two main adversaries in the debate under way: Rousseau and herself. That Staël has Rousseau specifically in mind here is made clear by the sentence that immediately follows: "If it were simply a matter of imposing domestic slavery on women, then one could rightly be afraid of increasing their intelligence, for fear that they might then be tempted to rebel against their lot; but since Christian society does not call for such tyranny in family relations, the more a woman's reason is enlightened, the more likely she is to obey moral laws" (I: 1). Staël disputes the traditional view espoused by Rousseau that knowledge leads to moral corruption, especially in women, because it encourages them to question authority. This reinforces her argument in Letter I that knowledge strengthens rather than corrupts morals; however, in the second preface, she extends this argument specifically to women.

In contrast to Rousseau, Staël maintains that study and writing are both effective means for women to control their emotions and to channel them into constructive outlets: "It is often the case that women with a superior mind also possess a passionate nature; however, the cultivation of literary talents diminishes rather than increases the dangers of such a character; the pleasures of the mind serve to calm the storms of the heart" (I: 1).[33] Moreover, Staël affirms that serious, constructive occupations of this kind offer solid protection against the frivolity and corruption of *la vie mondaine*—a means of rising above the superficiality of ordinary conversation, as well as an escape from the stifling effects of social conventions:

> The habits acquired among the elegant, leisured class wither our spirit unless we engage in studies that fortify and enliven it. If the manners of high society are not combined with a broad literary background, we simply learn to repeat commonplaces and clichés, to express our opinions in ready-made formulas and our character in superficial bows. If you don't have a superior education to compensate for all these drawbacks, . . . if you don't have access to a broader sphere of ideas, you are nothing but a well-trained doll always singing the same note. (I: 1–2)

This last sentence can be seen as an attack on the education of Sophie, who for lack of "enlivening studies" is nothing but a "poupée bien apprise"—a well-trained but mindless doll of whom Emile would soon tire.[34]

In the second preface, Staël again challenges the view presented in *Emile* that a man is happier with an uneducated but submissive wife than with a woman who is his intellectual equal:

> Even if it were true—which it is not—that a woman trained in this manner would be more likely to obey her husband, how can there be any kind of communion of the souls if the minds of a husband and wife have nothing in common? And what are we to think of a husband so proudly modest as to prefer a blindly obedient wife to one who offers him enlightened companionship? . . . Yet many men prefer to have a wife devoted solely to household duties; and, to ensure her complete submission, they would not mind if she were incapable of understanding anything else. (I: 2)

Staël vigorously decries the ignorance and domestic slavery to which women were condemned by an education such as Sophie's. She is perhaps alluding ironically here to Rousseau's relationship with Thérèse, whose intellectual and moral limitations were a source of such bitter regret to him and of such indignation to Staël. Whereas in the *Lettres* she expresses sympathy for Rousseau's unhappiness with Thérèse, in the second preface she suggests that it was his own fault for choosing a woman so inferior to himself intellectually—indeed a kind of fitting revenge against a man who advocated such a limited role and education for women. Contrary to Rousseau, Staël insists that intellectual parity between spouses leads to happier marriages. Like Wollstonecraft and Condorcet, she argues that men would benefit as much as women from improved female education. Perhaps recalling the intellectual partnership of couples like the Rolands and the Condorcets, victims of the Terror whose tragic fates were no doubt still in her mind, Staël adds: "The most touching examples of conjugal love have been offered by women capable of understanding their husbands and worthy of sharing their fate; a marriage cannot fully blossom unless it is founded on mutual admiration" (I: 2). In this idealized picture of companionate marriage, Staël no doubt also had in mind her parents' seemingly perfect match, as Gutwirth has suggested.[35]

At the end of the second preface, Staël returns to the issue of women writers. She begins by summarizing the traditional prejudices against them:

> "We don't object to women cultivating their minds," some people will say, "so long as these endeavors don't inspire them with the desire to become authors, distracting them from their natural duties and making them the rivals of men, whom they are destined solely to encourage and console." (I: 2)

Staël is clearly responding here to the reactionary views on women expressed in Book V of *Emile*—views that she restates matter-of-factly, no doubt with parodic intent.[36] Indeed, this passage could easily be mistaken as a quote from Rousseau's famous tirade against women writers and scholars. In her original comments on *Emile*, Staël had avoided responding to Rousseau's disapproval of such women. Given her position in 1788 as a well-known and already controversial *salonnière* making her literary debut, this omission is hardly surprising. Even at twenty-two, Staël was anything but a Sophie and was well aware of the fact. She would have been on shaky ground indeed if she had tried either to approve or refute Rousseau's criticism of women like herself who dared to have ambitions outside the domestic sphere and to compete with men in intellectual and literary pursuits. However, in 1814, Staël's battle as a woman author had been fought and won, and with great success. She no longer had to prove herself or apologize for her talents. This second preface constitutes a triumphant affirmation of her identity as a woman writer.

After summarizing the traditional prejudices against women authors, Staël suggests that the greatest obstacle to overcoming them lay in the complicity of women themselves with the status quo—particularly the fear of celebrity or, more often, the fear of failure and ridicule that caused many to retreat behind a mask of false modesty. She expresses respect and admiration for talented women (like her beloved cousin Albertine) who, through genuine modesty and devotion to their family, were content to develop their talents in private and who did not feel compelled (as did Staël herself) to seek public praise for their work. But Staël openly denounces the bad faith of women of mediocre talents who, through false modesty, pretend to fear or disdain celebrity and who, through envy, criticize more talented and ambitious women who do achieve success:

> One should disdain only what one can actually obtain. A man in Paris always bowed his head as he passed under the porte Saint-Denis, even though it was a hundred feet high; so it is with women who boast that they fear celebrity, without ever having the talents necessary to attain it. Such talents no doubt have their drawbacks, like all the finest things in this world; but even these drawbacks seem preferable to me than the languid indolence of a narrow mind that either denigrates what it cannot attain or else feigns what it is incapable of feeling. (I: 2)[37]

In contrast to—and defiance of—these small-minded women, these *esprits bornés*, portrayed so mercilessly here and in *Corinne*, Staël vigorously affirms her talents and her vocation as a writer, not simply to vindicate herself, but to offer a positive example to other women: "Finally, if we consider only our relationship with ourselves, a greater intensity of life always leads to greater happiness," she writes. "While it is true that suffering has a greater impact on characters of a more energetic nature, there is no one who should not be grateful to God for giving him or her an additional aptitude or talent" (I: 2).[38] This passage reflects a significant shift in audience; the *nous* ["we"] Staël is addressing here is no longer Rousseau and his admirers, but herself and other women, especially women with creative gifts. This passage also reflects a significant change in perspective: the female artist should look within herself, to her own creative powers, for the greatest and surest source of pleasure and self-fulfillment. One senses that Staël had at last come to terms with the tension that lay at the core of her life as a woman and a writer, which she had summed up in an oft-cited passage from *De l'Allemagne*: "for a woman, celebrity leads only to a tragic end of happiness."[39] In the second preface, this pessimistic view of the destiny of the woman artist doomed to unhappiness by her talents—played out so dramatically in *Corinne*—is finally overcome. And in its place, Staël offers a triumphant affirmation of female creativity as a God-given gift that infuses life with greater intensity and joy.

The differences in tone and perspective between the two prefaces reflect the evolution that had taken place in Staël's attitude toward both Rousseau and herself in the intervening years. In the first preface, she had suggested that Rousseau held a special appeal for young people because of their natural enthusiasm and idealism;[40] she had tried to justify her tribute to him on the grounds that if she waited until her talents were equal to the task, she might lose the youthful enthusiasm he inspired: "Who can predict the development of his or her mind? Why should we agree to wait and to postpone for some uncertain future time the expression of a feeling that propels us forward?" she had asked. "Time, no doubt, shatters our illusions, but . . . its destructive hand is not limited to our mistakes alone" (I: 1). This passage from the first preface curiously foreshadows Staël's later disenchantment with Rousseau's limited view of female destiny. Reading her second preface, one senses that she was no longer intimidated by him, nor convinced by his traditionalist discourse. Having developed her own strengths as a woman and as a writer, she finally dared to challenge Rousseau's narrow feminine ideals. It is above all when she wrote of her own literary career—of the pleasures it had brought her despite the pains—that the evolution in her viewpoint is most apparent. In her second preface, Staël was no longer a novice writer apologetically addressing her audience for the first time, but a mature and successful writer, sure of her opinions and talents and secure in her identity as a woman author.

Wollstonecraft's Review of Staël's Lettres sur Rousseau

Staël's *Lettres sur Rousseau* were translated into English in 1789 and found a hostile reviewer in Mary Wollstonecraft, another impassioned reader of Rousseau, who was also at the start of her literary career.[41] Writing in the *Analytical Review*, Wollstonecraft remarked deprecatingly on the young baroness's naive and self-serving enthusiasm:

> These remarks on Rousseau, consist of warm panegyrics, and answers to a few well-known objections. . . . These observations are written with timid caution, to steer clear of censure, while contending for a literary wreath, and sometimes so superficial, that indiscriminate admiration appears like the blind homage of ignorance to a great name. Rousseau's literary station has long been settled by time on a firm basis; his genius spreads flowers over the most barren tract, yet his profound sagacity and paradoxical caprice, his fascinating eloquence and specious errors, may be seen by their own light; a lamp is an officious twinkler when the sun has diffused his beams.[42]

In Wollstonecraft's opinion, Staël's praise for Rousseau was as undiscerning as it was presumptuous, and her comments on his works unoriginal and unperceptive. Singled out for attack is Staël's attempt to defend *La Nouvelle Héloïse* against charges of immorality by insisting on the work's didactic value and positive moral influence. Wollstonecraft argues that the moral issues of Rousseau's novel are by no means as clear-cut as Staël's account of them would suggest. To her reviewer, Staël's reading of Julie's character seemed as superficial and moralistic as her reading of Rousseau's own character. Using metaphors drawn from landscape imagery, Wollstonecraft describes Staël's literary criticism as having a bulldozer effect on Rousseau's writing, flattening out and burying the most salient features of his thinking and his portrayal of characters in her effort to render his depiction of human nature more palatable from an aesthetic and moral point of view:

> How little indeed do they know of human nature, who by their injudicious candour labour to destroy all identity of character, endeavouring to root out the tares, to soften apparent defects; they may seem to rub off some sharp corners, rude unsightly angles; but could they really succeed in their childish attempt,

they would only level original prominent features, and stupidly active, transform a sublime mountain into a beautiful plain. (360)

Wollstonecraft also disputes Staël's claim that Rousseau committed suicide, citing letters published at the end of the *Confessions* that "point out her mistake" (362).

By far the most acerbic comments in Wollstonecraft's review concern the long digression Staël makes in praise of her father: "The praises lavished on M. Necker are so extravagant, that they appear to be dictated rather by the head than by the heart; nay, they are indelicate, when we consider that they probably met his eye before publication; nor can we pay great deference to the Baroness's judgment after reading her opinion of her father, written in the bombast language of pride, instead of appearing to be the simple effusion of gratitude or tenderness" (361). To support her criticism, Wollstonecraft then cites the long tribute to Necker in its entirety. She undermines the value of Staël's *Lettres* by pointing to her lack of taste and judgment, and above all by questioning the motives behind her encomiums to Rousseau and her father. Adopting a Rousseauesque notion of sincerity, Wollstonecraft posits an ideal of genuine and spontaneous admiration, in contrast to what she describes as pompous and self-serving panegyrics. She suggests that the young author's chief motive in praising the reputation and talents of these two *grands hommes* was to enhance and mirror her own.[43] The inflated praise of Necker's *De l'importance des opinions religieuses* was no doubt irritating to Wollstonecraft, who had translated this work and had a low opinion of both the book and its author. Five years later in her study of the French Revolution, she would describe Necker as vain, greedy, and incurably small-minded and mock his literary pretensions and metaphysical speculations.[44]

The issue of Rousseau's sexual politics was not raised by Wollstonecraft in her 1789 review of Staël's *Lettres*. Either she felt this would be inappropriate in a short book review intended for the *Analytical Review*'s largely male audience, or else it simply was not an issue that concerned her at the time. However, three years later in her *Vindication of the Rights of Woman*, it was above all on this issue that she focused when she took a second look at Staël's book. Before discussing Wollstonecraft's response to Staël in the *Rights of Woman*, let us first examine the discussion of Rousseau's sexual politics that precedes it. For without a grasp of Wollstonecraft's main criticisms of Rousseau, one lacks the structural and philosophical framework needed

Portrait of Mary Wollstonecraft by John Opie. Courtesy of the Tate Gallery, London.

to fully understand her objections to Staël's *Lettres sur Rousseau*—objections largely derived from her analysis of *Emile*.

Wollstonecraft's Attack on the Sexual Politics in Emile

Chapter 5 of *A Vindication of the Rights of Woman*—titled "Animadversions on Some of the Writers Who Have Rendered Women Objects of Pity, Bordering on Contempt"—begins with a scathing, point-by-point critique of Rousseau's sexual politics, particularly the subordinate role and repressive education he proposes for women in *Emile*. Wollstonecraft underlines the contradictions between the egalitarian philosophy elaborated by Rousseau in the *Social Contract* and in the *Discourse on Inequality* and the unequal, oppressed status of women that he defends and attempts to justify, even to idealize, in *Emile*.

Challenging Rousseau's narrow views on female education, Wollstonecraft argues that women are moral beings who "ought to endeavour to acquire human virtues (or perfections) by the *same* means as men, instead of being educated like a fanciful kind of *half* being—one of Rousseau's wild chimeras."[45] She draws on the authority of her own experience as a woman and as an educator to argue against Rousseau's theories of feminine nature—the supposed "natural" weakness and passivity of girls, their alleged fondness for dolls and dress:

> I have probably had an opportunity of observing more girls in their infancy than J. J. Rousseau—I can recollect my own feelings, and I have looked steadily around me; yet, so far from coinciding with him in opinion, . . . I will venture to affirm that a girl whose spirits have not been dampened by inactivity, or innocence tainted by false shame, will always be a romp, and the doll will never excite attention unless confinement allows her no alternative. . . . Most of the women in the circle of my observation who have acted like rational creatures, or shown any vigour of intellect, have accidentally been allowed to run wild. (58)

In this last sentence, Wollstonecraft is no doubt alluding to her own unorthodox upbringing, in which through parental indifference, she was allowed "to run wild" both physically and intellectually.[46] Given the inadequacies of the standard female education of the period (which

Wollstonecraft criticizes in detail in the *Rights of Woman*), she suggests that women were better off educating themselves, as she herself had done. Anticipating de Beauvoir's famous dictum 150 years later—"One is not born a woman but becomes one"—Wollstonecraft argues that it is not nature but culture that renders women intellectually and physically weak. Like de Beauvoir, she adopts the metaphor of the golden cage to describe women's debilitating education and oppressed condition:

> Women are everywhere in this deplorable state; for, in order to preserve their innocence, as ignorance is courteously termed, truth is hidden from them, and they are made to assume an artificial character before their faculties have acquired any strength. Taught from their infancy that beauty is woman's sceptre, the mind shapes itself to the body, and roaming round its gilt cage, only seeks to adorn its prison. (59)

Wollstonecraft rejects the common view of women as essentially *sexual* beings—a view reflected in Rousseau's statement that "The male is only male at certain moments, while the female is female her entire life; everything brings her back constantly to her sex."[47] Wollstonecraft's response to this sexual characterization of women is to reverse the charge: not women, she argues, but *men* are dominated by their sexual impulses. In her view, Rousseau's insistence on women's "innate" desire to please and to yield is simply a projection of his own repressed desire. His arguments about women's "natural" inferiority are only rationalizations for the superior social position men have unjustly usurped, she maintains, and his talk of "natural" female wantonness is merely a cover for the sexual appetite men both fear and relish in themselves.

Wollstonecraft astutely analyzes how Rousseau simultaneously rationalizes his own sensuality and gratifies it, and then punishes the being who tempts him to this self-indulgence by making her responsible for sexual control.[48] Moreover, she intuits the dynamics of repression and compensation at work in his writings. As forbidden longings are censured, sexual desire erupts in sublimated form in his fiction: "Born with a warm constitution and lively fancy, nature carried him toward the other sex with such eager fondness that he soon became lascivious," remarks Wollstonecraft. "Had he given way to these desires, the fire would have extinguished itself in a natural manner; but virtue, and a romantic kind of delicacy, made him practice self-denial;

yet, when fear, delicacy, or virtue restrained him, he debauched his imagination, and reflecting on the sensations to which fancy gave force, he traced them in the most glowing colours" (114). This sublimation was as dangerous for Rousseau's readers as it was for himself, she claimed; for when the imagination becomes "debauched" in the name of virtuous self-denial, the artist seduces his reader as he indulges himself: "And so warmly has he painted what he forcibly felt, that interesting the heart and inflaming the imagination of his readers, they imagine that their understanding is convinced when they only sympathize with a poetic writer, who skillfully exhibits the objects of sense, most voluptuously shadowed or gracefully veiled" (114).

Wollstonecraft castigates the author of *Emile* as a sensualist who wished to deprive women of the power of reason to assure their complete subjugation by men and dependence upon them. In exchange for this female abdication of knowledge and autonomy, he offers women the questionable and often short-lived benefits of male love and adoration: "Rousseau declares that a woman should never, for a moment, feel herself independent, that she should be governed by fear to exercise her natural cunning, and made a coquettish slave in order to render her a more alluring object of desire, a sweeter companion to man, whenever he chooses to relax himself," writes Wollstonecraft (37–38). She maintains that both sexes are degraded by women's oppression, by their reduction to mere objects of male desire. In her opinion, this inequality leads to mutual deception and to the moral corruption of society. To Rousseau's claim that it is woman's lot to obey even a tyrannical husband, she responds: "Of what materials can that heart be composed, which can melt when insulted, and instead of revolting at injustice, kiss the rod? . . . Let the husband beware of trusting too implicitly to this servile obedience, for if his wife can with winning sweetness caress him when angry, . . . she may do the same after parting with a lover" (106). Alluding to Sophie's infidelity in the sequel to *Emile*, she argues that a woman who has been raised above all to please men and who has no inner resources upon which to draw is more likely to be unfaithful once her husband tires of her—which is almost inevitable, given her purely physical appeal.

Wollstonecraft calls Rousseau a "voluptuous tyrant" who, by cultivating women's sensibility and by making love the focus of their lives, made them the prey of their senses and more easily dominated by men.[49] She expresses deep ambivalence toward his attempt to confine women within the sphere of feelings (as opposed to the "masculine" sphere of reason and ideas); for she senses the implicit link of this dichotomy with the relegation of women to the domestic sphere, and indeed with the male self-interest and female repression that lay at the root of the gender hierarchy. Confined to the domestic sphere, "a woman's only occupation consists of affairs of the heart," observes Wollstonecraft. "The mighty business of female life is to please, and [because women are] restrained from entering into more important concerns by political and civil oppression, sentiments become events" (80).

This leads Wollstonecraft to what is probably her single most important insight and her most devastating critique of Rousseau: the dangers that his ideal of sensibility represented for his women readers. She denounces sentimentalism as a repressive system of social conditioning designed both to arouse and to control female desire. Sentimental novels, she claims, encourage girls to indulge in fantasies that make them vulnerable to seduction and lead them to project their desires uncritically onto a single man, a "hero" with whom they seek to realize their imaginative and sexual desires. In her view, sentimental novels like *Julie* undermine virtue by making reality seem unfulfilling. By engaging their readers' desire for immediate, vicarious gratification, such fictions disengage them from life; they feed wishful fantasies instead of initiating positive action, thereby imprisoning women further in the sphere of sensibility.

Expounded at length in *The Rights of Woman*, the dangers of sensibility and of sentimental novels are illustrated graphically in Wollstonecraft's novel *Maria*. Maria first projects her fantasies onto her husband (a dissolute gambler who marries her only for her money) and later onto her lover Darnford, who abandons her after she has sacrificed everything for him. It is no accident that Saint-Preux is taken as the model of the ideal lover Maria projects onto Darnford.[50] Moreover, *La Nouvelle Héloïse* serves as a means of communication (and ultimately of seduction) between the lovers, both imprisoned in a madhouse. They write to each other in the margins of Rousseau's novel—a means of communication emblematic both of women's marginal status in literary culture and of the novel's corrupting influence on morals through the exacerbation of women's sensibility and imagination. Although Maria had read *La Nouvelle Héloïse* before, "now it seemed to open a new world to her—the only one worth inhabiting" (88–89). Seduced by Rousseau's novel and by the man who sends it to her, she "flew to Rousseau as her only refuge" (89).

During Wollstonecraft's liaison with Gilbert Imlay, and later with William Godwin, a copy of *Julie* was similarly exchanged with her lover as a token of mutual affection. Writing about Rousseau in a letter to Imlay, Wollstonecraft confided: "I have always been half in love with him"[51]—a strange confession indeed coming from a woman who had only two years earlier written such a scathing attack on him in *The Rights of Woman*. The phrase "half in love" is nevertheless an apt description of Wollstonecraft's amorous enmity for Jean-Jacques. Her ambivalence toward Rousseau is apparent in her response to each of his main works. After reading the *Confessions*, she admitted: "It is impossible to peruse his simple descriptions without loving the man in spite of the weaknesses of character that he himself depicts, which never appear to have risen from depravity of heart."[52] To those who felt the need to apologize for the character flaws that Rousseau exposes so openly in his autobiography, Wollstonecraft replied: "A defense of Rousseau appears to us unnecesary—for surely he speaks to the heart, and whoever reading his works can doubt whether he wrote from it—had better take up some other book."[53] Similarly, despite her warnings concerning the ideal of sensibility extolled in *Julie*, her enthusiasm for Rousseau's novel prompted her to exclaim: "Rousseau alone, the true Prometheus of sentiment, possessed the fire of genius necessary to portray the passion, the truth of which goes so directly to the heart."[54] It is important to point out, however, that this statement is made by Darnford in a note to Maria in the margin of a particularly passionate letter from Saint-Preux to Julie. The context of this statement therefore undermines its content and reflects Wollstonecraft's ambiguous feelings toward *La Nouvelle Héloïse*, since she uses Rousseau's novel both as an actual means of seduction by Darnford and as an exemplary case of the novel's corrupting influence on morals through the exacerbation of women's sensibility and imagination.

Even *Emile* drew Wollstonecraft's praise when she read it for the first time in her mid-twenties: "I am now reading Rousseau's Emile, and love his paradoxes," wrote Mary to her sister.[55] Educational treatise, metaphysical essay, and sentimental novel all rolled into one, *Emile* appealed to her strongly at a time when she was preoccupied by pedagogical and metaphysical questions and before the full awakening of her feminist consciousness. In her twenties, it was above all as a sentimentalist that she judged—and most valued—the author of *Emile*: "He rambles into that *chimerical* world in which I have too often wandered—and draws the usual conclusion that all is vanity and vexation of spirit," she mused. "He was a strange, inconsistent, unhappy, clever creature—yet he possessed an uncommon portion of sensibility and penetration."[56]

Like Staël, Wollstonecraft seems to have identified strongly with Rousseau—especially with the image he presents of himself as a victim of his own intense sensibility and creative talent, doomed to unhappiness and solitude. This image recurs again ten years later (toward the end of her life) in a letter to Godwin after they first became intimate: "My imagination is forever betraying me into fresh misery," she confided. "You talk of the roses which grow profusely in every path of life—I catch at them, but only encounter the thorns." Alluding to Rousseau's *Rêveries du Promeneur Solitaire*, she then added: "Consider what has passed as a fever of your imagination and I will become again a *Solitary Walker*. Adieu!"[57] These two images of Rousseau—that of the Solitary Walker and the Prometheus of sentiment—remained intermingled in Wollstonecraft's mind, symbolizing both the attractions and dangers of the ideal of sensibility he promulgated and its dubious effects upon herself and other women readers. In *The Rights of Woman*, Wollstonecraft repeatedly underlines the pernicious effects of Rousseau's excessive sensibility on both himself and his readers: "All Rousseau's errors in reasoning arose from sensibility, and sensibility to their charms women are very ready to forgive! . . . The pernicious tendency of those books, in which the writers insidiously degrade the sex whilst they are prostrate before their personal charms, cannot be too often or too severely exposed" (114–15). Yet even at the end of her scathing attack on Rousseau in the *Rights of Woman*, she makes it clear that it is his ideas and not the man himself she is criticizing: "But peace to his manes! I war not with his ashes, but his opinions. I war only with the sensibility that led him to degrade woman by making her the slave of love" (115). Based on her own experience, Wollstonecraft viewed sensibility as a double-edged sword, source of pleasure and of pain, which could easily turn against even the deftest fencer in the endless battle of the sexes.[58]

Wary of the ideal of sensibility that Rousseau extols in *Julie* and rejecting the short-lived sensual power that he offers to women in *Emile* V, Wollstonecraft affirms the genuine and lasting benefits that improved female education and equality between the sexes would bring. Insisting that men are as degraded as women by female oppression, she calls for a "revolution in female manners" in order to bring about a general reform of society through the reform of domestic morals:

Women, . . . by practising or fostering vice, lose the rank which reason would assign them, and they become either abject slaves or capricious tyrants. They lose all simplicity, all dignity. . . . It is time to effect a revolution in female manners—time to restore to them their lost dignity—and make them labour by reforming themselves to reform the world. (60–61)

At first glance, Wollstonecraft's rhetoric of moral reform seems to resemble that of Rousseau in *Julie* and in Book I of *Emile*. However, their goals differ quite dramatically, as do the methods they would adopt to achieve them. Wollstonecraft's vision of social reform is much more ambitious and certainly more feminist, for it is based upon a radical reassessment and restructuring of women's education and role in society. In contrast to Rousseau, who maintained that women's education should be geared entirely to their relationships to men (as wives, lovers, and mothers), Wollstonecraft argued that it should serve above all as a means of assuring women's happiness and self-fulfillment. It was not an education like Sophie's she was proposing for women, but one like Emile's. "The most perfect education, in my opinion, is such an exercise of the understanding as is best calculated to strengthen the body and form the heart . . . to enable the individual to attain such habits of virtue as will render it independent," she writes. "This was Rousseau's opinion respecting men: I extend it to women" (33). To Rousseau's warning that women educated like men grow to resemble them and thereby lose their sexual charms, Wollstonecraft responds: "This is the very point I aim at. I do not wish them to have power over men; but over themselves" (81). Although Wollstonecraft (like Rousseau) considered marriage and motherhood a vital aspect of woman's destiny, hers was a far less reductive, less constraining view than his. She stressed women's right to an independent "life of the mind" and to participation in the broader cultural sphere beyond the home. Moreover, unlike Rousseau, she insisted on improved female education as a means of providing financial self-sufficiency for women who were not able to marry, as well as for widows and for women whose husbands were unable or unwilling to provide adequately for their family.[59]

Wollstonecraft's Second Response to Staël

After her probing analysis of the sexual politics in *Emile*, Wollstonecraft examines how Rousseau's traditionalist and often misogynic views on women had been uncritically adopted and advocated by various women writers. Staël is singled óut as a prime example of women's complicity with male oppression—of women who burnish their chains instead of seeking to break them. After a mordant attack on Hester Thrale's conservative views on women, Wollstonecraft writes: "The Baroness de Staël speaks the same language as the lady just cited, with more enthusiasm. Her eulogium on Rousseau was accidentally put into my hands, and her sentiments, the sentiments of too many of her sex, may serve as the text for a few comments" (127–28).[60]

Wollstonecraft begins her critique of Staël's *Lettres sur Rousseau* by citing the passage in *Lettre* I where Staël seems to approve the sexual politics outlined in the *Lettre à d'Alembert*—the superiority of the male sex, the principle of separate spheres, and the notion that love is woman's *raison d'être* and greatest source of happiness. Quoting from the English translation of the *Lettres sur Rousseau*, Wollstonecraft periodically interrupts Staël's text with cutting remarks or italicizes expressions that she finds particularly revealing of Staël's complicity with Rousseau. For example, in the concluding sentence of a long quotation from *Lettre* I, Wollstonecraft italicizes several key words ("yet when they come before him with all the *charms, weaknesses, virtues,* and *errors* of their sex, his respect for their *persons* amounts almost to adoration") and then caustically retorts:

> True!—For never was there a sensualist who paid more fervent adoration at the shrine of beauty. So devout, indeed, was his respect for the person, that excepting the virtue of chastity, . . . he only wished to see it embellished by charms, weaknesses, and errors. He was afraid lest the austerity of reason should disturb the soft playfulness of love. The master wished to have a meretricious slave to fondle, entirely dependent on his reason and bounty; he did not want a companion, whom he should be compelled to esteem, or a friend to whom he could confide the care of his children's education. . . . He denies woman reason, shuts her out from knowledge, and turns her aside from truth; yet his pardon is granted, because "he recognizes the passion of love." (128)

Wollstonecraft was reacting less to what Staël actually said than to what she failed to say—and especially to the fact that she overlooked the oppressive system of education and limited role Rousseau prescribed for women in her enthusiasm for his idealization of love.

According to Wollstonecraft, women had little enough for which to be grateful in Rousseau's idolization of their charms, since he "recognizes the passion of love only for the relaxation of men, and to perpetuate the species" (128).

For Wollstonecraft, Staël represents the typical female reader of Rousseau, who under his influence abdicates reason for emotion and sacrifices critical judgment to embrace his restrictive feminine ideals of beauty, love, subservience, and sensibility. She chides Staël for her gullibility, for letting herself be taken in so naïvely by Rousseau's seductive language. She cites a key phrase from Staël's *Lettres* to illustrate her point: " 'What signifies it to women,' pursues this rhapsodist [Staël], 'that his reason disputes with them the empire, when his heart is devotedly theirs?' " (128). Wollstonecraft is clearly portraying Rousseau as a seducer of women readers and Staël as one of his prime victims—but one who should have known better. Criticizing Staël's attraction to the dubious "empire" of love promised by Rousseau, Wollstonecraft vehemently replies: "It is not empire, but equality, that women should contend for" (128).

In her *Lettres sur Rousseau*, Staël frequently uses the term *empire*, which is also a favorite word in Rousseau's lexicon. Wollstonecraft is the first to have realized that, like Rousseau, Staël uses the term to denote two distinct but closely related concepts. Both use the term primarily to refer to woman's influence in the domestic sphere—to her role as supportive yet protected wife, who is dutiful and obedient, but who controls her partner indirectly by her physical attractiveness and her civilizing sensibility. Yet, as Wollstonecraft observes, they also use the word *empire* to refer to the dynamics of dominance and subjection in sexual relationships. Wollstonecraft points to the paradox imbedded in this dual usage of the term and to the dangers that could arise from the confusion of the two meanings. While she recognizes that a virtuous and intelligent woman's "empire" in the domestic sphere could have a positive moral influence on her family and on society as a whole, she is wary of the pernicious effects of the second type of "empire" because of the inequality it posits between the sexes. As in any unequal power relation, both parties are degraded and denatured, she maintains. As tyrant or as slave, idealized or vituperated by man, woman is in either case dependent upon and defined by her relationship to *him*, and is thereby denied her autonomy and dignity as a human being. In Wollstonecraft's opinion, only through equality—intellectual, moral, and social—could women hope to recover their

natural rights as human beings, their self-esteem, as well as the respect of men. Since love and sexual desire are so ephemeral, it is wiser
for women to develop intellectual and moral qualities that will earn
their husband's or companion's continued affection and esteem:

> Though beauty may gain a heart, it cannot keep it, even while
> the beauty is in full bloom, unless the mind lend at least some
> graces. When women are once sufficiently enlightened to dis-
> cover their real interest on a grand scale they will, I am per-
> suaded, be very ready to resign all the prerogatives of love that
> are not mutual . . . for the calm satisfaction of friendship, and the
> tender confidence of habitual esteem. (129)

The ideal advocated by Wollstonecraft of mutual esteem and affection is not unlike the model of companionate marriage presented in
Julie, which Staël herself had endorsed in her *Lettres*. Moreover, the
dialectic of desire and satiation to which Wollstonecraft points in this
passage is a central leitmotif in both of Rousseau's novels, and particularly in *Julie*. Yet in the *Rights of Woman*, Wollstonecraft chooses to
ignore *Julie* and to concentrate her criticisms on Book V of *Emile*—no
doubt because of the latter work's unambiguously misogynic content
and influence. Similarly, in her comments on Staël's *Lettres sur Rousseau*,
Wollstonecraft limits her discussion to Staël's appraisal of *Emile* V and
the *Lettre à d'Alembert*. This is not surprising given Wollstonecraft's
polemical and reformist goals in the *Rights of Woman*—her desire to
denounce the oppression of women in its many forms and to show
how improved female education could lead to a gradual amelioration
of their condition and to the reform of society as a whole. In the
context of her project, those two works by Rousseau were an important target for criticism because of the stultifying views they present
on women's role and education. On the other hand, *Julie* and Book I
of *Emile* present a more positive view of women, which might have
weakened Wollstonecraft's critique of Rousseau. She therefore chose
to ignore those two works, except in her discussion of the negative
influence of sentimental novels on female sensibility and imagination.

According to Wollstonecraft, Rousseau was incapable of writing
constructively about women because of his susceptibility to sexual fantasy. His tendency to fantasize—combined with his masculinist perspective and male self-interest—made him singularly unqualified to
prescribe women's role and education in a way that would serve their

needs and best interests, she maintained. In her view, Rousseau's intense sensibility and his extraordinary talent for communicating it made his writings even more pernicious for his female readers. Through his powers of persuasion and seduction, he led women to embrace his ideals of love and sensibility that only served to perpetuate their subjugation.

Highly critical of Rousseau's feminine ideals of love and sensibility, Wollstonecraft saw Staël's adoption of these ideals and her failure to challenge Rousseau's limited vision of woman's destiny as an even greater abdication of intellectual responsibility. She presumably knew nothing of Staël's championing of the rights of *la femme supérieure*, but she probably would have been unimpressed by it. The *Vindication* asserts the rights of all women and is specifically addressed to the undistinguished middle classes. Wollstonecraft's extreme hostility to Staël, the "officious twinkler," is symptomatic of the class differences that divided them and that gave rise to their very different outlooks on the "woman question"—at least at that point in time.

Wollstonecraft was one of the few writers of her generation to have consciously articulated women's oppression as a class, to have expressed compassion for the plight of working-class women (particularly of prostitutes), and to have emphasized the need for solidarity of women across classes and generations. In *Maria*, for example, the heroine is saved from despair through love for her daughter and through the friendship of her prison guard, a former prostitute. The importance of female solidarity is underlined in the *Rights of Woman*, where Wollstonecraft writes: "My arguments are dedicated by a disinterested spirit—I plead for my sex—not for myself" (7). Staël, on the other hand, was a self-centered individualist, a self-proclaimed "woman of genius" who expressed disdain for the common horde of ordinary women and showed little interest in their problems. Unlike Wollstonecraft, Staël expressed scorn for the political agitations of working-class women and feminist militants during the Revolution and tried to dissociate her name from theirs. In contrast to Wollstonecraft's novels, Staël's fictional works stress the dangers of female friendship and solidarity and the destructive force of female rivalry.[61]

Perhaps Wollstonecraft was better able than Staël to distance herself from Rousseau's influence because of her position as a cultural outsider. It was no doubt easier for her—from a safe distance across the Channel—to criticize the revolutionary's government's failure to extend civil rights to women than it was for French feminists like Méricourt and Gouges, who were severely punished for their militancy.[62] Well aware of Rousseau's determining influence on the revolutionary leaders' traditionalist attitudes and repressive policies toward women, she was quick to denounce the contradiction in their egalitarian rhetoric, which excluded woman from the rights of Man. It is significant, moreover, that Wollstonecraft dedicated her *Rights of Woman*—a work highly critical of Rousseau's sexual politics—to Talleyrand, and that she used the dedicatory preface as a forum to criticize the failure of the revolutionary leaders to grant equality to women, particularly in the realm of education. Although she praised Talleyrand's plan for public education as farsighted, she pointed to a glaring flaw: the fact that he had not included girls beyond the age of eight. At the end of her "dedication," Wollstonecraft boldly called for a revision of the French Constitution that would grant equal civil and educational rights to women.[63] Wollstonecraft's active engagement in the political discourse of her period on the issue of women's rights contrasts sharply with Staël's apparent indifference—or overt hostility—toward feminist militants and their demands.[64]

Ironic Parallels

Wollstonecraft's harsh criticism of Staël's *Lettres sur Rousseau* is doubly ironic in that Staël was not as uncritical of Rousseau as Wollstonecraft claimed, nor was Wollstonecraft herself as opposed to his views of women as the *Rights of Woman* might imply. In the course of her *Vindication*, not only did she ignore Staël's negative comments regarding Rousseau's views on female education, but she also ignored her own admiration for *Julie* and for Rousseau's ideals of sensibility and domesticity, which she shared with Staël—almost in spite of herself. A third irony is that, in the course of her career as a writer and public figure, Staël's views on women and on Rousseau would evolve along lines parallel to those of Wollstonecraft. Both Staël and Wollstonecraft began as passionate admirers of Rousseau; however, with the passing of time, they grew more critical of his limited views on women's role and education and regarded his ideals of sensibility and domesticity with increasing ambivalence. In the second preface to her *Lettres sur Rousseau*, Staël in fact outlines a number of the same criticisms of *Emile* developed by Wollstonecraft in the *Rights of Woman*. Moreover, in their mature works, both writers present incisive analyses of the condition of women in society and hold out for future generations a bold new vision of woman, which each strove to embody in her life and works.[65]

6

The Influence of Class and Politics on Women's Response to Rousseau:

Stéphanie de Genlis and Olympe de Gouges

How did women's class and political outlook influence their response to Rousseau? This chapter probes this question by comparing how two women from opposite poles of the social and political spectrum responded to his character and writings: Countess Stéphanie de Genlis, head tutor to the duc d'Orléans's children and staunch royalist, who fled France during the Terror, and Olympe de Gouges, a semi-literate woman of working-class origins turned courtesan and then playwright, whose radical feminist and republican manifestoes eventually led her to the guillotine. Both were highly prolific authors and controversial public figures who achieved considerable notoriety in the course of their careers. Their originality lies in their incisive analyses of women's condition in society and in the innovative reforms they proposed— Genlis in the field of female education, Gouges in her call for women's rights. Yet despite the celebrity they achieved in their lifetimes, the two women were largely forgotten until the mid-1980s when Gabriel de Broglie's monumental biography of Genlis and ground-breaking studies of Gouges by Olivier Blanc and Benoîte Groult aroused new interest in their lives and works.

Although products of very different socio-economic milieus, Genlis and Gouges experienced many of the same influences and tensions. Like other intellectuals of their generation, they were in uneasy tandem between the Enlightenment and the nascent Romantic movement, as well as between the ancien régime and the new social order ushered in by the events of 1789. Both initially greeted the French Revolution with hope and enthusiasm; however, as the bloody events of the Terror unfolded, they became increasingly disenchanted with the Revolution and critical of its leaders. As women writers and public figures, they were frequent targets for the wave of gynephobic attacks and misogynic slander that escalated under the Reign of Terror. Because of their association with the duc d'Orléans, the lover they had shared some twenty years earlier, Genlis and Gouges were attacked and ridiculed by Jacobins and Royalists alike.

Certainly the most striking parallel between Genlis and Gouges is that both were strongly influenced by Rousseau and responded repeatedly to his writings. Like Wollstonecraft and Staël, both were passionate admirers yet, at the same time, strong critics of Rousseau, but unwilling to recognize their own ambivalence. To probe Rousseau's paradoxical appeal to women of the revolutionary era, I examine how these two women from such very different backgrounds responded to his works and how he in turn influenced how each viewed herself as a writer, as well as her vision of women's proper role in society.

Both women were born in provincial France in the 1740s: Genlis near Autun in Burgundy in 1746, Gouges in Montauban north of Toulouse in 1748. Genlis's father, old nobility recently married into merchant money, lost his estate while she was still a child, and she spent her adolescence in embarrassing poverty. In her *Mémoires*, she recalls the humiliation of having to display her talents as actress and harpist in the salons of wealthy relations in order to provide room and board for herself and her mother and later to attract a suitable husband. Since she had no dowry, her beauty, charm, and talents were her only assets in a highly competitive marriage market. Marriage at seventeen to the future comte de Genlis made her position more secure and led to her entry into the royal court as *dame d'honneur* to the young duchess of Chartres in 1772. That same year, she began the affair with the duc de Chartres, the future Philippe-Egalité, which sealed her political and social fortunes. Her sharp intelligence and insistence earned her the job of governess to his daughters and later *gouverneur* (head tutor) to his sons, including the future king, Louis-Philippe. She thus became the first woman in France (or any other country) to direct the education of royal princes. From this prestigious position, she published a popular series of stories and plays for children and the best-selling pedagogical novel *Adèle et Théodore* (1782) that earned her an international reputation as an educator. This

professional activity had a determining influence on her vocation as a
writer; for, like *Adèle et Théodore*, nearly all of her early works were of
a pedagogical nature: theater pieces and didactic tales designed to
amuse and instruct her pupils, a variety of textbooks, and treatises on
education outlining her theories and methods. Forced to flee France
during the Terror and to support herself through her writing, Genlis
became a successful novelist during her exile. At the time of her death
at eighty-four in 1830, she had published more than 140 volumes in a
wide variety of genres and lived to see her pupil Louis-Philippe become king of France.

⋘◈⋙

Born Marie Gouze, the daughter of a butcher and a washerwoman,
Gouges received no formal education and (like Genlis) was entirely
self-taught. She was married at sixteen to an elderly business associate
of her father who died a year later, leaving her with an infant son. She
refused several advantageous remarriages, insisting that "mariage is
the tomb of confidence and love."[1] Gouges's metamorphosis from a
barely literate, provincial wife to revolutionary feminist began when,
under the protection of a rich lover, she moved to Paris and assumed
the name Olympe de Gouges. Refusing to keep the name of a husband
she had never loved or even liked, she used an approximation of her
maiden name, along with her mother's middle name Olympe, which
she felt had a "celestial ring to it." By assuming an aristocratic title,
she bestowed on herself the right to enter the world of Parisian salons,
where leading Enlightenment thinkers were disseminating their ideas.
There she received her only real education and was strongly influenced by the radical social critiques advanced by Mercier and
Condorcet, with whom she became close friends. Paradoxically, by
effacing her modest name and background under the mask of the
aristocrat, Gouges gained access to egalitarian and revolutionary
thought.[2] As an upper-class courtesan, she (like Ninon de Lenclos and
Théroigne de Méricourt) occupied the traditionally ambiguous position of the *hætera*: only outside the structure of marriage could a *déclassée*
woman gain access to a cultural discourse that might allow her to
transcend the limitations of her birth. At the age of thirty, Gouges
turned to playwriting to express her new political convictions. She
claimed to be the illegitimate daughter of the marquis Le Franc de
Pompignan, a minor playwright and member of the Académie Française
who had been her mother's godfather and childhood friend. By

Anonymous portrait of Olympe de Gouges painted in
1784. Courtesy of the Musée Carnavalet, Paris.

creating an affiliation with the socially respectable and culturally le-
gitimate marquis, she established a genealogy for her own ambitions
as a writer.

Gouges's Paradoxical Tributes to Rousseau

Although as a controversial political figure, feminist militant, and courtesan turned playwright, Gouges represented everything Rousseau despised, and although she rejected the ideal of marriage and domesticity
he advocated, she continued to idolize him and to view him as her
literary father. When friends tried to dissuade her from pursuing a career
as a dramatist, warning her of the theater world's prejudices against
women writers and the caprices of public opinion, Gouges invoked
Rousseau's example to strengthen her resolve: "Proud and strong-willed
like Jean-Jacques, I persisted in my ambitious plan nonetheless."[3] A firm
believer in the naturalist theories in vogue in the late eighteenth century, she spoke of herself as "a child of Nature" and "a natural talent"

in terms similar to his own in the *Confessions*. She viewed Rousseau as her spiritual father and literary model, just as she viewed her natural father, the marquis de Pompignan, as the source of her "natural talents." She identified with Rousseau above all as a *déclassée*, both socially and intellectually. Like him, Gouges felt out of place in the petit bourgeois world of her childhood and ardently aspired to a place in the Republic of Letters. Overcoming her lack of education, fortune, and connections, she persisted against all odds to achieve a certain measure of success and unquestionable notoriety as a writer. Her name was well known (although not always well respected) in Parisian literary circles, and several of her plays were performed in major theaters of the capital.

Gouges tried her hand at every genre available, from epic poetry to billboard writing, but her greatest ambitions were as a playwright and political writer—two genres traditionally dominated by men. Among the last of her thirty plays is *Les Rêveries de Jean-Jacques, la Mort de Rousseau à Ermenonville* (1791)—a paradoxical tribute to her literary father who disapproved so strongly both of women writers and of the theater. In 1792, Gouges sent this and other works to Bernardin de Saint-Pierre, who had been Rousseau's close friend and disciple. Perhaps aware that he shared his friend's disapproval of women writers, Gouges invoked the cult of nature for which Rousseau stood as if to excuse the irony of fate (or quirk of Nature) that had made her a writer, almost in spite of herself. "An enlightened man never disdains the literary fruit produced by Nature," she wrote him. "I consider myself one of Nature's favorite children, since I owe all my talents to her."[4] Like Genlis, who also corresponded with Bernardin de Saint-Pierre during the same period, Gouges seemed eager to win his advice and support for her literary endeavors. It is ironic indeed that both Genlis and Gouges attempted to establish a mentorship relation with a man who was generally regarded as Rousseau's literary successor and who shared his mentor's scorn for female writers. Like Henriette's appeal to Rousseau, their appeal to Bernardin de Saint-Pierre for approval of their work reflects an insecurity and ambivalence toward themselves as women writers. Their appeals for approval by male mentors reflects an anxiety of influence due in large part to the paucity of female predecessors to emulate and the lack of a strong female literary tradition on which to draw. Not surprisingly, their overtures met with a lukewarm reception. In fact, Saint-Pierre finally broke off his correspondence with Genlis because he was offended by her attacks on Rousseau.

One wonders what Bernardin de Saint-Pierre thought of Gouges's best-known play *Mirabeau aux Champs-Elysées* (1791), in which she implicitly rejects Rousseau's limited vision of female destiny. In the preface to the play, without specifically naming Rousseau, she paraphrases and then refutes his well-known tirade against women writers in *Emile*: "The sternest of our learned men grant us only the right to please," she writes. "They argue that we are fit only to run a household and that women with scholarly or literary pretensions are insufferable creatures. . . . But I believe that women can cultivate their minds and talents without neglecting their families and household duties."[5] Moreover, in the play itself, Gouges chides the revolutionary government for its failure to grant women equal rights and insists that the Revolution would not succeed unless women were allowed to play an active, constructive role in building a new society. "In vain the revolutionaries will overthrow kings and pass new laws," she maintained. "So long as nothing is done to elevate the souls of women, so long as the women themselves do nothing to become more useful and constructive, the State cannot prosper."[6] Significantly, these criticisms of the revolutionary leaders' Rousseau-inspired sexual politics are voiced in the play by Ninon de Lenclos, the famous seventeenth-century courtesan and *femme d'esprit* whom Rousseau attacked with such vehemence in the *Lettre à d'Alembert*. It is curious indeed that this same woman, whom Rousseau denounced as the most pernicious of models for his female contemporaries was Gouges's avowed role model and favorite *porte-parole* in her plays. Gouges in fact devoted an entire play to her entitled *Molière chez Ninon*, in which she again used Ninon to voice her discontent with the female condition: "I cannot bear the injustice of our condition. Men have kept all the important qualities for themselves and left only the most frivolous for us. So henceforth, I have resolved to be a man! I will no longer be ashamed of making the most of the precious gifts nature has given me."[7] The autobiographical allusions in these lines are unmistakable and echo Henriette's analysis of the female condition in her letters to Rousseau and her own decision to "become a man" for lack of satisfying options as a woman. This passage also recalls young Roland's letter to a friend in which she fantasizes about dressing as a man in order to study and travel abroad— and hence to escape the constraints of the female condition.

That Gouges could have two idols and role models so diametrically opposed as Rousseau and Ninon de Lenclos points to a fundamental tension in her view of woman's proper role in society and in her view of herself as a writer. Gouges is clearly torn between her admiration for Rousseau's importance as a precursor to the Revolution (which she celebrates in her play *Mirabeau*) and her rejection of his narrow views on women. Yet nowhere does Gouges openly acknowledge this tension in her feelings toward Rousseau. By avoiding criticizing Rousseau directly, Gouges (like Staël) was able to challenge his views on women without having to disavow her enthusiasm for his egalitarian ideals or his important influence on her development as a thinker and writer.

Despite the striking contrast in their views on woman's proper role, Gouges continued to identify intensely with Rousseau through her struggles as a writer and later as a political prisoner. During her trial, fearful that her son, an officer in the French army, might be implicated in her alleged counterrevolutionary activities, she refused to answer further questions. "I am a woman, I fear death, I dread torture," she declared, "but I have no confessions to make. My love for my son will sustain me. To die in order to accomplish one's duty is a way of extending motherhood beyond the tomb!"[8] Her claim of self-sacrifice for her son and invocation of maternal love extending beyond the tomb echo Julie's lofty pronouncements on her deathbed at the end of *La Nouvelle Héloïse*. In her last letter from prison, Gouges again invoked Rousseau and identified with his persona of persecuted virtue: "My dear son, I am going to die, victim of my ardent love for my country. . . . Like Jean-Jacques, I am sickly and feeble, and utterly lacking any talent for speech-making. Like him, I am virtuous and innocent."[9] Gouges clearly viewed Rousseau as a superior soul, victim of a narrow-minded public incapable of understanding or appreciating him, who aroused her compassion and symbolized her own frustrations as a woman writer. Like Mme Roland, executed the same week, Gouges strongly identified with Rousseau's egalitarian spirit and with his image as a scapegoat without realizing that it was in large part his narrow views on women and their decisive influence on the Jacobin leaders' policies toward women that had led to her persecution.

Genlis's Challenge to Rousseau's Views on Female Education

Gouges's enthusiasm for Rousseau forms a curious contrast to the harsh criticism of him by Genlis, who was far more traditionalist in her views on women's proper role. While Genlis was a firm advocate of the Rousseauian ideals of enlightened domesticity and motherhood, she rejected Rousseau's limited view of female capabilities and insisted on the liberating force of a solid education for women. In the preface to *Adèle et Théodore*, Genlis makes it clear that she wrote the novel in large part as a response to the principles of female education outlined in *Emile*. And in the novel itself, she proposes what was no doubt the most comprehensive, ambitious plan of studies for women in eighteenth-century France—a plan she had tested and perfected over a twenty-year period with her own daughters and pupils.

Preferring an exchange of letters in novel form to a formal theoretical treatise, Genlis used her mouthpiece, the baronne d'Almane, to illustrate what she considered the ideal education for aristocratic women of her period. The novel also chronicles the education of the d'Almanes' son by the baron and of a foreign prince by a family friend. However, the majority of the letters concern the baroness's

Portrait of Stéphanie de Genlis by Vestier. Courtesy of the Bibliothèque nationale, Paris.

education of her daughter Adèle, which she describes in minute detail over a twelve-year period in her correspondence with two close friends. In her letters, she also offers advice to these friends to help them in the education of their own children, to deal with the conflicting demands of society life and maternal responsibilities, and to recapture the affection of their wayward husbands.

Like her fictional alter-ego Mme d'Almane, Genlis had withdrawn from society to devote herself to the education of her children and pupils. Refusing to entrust their care to tutors and servants, she spent long hours teaching them their lessons, reading and conversing with them, drawing on all her talents and creativity to develop their minds and characters. Recalling her decision at age thirty to withdraw to the convent of Bellechasse with her two daughters and the four d'Orléans children, Genlis writes: "I had a such a strong inclination for scholarship and for artistic pursuits that this resolution cost me nothing. . . . I cultivated my mind and my talents with a new ardor in order to be of greater service to my students, as well as to my daughters."[10] She viewed her educational mission as an exalting, heroic, even historic task, to which she willingly devoted all her energy and remarkable gifts. On the wall above her desk hung her emblem of a lamp on a desk, with her motto below: *Pour éclairer, tu te consumes.* [You burn yourself up in order to give light.] Genlis's unselfish dedication to her pupils won her older daughter's praise and admiration: "It is curious indeed that at her age, when she was still young, pretty, and so talented, that she would renounce society life and all its pleasures in order to devote herself to her children and to their education," wrote Caroline in her journal in 1781. "I don't know how Mama withstands the life she leads: ten lessons to give every day, after which she works at her desk until two or three o'clock in the morning." Caroline then adds: "I prefer a thousand times more a quarter hour of conversation with Mama to all the parties and pleasures of Paris."[11]

Genlis was a demanding instructor and a rigorous disciplinarian who carefully monitored every moment of her students' day. However, thanks to her charismatic personality, boundless energy, and genuine affection for her charges, she was able to capture their love and enthusiasm, to draw the best from them, and to create a warm, closely knit group. Although her unexpected nomination as head tutor to the d'Orleans princes was at first widely criticized and ridiculed,[12] most people later agreed that she fulfilled her mission with great dedication and distinction. As one admirer remarked at her funeral in

December, 1830, six months after Louis-Philippe had become king: "To honor and celebrate Mme de Genlis's memory fittingly, one needs only to point out that the greatest tribute to her accomplishments now sits on the throne of France."[13] Perhaps the most eloquent tribute to Genlis's success as an educator comes from Louis-Philippe himself. Toward the end of his life, in a conversation with Victor Hugo, he recalled his arduous years as her pupil with humor, affection, and gratitude:

> She was a demanding teacher, I assure you. . . . She made us get up at six o'clock all year round. . . . She had me learn a whole range of manual skills; thanks to her, I know the basics of most trades: carpentry, masonry, blacksmithing, horse grooming. She was systematic and severe. I was afraid of her at first; I was a weak, lazy, cowardly boy; I was even afraid of mice! She turned me into a robust, hardy man with spirit. . . . My sister and I truly love Mme de Genlis.[14]

∽⊙⊙∾

Through her experience as an educator and mother, Genlis was acutely aware of the crucial influence of mothers on their daughters for good or for ill. Like Rousseau, she insisted that the moral reform of society depended above all on the positive example women set for their children; however, she argued that the education he proposed for women in *Emile* would make them singularly unfit to educate their own children and to fill the role of moral exemplar he ascribed to them in such glowing terms. Herself the victim of a negligent education, Genlis underlined the need to provide women with solid instruction to make them better wives and mothers, but also stronger and more self-reliant as individuals. In her view, the education Rousseau prescribed for women was designed to keep them in a position of inferiority and dependence and placed too much emphasis on the development of female wiles and coquetry: "Rousseau does not want women's natural cunning to be corrected because, in his view, they need it in order to captivate the men on which they depend."[15] Genlis found this view of women and of conjugal relations denigrating and pernicious, a clear prelude to marital strife and infidelities. She charged that Sophie's education in *Emile* was designed to make her a mere plaything for men. In her opinion, women had a higher destiny:

> Destined to run a household, to raise children, and to depend on a master who will expect both advice and obedience, women should be patient, prudent, and orderly, with a healthy and fair mind; it is necessary that they be familiar with a wide range of fields so that they can join in any kind of conversation with ease and grace, that they possess all the traditional feminine accomplishments [music, dance, drawing, embroidery, etc.], as well as a taste for reading. (*Adèle et Théodore*, I: 45–46)

Seizing on Rousseau's remark that woman is "the eye of man," Genlis argued that in order to fulfill this function women must receive a sound education that developed their intelligence and judgment.

The plan of education Genlis proposed for women was therefore an ambitious one, far more ambitious in fact than the education Rousseau outlined for Emile. Like the program Genlis followed with her real-life pupils, it is remarkable in its breadth, depth, order, and diversity—a rich blend of the Classical education advocated by Fénelon (history, mythology, geography, literature, Latin and Greek, etc.) and exposure to the latest discoveries in the sciences and technology, with frequent field trips to visit local artisans and factories (recalling the education of Rabelais's Pantagruel). To vary their activities and to give them an appreciation for manual labor, Genlis had her pupils at Bellechasse learn a wide range of crafts and trades, from carpentry and cabinet-making to basket-weaving. Herself an accomplished musician and artist, Genlis instructed her pupils in those areas and regularly invited famous artists such as Louis David and Hubert Robert to help in their instruction. To develop her pupils' memory, poise, and self-expression, Genlis composed a series of comedies and historical plays which they performed on a regular basis for family and friends.

Genlis attached particular importance to the study of foreign languages and was the first to popularize what would later be called the direct method (or oral approach) to language learning. In response to Rousseau's old-fashioned claim in *Emile* that few children can achieve fluency in a second language before the age of twelve or fifteen, Genlis replies: "At eight or nine years of age, all my students spoke three languages fluently and were able to read and explain prose works in all three languages."[16] In fact, at twelve years old, both Louis-Philippe and his sister Adélaïde spoke four languages fluently and translated Greek and Latin with ease. This remarkable fluency was achieved by having the children converse on a daily basis with native speakers of those languages, including a German gardener, an Italian chambermaid, and two English girls Genlis had adopted.[17] As in *Adèle et Théodore*, the day at Bellechasse was divided into four parts, each devoted to speaking a different language.

Like Rousseau, Genlis stressed the importance of good hygiene, comfortable clothing, and a healthy diet. And like Emile's tutor, she had her pupils engage in daily outdoor exercises, but with the important difference that all the exercices were coeducational, like most of their lessons. Indeed, it is the coeducational set-up of Genlis's school that constitutes its most innovative feature and that distinguishes it most strikingly from Rousseau's approach, in which girls and boys were strictly segregated and given completely different (and unequal) educations. Contrary to Rousseau, Genlis maintained that the two sexes were born with equal intellectual capacities. She contested his assertion that women were incapable of studying the exact sciences, arguing that their alleged weaknesses in these subjects were due not to any inherent intellectual inferiority, but simply to lack of training. To prove her point, she organized chemistry and physics classes for her female friends and later for her daughters and pupils. Genlis also contested Rousseau's assertion that women were incapable of exercising serious occupations: "What is to prevent women from being just as successful in every field as men, if not more so?" she asked. "There are women who have commanded armies, there are others who have ruled governments, who still reign with glory," she maintained, alluding to Catherine the Great of Russia.[18] Although Genlis remained fairly traditional in her view of woman's proper role, she recognized that improved female education was the key to the advancement of her sex. Like Wollstonecraft, she lamented the fact that so many of her female contemporaries had been denied adequate instruction and the opportunity to develop their natural talents.

Unlike Rousseau, Genlis stressed the benefits of emulation and sociability that came from educating children in groups. She charged that Emile's solitary education and his social isolation encouraged selfishness and a lack of concern for others. In response to Rousseau's claim that "Emile has all the virtue necessary to meet his own needs," Genlis retorts that this amounts to teaching egoism as a virtue: "The most despicable egoism is the foundation of the teachings underlying this work."[19] In response to Rousseau's assertion that man is born good but is corrupted by society, Genlis countered that only through education and the moral teachings of the Church could an individual become good and help build a healthy society. Like Fénelon, whose views on education strongly influenced her own, Genlis maintained that the primary function of education was to teach social responsibility and respect for others: "Education will always have the most powerful influence on the conduct and morals of a society and hence on the happiness of its people, since it serves to curb the egoism of individuals that is always so injurious to the community."[20] Convinced that children should be taught compassion for others and charity for the weak and unfortunate, Genlis made acts of charity an integral part of her pupils' education. One of these charitable acts involved Gouges, who wrote to Genlis in 1785 asking her to help secure the release of a family man imprisoned for debts. Gouges enclosed a copy of her play *L'Homme Généreux,* which told his story. Moved by the man's plight, Genlis and her pupils provided the thirty louis necessary for his release.

Genlis took issue with Rousseau's view that one should not try to teach a child too much and should never force a pupil to work against his or her will. "Children should be taught everything they are capable of learning," she maintains in her extended commentary on *Emile.* "Children must become accustomed to overcoming tedium in order to apply themselves to constructive activities; this is easily accomplished without tiring or frustrating them, provided one uses the right approach."[21] Indeed, the key to Genlis's success as an educator lay in her ability to keep her students constantly engaged in constructive activities that stimulated their interest and their desire to learn. Her educational plan, which covered infancy through adulthood, offers a remarkable balance of consistency and diversity, discipline and healthy recreation. Lessons, games, physical exercise, conversations and performances, arts and crafts all played an integral part of her program.

Like d'Epinay, Genlis underlined the fact that her own approach to education was drawn from her daily experience as the mother and educator of real children, which enabled her to join theory with practice and to gear her methods and goals to the real world. And like d'Epinay, she questioned the practical value of abstract theoretical formulations and pedagogical systems in works such as *Emile.* Always a pragmatist, Genlis maintained that the program of learning should be tailored to the individual needs and aptitudes of the student: "In education, one should be wary of absolute systems; one should reinforce a child's natural abilities, not constrain them."[22]

Herself an accomplished educator and devoted mother, Genlis found Rousseau's pretensions as a pedagogue irritating, especially in a man who openly admitted his limited experience—and questionable success—as a teacher and a parent. She nevetheless recognized Rousseau's importance as a popularizer of progressive educational ideas: "We owe to him a great number of useful precepts concerning education," she concedes in *Adèle et Théodore* (I: 389). Genlis adopted several of Rousseau's key principles, including the importance of developing a close, nurturing relationship between teacher and pupil, the value of daily walks and outdoor exercise, and the need to adapt the course of studies to the age and aptitudes of one's pupils. However, she maintains that Rousseau stole his most useful ideas from other educational theorists: "Rousseau took everything that is truly useful in his book from Seneca, Montaigne, Locke, and Fénelon," she charges (I: 199–200). In *Adèle et Théodore*, she calls attention to all the ideas that Rousseau took from each of these authors. Regarding Fénelon, for example, she comments: "Concerning women's natural weaknesses and the best way to correct them, as well as the talents and qualities that should be cultivated in them, Rousseau did little more than repeat Fénelon" (I: 200). Even Rousseau's most useful precept—not to overload a child with material beyond his comprehension simply to impress people—was taken from Montaigne, she claims. Genlis acknowledges nonetheless that Rousseau was responsible for popularizing this idea which, intelligently applied, had exerted a positive effect on educational practice. However, in her view, Rousseau had taken this notion too far in the education of Emile. "It is regrettable that, after offering such wise and useful advice, Rousseau did not realize the disadvantages of going to the opposite extreme," remarks Genlis. "In fact, he wound up proposing a plan of education as defective as the one he opposed (*Adèle et Théodore* I: 201–2). According to Genlis, Rousseau's poor judgment in this regard led to widespread misapplications of this same precept among his followers, with disastrous consequences for a whole generation of children raised in the 1770s and 1780s:

> I have seen children left entirely to themselves and displaying a rustic crudeness, an ineptitude, and a lack of discipline that left me dumbfounded; and what surprised me even more was to hear that they were being raised according to the teachings of Rousseau. . . . While it is true that Rousseau gives his students a

great deal of independence, he certainly does not intend for the teacher to leave them to their own devices; quite to the contrary, Rousseau wants the teacher to be with his students at all times, instructing them both through conversations and by example, and always keeping a watchful eye over them. (*Adèle et Théodore*, I: 389–90)[23]

Although Genlis acknowledges that she and other educators owed a great deal to Rousseau, she laments the fact that his pedagogical theories had been misunderstood and misapplied all too often by parents and educators alike.

In her memoirs, Genlis is especially critical of Rousseau's negative influence on the evolution of female education during the same period:

The education of girls has gone through many ups and downs as well. For a long time, people only wished to give them musical talents and social graces, without being at all concerned with cultivating their minds. . . . We went from this type of education to the opposite extreme, in which girls were taught only to be good housewives, as if ignorance and lack of refinement would guarantee their chastity, and as if it were impossible for an educated woman to run a house well. It was decided that women should neither read nor write, nor cultivate the arts. (*Mémoires*, Barrière ed., 344)

Regarding this second trend, clearly inspired by Book V of *Emile*, Genlis comments: "Yet wouldn't it have been a shame if Mme de Grollier and Mme Le Brun had never painted, if Mme de Mongeroux had never played the piano, if other women had never written?" One can read this as a justification of Genlis's own vocation as a writer and musician, who nevertheless was deeply devoted to her children and very conscientious about household management.

Despite these misgivings about Rousseau's pedagogical methods, Genlis frequently cites *Emile*, at times to challenge his views on education but, more often, to praise his ideas and their positive influence on childrearing practices. For example, after accusing him of plagiarizing Locke, Genlis concedes that Rousseau was more persuasive than the English philosopher and consequently more successful in spreading his progressive educational theories and methods than Locke himself. "The English philosopher seemed only to be offering advice, and no one in France adopted his method," remarks Genlis. "Rousseau reiterated the same views, but he did not advise, he ordered—and was obeyed" (*Adèle et Théodore*, I: 91). Similarly, Genlis praises Rousseau for encouraging mothers to take a more active role in the education and upbringing of their children. However, she feels he had exaggerated the importance of maternal breastfeeding, and she underlines the social inconvenience that nursing posed for some women. She herself had not breastfed her own children, noting that it had not yet become fashionable in the mid-1760s when they were born. Yet in every other way, Genlis (like her fictional representative Mme d'Almane) admirably fulfills the ideal of enlightened mother-educator that Rousseau had successfully popularized in *Julie*.

Genlis's Ambivalence toward Rousseau and His Works

Genlis's response to Rousseau was by no means limited to his views on education. In the course of a literary career that spanned more than five decades, she responded to all his major works, carefully analyzing their style, substance, and influence on the public, as well as what they revealed about his character. Her comments are a curious mixture of praise and blame and range in tone from profound admiration to violent scorn, reflecting a deep ambivalence toward Rousseau both as a writer and as a man.

Genlis's ambivalence toward Rousseau mirrors his own ambivalence toward women, of which she offers a penetrating analysis. In *Adèle et Théodore*, she underlines the paradoxical nature of her female contemporaries' enthusiasm for an author she considers a blatant misogynist: "It is above all to women that *Emile* owes its tremendous success; they generally praise Rousseau with enthusiasm, although no author has criticized them more," she observes (I: 203). Like Wollstonecraft, Genlis suggests that women forgave Rousseau's harsh criticisms because he wrote of them with such eloquence and passion, which in her view made his appeal to women all the more dangerous: "An author who sacrifices everything to the desire to impress and sway his readers is incapable of producing truly useful works, regardless of his talent," she insists. "It is therefore not surprising that Rousseau's writings have had such a pernicious influence on the public. There is certainly no novel more dangerous than his *Nouvelle Héloïse*."[24]

In the preface to *Adèle et Théodore*, Genlis launches a veritable tirade against Rousseau. Outraged by what she considers the immorality of his life and writings, by his hypocrisy and bad taste, Genlis cautions her female readers to resist his seductive eloquence:

> I wanted to protect young mothers, to whom I have dedicated this work, from a dangerous enthusiasm that can only lead them astray. A young woman who is convinced that Rousseau is one of the best writers of this century will read *Emile* and *La Nouvelle Héloïse* with profound admiration. Such enthusiasm is all the more pernicious when it is an unscrupulous author who inspires it. . . . What principles can there be in a man who, in one of his prefaces, claims: "A girl who, in spite of the title of this book, dares to read a single page, is forever lost to virtue"—and who then publishes this same work about which he has such an opinion? (ix–x)

Genlis is highly critical of the fact that Rousseau presents Wolmar, an atheist and dispassionate philosopher, as a model of human perfection. Not only does she find *Julie* immoral, but boring and poorly written as well, despite occasional flashes of brilliance: "What revolting details in *La Nouvelle Héloïse*, what emphatic and ridiculous phrases, not to mention that tedious episode about Laure!" (xii–xiii). She makes similar criticisms of the plot and style of *Emile*, underlining the incongruities between the work's stated pedagogical and moral function and the awkward novelistic frame in which it is presented: "What are we to make of the romantic portions of *Emile*, in a work that is supposed to have a strictly moral purpose?" she asks. "And what is the point of Sophie's extravagant passion for the fictional character Télémaque?" (xiii). This leads her to conclude matter-of-factly: "It is neither in the plots of his works, nor in his characters that Rousseau demonstrated that he had genius" (xiii). Most of these comments are made in long footnotes that invade the page, sometimes to the point that there is scarcely any text left to sustain the notes. With each successive edition of *Adèle et Théodore*, Genlis added further notes, which explains their excessive number and intrusive length.

Anticipating the ad hominem attacks of later Rousseauphobe critics like Sainte-Beuve, Genlis uses the blunt disclosures of personal failings in the *Confessions* as a point of departure for criticism of Rousseau's other works. Indeed, the moralist in Genlis makes the confusion of the man and his works inevitable. She describes Rousseau's autobiography as a monstrous and disgusting work that will forever tarnish his memory. She wonders if he wrote it out of envy and hatred for his enemies or simply out of sheer madness. In her view, Rousseau was a cynical hypocrite, whose behavior was in constant contradiction with what he preached: "Few men have pushed inconsistency and contradictions in character so far," she charged. "He has made admirable statements about good morals, and yet he wrote the most licentious novel; he has published attacks on stage productions of any kind, and yet he composed an opera; he has severely criticized fathers who failed to raise their children themselves, and yet he abandoned all his own. . . . " (xii). But nowhere is his hypocrisy more flagrant and revolting, she maintains, than in his *Confessions*:

> I do not think there is another work so pernicious as this abominable, insipid book. In other works of this kind, if vice reveals itself with such boldness, at least it does not assume the sacred name of virtue; but here is a man who accuses himself of having shown the basest ingratitude toward the most admirable benefactor, of having changed religions in exchange for money, of having violated basic morals, of having committed a theft and then falsely accused an innocent person, . . . and who, after all these confessions, concludes that no one on earth can in truth consider himself a better man than he. (xi)

In Genlis's view, Rousseau's boastful claim about absolute sincerity was a mere pretext for hypocrisy and for shameless self-exhibition. The prudish Countess was particularly outraged by Rousseau's pompous praise of Mme de Warens, whom he describes as a "celestial, pure, angelic soul," but whom Genlis refers to as "the shame and disgrace of her sex, a woman who cold-bloodedly indulges in the vilest licentiousness." (xi)[25] She then apologized to her readers for even citing such a work, but insisted that she felt compelled to expose its immorality to protect the public against its pernicious influence: "It is with regret that I cite a work of this sort; I resolved to do so only because, in my view, the different excerpts and judgments made available to the public have failed to show how despicable and revolting a work it is" (xi).

   Genlis's two other main charges against Rousseau were that he was both a plagiarist and a failed educator. She accused him of imitating Richardson in *Julie* and of plagiarizing Locke and other educational theorists in *Emile*. She wondered why everyone found his writings so original. Yet, as we have seen, Genlis frequently cited *Emile* in *Adèle et Théodore*, at times to challenge Rousseau's views on education but, more often still, to praise his ideas and their positive influence on childrearing practices. Moreover, despite her insistence in her *Mémoires* that *Emile* was the most boring book she had ever read, she praised it elsewhere as "Rousseau's loveliest and most useful work."[26] Finally, in stark contrast to her attacks on Rousseau in the preface to *Adèle et Théodore*, Genlis praised him—in a work written for her pupil Louis-Philippe—as a genius with a penetrating mind, who had been misunderstood and maligned by his contemporaries: "He possessed true genius; his mind was both noble and refined. He understood men and the world a thousand times better than the other *philosophes* who saw him only as a misanthropic boor."[27]

Genlis clearly was a victim of the same enthusiasm for Rousseau that she denounces so vigorously in her female contemporaries. She herself recognizes this ambivalence in the preface to *Adèle et Théodore*. To charges by Rousseau's admirers that she had not sufficiently praised *Emile* in her earlier writings, she replies: "Quite to the contrary, I feared I had not sufficiently criticized a book so reprehensible in so many ways; and in fact, deep down inside, I did not feel entirely impartial toward a man who, despite all his faults, errors, and indiscretions, possessed such superior talents and attractive personal qualities" (viii).

Genlis's Unlikely Friendship with Rousseau

Genlis's ambivalence toward Rousseau may have stemmed in part from her close but stormy friendship with him, which she describes in detail in the second volume of her ten-volume *Mémoires*.[28] There she relates how Sauvigny, a dramatist friend who knew Rousseau, revealed that her husband was planning to play a trick on her by bringing the actor Préville, disguised as Rousseau, to visit her. A few weeks later, Sauvigny mentioned that Rousseau had heard of her talents as a harpist and was eager to hear her play. She consented but, convinced that it would only be Préville in disguise, she was amused at the prospect of outwitting her husband. Yet it was the real Rousseau who came. Mme de Genlis felt perfectly at ease, far more relaxed and witty than she would have been had she known it was really Rousseau, given her usual shyness with strangers. After chatting with him gaily for a while, she played the harp and sang some arias from his *Devin du village*. Rousseau found her charming—"the gaiest, most natural, and least pretentious young woman he had ever met" he later told Sauvigny—and promised to dine with them the next day. No sooner had Rousseau left than Mme de Genlis burst out laughing. Her husband was dumbfounded by her behavior, but not less so than Mme de Genlis when she learned the truth. Embarrassed at her giddy behavior, she made her husband and Sauvigny promise never to tell Rousseau about the misunderstanding.

Rousseau returned to dine the following day as promised, after which (according to Genlis) he was a daily visitor in their home for six or seven months. Genlis's first impressions of Rousseau were extremely favorable, and her detailed account of his second visit expresses genuine affection and admiration for him. "I never met a more pleasant and less imposing man of letters," she recalls. "He spoke of himself in a simple, modest manner and of his enemies without bitterness" (II: 7). He spoke to her about his *Confessions*, portions of which he had recently read to private gatherings. However, he added that she was too young to obtain from him the same favor. He then asked if she had read any of his works. When she admitted she had not, he wanted to know why, which was especially embarrassing because he was looking straight at her: "He had small, piercing, deeply set eyes that seemed to penetrate into the eyes of others and to read into the depths of their soul. It seemed to me that he would have instantly detected a lie or subterfuge" (II: 7), she remarked, echoing the popular image of Rousseau as a *connaisseur du cœur humain*. Feeling it would be useless to lie, Genlis blushingly admitted that she had not read his works because they were thought to contain statements against religion. "I may not be orthodox in matters of religion," he replied, "but no one has spoken of the Christian faith with greater conviction or sensibility" (II: 8). Rousseau respected her candor, but wanted to know why she had blushed. She explained that she had been afraid of displeasing him. He praised her for this reply which he found so "naïve." In any case, he added, his works were not written for women of her age, but she would do well to read *Emile* in a few years (presumably to aid her in the education of her children). He went on to describe the intense pleasure he had experienced while writing *La Nouvelle Héloïse* and then recited his one-act play *Pygmalion* from memory "in a most spirited and convincing manner." (Genlis was so taken with Rousseau's play that she later wrote a sequel to it in 1798 titled *Galatée*, which was performed in the home of friends in Berlin during her exile there.) All in all, Genlis was charmed by her new friend: "I found him very sociable and vivacious; he had a charming smile, full of gentleness and finesse" (II: 9). Moreover, he was a true connoisseur of music, which he discussed with great passion and understanding, although (in her view) he was a far better lyricist than composer. Genlis proudly recalls that Rousseau later gave her a complete set of his songs, entirely copied in his hand—underscoring the fact that it was their common love for music (and not their literary affinities) that formed the basis of their friendship.

In a letter to Bernardin de Saint-Pierre in 1786, Genlis gives a far more somber account of this second meeting with Rousseau, particularly of his comments to her concerning his *Confessions* and his views on religion. In this account, she claims that Rousseau confided to her: "I alone had the courage to confess all my faults: that I stole, that I slandered innocence, that I changed my religion for money and advancement." Genlis claims that she was completely taken aback by Rousseau's disconcerting frankness: "While he spoke, I looked at him dumbfounded, and I shuddered down to my very soul. It was a terrible feeling that made an indelible impression on my memory."[29] The self-accusations Genlis attributes to Rousseau in her letter curiously echo the accusations she herself makes against him in the preface to *Adèle et Théodore* in her virulent critique of the *Confessions* cited earlier ("here is a man who accuses himself of . . . having changed religions in exchange for money, of having violated basic morals, of having committed a theft and then falsely accused an innocent person. . . . "). One could argue that Genlis fabricated this alternate account of her conversation with Rousseau, just as some critics claim she fabricated the one in her memoirs.[30] However, given Bernardin de Saint-Pierre's veneration for Rousseau and his irritation with anyone who dared criticize him, coupled with Genlis's eagerness to maintain her friendship with him, it seems unlikely that she would have invented such a story.

Why then did Genlis omit this portion of the conversation with Rousseau in her memoirs? Perhaps she wished to preserve the lighthearted tone of her earlier version, sensing it would better please the public, whose devotion to Rousseau was at a high point when she first published the account of their friendship in 1803. Her decision to retain essentially the same account in the final version of her memoirs published in 1825 may reflect the same reasoning. In a sales pitch to prospective readers, Genlis draws attention to her acquaintance with important eighteenth-century literary figures as a major selling point of her memoirs and insists on the veracity of her recollections: "I was personally acquainted with almost all the famous writers of the past century," she maintains. "I can therefore claim to leave authentic memoirs about the literary world spanning more than a half century" (I: 3). This may explain why she was unwilling to alter her earlier account of the friendship, despite challenges to her sequencing of events by Musset-Pathay in his 1821 biography of Rousseau.[31]

In any case, Genlis claims in her *Mémoires* that Rousseau had been coming to dine in their home almost every day for five months without showing any signs of susceptibility or capriciousness when the first falling-out occurred. He was fond of a particular wine from the Genlis country estate and agreed to accept two bottles as a gift. When her husband sent him twenty-five bottles instead, Rousseau felt insulted and returned them all. Mme de Genlis soothed his wounded pride by sending him two bottles with a long letter of apology, although he never completely forgave her husband.

According to Genlis, the friendship broke off completely two months later, again due to Rousseau's boorishness. She and her husband had persuaded him to attend the opening of Sauvigny's play *Le Persifleur* at the Comédie-Française. Although Rousseau insisted that he never went to the theater and avoided showing himself in public, he agreed to come when they promised to sit in a screened box with a private entrance. Yet when M. de Genlis began to close the grate, Rousseau objected and insisted that he would be hidden behind them. He kept advancing his head, however, and the audience soon recognized him, but his presence did not cause much of a stir. Although their friend's play was a great success, Rousseau grew irritable and after the performance refused to dine with them as he had promised. The next day, Rousseau angrily informed Sauvigny that he would never see Mme de Genlis again because she had taken him to the theater simply to exhibit him "like a wild animal at a fair." Genlis considered herself completely blameless and countered that Rousseau was suffering from wounded pride at his failure to attract attention. Tired of his capriciousness, she refused to see him again, despite his efforts to renew their friendship a few years later when, at his request, she obtained a key for him to the Mousseaux gardens. "Although deep in my heart I still felt a strong attachment to him, I was firm in my refusal to see him again" (II: 264).

⚬⊚⊚⚬

Some scholars question the veracity of Genlis's account of her friendship with Rousseau because of some rather obvious discrepancies in dates.[32] T. C. Walker even suggests that Genlis largely fabricated the account in order to attract a larger reading public for her memoirs when they were first published in serialized form in 1801–1803, at a time when she was in desperate financial straits and eager to re-establish herself as a literary figure after her return from exile. My own approach has been to take Genlis's account of the friendship more or less at face value (except for the dates, which are clearly in error) and to use her comments about Rousseau to better understand her ambivalence toward his character and writings.

What then does Genlis's account of her friendship with Rousseau reveal? As was the case with d'Epinay, Genlis's account of the beginnings of their friendship expresses genuine affection for him and appreciation for his positive qualities: his charm, candor, naturalness, and penetrating mind. Like d'Epinay, Genlis expresses great surprise and disappointment to discover the negative side of Rousseau's character: his hypersensitivity, excessive pride, and boorishness. And, as with d'Epinay, Genlis's irritation with Rousseau's capriciousness caused her affection for him to sour, giving way to a passionate animosity that later prompted her to attack his character and writings with startling vehemence. What distinguishes Genlis's description of Rousseau from Roland's and most other memorialists of the period is that she did not praise his literary talents—his most celebrated quality—claiming she had not yet read his works. This did not prevent her from adding a footnote attacking his writings on religion after reporting his defense of them to her during their second meeting: "If I had been familiar with his works, I would have agreed that he spoke of religion with the most touching eloquence," she writes, "but I would have had the courage to add that his baffling inconsistency in such matters was all the more reprehensible and revolting, since often in the same work, as in *Emile* for example, he placed eloquent praise for the Gospel side by side with blasphemies" (II: 8, n. 1). This footnote gives us a foretaste of Genlis's vigorous attacks on *Emile* in her later writings.

Unlike the majority of Rousseau's other friends and admirers, Genlis claims she was drawn to him by his talents as a composer and not by his talents as a writer—a point she emphasizes in her *Mémoires*. She begins her account of their friendship with what amounts to a disclaimer:

> Although I had not yet read a single line of his works, I felt a strong desire to meet such a famous man. He particularly interested me as the composer of *Le Devin du village*, a charming work that will always please those who value naturalness; for the lyrics of Rousseau's opera are perfectly suited to the music, a feat that has not been achieved since then to this degree of perfection except in Monsigny's comic operas and in the grand operas of Gluck. (II: 1)

This disclaimer served a dual purpose: it allowed Genlis to express her genuine affection and admiration for Rousseau as a person and composer without being embarrassed by her sharp criticism of what she later "discovered" about him in his writings (and notably the *Confessions*). At the same time, it allowed her to criticize his character and writings in her later works in accordance with her personal convictions without appearing to betray their earlier friendship. Thus Genlis, like Gouges, found an effective (although very different) strategy for dealing with her ambivalent feelings toward Rousseau and for masking the contradictions in her response to his writings without betraying her convictions.

When *did* Genlis finally read Rousseau? In her *Mémoires*, she notes that she still had not yet read either *Emile* or *Julie* at the beginning of her service as *dame d'honneur* to the duchess of Chartres in 1772. According to her biographer Gabriel de Broglie, Genlis did not read Rousseau's work until she was twenty-eight (and hence not before 1774).[33] In any case, she must have read *Emile* sometime before she took charge of the duc de Chartres's children in 1776, for in her *Mémoires* (III: 152, n. 1), she denies the charge made by the duc de Montpensier that she was raising the young princes "à la Jean-Jacques," although she admits that her plan did somewhat resemble that of *Emile*. However, it was not until the publication of *Adèle et Théodore* in 1782 that Genlis presented her first and most comprehensive critique of Rousseau's writings. In the preface, as we have seen, she offers detailed criticism of the *Confessions*, *Julie*, and especially *Emile*.

In the course of Genlis's ten-volume *Mémoires*, there are seventeen or eighteen passages referring to Rousseau, about half of which are to some degree unfavorable, the rest relatively favorable. They deal for the most part with her opinion of his works and make no further reference to her friendship with him. For example, toward the end of volume 1, Genlis offers her most balanced appraisal of Rousseau's talents as a writer. She praises the naturalness and harmony of his style, which she sees as a refreshing exception to the pompousness and artificiality that, in her view, characterized most other writers of the post-Enlightenment period:

> Almost all the works of this period suffer from a false brilliance and from a pedantic, bombastic tone. Even Rousseau did not escape these defects, but at least they do not dominate his usual style of writing, which in general is harmonious, natural, and unpretentious. However, as a stylist, he is far inferior to Buffon and to our other great prose writers; for, in addition to occasional lapses into grandiloquence, his works are flawed by awkward expressions and frequent errors in usage. (I: 374–75)

This fair-minded assessment of Rousseau's strengths and weaknesses as a writer contrasts with the one-sided and generally negative critiques of Rousseau found in Genlis's later works.

Genlis's Later Writings on Rousseau

Despite her disagreement with many of Rousseau's ideas, Genlis paid an affectionate tribute to him in her memoirs and in a five-act play titled *Jean-Jacques dans l'Ile de Saint-Pierre*, performed by the Comédie-Française in late 1791 to celebrate the inauguration of his statue in the Pantheon. (Gouges's *Rêveries de Jean-Jacques* was written during the same period, perhaps for the same event, but was never performed; like Genlis's play, it is drawn largely from Rousseau's own works and reflects his growing popularity during the revolutionary era.) In contrast to her sharp criticism of Rousseau in the preface to *Adèle et Théodore*, Genlis describes him in her play as "the most moral and religious of men." In her *Mémoires* (VI: 359), Genlis claims that her play rekindled the public's waning enthusiasm for Rousseau and that it was instrumental in gaining a place for him in the Pantheon. Arnold

Engraving by Porreau of Chéradane's portrait of Mme de
Genlis at age seventy. Courtesy of the Bibliothèque
nationale, Paris.

Rowbotham dismisses this claim as mere "wishful thinking" and, citing reviews of the play, insists that "the work obtained only a meagre
success, which the author owed more to the public's patriotism than
to her own taste or talents." However, his bias against Genlis is clear
when he refers, in Rousseau-like fashion, to "her insatiable desire to
become a writer," even though she was by then already a best-selling
writer with an international reputation. Rowbotham does convincingly
argue that Genlis hoped to capitalize on the public's enthusiasm for
Rousseau in order to promote her literary career.[34] (One could make
the same argument about Gouges's play and Staël's *Lettres sur Rousseau*.)
More importantly, I would argue, Genlis chose to pay public homage
to Rousseau to prove her devotion to republican ideals at a time when
she was increasingly under attack by enemies of the Orleanist faction.

This argument is supported by the fact that in her *Discours sur la Suppression des Couvents*, also published in 1791, Genlis denied La Harpe's claim that she had spoken of Rousseau with scorn: "I have never spoken of Jean-Jacques Rousseau with anything but the strongest admiration."[35] Given her scathing attacks on Rousseau a decade earlier in the preface to *Adèle et Théodore*, this assertion would appear completely incongruous were it not politically motivated.

That political opportunism lay behind Genlis's shifting responses to Rousseau is further illustrated by the fact that, toward the end of Napoleon's reign, when both republicanism and the author of the *Social Contract* had fallen out of favor, Genlis resumed her attacks on Rousseau with renewed vigor. For example, in *De l'Influence des femmes sur la littérature française* (1811), she criticized the exaltation of sensibility and desire in *Julie* because of the pernicious influence she felt it had had on public morals and aesthetic tastes—particularly as reflected in the politics and literature of the revolutionary era. "It was thanks to Rousseau that the vogue of exalted feelings and reckless love became so fashionable in literature," insists Genlis.

> The eloquence of political speech-makers completed the process of collective degeneration. In the eyes of the new literary hacks who suddenly flooded the public with their writings, emotional outpourings and exaggeration were seen as signs of sensibility, senseless gibberish as profoundness, extravagance and eccentricity as marks of genius. This deplorable state of literature . . . was but a salutary crisis. The political excesses of the Revolution made us realize the inestimable value of a firm, just, and paternal government, just as the literary excesses of the period showed us the danger of deviating from solid principles.[36]

In contrast to the passage in the *Mémoires* cited earlier where Genlis views Rousseau as a welcome exception to the literary trends of the revolutionary era, here she attacks him as a principal *source* of those trends.

To illustrate Rousseau's negative influence on French literature after the Revolution, Genlis provides a detailed critique of Mme Cottin's novel *Claire d'Albe*. It is a transparent imitation of *Julie*, with the important difference that Cottin's heroine yields to her adulterous passion on her deathbed and then dies after receiving her husband's generous forgiveness. Although Genlis is highly critical of *Claire d'Albe*, she recognizes its importance in literary history as a precursor to the Romantic novel (or what she refers to as *le genre passionné*): "Mme Cottin's novel is defective in every way, . . . revoltingly immoral and utterly lacking in verisimilitude," she remarks in *De l'Influence des femmes.* "However, it is impossible to pass over it in silence, for it had the sad distinction of launching a new school of novelists by representing for the first time . . . a virtuous heroine yielding without restraint or shame to an illicit passion" (346). Genlis attributes the flaws in Cottin's novel to the atmosphere of the Terror during which it was written, "a time during which tyrants had outlawed good taste as well as good morals . . . and during which writers, in a barbaric style, perverted every impulse of the soul. Their swordlike pens drenched in blood drew nothing but false, terrifying pictures" (345–46).

For a royalist like Genlis, who idealized the moral and aesthetic restraint of seventeenth-century French literature—exemplified by the flawless style of *La Princesse de Clèves* and the virtuous self-denial of Mme de La Fayette's heroine—Revolution and Romanticism went hand in hand. In her view, the moral and political excesses of the Revolution were clearly linked to a dangerous exaltation of sensibility and passion, which she traced back to Rousseau. Genlis's objections to the Rousseauian idealization of sensibility and romantic love were therefore moral and aesthetic in nature rather than feminist, although—like Mary Wollstonecraft—she viewed it as a serious obstacle to female autonomy and self-control.

At the age of seventy-five, Genlis embarked on an ambitious project to rewrite the *Encyclopédie* ("that monstrous collection of all the lies and misconceptions of the philosophes")[37] and the major texts of the *encyclopédistes* to purge them of their immoralism, atheism, and anarchism. For lack of time and support, she was forced to abandon her original project. However, in 1820, she did publish a three-volume version of *Emile*, laboriously edited with a large number of footnotes and many deletions (particularly of passages dealing with religion and sex). On the whole, the commentary in Genlis's footnotes is highly critical, but occasionally the tone shifts unexpectedly from blame to praise. "The description in this passage is exquisite," remarks Genlis at one point.[38] "This passage is quite remarkable," she comments in another (II: 94). Elsewhere we find: "Here the author is completely correct" (II: 230). And later: "These are all excellent observations" (III: 37). However, these rare notes of praise are lost in the mass of hostile criticism with which Genlis fills the bottom margins of the book. She is particularly critical of Rousseau's style, which she finds awkward, vague, pompous, and filled with improprieties. "What language! Such ridiculous expressions and phony sentiments," she exclaims at one point (III: 178). "It is impossible to express so many commonplaces so awkwardly," she declares elsewhere (III: 304). Yet, in her view, the impropriety of Rousseau's style perfectly reflects that of his ideas: "The coarseness of his language is perfectly suited to that of his ideas," she asserts. "One never finds such peculiar phrasing in the works of Fénelon, Massillon or Buffon" (II: 229, 394). Given Genlis's nostalgia for the restrained elegance and strict conventions of the high Classical style of Bossuet and Fénelon, it is not surprising that she would find fault with the author of *Emile*. One wonders why Genlis took such pains to edit and annotate a work which she describes in her *Mémoires* as the most boring book she had ever read, so full of sophisms and senseless exaggerations that it would require a note for every line to combat them (VI: 164). Perhaps Genlis felt that, in spite of its shortcomings, *Emile* was such a remarkable manual of pedagogy that, properly reshaped, it would provide an excellent vehicle for her own ideas on education.

Genlis's 1820 edition of *Emile* was followed by a similarly "corrected" version of Voltaire's *Siècle de Louis XIV* later the same year and in 1822 by *Les Dîners du Baron d'Holbach*, a series of satirical renditions of conversations among the philosophes of the d'Holbach circle. The sketches are both insightful and amusing, thanks to Genlis's careful readings of their works and her personal acquaintance with the key figures of the group. Rousseau is presented in a more positive light than in her other works of this period. Although Genlis pokes fun at his boorishness, she dissociates him from the other philosophes and praises him for the independence of his thought. In contrast to her laborious rewrites of Rousseau and Voltaire, which were largely ignored by the public and press, *Les Dîners du Baron d'Holbach* met with considerable success. Never had Genlis criticized and ridiculed the works and personalities of the *Encyclopédistes* with such force or wit. Her central criticism was that, with the exception of Rousseau's *Social Contract*, they offered no constructive alternative to the system they sought to demolish, which in her view had led to the political and moral chaos of the revolutionary era. Although the press was quick to dismiss her arguments as reactionary, the conservative public of the Restoration relished her witty satire of the d'Holbach circle.

Genlis's and Gouges's Insecurity as Writers

In his biography of Genlis, Gabriel de Broglie maintains that she was above all an autodidact, hard-working and brilliantly gifted, but deeply marked by her lack of formal instruction. Throughout her life, Genlis was haunted by a sense of intellectual inadequacy which neither her fame as an author and educator, nor a lifetime of voracious reading had overcome. Her insecurity may account for her rigid conformism to traditions and conventions, both literary and social, as Broglie has suggested.[39] What is certain is that Genlis was an overachiever in the best sense of the term, determined to offer her daughters, pupils, and readers the solid instruction she herself had been denied. Recalling the negligent education she received at home from her chambermaid, while her brother attended a prestigious boarding school in Paris, she later mused: "It is curious indeed that someone who has written so much was never really taught how to write" (*Mémoires*, I: 53).

This sense of intellectual inadequacy is deeper still in Gouges, whose humble Occitan origins proved an even greater handicap: "They never taught me anything," she later confided. "Brought up in a region where French is poorly spoken, I never learned its rules."[40] For this barely literate playwright, who held a pen with difficulty, the composition of texts was a laborious business indeed. Gouges's written French remained so rudimentary that she was forced to dictate most of her works to secretaries in her heavy Occitan accent; this may explain the spontaneous, declamatory, and at times unpolished quality of her style, her colloquialisms, and her tendency to digress. She was, moreover, painfully aware of the obstacles she faced in launching a literary career: "I don't know the art of composition; all I do is speak a natural language, with my imagination as my only guide," she acknowledged. "With few connections to help me and no mentor to guide me in my work, ... how do you expect me to succeed?"[41] Spurred on by the flow of a lively imagination and spontaneous wit, as well as by strong political convictions—feminist, republican, and abolitionist—Gouges persisted against all odds to achieve a certain measure of success and unquestionable notoriety. Rather than try to hide her failings as a writer, she defiantly called attention to them, even gloried in them with a kind of masochistic pleasure, adopting an attitude of mockery and self-mockery that recalled (and perhaps imitated) Rousseau's in his preface to *Julie*. "Let no one claim that I ever was foolish enough to believe that my plays are masterpieces," she declares in the preface to one play.[42] And in the preface to another, she attempts to disarm her critics by openly admitting her weaknesses as a writer: "I beg my readers' full indulgence for all the flaws in my writing: errors in French, weaknesses in construction and style, lack of knowledge, lack of wit, lack of interest. . . . Yet I am proud of my ignorance, for I write with my soul."[43]

On the whole, Genlis was far less willing than Gouges to openly express her feelings of intellectual insecurity—a difference that perhaps reflects a certain aristocratic pride. Aside from the passages in her memoirs where she laments her negligent education, Genlis hides her sense of inadequacy beneath a mask of exaggerated self-assurance. For example, in a letter promoting the sale of her memoirs to the British government for the vast sum of 130,000 francs, Genlis unabashedly vaunts their originality and interest: "If these memoirs are published by subscription, all of Europe will subscribe," she maintained, "for they are carefully written and strikingly original and will spark great curiosity both here and abroad."[44] In the memoirs themselves, Genlis continually boasts of the ease with which she wrote and the public's enthusiastic praise for her works.

Unlike Genlis, Gouges had nothing to lose by acknowledging her failings as a writer. In contrast to the countess's outward show of self-assurance, Gouges alternated between a mask of humility and one of bravado, according to circumstances and the whim of the moment. At times, she even managed to wear both masks simultaneously. For example, in the preface to her play *Le Philosophe Corrigé*, Gouges proclaims herself a natural talent, unspoiled by the slavish imitation of past masters, whose works she had not read: "I am the product of Nature. . . . I owe nothing to book learning: I am my own creation."[45] She pointed to her ignorance as both the source—and guarantee—of her originality: "People cannot deny my originality, since I owe it to my ignorance alone. I am proud to proclaim it publicly. And you, Messieurs the grand imitators, whose frozen style chills the heart without warming the mind, leave me that precious ignorance which constitutes my only merit." Gouges openly mocked the ideal of female modesty, as well as the vanity of her male colleagues: "I don't have the advantage of being educated. . . . And since I can't imitate my male colleagues' talents or their conceit, I'll heed the voice of modesty, which suits me better in every way."[46]

The prefaces to Gouges's plays are generally far more interesting and entertaining to the modern reader than the plays themselves. For together they constitute a running dialogue with her critics, in which Gouges was always assured the final word—a rostrum from which she could address the public at a time when other means of public address were being closed to women. In these prefaces, much like Rousseau in his, Gouges responded to her critics' objections and deftly turned their arguments against them, exaggerating and mocking any gibes they might make. This bombastic humility and exaggerated deference to critical standards was a mask Gouges assumed to ingratiate herself with theater directors and literary critics in an effort to get her plays performed—a mask she quickly dropped once her plays were either rejected or performed. Then her brazen self-confidence rang out loud and clear. For example, in the second preface to *Mirabeau aux Champs-Elysées* (her most successful play), Gouges boldly vindicated her career as a political writer, claiming equality with the "*grands hommes*" who had been persecuted alongside her for their outspoken criticism of government abuses:

> My countrymen should never forget that, at a time when our country was in bondage, it was a woman who first had the courage to take up the pen to break its chains. I attacked despotism, the machinations of the Cabinet, and government vices. . . . All my friends trembled for my safety, but nothing could shake my resolve. . . . In fact, the slander and lies spread to discredit my achievements are for me a source of pride, since they show that people view and persecute me as they would a famous man.[47]

Elsewhere, Gouges proudly declared (like Mme Roland) that her heroic self-sacrifice for her country guaranteed that her name "would live on in full glory among future generations."[48]

Ever conscious of decorum, Genlis was far more adept than Gouges at feigning modesty—another reflection of her aristocratic upbringing. Genlis began her literary career in the most acceptable, "ladylike" fashion by writing pedagogical works and *théâtre de société* (light plays for private gatherings). Only when forced to support herself in exile did Genlis move into the more "public" genres of novels, essays, history, and literary criticism. Gouges, by contrast, refused to enter the Republic of Letters through the back door. Her decision to begin her self-construction as an author by writing political plays, that most public of genres, was doubly transgressive, given the strong prejudices in France at the time against both women dramatists and female activists.

Gouges's choice of the theater as her preferred literary genre also reflects her identification with the play-writing Marquis Le Franc de Pompignan, the man she claimed was her father. Yet in her autobiographical novel, *Mémoire de Madame de Valmont*, Gouges recalls his strong objections to her literary career: "Don't expect me to be reasonable about this," he warned her. "Molière's *femmes savantes* were utterly ridiculous, and women who follow their example today are the scourge of society... Let women write if they must; but, for their own good and that of society, they should never indulge in literary pretensions."[49] Le Franc's disapproval of women writers echoes that of Rousseau in *Emile*: "It does not suit an educated man to take a wife with no education," writes Rousseau in *Emile*. "But I would prefer a simple and uneducated girl a hundred times over to a woman with intellectual and literary pretensions who would turn my home into a court of literature over which she would preside," he writes. "*Une femme bel-esprit* is the scourge of her husband, of her children, ... of everyone. From the sublime elevation of her genius, she disdains all her womanly duties and soon transforms herself into a man.... She is always ridiculous and is criticized quite justly."[50] Gouges's use of similar words and phrases ("scourge," "pretension," "ridiculous") suggests that she may well have had this passage from *Emile* in mind when she wrote her memoirs. Given the complex mixture of fact and fiction that pervades Gouges's memoirs, one wonders if this letter is a satiric version of a *real* letter she received from the marquis or a parody of one she imagines he *might* have sent her. The latter interpretation is supported by the satirical tone Gouges attributes to the marquis in another passage of the letter:

> If the members of your sex were to produce works of consequence and depth, what would become of us men? We'd lose our superiority of which we are so proud. Women would govern and control us.... For that reason, I hope that the Ladies will not presume to don the philosopher's cap and that they will maintain their frivolity even in their writings. So long as they lack common sense, women will always be adorable. (60)

It is unlikely that the real Marquis de Pompignan would have written anything so blatantly self-mocking. Whatever its origins, the letter reflects the hostility and ridicule that Gouges perceived among her male contemporaries toward her literary career. The letter ascribed to

Le Franc can also be read as a satire—conscious or unconscious—of Rousseau's tirade against women writers in *Emile*. On a deeper level, the letter plays out an anxiety of influence centered on the two key father figures in her life—Jean-Jacques Le Franc de Pompignan and Jean-Jacques Rousseau—with an interesting twist on the paternal interdiction embedded in *le nom/non du père*. Gouges seems to project Rousseau's disapproval of women writers onto Le Franc, mocking his paternal interdiction in order to negate its power over her.

Gouges's love-hate relationship with these two father figures spilled over into her relation with the public, which also showed little support for her writing. Comparing the relation between dramatist and spectator to one of seduction, Gouges felt she lacked the power to capture and hold the public's interest. In the preface to *Mirabeau*, she openly expresses her sense of inadequacy:

> I present this play to the public with the same zeal and the same weaknesses that one finds in all my other works. I know that this will hardly satisfy my audience, since it is not enough to arouse the public's curiosity: One must also excite its fancy. Yet I am utterly lacking in literary coquetry, which is very different from that of pretty women. This second type of coquetry requires only the attractions of youth, whereas the first type demands hard work, experience, and talent.

Rejecting the veils, masks, and coquetry needed to please the public, Gouges presents herself as she is, but fully aware that what she is may not be enough: "I present myself here as I have always have, with all the simplicity, disorder, and raw energy of nature, and always true to myself."[51] Here, as in so many other passages in her prefaces, Gouges opposes her own simple and "natural" talents to the more artful productions of her male colleagues, proud of her originality but painfully conscious of her shortcomings as a writer. She describes her vocation (and her relation to the public) as a stormy love affair in which artifice and coquetry play no part: "For me, literature is a passion that borders on delirium," she explains. "It's a passion that has preoccupied me constantly for the past ten years of my life. Like any love affair, it has its own anxieties and torments."[52]

Genlis's relations with the public were generally less stormy than Gouges's, due no doubt to her greater willingness to follow public tastes and expectations. Her conformism to traditional norms of femininity is reflected in her choice of Mme de La Fayette and Sévigné as her literary models. Both were "proper ladies" and prominent women of the aristocracy like herself, respected and admired as much for their character as for their talents. Genlis's model as educator was Mme de Maintenon, another aristocrat highly regarded by the public. Her choice of these aristocratic women as her female role models contrasts sharply with Gouges's strong identification with Ninon de Lenclos, who like herself was a demi-mondaine of humble origins, a woman of great charm and wit, but reviled by many because of her unconventional lifestyle and outspokenness. Like Gouges, Ninon never fulfilled her potential as a writer for lack of proper training and support. Gouges's choice of Lenclos as her female idol therefore carried with it a kind of self-fulfilling prophecy, much like Genlis's choice of the highly respected Mme de Sévigné and Mme de La Fayette as her models.

Despite her cautious conformism to social and literary norms, Genlis was not afraid to take on male-dominated institutions to defend her convictions. Deeply religious and a moralist to the core, she waged a lifelong, often solitary campaign against the atheism of the *Encyclopédistes* and what she viewed as their moral and social nihilism. In 1783, d'Alembert offered her a seat in the Académie Française and the Académie's prestigious Prix Montyon d'Utilité for *Adèle et Théodore* if she would abandon her attacks on the *Encyclopédistes*. Genlis proudly refused. The prize was given instead to d'Epinay's *Conversations d'Emilie*. As for the seat in the all-male Académie, no woman would be elected to that august body until nearly two centuries later. When she heard that the prize had been awarded to her rival, Genlis replied in Gouges-like fashion: "Such injustices toward authors are only further claims to fame."[53]

Genlis's conflict with the Encyclopedists parallels Gouges's prolonged battle with the Comédie-Française and the powerful slave-trade lobby. Gouges's experience with the Comédie-Française was one of continual frustration. Her first play *Zamore et Mirza, ou L'Esclavage des Noirs* was accepted in 1785; however, pressured by powerful protectors of the slave trade, the Comédie-Française delayed performance of Gouges's abolitionist drama for several years. Gouges entered into a bitter correspondence with its directors, who were often abusive in their language. Their hostility is illustrated by the comments of one official in his review of her play *Molière chez Ninon*: "I like pretty women; I like them even better when they are easy to seduce; but I dislike seeing them anywhere but at home, and certainly not performed on stage. I reject this play."[54] Each attack on Gouges made it perfectly clear that a woman's proper place was in the parlor or in bed, but not in the theater. During this same period, the influential actor Fleury publicly remarked: "Mme de Gouges is one of those women to whom one feels like giving razor blades as a present, who through their pretensions lose the charming qualities of their sex. . . . Every woman author is in a false position, regardless of her talent."[55]

Enraged by the Comédie-Française's attempts to thwart her career as a dramatist, Gouges defiantly declared: "I'm determined to be a success, and I'll do it in spite of my enemies, in spite of the critics, in spite of fate itself. Not even ten secretaries could keep pace with the richness of my imagination. I have at least thirty plays written or in the works."[56] Gouges tried to provoke Fleury to a duel and eventually took legal action to force the Comédie-Française to perform *L'Esclavage des Noirs*. The play finally opened in December 1789, but closed after three performances. Its success was sabotaged by mediocre acting and by hecklers paid by the slave-trade lobby, which for months had mounted a vicious press campaign against Gouges and her play. The day after the opening, *La Chronique de Paris* reported: "The public heckled the production without mercy. . . . We'll simply reiterate Piron's view that, to write a good play, one needs a beard."[57] Angered by the Comédie-Française's abuse of its monopoly on theater productions and by its flagrant bias against female dramatists, Gouges proposed the creation of a national theater company dedicated to promoting works by women.[58]

Genlis and Gouges were both outraged by charges that they had recourse to ghost-writers—an accusation frequently made against successful women writers of the period. Genlis's early works were falsely attributed to La Harpe and Gouges's to her friend Mercier. To an unknown fellow-traveler in a stagecoach who claimed to have written one of her plays in exchange for her favors (carefully adding grammar errors to make it seem more "authentic"), Gouges indignantly replied: "I'm that same Olympe de Gouges that you never even met and that you are not worthy of knowing. . . . Men like you are common enough, but never forget that it takes centuries to produce a woman of my caliber!"[59] Irritated that Gouges had composed a sequel to his *Barbier de Séville* and was trying to have it performed, Beaumarchais spread similar rumors about her and even insinuated that she was incestuously involved with her son (anticipating similar charges made against

Marie-Antoinette at her trial). He then succeeded in having her play rejected by the Comédie-Française, which earlier had expressed interest in it. Gouges angrily wrote to Beaumarchais: "Why is there such invincible prejudice against my sex? And why do you say that the Comédie-Française should not perform plays by women? . . . You even claimed that I was not the real author of my plays!"[60] To defend her reputation as a dramatist, Gouges challenged Beaumarchais to a public duel of wits in which each would write a play on the same subject within a given time limit—a challenge he prudently declined.

Because of their insecurity as women writers, Genlis and Gouges both tended to overreact to criticism of their work, responding in each successive preface to criticisms made of earlier works. In *L'Intrépide*, her journal of literary criticism published in 1820, Genlis took a certain masochistic pleasure in enumerating her numerous enemies: republicans, aristocrats, atheists, liberals, ultra-conservatives, anti-feminists, and Romantics. She presents herself as the perpetual target of partisan politics, but feels gratified by the general public's continued support for her writing: "As an author, I've had problems with everyone except the public. That's the true story of my career!"[61]

Gouges was less successful and more combative in her relations with the public and seemed to savor the controversy she provoked: "I know I've often been impulsive or imprudent, but I enjoy acting that way, even if it works against me. In fact, at times I put as much effort into being a non-conformist as others put into trying to conform," she admits.[62] Yet in her démêlés with the Comédie-Française and later with the Jacobin government, Gouges frequently appealed to the public for support and vindication of her rights. For example, following the controversy provoked in 1789 by her abolitionist drama *L'Esclavage des Noirs*, Gouges called upon the public to protest the premature closing of the play. However, without protectors in high places, Gouges was helpless against the rich and powerful slave-trade lobby. In fact, the vagaries of Gouges's career as a dramatist aroused more scorn than sympathy among the general public, as would her later career as a political pamphleteer.

The Challenge to Rousseau in Gouges's
Déclaration des droits de la femme

In 1791, Gouges issued her *Déclaration des droits de la femme et de la citoyenne* [Declaration of the Rights of Woman and the Female

Citizen], a bold feminist manifesto patterned after the *Déclaration des droits de l'homme*, which it was intended both to criticize and supplant. Strongly influenced by Condorcet's *Sur l'Admission des femmes aux droits de cité* [On the Admission of Women to the Rights of Citizenship], published the previous year, Gouges's *Droits de la femme* presents a radical vision of a world in which women would enjoy full equality: political, legal, educational, and professional. Inspired above all by the feminist implications of the egalitarian vision set forth in Rousseau's *Social Contract*—implications that Rousseau and his Jacobin followers chose to ignore—Gouges's fiery manifesto can be read as a gesture of revolt against Jean-Jacques's narrow feminine ideals, which the Jacobin government had endorsed in its denial of equal rights to women and in its brutal suppression of their political activities.

Although Condorcet's writings and friendship had a tremendous influence on the development of Gouges's feminist consciousness, Gouges's feminism springs above all from her own experience as a woman—from her frustration at being denied participation in the public sphere and her disenchantment with the failed promises of the Revolution. Marginalized by her humble birth and her Occitan origins, by her lack of education and connections, Gouges resisted her exclusion by defiantly transgressing accepted norms and barriers and claiming her right to speak.

In the Preamble to her *Déclaration*, Gouges apostrophizes the revolutionary leaders with biting invective. She rejects the naturalist arguments they invoke to justify the continued subordination of women:

> Man, are you capable of being just? It is a woman who is asking you this question, and you will not take away her right to do so. Who has given you the sovereign right to oppress my sex? your strength? your talents? Survey all of nature . . . and give me, if you dare, an example of such tyrannical authority. . . . Man alone has set himself up as an exception. Bizarre, blind, puffed up with knowledge, yet—in this century of enlightenment—fallen into the most crass ignorance, he wants to rule despotically over a sex that has received every intellectual faculty. We now claim our rights to equality and to the benefits of the Revolution.[63]

Gouges's tone in this opening passage is aggressive, sarcastic, and militant. She catches the readers' interest and draws them into the text through the use of short rhetorical questions and by alternating lofty-

Anonymous watercolor portrait of Olympe de Gouges painted in 1784. Courtesy of the Musée du Louvre, Collection Rothschild, Paris.

sounding lyrical phrases (such as "sovereign right" and "tyrannical authority") with earthy, pungent colloquialisms: *"fagoté," "boursouflé,"* and *"crasse"* [botched, puffed up, and crass]. The highly personal *tu*-form of address, juxtaposed with the blunt, impersonal apostrophe "Man," expresses Gouges's impatience with—and scorn for—her male addressees and underscores the equality of the sexes to which she lays claim. Challenging the patriarchal order and naturalist rhetoric which the *Rights of Man* merely perpetuated, Gouges redefined nature in such a way that it would serve as a guarantee of women's rights, rather than as a pretext for their continued oppression: "The exercise of woman's natural rights has no limits other than the perpetual tyranny that man imposes on her. These limits must be reformed according to the laws of nature and reason." She insisted, moreover, that women's inequality was fundamentally detrimental to the health of the body politic: "Ignorance, omission, or scorn of the rights of women are the sole causes of public misery and of the corruption of governments" (102).

Erica Harth has argued that Gouges's adoption of the Rousseauist discourse of nature in her Declaration left her "stuck in a set of contradictions" between rhetoric and reality and unable, consequently, to "move beyond the meliorist solution suggested by the use of 'oppression' as an undifferentiated category for slavery, for the condition of French women, and for the Old Regime."[64] I would argue, quite to the contrary, that Gouges explicitly challenged the contradictions of naturalist rhetoric in her preface and sought to reconceptualize nature in a way that minimized the importance of physical differences (particularly sexual, racial, and class distinctions) and reaffirmed "natural" rights to equality regardless of these differences. Moreover, as Joan Wallach Scott points out, Gouges underlines human responsibility for the imposition and institutionalization of these so-called natural categories. "The destabilizing implications of her redefinition of nature were undeniable," writes Scott. "Implicit in her critique was an interpretation of liberal political theory that countered the authoritarianism of Rousseauian doctrines of the general will with more conflictual . . . notions of politics."[65] Like many writers of feminist pamphlets of her day, Gouges demanded not the institution of new rights for women, but the restoration of original natural rights of which they had been deprived.

In the body of her *Déclaration*, Gouges rewrites the seventeen articles of the *Rights of Man* from a feminist perspective. Beginning with the assertion that "Woman is born free and remains equal to man in rights," she insists that women have the same right as men to liberty, property, and resistance to oppression (102). Equal before the law and sharing the same taxes and public responsibilities, they have the right to be admitted to all positions and honors, to make the laws, and to serve as judges, she argues. Finally, Gouges maintains that full participation in public life requires full and equal education. In rewriting the *Rights of Man*, Gouges did not simply substitute the word "woman" for "man," but went far beyond the scope of the original document to complete the civil rights it guaranteed with individual rights, such as the right of an illegitimate child to inherit a portion of the father's estate and an unwed mother's right to name the father of her child and to collect child support. Insisting that "marriage is the tomb of love and trust," Gouges proposed legalizing divorce and replacing marriage with a "social contract" that would unite a couple in a form of legal cohabitation and provide for equal division of property upon separation. In these radical proposals, Gouges could not be farther from Rousseau's traditionalist views on marriage and from his narrow vision of woman's proper role in society. Indeed, her use of the term "social contract" to describe this radical departure from traditional family and gender structures can be read as a direct challenge to Rousseau's paternalistic view of relations between the sexes.

In her "Postambule," Gouges called on her fellow *citoyennes* to end the subjugation of women once and for all: "Women, rouse yourselves; the tocsin of reason is sounding. It is time to claim your rights," she urged. "Whatever the barriers put up before you, it is in your power to overcome them; you have only to desire it" (106–7). She denounced the hypocrisy and self-interest of the revolutionary leaders and insisted that the promises of the Revolution could not fully be realized until all women were allowed to exercise their rights as citizens: "O women, women, when will you stop being so blind? What advantages have you gained from the revolution? Only greater scorn, a more conspicuous disdain" (106). Anticipating feminist arguments advanced two centuries later, Gouges maintained that consciousness raising, willpower, and solidarity among women were the key to gaining equal rights. Given the iconoclastic nature of her proposals, it is paradoxical that Gouges chose to end her tract with a strong familial metaphor in which all political tensions promised to be resolved. Linking the cause of slaves and women, of the monarchy and the Assembly, Gouges concludes by declaring that the executive and legislative powers "like man and woman, should be united, but equal in strength and virtue, in perfect marriage" (112). Commenting on this passage, Joan Landes observes: "such is the power of republican rhetoric in this period, that the least domestic of women is moved to couch her demands in this form."[66]

Gouges had no illusions about how her text would be received: "As I read through this strange document, I see rising up against me the pious hypocrites, the prudish prigs, the clergy, the whole infernal band" (110). Yet her *Déclaration* failed to arouse much controversy, for it was all but lost in the stream of pamphlets and petitions that flooded the public during the first years of the Revolution. It is fairly certain, however, that Gouges's text was read by Mary Wollstonecraft, who was living in France in the summer of 1791 when it appeared and that it influenced her own *Vindication of the Rights of Woman* published in February of the following year. Other than inspiring a few parodies such as *Les Droits des Poissardes des Halles*, Gouges's text attracted little attention and was largely forgotten after her death. Ironically, Gouges's text was best remembered for a line that Michelet erroneously attributed to Sophie de Condorcet: "Woman has the right to mount the scaffold; she should also have the right to go to the rostrum and address the Assembly."[67] Of the two rights she claimed, Gouges was granted only the former. Imprisoned for her verbal attacks on Robespierre and Marat and convicted of treason for alleged political crimes, Gouges was guillotined in November 1793, the same month as Mme Roland, Marie Antoinette, and Mme du Barry, former mistress to Louis XV.

Commenting on this rapid succession of executions, all involving important female public figures, Carol Blum writes: "A symbolic foursome, they stood for women's ambitions in their principal manifestations: two who had incarnated old-style success, by embodying royalty or seducing it, and two who had essayed republican paths. . . . All four were guillotined, and their execution lent weight to the condemnation of female claims."[68]

Although Gouges's alleged political transgressions were the pretext for her trial, the accounts of her execution in the press clearly suggest that she (like Mme Roland) was punished above all for her transgression of traditional gender barriers. Both women were widely criticized for their political activities and their ambition and denounced as viragos, unnatural mothers, and whores. For example, in *La Feuille du Salut Public*, we read: "Born with an exalted imagination, Olympe de Gouges mistook her delirium for an inspiration of nature. . . . She aspired to be a statesman, and the law has punished her for having forgotten the virtues appropriate for her sex."[69] Like Roland's execution, Gouges's execution was used to warn other women to stay within the narrow limits prescribed for them by the new regime.

When a deputation of women headed by Claire Lacombe appeared before representatives of the Paris Commune to protest the ban on women's political clubs and demonstrations, they were chastised for their unfeminine behavior by Pierre-Gaspard Chaumette, Procureur de la Commune:

Since when are women allowed to renounce their sex and to turn themselves into men? And since when is it the custom for women to abandon the sacred duties of their households and the cradles of their children to enter the public sphere, the rostrum of the Assembly and the Senate, the ranks of our armies, in order to perform the duties that nature assigned to man alone? . . . In the name of nature, stay as you are, and far from envying the perils of our stormy life, be content to help us forget them in the bosom of our family. . . . Only when you are what nature intended you to be will you become truly worthy of esteem.

Chaumette evoked Rousseau's idealization of the domestic sphere as a privileged feminine space and his naturalistic arguments against women's participation in the public sphere, as if to refute Gouges's arguments against such barriers in her *Droits de la femme*. That he had Gouges in mind becomes clear at the end of his harangue, where he threatened the women before him with her unenviable fate: "Remember that virago, that man-woman, the impudent Olympe de Gouges, who was the first to set up women's societies, who abandoned the duties of her household to meddle in politics, and whose head fell beneath the avenging knife of the law."[70] According to Olivier Blanc, Chaumette was mistaken in his claim that Gouges was a founder of women's revolutionary clubs; in fact, it is doubtful whether she ever officially belonged to such a club. However, it is clear from all these commentaries that Gouges's execution, like that of other "public" women, was being used as a warning to women activists: If they did not give up their political activities and conform to the passive domestic role prescribed for them by the revolutionary government, they too would risk imprisonment and death.

Women's Role in the Public Sphere through the Eyes of Genlis and Gouges

The radical feminist vision of sexual equality that Gouges puts forth in her *Déclaration des droits de la femme* forms a sharp contrast to Genlis's equally idealized but backward-looking nostalgia for the court of Louis XIV and the salons of the ancien régime, in which aristocratic women were the supreme arbiters of manners, morals, and the arts, yet careful to stay within the bounds of decorum. In *Adèle et Théodore* and other early writings, Genlis prescribed strict boundaries (social, moral, and political) for other women to follow, which she herself discreetly ignored or blurred in her own life. Through her crucial roles as head tutor to Louis-Philippe and as secret political advisor to the duc d'Orleans, Genlis exercised considerable influence on the Orleanist faction. For example, after the King's attempted flight, Genlis dissuaded the duc d'Orléans from accepting power when it was offered to him, partly out of her belief in the divine right of kings, partly because she felt Philippe-Egalité was incapable of providing effective leadership under such difficult circumstances. To charges in the Jacobin press that she had been the leader of an Orleanist plot to seize the throne, she sarcastically replied "I didn't take part in the Revolution; for, with nine children to raise and twenty volumes to write, I didn't have time to overthrow governments!"[71] In her *Précis de ma conduite depuis la Révolution*, published in 1796, Genlis tried to dispel rumors that she had encouraged an Orleanist coalition, claiming that she had urged both Louis-Philippe and his father to withdraw from public life. Mimicking the revolutionary leaders' disapproval of female activists, she insisted on her non-partisan loyalty to whatever government had been in power: "I have always led a quiet, solitary life, solely occupied by my writing. . . . A woman should always respect the established government and obey it in good faith; this was always the rule I followed." She even made a pretense of renouncing her royalist sentiments altogether: "When the French Republic was proclaimed, I genuinely hoped that it would prevail. . . . After all it has done, the French nation would be the lowest people on earth if it restored the monarchy," she added with bitter irony—perhaps recalling the execution of her husband, the duc d'Orléans, and so many others close to her.[72] Genlis sent her *Précis* to the Minister of Justice in Paris in an unsuccessful effort to exonerate herself in the eyes of the Directoire and to gain permission to return to France.

It was only in 1800 that Genlis finally was allowed to return to Paris through the influence of her daughter Pulchérie, who had become a prominent figure in the inner social circle of the Directoire. Four years later, after supporting herself through arduous literary labors, Genlis received a generous pension and living quarters at the Arsenal from the Emperor in exchange for weekly letters in which, at his request, she offered him her opinion and advice on a variety of subjects: politics, literature, education, court etiquette, and the arts. Although she secretly viewed Napoleon as a usurper and later rejoiced at the restoration of the monarchy, she did not hesitate to flatter the Emperor to further her own interests and those of her friends and relatives, many of whom received posts or pensions from him at her request. In short, Genlis—unlike Gouges—was a political opportunist who was willing to compromise her political views in order to assure her personal and financial security.[73] By offering submission to the new regime on behalf of her sex and class, Genlis was able to write herself out of exile and into Napoleon's good graces. Through her strategy of accommodation and compromise, she ensured her power to speak and indeed her very survival—in contrast to Gouges's unyielding and aggressive political militancy, which led quite inescapably to her silencing under the Reign of Terror.

In contrast to Genlis's discreet political maneuvering behind the scenes, Gouges insisted on women's right to participate openly in the public sphere on an equal footing with men. She denounced the covert political influence of aristocratic women like Genlis as pernicious and ultimately self-defeating. With her usual brazenness, she publicly criticized Genlis for her influence on the duc d'Orleans. In her *Droits de la femme*, Gouges offers a scathing critique of the sexual politics of the ancien régime: "Through their feminine wiles, women took back what men robbed from them by force," she asserts. "For centuries, the French government was at the mercy of women and their noctural rule. . . . Everything that characterized the stupidity of men, both sacred and profane, was subjected to the avarice and ambition of the female sex" (107).

At times, Gouges seems to embrace Rousseau's ideal of motherhood and domesticity and even to echo his misogynic rhetoric. For example, in "Le Cri du sage, par une femme," one of her earliest political pamphlets, Gouges blames women's negative influence on men for the National Assembly's failure to overcome its internal divisions:

> Oh women! What have you done? . . . You have abandoned the reins of your households and driven your children away from your maternal breasts. . . . Oh seductive and perfidious sex that is both weak and all-powerful, both deceiver and deceived! You led men astray and they are now punishing you for it with their scorn. . . . You taught men your failings, subterfuges, ruses, and deceits, and in the end they have become women too.[74]

With its rhetoric of contradiction and misogynic tone, this passage easily could be mistaken for an excerpt from Rousseau's *Lettre à d'Alembert*. The main thrust of Gouges's message is to criticize the deputies' failure to provide constructive leadership. However, to make this criticism more palatable to her male readers, Gouges ascribes their lack of courage and integrity to the feminizing or castrating effect of women who have abandoned their proper domestic sphere of activity to invade the public sphere. It seems incongruous that this most undomestic, public, and progressive of women should adopt such traditionalist and misogynic language, even as a rhetorical device with which to veil her criticism of the male deputies. Yet despite her personal aversion to marriage and domesticity, Gouges was nevertheless a firm believer in Rousseau's program of moral reform. Like Rousseau and Wollstonecraft, Gouges viewed women as a main source of corruption in society, but also as the key to its regeneration. In her view, only by criticizing her sex could she best serve its interests: "I will betray it now to serve it later," she explains.[75] Like Wollstonecraft, Gouges would become one of women's boldest champions, while remaining one of their severest critics.

Joan Scott points to the contradictions in the view of women presented in the *Rights of Women*. "Gouges never escaped the ambiguity of feminine identity in its relationship to universal 'Man' and she often exploited it. On the one hand, she attacked women as they were— indulgent, frivolous, seductive, intriguing, and duplicitous—insisting that they could choose to act otherwise (like men); on the other hand, she appealed to women to unite to defend their special interests." According to Scott, one of Gouges's key strategies in her Declaration was to play with Rousseauian distinctions between artifice and nature in order to disentangle the feminine from prevailing associations with artifice and aristocracy and to identify women instead with republican virtues.[76]

In a speech before the Assemblée Législative in May 1792, Gouges argued that the Revolution would not be complete until women worked together to build a better society and to recover their natural rights and dignity: "Women, isn't it high time for a revolution to take place among us too?" she asked. "Will women always be as isolated from each other? Will they never join together except to slander their own sex and to inspire pity in men?"[77] Gouges saw women's lack of solidarity due to female rivalry, class divisions, and complicity with their male oppressors as the greatest obstacle to the attainment of equal rights. She urged her fellow *citoyennes* to be supportive of each other and more receptive to efforts by reformers like herself to improve their condition and raise their consciousness:

Women . . . have no greater enemy than themselves. Seldom do
they applaud a generous act or the accomplishment of another
woman. Few women ever learn to think like men, while most of
the others join forces with the dominant sex against their own. . . .
Oh women, of whatever rank you may be, try to be more straightforward, more generous toward each other. I can already imagine you gathered round me, like so many furies hunting me
down, ready to punish me for the audacity of offering you
advice.[78]

Despite her devotion to the cause of women's rights, Gouges remained
ambivalent toward her sex and pessimistic regarding her efforts to
bring about a second revolution within the Revolution. Her frustration may explain why here and in certain other key passages of her
Déclaration, Gouges adopts (unwittingly perhaps) the misogynic tone
and language of the very leaders whose policies she was striving to
combat.

In contrast to Gouges's calls for female solidarity and militancy,
Genlis expressed scorn for the political agitations of working-class
women and feminist activists during the Revolution and tried to dissociate her name from theirs. A staunch supporter of the class and
gender structures of the ancien régime, Genlis viewed calls for the
equality of the classes and sexes as attempts to pervert the natural
order. While Gouges insisted on the need to overcome female rivalry
and to break down class barriers among women, Genlis tended to
mistrust others of her sex and particularly servants: "We cannot regard a person without any education as our friend," she cautioned her
readers in *Adèle et Théodore*. "I know of nothing more dangerous for a
young lady than being on familiar terms with servants, since she will
only pick up from them trivial and ridiculous expressions, vulgar
sentiments, and a taste for bad company" (I: 230–31). Despite her life-
long commitment to educational reform, Genlis viewed education for
working-class women above all as a means of keeping them in their
place. In *Adèle et Théodore*, she dealt only with the upbringing and
education of the aristocracy and the haute bourgeoisie. After the Revolution, Genlis published a *Discours sur l'éducation publique du peuple*
(1791), in which she advocated free public schooling for girls and boys
alike, but maintained that the education of working-class children
should be largely vocational and not encourage aspirations beyond
their station. Although one finds feminist undercurrents in many of

her works, Genlis never explicitly articulated a call for social reform, except in the realm of morals and public education. Indeed, the achievement of equal civil rights for women seemed to her a remote possibility—and not a particularly desirable one.

In contrast to Genlis's mask of decorum and her delineation of strict boundaries for female activity, Gouges deliberately transgressed such bounds through her fierce independence and unabashed self-dramatization. Her passionate calls for equality between classes, sexes, and races are interspersed with accounts of her personal struggles in the flood of political pamphlets she distributed on streetcorners or plastered on the walls of the capital. All this rhetorical excess reflects the frustrations of a woman trying to enter a sphere of activity traditionally reserved for men. In Gouges's view, the aim for women entering revolutionary discourse was above all to escape forced powerlessness and ignorance. "Men have all the advantages," she writes. "Women have been excluded from all power and knowledge, but fortunately writing has not been taken away from us—at least, not yet."[79] In a world in which women were deprived of the right to vote and to hold public office, writing remained their sole means of political expression. Gouges's voice was mocked by her contemporaries and silenced by the guillotine, but her writing carried her utopian vision of radical egalitarianism far into the future to readers who only now are able to appreciate the truly revolutionary implications of her message.

Genlis's Ambivalence toward Literary Women

Despite her own ambitions and success as an author and educator, Genlis openly disapproved of other women who ventured beyond the domestic sphere. Moreover, despite her strong advocacy of improved female education, she was uneasy about the effects such reforms could have on society. In *Adèle et Théodore*, Genlis expressed the fear that improved education might make women discontent with their condition and lead them to neglect what she considered their proper role— that of wives, mothers, and educators of their children. If women were to be happy, argued Genlis, they must be trained to accept their lot in life, avoiding anything that might lead to frustration and discontent. "One should carefully avoid inflaming women's imagination; for they are destined to lead a monotonous and dependent life," she warns.

"Genius is for them a useless and dangerous gift; it perturbs their natural state and serves only to make them aware of its constraints. The desire for knowledge stigmatizes women and distracts them from their domestic duties and social obligations." These conservative pronouncements—which seem to echo Book V of *Emile*—did not prevent Genlis from advocating what was undoubtedly the most ambitious plan of studies for women in eighteenth-century France. Yet the ideal of enlightened motherhood represented by the baronne d'Almane (Genlis's alter-ego in *Adèle et Théodore*) and the ambitious education she gives her daughter Adèle were in no way incompatible with the subordinate social position of eighteenth-century women. Indeed, in Genlis's view, the only constructive and rewarding role open to the women of her class and period was that of enlightened mother and educator.

Until relatively late in her career, Genlis expressed a deep ambivalence toward herself as a writer. Although her fame as an educator rivaled Rousseau's among her contemporaries, she was mocked by many as a bluestocking. In her memoirs, she recalls the humiliation of being booed as she entered a performance of Molière's *Femmes Savantes*. As the play continued, each reference to pedantic women drew further jeers from the crowd. It is no wonder that Genlis warned that genius in a woman was "a useless and dangerous gift"—a *cri du cœur* that echoes Mme de Staël's warning that "for a woman, celebrity leads only to a tragic end to happiness."[80] Yet toward the end of her career, Genlis reversed her attitude. This shift is particularly evident in her history of French women writers, *De l'Influence des femmes sur la littérature française*, published in 1811. "Why should women be forbidden to write and publish?" she asks. "I know all the arguments used to discourage women from pursuing literary ambitions, since I once made these same arguments myself . . . ; now, at the end of my career, I can speak more freely on this subject, because I feel completely objective about a cause I no longer consider my own" (xxi). In this tribute to her literary "mothers," Genlis defied male critics' negative view of women writers and claimed their rightful place in literary history. Indeed, this work constitutes one of the earliest attempts to rewrite women back into the canon.

Genlis chose to apply the same moral standards to authors of both sexes, thereby challenging the reigning double standard that required chastity and discretion of women authors, while giving men far greater freedom in their writings and behavior. In *De l'Influence des femmes*,

Genlis defends women writers against the misogyny of male critics who denigrate their lives and works. In response to one critic who (echoing Rousseau) claimed that "women writers deserve no respect whatsoever; by becoming authors, they renounce their sex and give up their rights as women," Genlis exclaims: "What! Mme de La Fayette, Mme de Lambert, Mme de Graffigny, these charming women with such irreproachable conduct and such distinguished talent, *renounced their sex by becoming authors and no longer deserve our respect!*" Genlis then adds, with biting sarcasm:

> What then can be expected by women authors who have neither such rare talent, nor such personal distinction? Should they expect to be mercilessly persecuted, insulted, and mocked? And what would be the fate of those unfortunate enough to write inferior works containing reprehensible errors? No doubt they would be stoned to death! (xxxi–xxxii)

Genlis concludes by calling for the same critical standards and public respect for all authors, regardless of their sex. This vindication of the rights of women writers to equality in the eyes of the public and the press constitutes a bold act of self-affirmation, as well as a surprising show of solidarity on the part of a woman who had expressed such ambivalence toward female authors earlier in her career.

In her preface to *De l'Influence des femmes*, Genlis attributes the scarcity of women geniuses to the inequality of female education. However, she insists that women have their own brand of genius, which consists of "all the qualities that are not denied to them and that they can possess to the highest degree: imagination, sensibility, loftiness of soul" (ix). For Genlis, women are equal to men in imagination and feeling, as well as in moral and aesthetic understanding: "The capacity to feel and admire what is great and beautiful and the capacity for loving are the same in both sexes; there is complete moral equality between them," she maintains (xiv). Commenting on these passages, Erica Harth argues that Genlis's strategy here is not to claim equality of reason for women, since this would risk masculinizing them, but instead to emphasize the essentially "feminine" ingredients of genius. According to Harth, Genlis is voicing support here for the conventional view of women as creatures of sensibility and for "a system of unequal but complementary gender relations in which masculine reason is counterposed by feminine sentiment."[81] I disagree with this interpretation. For, as I pointed out earlier, Genlis was wary of attempts by Rousseau and others to confine women within the sphere of feelings and impressions (as opposed to the "masculine" sphere of reason and ideas); for she saw this exaltation of sensibility not only as a serious obstacle to female autonomy and self-control, but also as a corruptive influence on public morals and aesthetic tastes. I would argue, quite to the contrary, that Genlis's strategy here and in her other works is to claim that women are equal to men in imagination and feeling and to insist that, with equal education and training, they would become equal as well in reasoning, argumentation, and other skills in which men were traditionally superior because of their superior education.

Rejecting the common argument (which she herself had espoused in *Adèle et Théodore*) that study and writing interfered with a woman's domestic duties, Genlis argued that women writers and scholars were likely to spend more time at home and to lead healthier, less dissipated lives than society women. Better educated and happier with themselves because of their creative outlet, such women were, in Genlis's view, likely to be better spouses and mothers and to find greater pleasure than most women in the simple joys of domesticity: "Sedentary tastes are unlikely to distract women from their domestic duties," she maintained. "Let them write, if for this diversion they give up balls, gambling, useless visits, and trips to the theater—frivolous and dangerous pastimes that prevent women from raising their children properly and that break up families and bring them to financial ruin" (xxii). Genlis affirmed that serious, constructive occupations like study and writing offered solid protection against the frivolity and corruption of *la vie mondaine*, a means of rising above the superficiality and sterility of ordinary conversation, as well as an escape from the stifling effects of social conventions. Based on her own experience, she saw no reason why a woman writer could not gain due recognition for her work, while practicing her craft within the confines of the domestic sphere, with the modesty appropriate to her sex (xx–xxi).

Retracting her earlier disapproval of women who pursued literary vocations, Genlis went on to argue that the benefits and satisfactions of a literary career far outweighed the dangers, particularly for women with genuine talent: "The gifts of nature are so precious that they should never be squandered," she maintains. "Any true gift or artistic talent deserves to be cultivated, because then one is sure of possessing the noblest resource against adversity and the most innocent source of pleasure. . . . " (xxiii). Just as Genlis's earlier warnings resembled Staël's concerning the pitfalls faced by women writers, so too Genlis's more positive view of them at the end of her career parallels the shift in Staël's attitude in the second preface to her *Lettres sur Rousseau*. One senses that at the end of their careers, each had at last come to terms with the tension that lay at the very core of her life as a woman and writer. Having enjoyed the public triumphs and personal satisfactions of a successful literary career, each finally dared to challenge the negative view of women writers voiced by Rousseau and other male critics. Like Staël, Genlis came to the conclusion that the woman artist should look within herself, to her own creative powers, for the greatest (and surest) source of pleasure and self-fulfillment.

Reluctant Admirer and Unlikely Disciple

Genlis's aristocratic background and royalist sentiments had a determining influence on her response to Rousseau, just as did Gouges's working-class origins and her egalitarian ideals and aspirations. Gouges viewed Rousseau as a fellow plebeian who offered her an inspiring model of success, as well as a new egalitarian vision of society. Despite the limitations of his background and education, he was able to rise to prominence as a writer and intellectual through his natural talents, hard work, and persistence in the face of persecution. She identified with Rousseau above all as a *déclassée*, both socially and intellectually. Like him, Gouges had felt out of place in the humble milieu of her parents and ardently aspired to a place in the Republic of Letters. At the same time, Gouges clearly viewed Rousseau as a superior soul, victim of a narrow-minded public incapable of understanding or appreciating him, and as a scapegoat who aroused her compassion and who symbolized her own frustrations as a writer.

In contrast, Genlis viewed Rousseau as an ill-mannered, unprincipled plebeian intruder into the aristocratic confines of the French intelligentsia. In her view, he was a hypocritical arriviste, who was willing to abandon his convictions, his friends, even his children in order to gain celebrity: "He wished to set himself apart from others," she charged. "He sacrificed reason, truth, and his own convictions to the desire to gain celebrity quickly."[82] Genlis's aristocratic bias against Rousseau explains why her attacks focus more on his character and literary style than on the substance of his writings—except for their alleged immorality and lack of taste. Furthermore, because of Rousseau's plebeian Swiss origins and the republican ideals he advocated, Genlis viewed him as a dangerous precursor to the Revolution and to the social, moral, and cultural upheavals it provoked.

Gouges, on other hand, hailed Rousseau as a precursor to the Revolution. Even after she became disenchanted with the revolutionary government, she did not lose faith in Rousseau's republican ideals. Unlike Genlis, Gouges refused to hold Rousseau responsible for the excesses of the Terror; she underlined his pacifism and his opposition to bloodshed. Alarmed by the mounting tide of political persecutions and violence in the spring of 1792, Gouges evoked Rousseau's ideal of a bloodless revolution in an effort to stem that tide: "Like the author of the *Social Contract*, I hoped that the Revolution would take place without bloodshed; for, like Rousseau, I feared that the spilling of a single drop of blood would unleash torrents of blood."[83] Moreover, it was Gouges's unwavering faith in Rousseau's egalitarian ideals and the utopian vision he presented of social reform that sustained her through the darkest hours of the Terror and her months of imprisonment.

Acutely aware of the interconnections between literary and social trends, Genlis viewed Rousseau's exaltation of sensibility and desire in *Julie* and the breakdown of class structures he seemed to advocate as a key source for both the Revolutionary and Romantic movements. In her view, Rousseau's novel had a deeply pernicious influence on public morals and aesthetic tastes—an influence that was particularly evident in the politics and literature of the Revolutionary era. For a royalist like Genlis, who idealized the strict conventions of seventeenth-century French literature and court life, Revolution and Romanticism went hand in hand. In her view, the moral and political excesses of the Revolution were clearly linked to a dangerous exaltation of sensibility and passion, as well as to a breakdown of traditional structures and conventions (political, moral, social, and literary), which she traced back to Rousseau.

In contrast to Genlis's staunch anti-revolutionary, anti-Romantic stance, Gouges was a Romantic and a revolutionary to the core. Indeed, her declaration that "marriage is the tomb of confidence and love" later earned her the dubious title of "la Bovary du Midi" [the Madame Bovary of Southern France].[84] Rousseau's exaltation of sensibility and romantic love appealed to her intensely and strongly marked both her character and her writings. Although unaware of it herself perhaps, Gouges was in many ways an embodiment of the nascent Romantic movement. Her exaltation of the self and of feelings, her utopian dreams of human progress, her revolt against literary and social conventions, and her militant compassion for human suffering among the disenfranchised and the oppressed (slaves, indigents, bastard children, abandoned women)—all these traits mark her as one of the early Romantics.

In short, we have the aristocratic woman on the one hand, the plebeian on the other, and a great deal of irony in their respective positions regarding Rousseau. Gouges identified with him on a personal level because of the parallels in their social origins and political outlook, but she challenged him intellectually (albeit indirectly) because of her feminist ideals. Genlis's position is much the reverse. Because of differences in class and political outlook, she tended to scorn him as a person, but seemed more drawn to him than Gouges on an intellectual level, particularly by his ideas on education and by his ideal of enlightened domesticity. At the same time, Genlis's disdain for Rousseau's character and humble birth enabled her to appropriate his pedagogical theories and rhetoric of moral reform with greater ease because she felt less inhibited than others by his fame as an educator and his stature as a cult figure. By portraying him as a failed educator, she was able to criticize his narrow views on women's role and education with greater confidence and directness than most of her contemporaries. Similarly, by portraying Rousseau as a misogynist in disguise and as a hypocritical arriviste bent on swaying his readers to advance his career, Genlis could more effectively denounce his idealization of sensibility and romantic love as an obstacle to female autonomy and self-control.

In contrast, Gouges was so caught up in her passionate admiration for Rousseau that she seemed unable to distance herself enough to see the contradictions in his sexual politics or their negative impact on the status of women in revolutionary France. Although her views on women differed far more dramatically from his than Genlis's, Gouges lacked the courage or the insight (or both) to criticize Rousseau directly. No doubt her profound respect for him as a political thinker and her strong identification with him as a fellow plebeian made such frontal attacks unthinkable for her and caused her to resort instead to subtle subversions of his sexual politics and oblique challenges to the works with which she disagreed. Like other feminist militants of her period, Gouges found herself caught up in the contradictions between the revolutionary leaders' egalitarian rhetoric and their gynephobic policies, or what Carole Pateman has referred to as the "double bind of the fraternal social contract."[85] These contradictions can be traced back directly to the feminist implications of the egalitarian vision set forth in *The Social Contract*—implications which both Rousseau and his Jacobin followers chose to ignore, even to deny.

Despite their very different backgrounds and political outlooks, Genlis and Gouges experienced many of the same influences and tensions as women and as writers. Both were true amazons of the pen, driven to arduous literary vocations by their ambitions and fervent (although very different) convictions. Neither was afraid to take on male-dominated institutions or male figures of authority in order to defend those convictions. Both women lived their lives to the fullest, passionately engaged in the issues of their day. In a tribute to Genlis after her death, her niece Georgette Ducrest wrote: "She never wasted a minute. By making the most of every day, she doubled her long lifetime."[86] Although Gouges's life tragically was cut short by the blade of the guillotine, this tribute holds true for her as well. The parallels between the two women continue even beyond the grave, for their works were later devalued or dismissed by literary historians because they were considered politically incorrect and failed to conform to accepted norms of femininity: Gouges because of her strident outspokenness and feminist militancy, Genlis because of her prudish moralism and strong aristocratic bias. Perhaps the most striking parallel between Genlis and Gouges is that both were strongly influenced by Rousseau and responded repeatedly to his writings. Like Wollstonecraft and Staël, they were both passionate admirers yet, at the same time, strong critics of Rousseau, but largely unaware of their own ambivalence.

Conclusion

Engendering a Self:

Rousseau's Influence on Women and Their Writing

To most readers today, Rousseau's sexual politics appear reactionary, paternalistic, even blatantly misogynic; yet, among his female contemporaries, his works often met with enthusiastic approval and had tremendous impact on their values and behavior. To probe Rousseau's paradoxical appeal to eighteenth-century readers, I have examined how seven women authors responded to his writings and sexual politics and have traced his influence on their lives and works. My purpose in this concluding chapter is to compare their responses to Rousseau and to explore differences in the way he affected their development as writers. Specifically, I will examine how their upbringing and class origins influenced their reception of Rousseau and their view of themselves as women writers, whether his ideal of sensibility and his negative opinion of women writers stimulated or inhibited their self-expression, and the extent to which these women adopted, rejected, or transformed Rousseau's feminine ideals. I will also explore certain gender- and genre-linked differences in the way they responded to conflicting motivations and conventions in their writing, particularly in their autobiographical works.

Differences in Outlook: The Impact of Upbringing and Class

I have suggested that Rousseau's popularity among eighteenth-century women readers may have stemmed in part from a deeply rooted moral and social conservatism conditioned in them by their upbringing, from a tacit (albeit self-defeating) support for the status quo. Such conservatism certainly characterized the mothers of several women I have studied,

293

particularly Mme d'Esclavelles (d'Epinay's mother), Mme Phlipon (Roland's mother), and Mme Necker (Staël's mother), whose strict sense of propriety and conformity to traditional views were to have so constraining an effect on their daughters' psychological and artistic development. Only by rejecting the limited social role prescribed by their mothers and by Rousseau were these women able to develop their potential as writers. Although we have no direct references to Henriette's mother, we know that she, too, had raised her daughter to view marriage as a woman's only true path to self-fulfillment—a view that would cause Henriette considerable anguish when she was later unable to marry and felt compelled to seek less conventional means of self-fulfillment.

In contrast, the childhoods of Wollstonecraft, Gouges, and Genlis were characterized by a general lack of structure in their upbringing and by their mothers' benign indifference to their education. This lack of maternal constraint helped make them more independent and self-confident than the other women I have studied and less anxious about transgressing traditional gender boundaries—qualities that later proved to be significant advantages in their creative development. The striking similarities among these three women, who (like d'Epinay) were almost entirely self-taught and who developed such strong minds and talents despite their lack of formal instruction, lends support to Wollstonecraft's arguments regarding the superiority of self-educated women in the eighteenth century. Moreover, because of their experience as children and later as educators, these women were acutely aware of the crucial influence, for good or for ill, of mothers on daughters. Like Rousseau, they insisted that the moral reform of society depended on the positive example women set for their children, but they argued that the education Rousseau proposed for women would make them singularly unfit to educate their own children and to fill the role of moral exemplar he ascribed to them in such glowing terms. Given the inadequacies of the standard female education of the period, they maintained that women were better off educating themselves and their daughters at home.

ဆင်္ချ

Even more than their upbringing, class differences seem to have had a determining influence on how these women viewed Rousseau. The women of middle-class background (Wollstonecraft, Roland, and Henriette) generally responded with greater enthusiasm to his ideals of domesticity and motherhood and to his rhetoric of moral reform, while the women of aristocratic origins (particularly d'Epinay and Staël) were more ambivalent in their response. Their ambivalence can be traced in part to the pressures they felt to conform to the norms of their milieu, in which *la vie mondaine* and *la morale mondaine* were still dominant, despite the Rousseauian home-and-hearth ethic that was emerging during this period among the bourgeoisie.

Genlis, through her experiences as an educator, was a firm advocate of the Rousseauian ideals of domesticity and motherhood, although she was fully conscious of the strong pressures on women of her class to conform to the moral codes and social obligations of high society. In her novel *Adèle et Théodore*, the joys of enlightened motherhood are extolled by the baronne d'Almane (whom Genlis clearly identifies as her *porte-parole*), while the demands and illusory pleasures of society life are expressed by the baronne's closest friend, the Vicomtesse de Limours. One finds similar pairings of female characters in the novels of other aristocratic women (notably Staël, d'Epinay, and Isabelle de Charrière), but in their works (unlike Genlis's) the author's *porte-parole* is inevitably a woman of superior talents and aspirations who, both by character and by circumstances, feels compelled to resist confinement within a domestic, maternal role. The parallels among Staël's Corinne, Charrière's Caliste, and d'Epinay's Emilie de Montbrillant are quite striking in this respect.[1] In each case, the heroine is impelled by her very nature to resist conformity to the narrow gender roles prescribed for her—domestic and maternal duties, as well as the demands of society life—and to seek transcendence through some form of artistic expression.

Gouges's response to Rousseau's sexual politics was more complex and more ambivalent. Although as a courtesan, woman writer, and controversial political figure, she represented everything Rousseau despised, and although she rejected the ideal of marriage and domesticity he advocated, she continued to idolize him and to view him as her spiritual father. Like Roland, Gouges identified intensely with the Genevan's egalitarian spirit and with his persona of persecuted virtue without realizing that it was in large part his narrow views on women and their strong influence on the Jacobin leaders' policies toward women that had led to her persecution.

The aristocratic backgrounds of Genlis, Staël, and d'Epinay therefore had a determining influence on their response to Rousseau, just

as did the humbler origins of Gouges, Roland, and Wollstonecraft. The
second group viewed Rousseau as a fellow plebeian who offered them
an inspiring model of success, as well as a new egalitarian vision of
society. They identified with Rousseau above all as *déclassées*, both
socially and intellectually. Like him, they had felt out of place in the
petit bourgeois milieu of their parents and ardently aspired to a place
in the Republic of Letters. All three were strongly marked by Rousseau's
political writings and hailed him as a key precursor to the French
Revolution. Even after they became disenchanted with the revolutionary government, they did not lose faith in his republican ideals. Because of the parallels in their social origins and political outlook, they
identified with Rousseau on a personal level, but they challenged him
intellectually (albeit indirectly) because of their more progressive view
of women's role.

In contrast, Genlis and d'Epinay viewed Rousseau as a plebeian
intruder into the aristocratic circles of France's cultural elite. In their
view, he was an unprincipled opportunist who was willing to abandon his convictions, his friends, even his children in order to advance his career. Their aristocratic bias against Rousseau explains
why their attacks focus more on his character and literary style than
on his ideas—except, in Genlis's case, for his political ideas. Because
of his ardent republicanism, Genlis viewed Rousseau as a precursor
to the Revolution and to the social and moral turmoil it provoked.
Because of their own republican inclinations, Staël and d'Epinay were
more favorably disposed toward Rousseau's political writings; yet
their aristocratic bias against him surfaced in their criticism of his
fictional characters' imperfect diction and their lack of social polish
and savoir-faire. Whatever their political inclinations might be, these
women did not hesitate to capitalize on Rousseau's popularity in
order to promote their own literary careers. We have seen, for example, how Staël successfully launched her career with the *Lettres
sur Rousseau* and how both Gouges and Genlis wrote plays about
him in an attempt to curry favor with the public and to prove their
devotion to republican ideals at a time when they themselves were
increasingly under attack.

࿐

Let us now turn to the central question of Rousseau's influence on
the development of women's writing and, more specifically, his impact on the literary careers of the seven women in this study.

Rousseau's Influence on Women's Writing

Rousseau's narrow vision of women's proper role and his ideals of female modesty and self-effacement clearly had a repressive influence on the literary careers of several of these women. His tirade against female writers in *Emile* caused Roland and d'Epinay to postpone publishing their work or to publish anonymously; it impelled Henriette to give up writing altogether. Although well aware of their literary talents and eager to develop them, these women were "closet writers" for most of their lives. Haunted into silence by the specters of *Emile* and the Proper Lady, they were not able to overcome Rousseau's repressive influence until late in their lives, when they felt they had nothing more to lose; only then did they feel free to write and publish for a public audience. One can only speculate as to how many other literary vocations and works of art by women were stifled in this way by men like Rousseau.

The four other women—Wollstonecraft, Gouges, Genlis, and Staël— were ambitious professional writers who published widely from the beginning of their careers. All four were irresistibly drawn to the power and prestige of the printed word. One of the main reasons behind their success was that they had the self-confidence and strength of character to defy the traditional prejudices against women writers expressed so vehemently by Rousseau and shared by many of their contemporaries. Success did not come easily, however, to female writers of the period. For each of these women, defiance of traditional gender norms entailed some kind of personal suffering: emotional insecurity, financial hardship, social ostracism and public mockery, political persecution, even death. Indeed, Gouges suffered all of these hardships for the sake of a career that was always precarious and marginal, despite her notoriety. Genlis, though her fame as an educator rivaled that of Rousseau, was nevertheless mocked by many as a bluestocking. It is no wonder she warned her readers that genius in a woman was "a dangerous and useless gift."

Even Staël, despite her bravado and undeniable success, continued until relatively late in her career to be plagued by a deep ambivalence toward herself as a writer. Hers is a particularly illuminating example of Rousseau's contradictory influence on women writers; for not until the second preface to her *Lettres sur Rousseau* did she succeed in exorcising the ghosts of Rousseau and of her parents, whose disapproval of women writers had haunted her since the original writing and publication of the *Lettres* twenty-six years earlier. In this second preface, after summarizing the traditional prejudices against women authors, Staël suggests that the greatest obstacle to overcoming them lay in the complicity of women themselves with the status quo. Like Gouges and Wollstonecraft, Staël points to the fear of celebrity and to the even greater fear of failure and ridicule that caused many to retreat behind a mask of false modesty and to criticize more talented and ambitious women who did achieve success. Reading her second preface, one senses that Staël was no longer intimidated by Rousseau's negative view of women writers. Having enjoyed the public triumphs and personal satisfactions of a successful literary career, she finally dared to challenge his limited view of female destiny.

This shift in Staël's view of herself as a writer parallels that expressed by Roland, d'Epinay, and Genlis toward the end of their careers. Perhaps the most striking change in attitude is found in Genlis's later writings. In *De l'Influence des femmes sur la littérature*, she retracted her earlier Rousseau-like disapproval of women writers, insisting (like Staël) that the benefits and satisfactions of a literary career far outweighed the dangers, particularly for women of genuine talent.

The Stumbling Block of Sensibility

Like Rousseau's ideal of enlightened domesticity, his ideal of sensibility was empowering for some women but inhibiting for others, depending on the character and circumstances of each. In Rousseau's own experience, the sublimation of his unfulfilled desires through the exaltation of sensibility and the self had a liberating effect and served as the creative impetus for his greatest fiction. Capsulized in his life and works, the Rousseauian ideal of sensibility was also to have a potentially liberating effect on women authors of the period, provided they had the self-confidence and strength of character needed to rise above traditional gender barriers. By transcending the traditional conventions of female modesty and silence, these women were able to express their unfulfilled aspirations and desires through their writing, to transform their personal suffering into works of art. This was certainly true of Staël, Wollstonecraft, and Gouges; later in their lives, it was also true of d'Epinay and Roland. However, for women like Henriette, who lacked the strength of character and self-confidence to rise above traditional prejudices against female authors and to express their longings in writing, the Rousseauian ideal of sensibility constituted a major stumbling block—a source not of transcendence but of further oppression. For it impelled them to turn back upon themselves, to indulge masochistically in their own suffering. Indeed, in her response to Rousseau's letters, Henriette tried to explain that far from relieving her problems, the narcissism and introspective exaltation of sensibility he recommended would only exacerbate them.

Despite its artistic benefits, Rousseau's exaltation of sensibility continued to be problematic for all the women writers in my study. All seven were ambivalent about his attempt to confine women within the sphere of feelings and impressions (as opposed to the "masculine" sphere of reason and ideas); for they sensed the implicit link of this dichotomy with attempts to relegate women to the private sphere and, indeed, with the male self-interest and female repression that lay at the root of the gender hierarchy.[2] This ambivalence was articulated most explicitly by Wollstonecraft in *The Rights of Woman*. There, she referred to Rousseau as a "voluptuous tyrant" who, by cultivating women's sensibility and making love the focus of their lives, made them the prey of their senses and more easily dominated by men's will and desires. In her view, sentimental novels like *Julie* undermined virtue by making reality seem unfulfilling. She argued that by indulging their readers' desire for vicarious gratification, such fictions disengaged them from life; by feeding wishful fantasies instead of initiating positive action, they imprisoned women even more narrowly in the sphere of sensibility.

Genlis echoed Wollstonecraft's warnings against the pernicious influence of sentimental novels in general and of *La Nouvelle Héloïse* in particular. Portraying Rousseau as a misogynist in disguise and as a hypocritical arriviste bent on swaying his readers to advance his career, she urged her women readers to resist his seductive eloquence. She argued, moreover, that his exaltation of sensibility had exerted a corruptive influence on public morals and aesthetic tastes, which had culminated in the degenerate politics and literature of the revolutionary era. In her view, the moral and political excesses of the Revolution were clearly linked to a dangerous exaltation of sensibility, which she traced back to Rousseau. Her objections to his ideal of sensibility were therefore moral and aesthetic in nature, rather than consciously feminist, although, like Wollstonecraft, Genlis denounced Rousseau's celebration of sensibility and romantic love as a serious obstacle to female autonomy and self-control.

ℭℴℊℴℭ

To overcome the stumbling block of excessive sensibility, these women came to view study and writing as important means of self-discipline that would enable them to channel their energies and emotions into constructive outlets instead of turning them masochistically inward upon themselves. Conscious that they were transgressing traditional gender roles through their literary activities, they came to view writing as an act of self-affirmation and of resistance to the various forms of oppression they had endured as women. Contrary to traditional eighteenth-century views of women as victims of their imagination, emotions, and sexual desires (views clearly reflected in Rousseau's portrayal of Sophie and Julie), these women underlined their belief in the primacy of reason and turned to writing and study as a means of self-control. Throughout their lives, and particularly in times of crisis, these activities served as an inner source of order, consolation, and strength. For example, describing her early literary efforts after the death of her mother, Mme Roland recalls: "I felt the need to write. Writing helped me probe my ideas and understand them better. With the aid of my pen, I was able to channel my imagination and to pursue lines of reasoning."[3] Similarly, at the end of her first letter to Rousseau, Henriette openly expresses the pleasure that she had experienced in writing to him, the consolation and sense of purpose it had given her: "Writing to you has clearly proven to me that a serious, stimulating occupation is necessary to my well-being. . . . [It] has given me a mental activity absorbing and stimulating enough to help me forget my unhappiness."[4] And writing of her cousin, Mme Necker de Saussure comments: "For Mme de Staël, writing and study were a necessary resource, a way to calm and renew her agitated spirit and to maintain the true elevation of her mind."[5]

These women also viewed study and writing as remedies for that most pernicious female malady of their time, ennui: "I sometimes feel bored or restless; to escape from my ennui, I force myself to write," notes Mme Roland. "I write everything that comes into my head; it purges my thoughts."[6] Similarly, in her conversations with her granddaughter, d'Epinay underlines the value of study as an effective antidote to ennui, as well as an inner source of strength and independence: "When you take care to cultivate your mind and to enrich it with useful knowledge, you give yourself new sources of pleasure and satisfaction, as well as valuable resources against boredom and adversity," she explains. "These are treasures that no one can take away from you and that free you from dependence on others."[7] Despite her ambivalence toward women writers and scholars, Genlis also stressed the benefits of study and writing as "valuable resources against idleness and ennui."[8] She insisted, moreover, that serious, constructive occupations of this kind offered solid protection against the frivolity and corruption of society life; for they enabled women to rise above the superficiality of ordinary conversation and to escape the stifling effects of social conventions.

Henriette was the only one of the seven who did not continue to find solace in study and writing, which she abandoned at Rousseau's urging. A prisoner of her own excessive sensibility, she complained of suffering from intense ennui, indeed of being "la personne au monde la plus ennuyée de son existence."[9] Thanks to their greater independence of mind and spirit, the other women developed a sensibility that did not fall back passively on itself—a healthy exaltation of the self that gave them strength and that inspired positive action and artistic self-expression.

Put to positive use in this way, the Rousseauian ideal of sensibility opened up exciting new possibilities of self-expression. The pre-Romantic style made fashionable by Rousseau was widely imitated by writers of both sexes and generated enormous enthusiasm, particularly among his female readers. For many women, as for Wollstonecraft, the creator of *Julie* was "the true Prometheus of sentiment" they strove to emulate in both their lives and works. Rousseau's influence on women's writing was particularly strong in the areas of autobiography and autobiographical fiction, to which we now turn our attention.

Strategies of Self-Representation: The Influence of Rousseau's Confessions *and the Woman Autobiographer's Double Bind*

For most literary historians, autobiography officially begins as a distinct genre in France in the 1780s with the posthumous publication of Rousseau's *Confessions*.[10] Rousseau not only inaugurated this new genre, but served as a model against which future autobiographies would be measured. "Rousseau is the only one to say aloud what everyone thinks in private," remarks Philippe Lejeune. "All the autobiographical pacts that follow are written against his disastrous frankness."[11] In the original introduction to his *Confessions* (the Préambule du manuscrit de Neuchâtel, written in 1764), Rousseau offers a bold vision of the autobiographical venture that clearly sets it apart from earlier self-reflective forms of writing:

> I have resolved to lead my readers one step farther in the knowledge of human nature.... I know of no other man who has dared attempt what I have set out to do. Histories, life stories, portraits, character sketches! What are they, after all? Clever fictions built upon a few exterior acts, a few speeches, ... in which the author tries to give a flattering picture of himself rather than to seek the truth.

Rousseau then articulates his famous autobiographical pact:

> I will be truthful without reserve.... How many insignificant acts, how many revolting, indecent, childish, even ridiculous details will I need to reveal in order to fully explain the development of my character? I blush even to think of the humiliating confessions I will need to make, and I know some readers will consider me impudent; but I must openly admit these things or else conceal them entirely; for if I hide anything, my readers will not know me at all, since everything in my character is so completely intertwined.[12]

The publication of the *Confessions* created a major literary sensation, captivating countless readers, scandalizing many others. In France, Rousseau's autobiography provoked a moralistic reaction against the genre as a whole, causing it to be associated with a tendency toward exhibitionism and provocation, overbearing pride and *impudeur*—a peculiarly French mixture of impudence and indecency. According to Lejeune, in England and Germany, where the first great autobiographies were of a less controversial nature, there was no such reaction.

For the writers of his period, Rousseau's *Confessions* opened up hitherto unexplored modes of self-analysis and self-revelation. Following his example, certain women writers dared to transgress social and literary conventions in order to reveal their most intimate thoughts, feelings, and experiences in ways that both shocked and thrilled their readers. Inspired by the *Confessions*, Mme Roland gave free rein to her thoughts and feelings in her memoirs and, like Rousseau, attempted to justify herself in the eyes of posterity by presenting an accurate self-portrait and self-analysis to counter what she perceived as misrepresentations of her character and motives by her political enemies. In a note accompanying her memoirs, she underlines her conscious effort to emulate Rousseau's frankness in her portrayal of herself and others. "These memoirs will be my *Confessions*, for I will not conceal anything," she declares. "It's true that one cannot always divulge secrets about oneself without revealing those of others; it's sometimes a delicate matter. But I've thought about it carefully and made up my mind. I will tell all, absolutely everything. That is the only way to be useful."[13]

Roland's determination to follow Rousseau's example, even at the risk of indiscretion, contrasts sharply with the negative reaction of other women autobiographers to his *Confessions*. In *L'Histoire de ma vie*, for example, George Sand asks: "Who can forgive Rousseau for having revealed Mme de Warens's secrets while revealing his own?"[14] Sand then warns scandalmongers that they will be disappointed in her own autobiography, for she vows to maintain a rigorous discretion in recounting her life story: "I am neither humble enough to write confessions like Jean-Jacques nor impertinent enough to praise myself like the literary lights of the century. Furthermore, I don't believe that private life should fall within the purview of the critics."[15]

The traditional conventions of female discretion and *pudeur* expressed so forcefully in Rousseau's earlier writings clearly had a repressive effect on the autobiographical writings of a number of women. In d'Epinay's *Histoire de Madame de Montbrillant*, for example, self-justification and respect for social and literary conventions far outweigh self-revelation and self-analysis as motivating and structuring principles in her self-portrayal. Yet Rousseau motivated d'Epinay to write nonetheless, even if she did not choose to emulate his unprecedented candor. Indeed, *Montbrillant* can be read as a narrative of self-justification against his criticism of women writers in general and of Mme d'Epinay in particular—a defensive celebration of the self similar to what one finds in Genlis's memoirs and Henriette's letters to Rousseau.

Writing in her diary in 1863, Marie d'Agoult (better known by her *nom de plume* Daniel Stern), acknowledges the conflicting influences of Rousseau's example and the social conventions of female modesty on the autobiographical venture: "I had envisioned a daring book. Female confessions as frank as Jean-Jacques's, and consequently far bolder (because of public opinion). . . . But *I* cannot do it."[16] The book does get written, however, and in the preface to *Mes Souvenirs*, Stern explains her hesitations: "As a woman, I did not feel bound to the rule of virile sincerity. But when a woman's life is not governed by the common rule and, because of exceptional circumstances or talents, she emerges from obscurity, that woman becomes more responsible than a man in the eyes of all and thereby contracts virile duties."[17] By "virile sincerity" and "virile duties," Stern is referring to the Rousseauian autobiographical pact to tell all, the obligation to be as frank as possible in recounting one's life's story. Yet in the memoirs themselves, she insists that a woman's pen is more constrained than a man's and that, consequently, she felt neither the right nor the desire in recalling her own memories to divulge those of others.[18] Like Sand, Stern rejects Rousseau's "tell-all" stance and maintains a scrupulous discretion regarding past loves and lovers. This is precisely the strategy that d'Epinay (like Genlis) adopts in reverse, for she is coyly discreet in recounting her own life, but selectively *indiscreet* in revealing the private lives of others (notably Rousseau and Duclos)—a tactic that enables her to present herself in the best light and her enemies in the worst.

The contrast between the self-portrayals of d'Epinay on the one hand, and of Rousseau and Roland on the other, reflect the determining influence of genre and narrative voice on the autobiographical project. Whereas the "tell-all" stance of the confessional genre adopted by Rousseau and later by Roland gave them the freedom—indeed a consciously assumed obligation—to reveal the truth, d'Epinay's decision to write an autobiographical novel rather than a strict autobiography gave her the freedom to deviate from the truth and to refashion it as best suited her personal and polemical objectives. In the *Confessions*, Rousseau's use of a single-voiced first-person narrative clearly aimed at a public audience gives his self-portrayal an intensity and directness that serve to underline his sincerity and to excuse his sometimes brazen frankness. The same is true of Roland's memoirs, although her frankness met with greater criticism because she was a woman. In contrast, d'Epinay's use of fictional names and her frequent shifts in narrative viewpoint and genre serve as distancing devices, enabling her to portray herself in the most flattering light, illuminating the most positive facets of her character, while casting a deep shadow on less admirable traits and actions. The novel that results is a complex mixture of fact and fiction, of male and female voices, of "public" and "private" writings, presented in a rich patchwork of narrative styles and genres. Fragments from Emilie's journal, letters exchanged among a dozen or so correspondents, theatrical dialogues, stylized portraits, and brief summaries of events narrated by her tutor are alternated and intertwined to reshape d'Epinay's life into a more satisfying story. The novelistic form she adopts enables her to fill the emotional void and dull ending of own life with a melodramatic fictional dénouement that satisfies both literary conventions and the unfulfilled longings of her own heart.

The artificial closure that marks the end of d'Epinay's novel— Emilie's death from grief over her lover's political exile—forms a striking contrast to the gripping true-life ending imposed by Mme Roland's execution. The blade of the guillotine hovers over Roland through much of her narrative, giving her memoirs an immediacy and urgency that would be difficult to achieve through purely literary means, as well as an increasingly stronger impulse and justification to reveal her most secret ambitions and desires. Similarly, the closing chapters of Rousseau's *Confessions* are punctuated by his successive flights into exile, each followed by a deeper phase of paranoia and ever more probing looks within himself. In this way, the events of the autobiographer's life and inner reactions to them shape the trajectory of his or her narrative, even the very form chosen to convey it, just as the author's sex and moral posture have a determining influence on the degree of frankness in which he or she is willing to engage.

It has been argued by critics as diverse as Virginia Woolf and Pierre Fauchery that women writers are instinctively drawn to certain "personal" genres (notably autobiography and letters). If this indeed is the case, how does this predilection reflect their experience as women and in turn shape their writing? To what extent does their sex affect the way their writings are subsequently read and judged by the public? In probing these questions, I have examined the hierarchy of genres and genders implicit in the negative judgment of women's autobiographical writing by male critics. Fauchery, for example, maintains that autobiographical novels constitute a feminine genre, inferior, for lack of imagination, to "true" novels (i. e., non-autobiographical ones)— a genre in which male authors excel, he claims, because of their ability to transcend the narrow confines of their daily life through the power of imagination. Citing *Histoire de Madame de Montbrillant* as a case in point, Fauchery points to the inability of women writers to distance themselves from their personal experiences and frustrations, to go beyond the confines of their familial and social milieu, as a major obstacle to the creation of truly original, imaginative work: "This myopia is reflected in their obsessive preoccupation with certain landscapes, especially those of their childhood," he claims. "Although a woman novelist is certainly capable of giving a candid description of the female condition, the woman she thinks she is imagining is never anyone but herself." Alluding obliquely to d'Epinay's quarrels with her husband and with Rousseau, Fauchery then adds: "Many women's novels are really nothing but pretexts to express bitterness toward their family or to satisfy a desire for revenge."[19] Similarly, commenting on Staël's novels, Starobinski claims that she is incapable of the "artistic suicide" that liberates works from their author, giving them a life and character of their own.[20] Yet one could argue that this alleged myopia of women writers—which supposedly prevents them from distancing themselves from their personal experience—would serve to guarantee the authenticity of the view they present of women's condition, frustrations, and aspirations.

Colette, responding to this common prejudice against women's autobiographical writings, pointedly remarks: "Man, my friend, you willingly make fun of women's writings because they can't help being autobiographical. On whom then were you relying to paint women for you? . . . On yourself?" She then suggests that women's tendency toward self-dramatization in their writings is in fact a strategy designed to conceal other facets of their lives and personalities: "Why do men still show surprise that a woman should so easily reveal to the public love-secrets and amorous lies and half-truths?" she asks. "By divulging these, she manages to hide other important and obscure secrets which she herself does not understand very well."[21] Commenting on this passage, Nancy Miller argues that women writers have a different standard of sincerity and self-disclosure than male writers and a different style of autobiography as a result. "Female autobiographers know that they are being read as women," writes Miller. "The concern with notoriety, then, functions as an additional grid or constraint placed upon the truth . . . upon the shaping of the past as truth."[22]

If this indeed is the case, what are some of the gender-linked differences we can discern in the autobiographical writings of Rousseau and the women in my study? How did their sex affect the way they responded to conflicting motivations and conventions in their self-portrayals and the way their autobiographical writings were subsequently read and judged by the public? A detailed discussion of these questions would obviously go beyond the scope of this study, but a preliminary response can be reached by comparing how the problem of illegitimate children is dealt with by these women and Rousseau in their writings. Whereas in his *Confessions*, Rousseau openly admits having fathered and then abandoned several children, d'Epinay carefully avoids all reference to her illegitimate children in her autobiographical novel. By compressing the events of 1747–48 in her narration and by fusing the characters of her first daughter (who died in infancy) and her second, illegitimate daughter (born the following year, but raised as d'Epinay's child), she deftly avoids embarrassing issues. As for her subsequent pregnancies and births, they are as carefully concealed in d'Epinay's novel as they were in her life. The same is true for Genlis and Staël, who carefully avoid any mention of their illegitimate children in their writings, except in personal letters not made public until long after their death.

Wollstonecraft, on the other hand, alludes frequently to her liaison with Imlay and to their illegitimate daughter in *A Short Residence in Sweden*, addressed to Imlay and published in 1796. The negative effect this candor had on her reputation both as a woman and as a writer was dramatically heightened by Godwin's publication after her death of his biography (*Memoirs of the Author of "The Rights of Woman"*) and her personal letters, which deal quite openly with her liaison with Imlay, the illegitimacy of their daughter, and her subsequent affair with Godwin. His biography aroused a great scandal and caused Wollstonecraft's reputation as a writer to plummet.[23] *Maria* and even the *Rights of Woman* were branded as morally pernicious books, which girls were warned against reading.

To be as daringly frank as Rousseau in sexual matters, a woman autobiographer needed to be as morally irreproachable as Mme Roland, or else fall victim to the double standard by which male and female writers were judged. Even though she had nothing strictly immoral to hide, Roland was nevertheless criticized for imitating Rousseau's brazen example. D'Epinay and Genlis, on the other hand, were later charged with hypocrisy by editors and critics for trying to whitewash their infidelities (both to their husbands and to the truth of their stories),[24] when they were simply obeying the same conventions of female discretion that Roland and Wollstonecraft were criticized for transgressing. For women writers, there seemed to be no escape from this double standard and this double bind. As a man, Rousseau was able to reveal far more about himself than could a woman autobiographer.

That male and female authors of the period were subject to different moral standards and to different standards of sincerity in their writing is made clear by various critics who later evaluated their works. We have seen, for example, how Roland's disclosure of two incidents of sexual molestation experienced when she was eleven years old, was vehemently criticized when these accounts (censored from earlier editions of her memoirs) were finally published in 1863. According to Sainte-Beuve, the inclusion of these episodes was morally reprehensible, as well as socially unacceptable. In his opinion, traditional gender restrictions—and particularly the literary and social conventions of *pudeur*—outweighed the need for sincerity, indeed its very desirability. Sainte-Beuve was not alone in his criticism of these passages. A few years later, his objections were reiterated by Elme-Marie Caro in a review of Roland's memoirs. "Confessions of this sort that are so unnecessary and developed in such a cold-blooded manner reveal the absence of delicacy in highly delicate matters," maintains Caro. "Rousseau's example is sometimes invoked to excuse such brazenness. Yet what is already intolerable in his *Confessions* is doubly so in Roland's memoirs. This type of 'natural history,' which may have its place in impersonal scientific treatises, is revolting in the memoirs of this woman, whose confessional style brings her back to life in far too realistic a manner."[25]

The disapproval of Roland's candor expressed by Sainte-Beuve and Caro parallels that voiced by Wollstonecraft's critics after the posthumous publication of her letters and her memoirs by Godwin. Similarly, the strong objections of numerous critics to Corinne's sexual freedom and her disdain for the Rousseauian ideals of domesticity and motherhood were heightened by their interpretation of the heroine as a brazen fictionalized self-portrait by Staël. "Since the novels have been interpreted almost exclusively as fictional projections of self," notes Gutwirth, "Mme de Staël's personal reputation has had a decided influence upon that of her novels."[26] In her study of the critical reception of Staël's works, Noreen Swallow has found attitudes ranging from the "prophetic sexism of Jacques Necker in 1785, to the patronizing chauvinism of Le Breton in 1901, to the misogynous hysteria of Anthony West in 1975."[27] Charlotte Hogsett attributes this sexist denigration of Staël's character and works to what she calls "the lightning rod of her gender."[28] Despite Staël's early efforts (particularly in

Delphine) to create heroines who conformed—outwardly, at least—to her period's ideals of femininity and discretion, these efforts were of no avail, for her female characters were always viewed as Staël's self-portraits and criticized as such. Like Gouges, Staël later chose to defy the double standard in both her life and works (notably in *Corinne*)— a revolt that was vigorously criticized by certain critics and viewed by many others with ambivalence well into the twentieth century.

Conscious of the double standard applied by male critics to the lives and works of women authors, d'Epinay and Genlis chose to shroud their liaisons under a veil of moral respectability when they wrote their autobiographies. This strategy caused certain of their critics to accuse them of hypocrisy and to mock them openly in reviews of their works. Genlis responded by applying the same moral code to authors of both sexes, thereby challenging the double standard that required chastity and discretion of women authors while giving men much greater freedom in their writings and behavior. Her condemnation of the immorality and indiscretion that she found in Rousseau's *Confessions* was in many ways stronger than her disapproval of similar writings by women,[29] for she considered Rousseau's example far more pernicious because of the tremendous popularity of his works and their powerful influence on the public. At the same time, Genlis defended women writers against misogynic male critics who denigrated their character and works. In *De l'Influence des femmes sur la littérature française*, she called for the same critical standards and the same respect for all authors, regardless of their sex. This call for equal treatment of women writers by the public and the press constituted a bold act of self-affirmation—and a surprising show of female solidarity— on the part of an author who, earlier in her career, had disapproved so strongly of women with literary ambitions.

In her discussion of women's autobiographies, Mary G. Mason claims that the disclosure of the female self is invariably linked to the influence of some significant male "Other" (husband, father, lover, or mentor) and hence that Rousseau's style of autobiography, "where characters and events are little more than aspects of the author's self-discovery and evolving consciousness, finds no echo in women's writing about their lives."[30] I disagree with this claim. Quite to the contrary, the women in my study consciously adopted Rousseau's view of autobiography as a radical process of self-affirmation and self "re-creation"—a probing look into the past in order to better understand and reshape the present self. Moreover, in the course of her autobiographical venture, each of these women gradually learned to speak in her own voice, independently of the male voices of authority that had guided her early literary efforts. Indeed, it was only after overcoming the constraining influence of these significant male "Others"—and especially Rousseau, their common mentor—that each woman was finally able to write for herself in her own name.

Toward an Ecriture Féminine

During the past three decades, feminist critics have approached women's writing with a commitment to explore what, if anything, makes it different from writing by men. Sharing a general feeling that significant differences do exist, they have begun to revise traditional accounts of literary history in order to recognize the important contributions made by women authors.[31] In *The Madwoman in the Attic*, for example, Gilbert and Gubar carry out a feminist revision of Harold Bloom's Oedipal model, which regards literary history as a conflict between fathers and sons. In its place, they advance a psychoanalytic model of the woman artist as displaced, disinherited, and excluded and see the nature and "difference" of women's writing in its troubled and even tormented relationship to female identity. The woman writer experiences her gender as "a painful obstacle or even a debilitating inadequacy," they maintain.

> Thus the loneliness of the female artist, her feelings of alienation from male predecessors coupled with her need for sisterly precursors and successors, her urgent sense of need for a female audience together with her fear of the antagonism of male readers, her culturally conditioned timidity about self-dramatization, her dread of the patriarchal authority of art, her anxiety about the impropriety of female invention—all these phenomena of "inferiorization" mark the woman writer's struggle for artistic self-definition and differentiate her efforts at self-creation from those of her male counterpart.[32]

According to Gilbert and Gubar, the quest for self-definition is a distinguishing feature of writing by women. Although they are dealing specifically with nineteenth-century Britain, their observations apply equally well to female authors of eighteenth-century France.

In "Feminist Criticism in the Wilderness," Elaine Showalter has stressed the need for subtler, suppler accounts of literary influence, not only to better trace the evolution of women's writing but also to better understand how male writers and critics have denied the influence of female precursors: "We must go beyond the assumption that women writers either imitate their male predecessors or revise them and that this simple dualism is adequate to describe the influences on the woman's text,"she maintains.[33] Although she agrees with Virginia Woolf's notion that, in order to write, a woman must think back through her mothers, Showalter insists that a woman writer unavoidably thinks back through her fathers as well. To help remedy the inadequacies of previous models of literary history, Showalter has proposed a dual-culture model, according to which women's writing can be read as a double-voiced discourse, reflecting both the dominant male culture and a muted or repressed female culture. "Women writing are not, then, *inside* and *outside* of the male tradition," she maintains, "they are inside two traditions simultaneously."[34]

My study of these seven women and their reception of Rousseau has been guided by this view of women as participants in a dual literary heritage and of their writing as an intertwining of dominant male and repressed female discourses. I have examined how each of these seven authors responded to Rousseau on both a literary and ideological level and how their responses are in turn reflected in the style and structure of their writings. I have suggested, for example, that d'Epinay's autobiographical novel *Histoire de Madame de Montbrillant* represents the strivings of a woman writer to create within the confines of male-dominated novelistic genres a *roman de femme*, in which the experiences and dilemmas of women might be expressed in a more authentic manner. The same search for a distinctly feminine form of expression is reflected in the novels of Wollstonecraft, Staël, and Genlis (particularly in *Maria, Corinne,* and *Adèle et Théodore*), in Roland's and Gouges's memoirs, and in Henriette's letters to Rousseau (which can be read as *lettres-mémoires*). By recording their experiences in their writings, these women were able to distance themselves from the problems and tensions inherent in the female condition of their period and to begin to resolve them, at least at the narrative level. Each was able to re-create herself through her writing, reshaping her life according to her deepest longings and aspirations.

Aside from the novels of Mmes de Lafayette, de Graffigny, and Riccoboni, there were few models for these women to follow in elaborating what was essentially a woman's story. Their originality lies in their effort to develop a style that would enable them to articulate their feelings and perceptions from a distinctly feminine point of view. Contrary to Michèle Duchet's claim "that it would be difficult to find eighteenth-century texts in which the feminine voice seeks to express itself authentically," I have argued that d'Epinay's writings— and her novel in particular—are exemplary *"textes au féminin"* in which the feminine resolutely seeks to express itself through alternative modes of discourse. D'Epinay's use of gaps, silence, "body language," and an original mixture of styles, genres, and voices anticipates the *écriture féminine* of contemporary feminist writers such as Hélène Cixous, Marguerite Duras, and Luce Irigaray. The six other women also produced striking examples of eighteenth-century *"textes au féminin."* Although their styles vary considerably depending on the genre adopted (novel, autobiography, letter, essay, play, political manifesto), their implied reader, not to mention their very different personalities and experiences, their works share certain fundamental traits. What are these common traits and to what extent are they distinctively feminine?

In reaction to the prescriptive tendencies of male writings on women—a tendency particularly marked in Rousseau's works and in the conduct books that proliferated in the late eighteenth century[35]— these female authors drew on the authority of their own experiences as daughters, wives, mothers, and lovers in an effort to present a more authentically descriptive, feminocentric view of women's lives. Instead of passively allowing male authors to tell them how they should be, they sought to describe how they actually were—or how they perceived themselves and other women to be. For example, in contrast to Rousseau's prescriptive, moralistic pronouncements in favor of maternal breastfeeding, d'Epinay, Roland, and Genlis describe in realistic detail the practical problems (both social and physical) that women encountered when they tried to nurse their babies themselves, instead of hiring a wet-nurse.[36] The physical realities of the female condition (pregnancy, childbirth, motherhood, aging) are recurring themes in the writings of these women—details from daily life generally ignored in male-authored texts of the period. In contrast to the idealized view of conjugal felicity presented by Rousseau, these women present a far more realistic (and generally more pessimistic) view of the realities of married life: financial and legal dependence upon irresponsible husbands, the injustices of the double standard, the frustrations of motherhood, and the daily misery of being tied for life to a man one does not love or even like. In their works, one finds recurring images of confinement (cage, prison, asylum, convent) that reflect the oppressed state of women in eighteenth-century society, their imprisonment within constraining roles and structures. These images of confinement and powerlessness in women's texts contrast sharply with the recurring allusions to Julie's "empire" and moral authority in *La Nouvelle Héloïse*. Yet their portrayal of this oppression in their writings constituted an act of individual and collective empowerment, a vehicle for social protest and social change.

Rejecting or subverting the traditional conventions of female modesty and silence advocated by Rousseau, these women strove to convey repressed female desires, thoughts, and emotions—to go beyond existing possibilities of expression by defying literary and social *bienséances* of what was considered "proper" for a woman to articulate. Their writing thus functions simultaneously as a historical record of their oppression and a mark of their defiance.[37] Each writer attempted to develop a style in which her grievances and longings could be expressed from within rather than viewed from outside through the distorting lens of male desire and self-interest. In order to do so, they needed to overcome the interiorized feelings of inferiority, the traditional prejudices against women writers, and the fear of censure conditioned in them by society—negative gender stereotypes that Rousseau's writings both reflected and intensified. Their strategies for overcoming these feelings of insecurity ranged from denial of literary ambitions (as with Roland and Henriette) to pompous claims to genius (as with Staël and d'Epinay) to equally exaggerated admissions of inferiority (as with Gouges).

By questioning male figures of authority in general—and Rousseau in particular—these women gradually gained confidence in their own experience and point of view. No longer taking Rousseau and other male authors as their sole literary models, they gradually developed a sense of belonging to a female literary heritage. This shift in identification is particularly striking in the works of Roland and Wollstonecraft, who both adopted Catherine Macaulay as their preferred literary model after earlier choosing Rousseau—a significant shift, since Macaulay was principally a writer of history, traditionally a male-dominated genre. Similarly, when Genlis turned to novel writing to support herself during her exile, she looked back to Graffigny and Mme de LaFayette as her main literary models, just as she had earlier emulated Mme de Maintenon in her vocation as an educator. A similar shift occurred in Staël's career when she chose a passage from her mother's writings to serve as the epigraph to *Delphine*, her first novel. For Staël, who until then had been very much a male-identified author, this was a way of recognizing her mother's talents as a writer (talents her father had largely stifled) and her own female literary heritage—an act of self-affirmation she would re-enact more dramatically, at the end of her career, in the second preface to her *Lettres sur Rousseau*.

According to Judith Gardiner, women's writing generally fosters stronger identification and more intimate connections among authors, characters, and readers than male texts, due to their shared experiences and problems as women. Using the mother-daughter bond to describe the relationship between a woman author, her female literary predecessors, her female characters and women readers, Gardiner suggests that "the heroine is her author's daughter" as a paradigm for women's literary creation.[38] This metaphor accurately depicts the relationship between these seven women writers and their public; for in the course of their careers, they became more "woman-identified" as writers and in relation to their readers. This is clearly reflected in d'Epinay's *Conversations d'Emilie*, Wollstonecraft's *Rights of Woman* and *Maria*, and Gouges's feminist manifestos. This shift is more striking still in Genlis's *De l'Influence des femmes* and in the second preface to Staël's *Lettres sur Rousseau*.

Each woman's individual story (or fictional projection of it) leads to social commentary on the condition of women in general and to a mixture of realistic description with idealistic longings. In their writings, one often finds a blurring of the public/private distinction in the relation between author and audience, as well as a breakdown of generic boundaries (between fiction, autobiography, and essay). Because of the continual crossing of self and self-representation, of self and other, their lives, journals, letters, and fictions overflow one into the other. This is particularly striking in the works of d'Epinay, Roland, Genlis, and Wollstonecraft. It is hardly surprising, then, that the fictional and autobiographical writings of these women do not conform to the generic prescriptions of the male canon. Their writings tend to be less linear, unified, and chronological than those of their male contemporaries. Rousseau's *Confessions*, for example, follow a fairly straightforward chronological progression. In contrast, Mme Roland's *Mémoires* jump backward and forward in time and are often interrupted by exterior events that intrude into the narrative or by memories from the past in which she consciously seeks refuge from her painful experiences in prison. The same can be said of Henriette's letters to Rousseau and Wollstonecraft's letters to Imlay, which reflect their inner state of mind far more than external events and which present their experiences in spiral, rather than linear, fashion.

Perhaps the most distinctive common feature of the writing by these seven women (particularly the five fiction writers among them) is its multivocal quality. Engaged in a process of trying out different identities, chosen from among many imaginative possibilities, these women used their texts as a means of self-discovery and self-definition. Their texts begin as narcissistic extensions of themselves, in which different possible identities are projected onto the heroine and various secondary female characters. The personalities of these characters are shaped by literary conventions and social realities, as well as by the author's own ideals and view of herself. In the course of this narrative self-"re-creation," the author shifts her self-projection from one character to another, often shifting at the same time from first- to second- to third-person narration. These narrative shifts are especially noticeable in *Histoire de Mme de Montbrillant*, *Maria*, and *Corinne*, but also occur in Genlis's *Adèle et Théodore* and Roland's memoirs. Such shifts in voice serve as distancing devices that allow the woman writer to experience her literary self-representation as separate from herself, to use it as a form of self-therapy and as a means of change. By imagining and portraying herself as freer, more self-confident, more gifted, happier, *different* from what she is (or from what she perceives herself to be), the author takes an important step toward fulfilling her aspirations and effecting both personal and social change. For, as Hélène Cixous has suggested, "writing is precisely the very possibility of change, the space that can serve as a springboard for subversive thought, the precursory movement of a transformation of social and cultural structures."[39]

If, at the end of her novel, d'Epinay is able to declare: "I have begun to dare to be myself," it is because she has recreated herself through her fictional alter-ego, just as Staël has through Corinne, Genlis through Mme d'Almane, and Gouges in her plays through the character of Ninon de Lenclos. Madame Roland ends her memoirs with a similar affirmation of her identity as a writer: "And *I too* will live on for future generations," just as Gouges proudly declared that her heroic self-sacrifice for her country guaranteed that her name "would live on in full glory among future generations." For each of these writers, the decision to write and to publish constituted a courageous act of self-affirmation in a period in which female self-expression was often mocked and scorned. All seven writers gradually came to the conclusion that the woman artist should look within herself, to her own creative powers, for the greatest and surest source of pleasure and self-fulfillment.

From Passionate Disciples to Resisting Readers

With the passing of time, these seven women came to view Rousseau's ideal of sensibility and his limited vision of female destiny with increasing ambivalence. With the insights brought to them by their careers as writers and their experiences as women, they gradually moved from a position of admirer or even passionate disciple of Rousseau to one of resisting reader and protesting writer. This was especially true of Wollstonecraft, d'Epinay, Staël, and Genlis, who were openly critical of Rousseau's views on women and women writers by the end of their careers.

The challenge to Rousseau's views by Henriette and Mme Roland was more subtle but no less eloquent. Henriette's decision to publish her correspondence as a "tribute of gratitude" to the man who had stifled her talents and her literary ambitions is an ironic (and perhaps unconscious) gesture of self-affirmation and revolt. Similarly, Mme Roland's imitation of Rousseau's bold confessional style, coupled with her active involvement in politics and her decision to record her life and times for posterity, can also be seen as an act of defiance. Although on the surface she appeared devoted to Rousseau's ideals of sensibility and domesticity, Roland subtly subverted and reshaped his views to serve her own needs and ambitions. Indeed, all seven women appropriated some aspects of his sexual politics, while rejecting others, and then transformed his views to suit their own purposes. Drawing on their experiences as daughters, wives, mothers, and lovers, and responding to the powerful impulse of their talents and aspirations, each of these women eventually challenged Rousseau's limited view of female destiny.

Notes

Introduction

1. See, for example, the study of Rousseau's sexual politics by Maïté Albistur and Daniel Armogathe, in *Histoire du féminisme français du moyen âge à nos jours* (Paris: Eds. des femmes, 1977), v. I, pp. 277–78; Michèle Coquillat, "Nature et sexe chez Rousseau. Au commencement était le phallus," in *La poétique du mâle* (Paris: Gallimard, 1982), pp. 119–35; Eva Figes, "Rousseau, Revolution, Romanticism, and Retrogression," in *Patriarchal Attitudes* (London: Macmillan, 1986), pp. 92–110; Elisabeth de Fontenay, "Pour Emile et par Emile, Sophie ou l'invention du ménage," *Les Temps Modernes* 358, 2 (1976): 774–95; Sarah Kofman, "Rousseau's Phallocratic Ends," *Hypatia, A Journal of Feminist Philosophy* 3, 3 (Winter 1989): 123–36; Joan Landes, "Rousseau's Reply to Public Women," in *Women and the Public Sphere in the Age of the French Revolution* (Ithaca: Cornell Univ. Press, 1988), pp. 66–89; Lynda Lange, "Women and the 'General Will,'" *University of Ottawa Quarterly* 49, 3–4 (1979): 401–11; Nannerl Keohane, "'But for Her Sex . . . ' The Domestication of Sophie," *University of Ottawa Quarterly* 49, 3–4 (1979): 390–400; Aubrey Rosenberg, "Property, Possession, and Enjoyment: Woman as Object, Subject, and Project in the *Emile*," in *Rousseau et l'éducation: Etudes sur l'Emile*, ed. Jean Terrasse (Sherbrooke, Canada: Naaman, 1984), pp. 102–13; and Nancy Senior, "*Les Solitaires* as a Test for Emile and Sophie," *French Review* 49, 4 (March 1976): 528–35.

2. See, for example, Jean H. Bloch, "Women and the Reform of the Nation," in *Woman and Society in Eighteenth-Century France*, ed. Eva Jacobs et al. (London: Athlone Press, 1979), pp. 3–18; Mary Louise Butler, *Rousseau's Vision of Woman* (Ph.D. diss., Univ. of Connecticut, 1980); Ruth Graham, "Rousseau's Sexism Revolutionized," in *Woman in the 18th Century and Other Essays*, ed. Paul Fritz and Richard Morton (Toronto: Hakkert, 1976), pp. 127–39; Gita May, "Rousseau's 'Anti-Feminism' Reconsidered," in *French Women and the Age of Enlightenment*, ed. Samia I. Spencer (Bloomington: Indiana Univ. Press, 1984), pp. 309–17; Colette Piau-Gillot, "Le Discours de J. J. Rousseau sur les femmes et sa réception critique," *Dix-huitième siècle* 13 (1981): 317–33.

3. See Anna Attridge, "The Reception of *La Nouvelle Héloïse*," *Studies on Voltaire and the Eighteenth Century* 120 (1974): 227–67; Margaret Darrow, "French Noblewomen and the New Domesticity, 1750–1850," *Feminist Studies* 5, 1 (Spring 1979): 41–65; Peter Jimack, "The Paradox of Sophie and Julie: Contemporary Response to Rousseau's Ideal Wife and Ideal Mother," in Jacobs, *Woman and Society*, pp. 152–65; Marie-Laure Swiderski, "La dialectique de la condition féminine dans *La Nouvelle Héloïse*," in *Rousseau et la société du XVIIIe siècle*, ed. Jean Terrasse (Ottawa: Univ. of Ottawa Press, 1982), pp. 109–26; and the studies by Bloch, Graham, May, and Piau-Gillot cited in note 2.

4. Condorcet (Antoine Caritat de), *Lettres d'un bourgeois de Newhaven à un citoyen de Virginie* [1787], in *Œuvres de Condorcet* (Paris: Firmin Didot, 1847–49; reprinted Stuttgart: Frommann Verlag, 1968), v. IX, p. 20.

5. Carol Blum has examined this tendency in detail in *Rousseau and the Republic of Virtue: The Language of Politics in the French Revolution* (Ithaca: Cornell Univ. Press, 1986). Blum's study is cited and discussed in Chapter 1.

6. In my investigation into the breakdown of traditional boundaries brought about by women writers, I share Joan DeJean's dissatisfaction with the compartmentalization of discourses normally operative today and agree with her assertion that "absolute distinctions between word and event, between history and literature, between public and private (history), between domestic economy and political life cannot be maintained to account for situations that developed in violation of these traditional boundaries." See Joan DeJean, *Tender Geographies. Women and the Origins of the Novel in France* (New York: Columbia Univ. Press, 1991), p. 18.

On the development of public and private spheres in eighteenth-century society, see Jürgen Habermas, *The Structural Transformation of the Public Sphere: An Inquiry into a Category of Bourgeois Society*, trans. Thomas Burger with Frederick Lawrence (Cambridge: MIT Press, 1989), pp. 27–56, and Joan B. Landes, *Women and the Public Sphere in the Age of the French Revolution* (Ithaca: Cornell Univ. Press, 1988). For critiques of Habermas's model and the ongoing debate over the relationship of women to the public sphere, see Lawrence E. Klein, "Gender and the Public/Private Distinction in the Eighteenth Century: Some Questions about Evidence and Analytic Procedure," *Eighteenth-Century Studies* 29, 1 (Fall 1995): 97–109; Dena Goodman, "Public Sphere and Private Life: Toward a Synthesis of Current Historiographical Approaches to the Old Regime," *History and Theory* 31 (1992): 1–20; Joan DeJean's study cited above, particularly Chapter 1: "Women's Places, Women's Spaces," pp. 17–70; Jennifer M. Jones, "Repackaging Rousseau: Femininity and Fashion in Old Regime France," *French Historical Studies* 18, 4 (Fall 1994): 939–67; and the forum of articles on "The Public Sphere in the Eighteenth Century" by Sarah Maza, Daniel Gordon, and David Bell in *French Historical Studies* 17, 4 (Fall 1992): 882–956.

7. Isabelle de Charrière, *Eloge de Rousseau* [1790], in *Œuvres complètes*, ed. Jean-Daniel Candaux (Amsterdam: Van Oorschot, 1981), v. X, p. 204.

8. Ibid.

9. See Robert Darnton, "Readers Respond to Rousseau: The Fabrication of Romantic Sensitivity," in *The Great Cat Massacre* (New York: Basic Books, 1984), and Claude Labrosse, *Lire au XVIIIᵉ siècle. La Nouvelle Héloïse et ses lecteurs* (Lyon: Presses universitaires de Lyon, 1985). Both works are cited and discussed in Chapter 1.

10. See Judith Fetterley, *The Resisting Reader: A Feminist Approach to American Fiction* (Bloomington: Indiana Univ. Press, 1978), and *Gender and Reading. Essays on Readers, Texts, and Contexts*, ed. Patrocinio P. Schweickart and Elizabeth A. Flynn (Baltimore: Johns Hopkins Univ. Press, 1986), esp. Schweickart's essay, "Reading Ourselves: Toward a Feminist Theory of Reading," pp. 31–62.

Chapter 1

1. Both tendencies are apparent in the discussions of Rousseau's sexual politics by Maïté Albistur and Daniel Armogathe in *Histoire du féminisme français du moyen âge à nos jours* (Paris: Eds. des femmes, 1977), v. 1, pp. 277–78, and in Ron Christenson, "The Political Theory of Male Chauvinism: J.-J. Rousseau's Paradigm," *Midwest Quarterly* 13, 3 (April 1972): 291–99; Michèle Coquillat, "Nature et sexe chez Rousseau. Au commencement était le phallus," in *La poétique du mâle* (Paris: Gallimard, 1982), pp. 119–35; Eva Figes, "Rousseau, Revolution, Romanticism, and Retrogression," in *Patriarchal Attitudes* (London: Macmillan, 1986), pp. 92–110; Sarah Kofman, "Rousseau's Phallocratic Ends," *Hypatia, A Journal of Feminist Philosophy* 3, 3 (Winter 1989): 123–36; and Joan B. Landes, "Rousseau's Reply to Public Women," in *Women and the Public Sphere in the Age of the French Revolution* (Ithaca: Cornell Univ. Press, 1988), pp. 66–89.

2. Stephen Salkever, "Interpreting Rousseau's Paradoxes," *Eighteenth-Century Studies* 11 (1977/78): 208–9.

3. Colette Piau-Gillot, "Le Discours de Jean-Jacques Rousseau sur les femmes, et sa réception critique," *Dix-huitième siècle* 13 (1981): 317–18.

4. See Paul Hoffmann, "Le mythe de la femme dans la pensée de Jean-Jacques Rousseau," in *La femme dans la pensée des lumières* (Paris: Editions Ophrys, 1977), pp. 359–446, and Joel Schwartz, *The Sexual Politics of Jean-Jacques Rousseau* (Chicago: Univ. of Chicago Press, 1984), esp. Chap. 6, pp. 142–54.

5. Jean-Jacques Rousseau, *Julie, ou la Nouvelle Héloïse*, in *Œuvres complètes*, 4 vols., ed. Bernard Gagnebin and Marcel Raymond (Paris: Gallimard, Bibliothèque de la Pléiade, 1961), v. II, p. 27.

6. Thomas Kavanagh argues that it is Rousseau's quest to write the truth that constitutes the central preoccupation of his works. See *Writing the Truth: Authority and Desire in Rousseau* (Berkeley: Univ. of California Press, 1987).

7. *Emile ou de l'éducation*, in *Œuvres complètes* (Paris: Gallimard, Bibliothèque de la Pléiade, 1969), v. IV, p. 323. The Pléiade edition of Rousseau's complete works will be referred to hereafter as *OC*. Subsequent references to this edition will be referred to parenthetically in the text by volume and page number, except for initial references to works not yet cited. Hence, the *Confessions* will be referred to as vol. I, *Julie* as vol. II, and *Emile* as vol. IV.

8. The appeal to nature in Rousseau's thought has been well documented by Rousseau scholars. See, for example, Sarah Kofman, *Le Respect des femmes. Kant et Rousseau* (Paris: Eds. Galilée, 1982) and her "Rousseau's Phallocratic Ends" cited earlier; James Hamilton, "Literature and 'Natural Man' in Rousseau's *Emile*," in *Literature and History in the Age of Ideas: Essays on the French Enlightenment*, ed. Charles Williams (Columbus: Ohio State Univ. Press, 1975), pp. 194–206; Genevieve Lloyd, *The Man of Reason. "Male" and "Female" in Western Philosophy* (Minneapolis: Univ. of Minnesota Press, 1984), pp. 62–64; Juliet Flower MacCannell, "Nature and Self-Love. A Reinterpretation of Rousseau's 'Passion Primitive,'" *PMLA* XCII (1977): 890–902; Janine Rossard, "La Pudeur Naturiste de *La Nouvelle Héloïse*," in *Une Clef du Romantisme: La Pudeur* (Paris: Nizet, 1975), pp. 21–48; Nancy Senior, "Sophie and the State of Nature," *French Forum* 2 (1977): 134–46; and the studies by Coquillat and Piau-Gillot cited earlier.

9. Lloyd, pp. 62, 64.

10. In the *Social Contract*, Rousseau writes: "The strongest is never strong enough to remain the master unless he transforms his dominance into law and the obedience of others into a duty. From this arises *le droit du plus fort*— the law of the strongest, the principle that might is right" (*Du Contrat social*, in *OC*, III: 354). All translations are mine unless indicated otherwise.

11. Bernard Guyon, notes to *Julie*, in *OC*, II: 1635.

12. See *Emile*, IV: 749. But how are we to interpret the fact that Saint-Preux, like Rousseau himself, confesses a special fondness for dairy products, normally reserved for female consumption?

13. Rousseau, *Lettre à d'Alembert*, ed. M. Fuchs (Geneva: Droz, 1948), pp. 120, 130.

14. Pierre Burgelin,"L'éducation de Sophie," *Annales J.-J. Rousseau* 35 (1959–62): 125.

15. See *Emile*, in *OC*, IV: 699.

16. Elsewhere, Rousseau blames society more than women themselves for these practices. In the Second Discourse, he writes: "Viewing children as a burden to their parents, society kills them before their birth," and later adds: "The laws of abstinence and honor in fact encourage debauchery and recourse to abortions" (*Discours sur l'inégalité*, in *OC*, III: 135, 159). On the use and consequences of contraceptive methods in eighteenth-century France, see Jean-Louis Flandrin, *Familles: Parenté, maison, sexualité dans l'ancienne société* (Paris: Hachette, 1976), pp. 190–233; A. Chamoux and C. Dauphin, "La Contraception avant la Révolution française," *Annales, Economies, Sociétés, Civilisations* XXIV, 3 (1969): 662–84; and Edward Shorter, "Female Emancipation, Birth Control, and Fertility in European History," *American Historical Review* (June 1973): 605–40.

17. This is the picture of family structures in mid-eighteenth-century France that emerges in Philippe Aries's seminal study *L'enfant et la vie familiale sous l'Ancien Régime* (Paris: Eds. du Seuil, 1960) and in more recent studies on the history of the family. See, for example, Louis Trenard, "La famille au XVIIIᵉ siècle," in *Actualité du XVIIIᵉ siècle*, ed. Jean Balcou (Brest, 1982), pp. 105–74; François Lebrun, *La vie conjugale sous l'Ancien Régime* (Paris: A. Colin, 1975); A. Lottin, *La désunion du couple sous l'Ancien Régime* (Lille: Université de Lille III, 1975); James Traer, *Marriage and the Family in Eighteenth-Century France* (Ithaca: Cornell Univ. Press, 1980); and Flandrin cited above. For a good overview of the subject, see Barbara J. Harris, "Recent Work on the History of the Family: A Review Article," *Feminist Studies* 3, 3/4 (Spring–Summer 1976): 159–72.

18. In the mid-1750s, well before the publication of *Emile*, l'abbé Picardet and l'abbé Poncelet published works in which they maintained that it was women's moral duty to breastfeed their children. Before *Emile*, the health benefits of maternal nursing were stressed by numerous doctors, including Vandermonde, Dessessartz, and Ballexserd.

19. For further discussion of Rousseau's contribution to the breastfeeding movement, see Jean H. Bloch, "Rousseau's Reputation as an Authority on Childcare and Physical Education in France before the Revolution," *Paedagogica historica* XIV, 1 (1974): 5–33; Nancy Senior, "Aspects of Infant Feeding in Eighteenth-Century France," *Eighteenth-Century Studies* 16 (1983): 367–88; and George Sussman, "The Wet-Nursing Business in Nineteenth-Century France," *French Historical Studies* 9, 2 (Fall 1975): 304–28.

20. Carol Blum, *Rousseau and the Republic of Virtue: The Language of Politics in the French Revolution* (Ithaca: Cornell Univ. Press, 1986), p. 47. See especially the chapter titled "The Sex Made to Obey," pp. 204–15.

21. Letter to Mme de Berthier, 17 Jan. 1770, in *Correspondance Complète de Jean-Jacques Rousseau*, ed. R. A. Leigh (Geneva: Institut Voltaire, 1967), v. 37, pp. 205–7. This edition will be referred hereafter to as *CC*.

22. Letter to Anne-Marie d'Ivernois, 13 Sept. 1762, in *CC*, XIII, p. 60. Also see the *Confessions*, in *OC*, I: 602.

23. *La Mort de Lucrèce*, in *OC*, II: 1024.

24. As early as 1730, l'abbé de Saint-Pierre had proposed a *Projet pour multiplier les collèges de filles* that called for the establishment in France of twenty girls' schools composed of twelve classes of fifteen students each, to be administered by a central government agency in Paris. (See his *Œuvres* [Rotterdam, 1733], v. IV, pp. 269–81).

Rousseau opposed boarding-school educations for girls and boys alike: "There are no boarding schools for girls? What a pity! If only there weren't boarding schools for boys either, they'd be brought up much better!" (*OC*, IV: 701).

25. However, it is not so much Sophie's education that fails her in Paris as Emile himself, first by taking her there against her will and then by leaving her alone much of the time. For different perspectives on the failure of Sophie's education, see Nancy Senior, "*Les Solitaires* as a Test for Emile and Sophie," *French Review* 49, 4 (March 1976): 528–35; Pierre Burgelin, "L'Education de Sophie," *Annales J.-J. Rousseau* 35 (1959–62): 113–30; James Hamilton, "Rousseau's *Emile et Sophie*: A Parody of the Philosopher-King," *Studi francesi* 22, 2 (May–Dec. 1978): 392–95; and Jean-Louis Lecercle "Les Solitaires," in *Rousseau et l'art du roman* (Paris: A. Colin, 1969), pp. 351–59.

26. See Rousseau's reflections in the *Confessions* concerning Thérèse after their move to l'Ermitage: "It was then that I realized how wrong I had been, during our early days together, not to have taken advantage of the docility love gave her to cultivate knowledge and talents in her that would later have drawn us together in our seclusion and pleasantly filled her time and mine, without letting us grow bored when we were alone together. We did not have enough ideas in common to draw on for long. . . . It is particularly in solitude that one feels the advantage of living with someone who can think" (*OC*, I: 421).

27. In *Emile*, Rousseau declares: "The search for abstract and speculative truths . . . is not at all within women's reach; their studies should be limited to practical knowledge" (*OC*, IV: 736).

28. While, in this passage from *Emile*, Rousseau suggests that girls are naturally curious to learn to read and write, on the preceding page he affirms just the opposite: "Nearly all little girls detest learning to read and write, but they are always delighted to learn how to sew. They are pleased at the thought that these talents later will be useful in adorning themselves and enhancing their charms" (IV: 707). Evidently, in Rousseau's view, women's vanity outweighs their intellectual curiosity. The contradiction between these two passages reveals Rousseau's bad faith—the extent to which he purposely

confuses the social conditioning of women with their natural capabilities and inclinations.

29. The meaning—and veiled ambiguity—of this passage becomes clearer when read in conjunction with another passage in *Emile*: "All the thoughts of women not directly pertaining to their domestic duties should be directed toward the study of men or toward the attainment of female accomplishments. . . . Women must know how to make us give them whatever they cannot obtain for themselves that is necessary or desirable to them; they must therefore study men carefully and learn how to penetrate their thoughts and feelings" (IV: 736–37).

30. Begun in the spring of 1756, *Julie* was not completed until 1760, after Rousseau had already been working on *Emile* for nearly two years. *Julie* was published in 1761, *Emile* the following year.

31. That the implied reader of *Emile* is generally male and its point of view distinctly masculine is particularly well illustrated by a passage on pp. 700–1, in which male readers are referred to as "we" or "us" [*on* or *nous*], while women readers are referred to as "you" [*vous*] or "they" [*elles*].

32. Jean-Louis Lecercle, "La femme selon Jean-Jacques," in *Jean-Jacques Rousseau. Quatre études* (Neuchâtel: Editions de la Baconnière, 1978), p. 42.

33. See Hoffmann, pp. 390–91, 562.

34. Any such attempt at categorization is always somewhat artificial. The four views of women outlined here should not be seen as rigid, mutually exclusive doctrines, but rather as distinct, yet at times overlapping currents of thought. Hence certain authors may fall into more than one category depending upon the specific question or text under consideration. There are of course other possible classification schemes. Jean Portemer, for example, outlines three tendencies in eighteenth-century views on women: rigorist, rationalist-feminist, and pragmatist-reformist. See "Le statut de la femme en France depuis la réformation des coutumes jusqu'à la rédaction du code civil," *Recueils de la Société Jean Bodin* 12 (1962): 447–97, esp. 448–49. See also Eva Jacobs's distinction between the rationalist-feminist position of Condorcet and the empirical-pragmatist position of Diderot in "Diderot and the Education of Girls," in *Women and Society in Eighteenth-Century France*, p. 95. Paul Hoffmann proposes a far more complex scheme involving multiple poles or currents of thought: naturalist vs. rationalist-egalitarian, novelistic vs. theoretical, empiricist vs. moralistic, pragmatist vs. utopian. See Hoffmann, pp. 559–63.

35. The most emphatic expression of the traditionalist view on women in eighteenth-century French literature is to be found in the works of Restif de la Bretonne, particularly his *Gynographes* (1777). Also see Voltaire's article "Femme," in his *Dictionnaire philosophique*, in *Œuvres complètes* (Paris: Garnier,

1877–1885), v. XIX, p. 98, and Antoine-Léonard Thomas's *Essai sur le caractère, les mœurs et l'esprit des femmes dans les différents siècles* (Paris, 1772). Thomas's views are discussed in Chapter 3.

36. For discussions of the sexual politics of these writers, see P. Charbonnel, "Répères pour une étude du statut de la femme dans quelques écrits théoriques des philosophes," in *Etudes sur le XVIIIᵉ siècle* [Université de Bruxelles] 3 (1976): 93–110; Elizabeth J. Gardner, "The *Philosophes* and Women: Sensationalism and Sentiment," in Jacobs, pp. 19–27; Anne Marie Jaton, "La femme des lumières, la nature et la différence," in *Figures féminines et roman*, ed. Jean Bessière (Paris: Presses universitaires de France, 1982), pp. 75–87; Abby R. Kleinbaum, "Women in the Age of Light," in *Becoming Visible: Women in European History*, ed. Renata Bridenthal and Claudia Koonz (Boston: Houghton Mifflin, 1977), pp. 217–35; Jeannette Geffriaud Rosso, "Montesquieu, Rousseau et la féminité. De la crainte à l'angélicisme," in *Etudes sur la féminité* (Pisa: Golardica, 1984), pp. 126–46; Sheila Mason, "The Riddle of Roxanne," in Jacobs, pp. 28–41; Robert F. O'Reilly, "Montesquieu: Anti-feminist," *Studies on Voltaire and the Eighteenth Century* 102 (1973): 143–56; Leon Schwartz, "F. M. Grimm and the Eighteenth-Century Debate on Women," *French Review* 58, 2 (December 1984): 336–43; David Williams, "The Politics of Feminism in the French Enlightenment," in *The Varied Pattern: Studies in the 18th Century*, ed. Peter Hughes and David Williams (Toronto: Hakkert, 1971); and the studies already cited by Albistur and Armogathe, Hoffmann, and Portemer.

37. See Condorcet's *Lettres d'un bourgeois de Newhaven à un citoyen de Virginie*, in *Œuvres de Condorcet* (Stuttgart: Frommann Verlag, 1968), v. IX, and his essay *Sur l'admission des femmes au droit de cité*, in *Œuvres*, v. X.

38. See, for example, Helvétius's essay *De l'Homme*, in Helvétius, *Œuvres complètes* (London, 1776), v. III, esp. pp. 184–85; Laclos's *De l'éducation des femmes*, in *Œuvres complètes*, pp. 403–58; and Diderot's essay *Sur les femmes*, ed. J. Assézat (Paris: Garnier, 1875), in Diderot, *Œuvres complètes*, v. II, pp. 252–62. For an analysis of the pseudo-feminist aspects of Diderot's essay, see my article "Sexual/Textual Politics in the Enlightenment: Diderot and d'Epinay Respond to Thomas's Essay on Women," *Romanic Review* 84, 2 (March 1994): 98–116.

39. See Pierre Roussel, *Système physique et moral de la femme* (Paris: Vincent, 1775), and Paul-Victor de Sèze, *Recherches physiologiques et philosophiques sur la sensibilité* (Paris: Prault, 1786). Also see Lindsay B. Wilson, *Women and Medicine in the French Enlightenment: The Debate over "Maladies des Femmes"* (Baltimore: Johns Hopkins Univ. Press, 1993), and the discussions of eighteenth-century French medical discourse on women by Portemer, Hoffmann, and Jaton (cited earlier).

40. See Joseph Pothier, *Traité de la puissance du mari sur la personne et les biens de la femme et des donations entre mari et femme* (1770), in Pothier, *Œuvres*, ed. Bugnet (Paris, 1861). Also see the discussion of eighteenth-century French legal discourse on women by Portemer and Hoffmann in the studies cited above.

41. "In Rousseau's discourse, marriage goes beyond the realm of sentiment to attain the realm of politics," remarks Colette Piau-Gillot. "In his view, emotional and sexual problems cannot be resolved independently of class conflicts." See Piau-Gillot, "Le Discours de Rousseau sur les femmes et sa réception critique," *Dix-huitième siècle* 13 (1981): 326.

42. The French in this passage reads: "Je suis lasse de servir aux dépends de la justice une chimérique vertu.... Nature, ô douce nature, reprends tous tes droits! j'abjure les barbares vertus qui t'anéantissent.... Devoir, honneur, vertu, tout cela ne me dit plus rien.... Qu'un père esclave de sa parole et jaloux d'un vain titre dispose de ma main qu'il a promise; que l'amour seul dispose de mon cœur" (II: 334–35).

43. Marie-Laure Swiderski, "La dialectique de la condition féminine dans *La Nouvelle Héloïse*," in *Rousseau et la société du XVIIIᵉ siècle*, ed. Jean Terrasse (Ottawa: Univ. of Ottawa Press, 1982), p. 116.

44. See Blum, p. 64. The French passage reads: "J'espère me réunir à toi pour le reste de nos jours. Petite ingrate, c'est que tu me consoles de tout, et que je ne sais plus m'affliger de rien quand je te possèdes. Ton empire est le plus absolu que je connaisse; tu m'en imposes, tu me subjugues, tu m'atterres" (II: 408–9).

45. See *Julie* (II: 599): "Claire rushed to help Julie as she fainted, and fell on her in the same state. Despite his usual coldness, even Wolmar felt moved. Instead of running to Julie, this happy spouse threw himself in a chair to greedily contemplate this ravishing sight. Don't be alarmed, he said, noticing our concern. These scenes of joy and pleasure present no danger; they drain nature only for an instant in order to revive it with new vigor. Let me enjoy the happiness I feel and which you share." For further discussion of the homoerotic nature of Claire's friendship for Julie, see Jean Hagstrum, *Sex and Sensibility* (Chicago: Univ. of Chicago Press, 1980), pp. 232–34.

46. Compare Saint-Preux's letter with the passage describing "l'idylle des cerises" in the *Confessions*, in *OC*, I: 137–38.

47. The abnormal aspects of Rousseau's sex life—his excessive timidity toward women, his possible impotence in later life due to a genetic urinary malformation, his exhibitionism, onanism, voyeurism, transvestism, sado-

masochistic tendencies, and intense homophobia (toward male homosexuals), along with his decided predilection for *ménage à trois* relationships—have all been described in detail by numerous scholars and by Jean-Jacques himself in the *Confessions*. For different perspectives on Rousseau's complex psychosexual makeup, see Georges Dupeyron, "Jean-Jacques et la sexualité," *Europe* 39, 391–92 (Nov.–Dec. 1961): 33–42; Jenny H. Batlay, "Madame de Warens, femme savante ou femme fatale?," in *J.-J. Rousseau et la société du XVIIIe siècle*, pp. 127–36; Georges Benrekassa, "L'individu et le sexe: du discours de l'*Emile* au texte des *Confessions*," *Revue des sciences humaines* 41, 161 (Winter 1976): 45–61; Charly Guyot *Plaidoyer pour Thérèse Levasseur* (Neuchâtel: Ides et Calendes, 1962); Anne Srabian de Fabry, "Amours et mathématiques: Rousseau et les femmes," *Rice University Studies* 59, 3 (Summer 1973): 27–36; and especially Jean Starobinski, *J.-J. Rousseau. La Transparence et l'obstacle* (Paris: Gallimard, 1971).

48. See Pierre Fauchery, *La Destinée Féminine dans le Roman Européen du Dix-Huitième Siècle* (Paris: A. Colin, 1972), p. 212, and Paul Hoffmann, *La femme dans la pensée des lumières* (Paris: Editions Ophrys, 1977), pp. 563–64.

49. The incestuous undercurrents in Julie's relation with her father are particularly apparent in the scene where M. d'Etanges pulls Julie onto his lap after he has brutally beaten her (to the point of provoking a miscarriage): "Catching me by my skirt and pulling me to him without a word, he seated me on his lap. . . . From time to time, I felt his arms press against my sides with a muffled sigh. I don't know what misguided shame prevented those paternal arms from yielding to such sweet embraces; a certain embarrassment that we dared not overcome put between father and daughter this charming awkwardness that love and sexual modesty [*pudeur*] give to lovers. I pretended to slip; to keep myself from falling, I threw my arms around my father's neck; I turned toward his venerable face, which in an instant was covered with my kisses and flooded with my tears." When her father later apologizes for having beaten her, Julie replies: "For such a reward, I would be only too happy to be beaten every day" (II: 175–76). This statement points to the sadomasochistic undercurrents in their relationship and prefigures similar, although subtler undercurrents in her relationship with Wolmar.

50. See *Julie*, in *OC*, II: 301–2.

51. Anna Attridge, "The Reception of *La Nouvelle Héloïse*," *Studies on Voltaire and the Eighteenth Century* 120 (1974): 258.

52. For an overview of the social history of women in eighteenth-century France, see Albistur and Armogathe, v. I, pp. 248–65, and the collection of essays edited by Samia I. Spencer, *French Women and the Age of Enlightenment* (Bloomington: Indiana Univ. Press, 1984). Also see Evelyn Gordon Bodek,

"Salonnières and Bluestockings: Educated Obsolescence and Germinating Feminism," *Feminist Studies* 3, 3/4 (Spring–Summer 1976): 185–99; Margaret Darrow, "French Noblewomen and the New Domesticity, 1750–1850," *Feminist Studies* 5, 1 (Spring 1979): 41–65; Jules and Edmond Goncourt, *La femme au dix-huitième siècle* (Paris: Flammarion, 1982); Dena Goodman, "Enlightenment Salons: The Convergence of Female and Philosophic Ambitions," *Eighteenth-Century Studies* 22 (Spring 1989): 329–50; Erica Harth, *Cartesian Women: Versions and Subversions of Rational Discouse in the Old Regime* (Ithaca: Cornell Univ. Press, 1992); Olwen Hufton, "Women and the Family Economy in 18th-Century France," *French Historical Studies* (Spring 1975): 1–25; Roderick Phillips, "Women's Emancipation, the Family, and Social Change in Eighteenth-Century France," *Journal of Social History* 12, 4 (Summer 1979): 553–68; Paul Rousselot, *Histoire de l'éducation des femmes en France* (Paris: Didier, 1883; reprinted New York: Burt Franklin, 1971), esp. v. 2, pp. 1–91; the articles by Barbara C. Pope and Mary D. Johnson in *War, Women, and Revolution; Women in Revolutionary Paris, 1789–1795*, ed. Darline Gay Levy *et al.*; and the studies cited above by Ariès, Flandrin, Lebrun, Lottin, Portemer, Traer, and Trenard.

53. Concerning the connections between the literary representation of women and their condition in eighteenth-century French society—and, more specifically, the mediations between fiction and reality in *Julie*—see Georges Benrekassa, "Sphère publique et sphère privée. Le romancier et le philosophe interprètes des Lumières," *Revue des sciences humaines* 182, 2 (1981): 7–20; Janet Bowman, "*La Nouvelle Héloïse*. Etude sociocritique par Rousseau," *Chimères* XIII, 2 (Spring 1980): 45–53; Geoffrey Bremner, "Rousseau's Realism or a Close Look at Julie's Underwear," *Romance Studies* 1 (Winter 1982): 48–63; Elizabeth Fox-Genovese and Eugene Genovese, *Fruits of Merchant Capital: Slavery and Bourgeois Property in the Rise and Expansion of Capitalism* (Oxford Univ. Press, 1983), esp. the chapter titled "The Ideological Bases of Domestic Economy: The Representation of Women and the Family in the Age of Expansion," pp. 299–336; Paul Hoffmann, ed., *The Portrayal and Condition of Women in Eighteenth-Century France*, SVEC 193 (1980): 1881–2040; John Lechte, "Fiction and Woman in *La Nouvelle Héloïse*," in *1789: Reading Writing Revolution*, ed. Francis Barker (University of Essex, 1981), pp. 38–51; Louise Marcil-Lacoste, "Les coefficients idéologiques de l'appel au sentiment," in *J-J Rousseau et la société du XVIIIᵉ siècle, op. cit.*, pp. 21–49; Gita May, "Rousseau's 'Anti-Feminism' Reconsidered," in Spencer, pp. 309–17; Marlene LeGates, "The Cult of Womanhood in 18th-Century Thought," *Eighteenth-Century Studies* 10 (1976): 35; Horst-Werner Nöckler, "Le Conflit entre l'idéal et la réalité bourgeoise dans *La Nouvelle Héloïse*," in *Ecriture des Marges et Mutations Historiques* (Besançon, 1983), pp. 85–91; Warren Roberts, *Morality and Social Class in 18th-Century French Literature and Painting* (Toronto: Toronto University Press, 1974); Leslie W. Rabine, *Reading the Romantic Heroine: Text, History, Ideology* (Ann Arbor:

Univ. of Michigan Press, 1985); and the studies cited earlier by Bloch, Hoffmann, LeGates, Portemer, and Swiderski.

54. Letter to Rousseau (6 April 1761) in *CC*, VIII, p. 296.

55. Letter from Mme de Polignac to Mme de Verdelin (3 Feb. 1761), in *CC*, VIII, pp. 56–57. Rousseau alludes to this letter, which Mme de Verdelin later sent to him, in a passage of the *Confessions* (*OC*, I: 546).

56. Blum, p. 137.

57. Robert Darnton, "Readers Respond to Rousseau: The Fabrication of Romantic Sensitivity," in *The Great Cat Massacre* (New York: Basic Books, 1984), pp. 248–49.

58. Jean Roussel, "Le Phénomène d'identification dans la lecture de Rousseau," *Annales J. J. Rousseau* 39 (1972–77): 65–66. For further discussion of reader response to Rousseau, see Jean Lecercle, "Rousseau et ses publics," in *Jean-Jacques Rousseau et son œuvre: Problèmes et recherches* (Paris: Klincksieck, 1964), pp. 283–301, and Albert Soboul, "L'Audience des lumières sous la Révolution: Jean-Jacques Rousseau et les classes populaires," in *Utopies et institutions au dix-huitième siècle: Le Pragmatisme des lumières*, ed. Pierre Francastel (Paris: Mouton, 1963), pp. 289–303.

59. Letter from Françoise Constant de Rebeque to her husband (9 Feb. 1761), in Rousseau, *CC*, VIII, p. 72.

60. Hippolyte Buffenoir, *La Maréchale de Luxembourg* (Paris, 1924), p. 84.

61. See the letters of 28 and 29 Sept. 1761, in *CC*, IX, pp. 132–33 and 136–37.

62. Claude Labrosse, *Lire au XVIIIᵉ siècle. La Nouvelle Héloïse et ses lecteurs* (Lyon: Presses universitaires de Lyon, 1985), pp. 113, 117.

63. Bernardin de Saint-Pierre, *Vie et œuvres de Jean-Jacques Rousseau* (Paris: Cornély, 1907), pp. 18–19.

64. Germaine de Staël, *Lettres sur les écrits et le caractère de J. J. Rousseau*, in *Œuvres complètes* (Paris: Firmin-Didot, 1838), v. I, p. 12.

65. Madame Panckoucke, *Sentiments de reconnaissance d'une mère*. Cited by Peter Jimack in "The Paradox of Sophie and Julie: Contemporary Response to Rousseau's Ideal Wife and Ideal Mother," in Jacobs, p. 162.

66. See Fauchery, p. 553.

67. Bernard Guyon, Notes to *Julie*, in *OC*, II: 1774.

68. See, for example, Diderot's essay *Sur les femmes* cited earlier and Restif de la Bretonne's *Gynographes, ou idées de deux honnêtes femmes sur un projet de*

règlement proposé à toute l'Europe, pour mettre les femmes à leur place (The Hague, Netherlands, 1777).

69. D'Alembert contests Rousseau's view that women are by nature inferior to men, insisting that any moral or mental deficiencies displayed by women resulted not from nature, but from the oppressive cultural conditioning to which they had been subjected: "But if, unfortunately, you are right, what would be the sad cause for these weaknesses? They stem from the servitude and degrading condition in which we have placed women, the obstacles we put in the way of their mind and spirit, the trivial and humiliating banter to which we have reduced our interaction with them. . . . Their weaknesses are due above all to the disastrous, almost deadly education we prescribe for them, . . . in which all they learn is to disguise their true selves at all times, to repress their feelings, to hide all their thoughts and opinions." (Jean Le Rond d'Alembert, *Lettre à J.-J. Rousseau sur l'article "Genève"* [1759], reprinted in *Œuvres complètes de d'Alembert* [Berlin, 1822], v. IV, pp. 450–53.)

70. Staël's and Wollstonecraft's responses to this passage are discussed in Chapter 6.

71. This is borne out by Laure's parting words to Bomston: "You hoped to marry me. . . . But your friend has made my duty clear. By dishonoring you, I would have made my life unhappy; by leaving your good reputation intact, I will feel that I am sharing in it. The sacrifice of my happiness to this cruel duty has made me forget the shame of my past" (II: 652–53).

72. For discussions of Julie's death as a form of suicide, see Aram Vartanian, "The Death of Julie: A Psychological Post-Mortem," *L'Esprit Créateur* 6 (1966): 77–84; Michèle Duchet, "Clarens, le lac d'amour où l'on se noie," *Littérature* VI, 21 (February 1976): 79–90; Ruth P. Thomas, "The Death of an Ideal: Female Suicides in the Eighteenth-Century French Novel," in Spencer, pp. 321–31; and Robert Favre, *La Mort dans la littérature et la pensée françaises au siècle des lumières* (Lyon: Presses universitaires de Lyon, 1978), pp. 167–89.

73. See Julia Kristeva, "Héréthique de l'amour," *Tel Quel* 74 (1977): 30–49.

74. Although the children born to Thérèse may not have been fathered by Rousseau, he was responsible for them nonetheless (as he himself recognized), since they were living together at the time. The controversy concerning Rousseau's children is of course a complex one, given his character and financial circumstances. For different perspectives on this question, see Staël, *Lettres sur Rousseau*, pp. 98–99; Blum, pp. 74–82; Jean Fabre, "Le J.-J. Rousseau de Lester Crocker," *Dix-huitième siècle* 3 (1961): 176; Albert Meynier, *Jean-Jacques Rousseau, révolutionnaire* (1912), p. 30; and the *Confessions* (I: 345; 357–59; 558; etc.) and the commentary on these passages by Gagnebin and Raymond in the Pléiade edition.

75. Margaret Darrow convincingly argues that following the Revolution, many French noblewomen consciously adopted domesticity as a class ideal in an effort to answer middle-class criticism of the nobility, and hence as a means of proving their patriotism and, in some cases, of ensuring their very survival. See Darrow, especially pp. 42 and 53.

76. The anti-family undercurrents in Rousseau's thought are particularly apparent in his *Considérations sur le gouvernement de Pologne*: "It is education that must give people a sense of national identity and control their opinions and tastes to such an extent that they become patriots by inclination, passion, even necessity. . . . In such a society, people see nothing but their fatherland and live for nothing else. . . . Since everyone is equal under the constitution, they should be raised together and in the same way. . . . These public boarding schools are the hope of the republic; on them depends the glory and fate of the nation" (*OC*, III: 966–67). Similarly, in the *Discours sur l'économie politique*, Rousseau writes: "An even greater reason for not abandoning the children's instruction to their fathers' limited abilities and prejudices is that education is more important to the State than to the parents; for, following the normal course of nature, the father's death often robs him of the final fruits of that education, whereas the nation feels its effects sooner or later. Thus the State remains, while the family dissolves" (III: 260).

77. Michel Le Pelletier de Saint-Fargeau, cited in translation by Blum, p. 187.

78. *Bouche de Fer* (October 1790), p. 348.

79. Regarding the debate surrounding Rousseau's views on women in the decade following the Revolution, see Ruth Graham "Rousseau's Sexism Revolutionized," in *Woman in the 18th Century and Other Essays*, ed. Paul Fritz and Richard Morton (Toronto: Hakkert, 1976), pp. 127–39, and the studies cited earlier by Bloch, Blum, Figes, Landes, and Piau-Gillot.

80. Robespierre, cited in French by Graham, pp. 138–39.

81. Prudhomme, cited and translated by Blum, pp. 209–10. The exchange between Prudhomme and Blandin-Demoulin was originally reported in *Les Révolutions de Paris*, no. 185 (25 Jan. 1793), pp. 19–26, and is reproduced in its entirety by Paule-Marie Duhet in *Les Femmes et la Révolution, 1789–1794* (Paris: Julliard, 1971), pp. 150–58.

82. Blandin-Demoulin, cited and translated by Blum, pp. 209–10. In her reply to Prudhomme, Blandin-Demoulin may have been inspired by Wollstonecraft's response to Rousseau in *The Rights of Woman* (published one year earlier in 1792), and particularly by the following passage: "Women, by practicing or fostering vice, become either abject slaves or capricious tyrants.

They lose all simplicity, all dignity. It is time to effect a revolution in female manners—time to restore to them their lost dignity—and make them, as a part of the human species, labour by reforming themselves to reform the world" (pp. 60–61). The similarities between the two texts in both style and content seem too striking to be coincidental.

83. Fox-Genovese, "Introduction," in Spencer, p. 16.

Chapter 2

1. Their correspondence consists of five letters from Henriette (dated 26 March 1764, 10 Sept. 1764, 5 Feb. 1765, 28 March 1765, and 18 Dec. 1765) and three responses from Rousseau (dated 7 May 1764, 4 Nov. 1764, and 25 Oct. 1770). This last response was to a note that Henriette sent to Rousseau upon his return to Paris in September 1770. The note seems to have been lost, but Henriette summarizes its contents and her reaction to his response in the preface to the revised edition of their correspondence that she later prepared for publication. This *édition remaniée* and Henriette's preface to it was reprinted a century later by Hippolyte Buffenoir in a book titled *J.-J. Rousseau et Henriette, jeune Parisienne inconnue, manuscrit inédit du XVIIIᵉ siècle* (Paris: H. Leclercq, 1902). Buffenoir maintains that Henriette's version of the correspondence was never published before his own edition appeared, but this claim has not yet been substantiated. Unless otherwise indicated, I have used R. A. Leigh's edition of Rousseau's correspondence.

At Henriette's request, Rousseau addressed his responses to "Mˡˡᵉ demaugin chés Mᵈᵉ Du hossay, rue traversière, près la rue clos georgeot butte Sᵗ Roch à Paris." Leigh maintains that de Maugin was not Henriette's surname and that Mlle Maugin was merely an intermediary. Leigh suggests that Mme du Hossay may have been a relative with whom "Henriette" lived. Another possible clue to the mystery is that Henriette's first letter to Rousseau was given to him by an English acquaintance, Daniel Malthus, who visited him in Môtiers after stopping in Paris. It is not clear, however, how Malthus received the letter from Henriette. (See "Notes explicatives," in *Correspondance Complète de Rousseau*, ed. R. A. Leigh [Geneva: Institut Voltaire, 1967], v. XIX, p. 254; "Remarque," v. XXI, pp. 128–30; and "Notes explicatives," v. XX, p. 25.) The Leigh edition of Rousseau's correspondence will be referred to hereafter as CC.

2. Letter of Henriette to Rousseau, 26 March 1764, in CC, XIX, p. 242. All translations are mine.

3. *Le Petit Robert* gives the following definition for the term *honnête homme*: "Essential notion of *la morale mondaine* in eighteenth-century France. A man of

good breeding, pleasant and distinguished in both mind and manners." (Paul Robert, *Dictionnaire alphabétique et analogique de la langue française*, ed. Alain Rey [Paris: Société Nouveau Littré, 1976], p. 847.) Lagarde and Michard offer a more detailed definition: "Cultivated without being pedantic, distinguished without being affected [*précieux*], *l'honnête homme* is serious-minded, moderate, discreet, courteous, honest, courageous, and modest. He is characterized by an elegance that is both outward and within, that is only found in a highly civilized, highly disciplined society." (André Lagarde and Laurent Michard, *XVIIᵉ Siècle. Les Grands Auteurs français du programme* [Paris: Bordas, 1970], pp. 8–9.) Henriette is clearly referring to this seventeenth-century notion, which still served as a model for masculine behavior in eighteenth-century France.

4. Letter of Henriette to Rousseau, 26 March 1764, in *CC*, XIX, p. 243.

5. "I no longer regret my inability to marry because my knowledge of morals and manners in today's society has shown me that one is not likely to find the happiness in marriage that I once imagined" (Ibid., p. 245).

6. Henriette to Rousseau, 26 March 1764, in *CC*, XIX, p. 247.

7. *Emile*, p. 768. See the discussion of this key passage in Chapter 1.

8. Henriette to Rousseau, 26 March 1764, in *CC*, XIX, p. 240.

9. Rousseau's correspondence richly attests to the reputation he enjoyed as an astute judge of human nature. See, for example, the letters he exchanged with Mme de Berthier, who (like Henriette) was convinced that Rousseau alone could understand and help her. (See esp. his letter of l7 Jan. 1770, in *CC*, XXXVII, pp. 205–7.) In contrast, Mme de Staël strongly contested the popular image of Rousseau as *un connaisseur du cœur humain*: "Rousseau was even more lacking than most people in the divine power to read into the hearts of others," she affirms (*Lettres sur Rousseau*, I: 19–20). In her view, Rousseau's intense imagination and introverted character made him unable to truly understand or relate to the people around him. Staël saw Rousseau much as he saw himself—and as Henriette viewed *herself*—as the victim of his own talents and excessive sensibility, which proved to be more of a curse than a blessing. See the discussion of Staël's view of Rousseau in Chapter 5.

10. Henriette to Rousseau, 26 March 1764, in *CC*, XIX, pp. 240–41. Later in the same letter, she adds: "I don't play the learned lady who puts on airs, always talking, judging, and dominating the conversation. . . . Any ostentatious display of knowledge appears ridiculous to me. . . . I protest against any charge of vanity. I'm not trying to set myself up as a philosopher or wit, but merely to acquire inner resources to help myself. . . . It is true that this occupation is not within the natural order of things, but then I am not in my natural place either, which is hardly my fault" (Ibid., pp. 247, 250–51).

11. The portrait Henriette draws of herself in her first letter to Rousseau presents interesting parallels with Jean-Jacques's self-portrait in the *Confessions*: "I am of an intensely passionate nature, . . . extremely sensitive, proud, and strong-willed, with a lively imagination and an overly tender heart. . . . I am eager to win the consideration and esteem of others, indifferent to the prestige conferred by wealth, yet desiring wealth nonetheless for the greater independence it offers. . . . Harsh when I am offended, stubborn in the face of tyranny and threats, embittered by setbacks, I am nevertheless intensely loyal and generous to my friends. I am often in the wrong, but I readily admit my mistakes. I find it unbearable that I have no one to care for and no one to care for me, always searching for friendship and finding to my despair that it is only an illusion. . . . I have little concern for prejudices and for public opinion in general, but I do care a great deal about the individual judgments of people I respect and whose esteem I value" (Ibid., pp. 244–45). The mimetic quality of Henriette's style and self-portrayal is further discussed later in this study.

12. Letter to Rousseau, 5 February 1765, in *CC*, XXIV, p. 296.

13. Before her marriage to Necker at the age of twenty-five, Suzanne Curchod's beauty, wit, and learning had made her the center of a distinguished circle of admirers, including the English historian Edward Gibbon to whom she had been engaged for several years. However, her precarious financial situation after the death of her father had dimmed her hopes of marriage and had forced Curchod to earn her living as a governess. Her lack of fortune and social standing had caused Gibbon's father to disapprove of the match, which led Gibbon to break off their engagement. Mlle Curchod had confided her deep disappointment to Rousseau during one of his visits to the Moultous.

14. Rousseau to Henriette, 7 May 1764, in *CC*, XX, p. 18.

15. Ibid., pp. 19–20. Rousseau is responding here to a passage in Henriette's first letter where she attempts to justify her studies: "There was nothing so humiliating than to look like a girl who has been forgotten, who is waiting for someone who never comes," she writes. "The studious life I adopted helped me avoid the humiliation I so feared. It gave me a certain philosophical air that made me appear to have become by choice what I was in fact by necessity" (Letter of 26 March 1764, in *CC*, XIX, p. 243).

16. Rousseau's sharp criticism here of *les femmes qui veulent se faire hommes* (women with "masculine" aspirations) echoes that of Julie in a letter to Saint-Preux: "A perfect woman and a perfect man should not resemble each other in character any more than in their appearance; these vain imitations of the opposite sex are utterly ridiculous; they make the wise man laugh and scare suitors away. Unless one is five and a half feet tall, with a deep voice and a

beard, one has no business trying to be a man" (*Julie*, in *OC*, II: 128). Similarly, in *Emile* (IV: 701), Rousseau warned that women who strove to cultivate the qualities and talents of men and to usurp their prerogatives only worked against their own interests, since (in his view) such behavior deprived them of their feminine charms and hence of their power to subjugate men. See the discussion of these passages in Chapter 1.

17. For example, in his *Essai sur les femmes*, Diderot writes: "There are women who are men, and men who are women; and I admit that I will never take a man-woman as my friend" (Diderot, *Sur les femmes* in *Œuvres complètes*, ed. J. Assézat [Paris: Garnier, 1875], v. II, p. 260). For further discussion of the deep-seated fear of the "man-woman" during this period, see Mary Sheriff, "Woman? Hermaphrodite? History Painter? On the Self-Imaging of Elisabeth Vigée-Lebrun," *The Eighteenth Century* 35, 1 (1994): 3–27.

18. Rousseau to Henriette, 7 May 1764, in *CC*, XX, pp. 19, 22.

19. "It is as impossible to return to ignorance and simplicity of mind as it is to childhood. . . . Once the mind is stirred up, it always remains so, and anyone who has acquired the habit of reflexion is condemned to be a thinker all his life" (Ibid., p. 19).

20. Henriette to Rousseau, 10 Sept. 1764, in *CC*, XXI, pp. 124–25.

21. Henriette to Rousseau, 5 Feb. 1765, in *CC*, XXIII, p. 299.

22. Henriette to Rousseau, 10 Sept. 1764, in *CC*, XXI, p. 125.

23. Letters to Rousseau of 26 March 1764 and 10 Sept. 1764, in *CC*, XIX, p. 247 and XXI, p. 124.

24. Rousseau to Henriette, 4 Nov. 1764, in *CC*, XXII, pp. 8–9.

25. See *Emile*, in *OC*, IV, p. 769.

26. Rousseau to Henriette, 4 Nov. 1764, in *CC*, XXII, p. 9. The advice Rousseau offers Henriettte presents an interesting parallel to Julie's masochistic exaltation of sensibility on her deathbed: "Heightened sensibility always brings with it a certain satisfaction with oneself regardless of fortune or events. How I suffered! How many tears I cried! And yet, if I had to live my life over again, the sin that I committed would be all I would wish to erase: my suffering would be still be worth reliving and would even bring a certain pleasure to me" (*Julie*, in *OC*, II, pp. 725–26).

27. Henriette to Rousseau, 5 Feb. 1765, in *CC*, XXIII, pp. 297–98.

28. Henriette to Rousseau, 10 Sept. 1764, in *CC*, XXI, p. 125. Similarly, in her first letter to Rousseau, Henriette writes: "One cannot control one's heart, it is only interested in what it wants and remains unhappy if its desires are never satisfied" (26 March 1764, in *CC*, XIX, p. 245).

29. Henriette to Rousseau, 5 Feb. 1765, in *CC*, XXIII, p. 298.

30. Henriette to Rousseau, 26 March 1764, in *CC*, XIX, p. 251.

31. Henriette to Rousseau, 10 Sept. 1764, in *CC*, XXI, p. 123.

32. In 1764, the *Confessions* were of course not yet published or even written; however, a distinctly confessional style and self-justifying tone are already apparent in Rousseau's *Lettre à Christophe de Beaumont* (published in 1763), his *Lettres écrites de la Montagne* (1764), and in his two novels (1762 and 1764). Henriette had read these four works and comments on them in the course of her letters.

33. Henriette to Rousseau, 26 March 1764, in *CC*, XIX, p. 251.

34. Henriette to Rousseau, 18 Dec. 1765, in *CC*, XXVIII, p. 68.

35. Henriette to Rousseau, 5 Feb. 1765, in *CC*, XXIII, p. 295.

36. Ibid, p. 299. In her next letter, Henriette is even more insistent in her portrayal of Rousseau as her spiritual guide and savior: "I am spending the entire summer in the country. . . . Your advice would be so tremendously helpful to me! How I yearn to hear from you. . . I feel as though I am perhaps destined to be reborn here, to begin a new life; . . . that breathing the fresh country air and reflecting upon your teachings, I may gradually lose myself and find myself transformed into a new person. But without you, there is no air nor sun nor greenery that can have any effect on a heart like mine that stubbornly feeds on its own sorrows. Only the strength of your arguments can touch it and cause it to change" (Letter of 28 March 1765, in *CC*, XXIV, pp. 321–22).

37. Rousseau to Henriette, 4 Nov. 1764, in *CC*, XXII, p. 10.

38. Henriette to Rousseau, 18 Dec. 1765, in *CC*, XXVIII, p. 68.

39. Preface to the 1902 edition of Henriette's correspondence with Rousseau, ed. Buffenoir, I, pp. 39–40.

40. Ibid.

41. In her preface to her correspondence with Rousseau, Henriette later recalled: "When I learned of his return to Paris in September 1770, I was very eager to see him. But but how should I arrange it? I heard every day about people whom he had received very badly. . . . Finally, after a long and vain attempt to become acquainted with one or another of his friends, I decided simply to write to him directly to ask him if he would allow me to visit him." (Reprinted in Buffenoir, I, pp. 37–38.)

42. Rousseau to Henriette, 25 Oct. 1770, in *CC*, XXXVIII, p. 124.

43. Buffenoir, I, pp. 39–40.

44. Henriette to Rousseau, 28 March 1765, in *CC*, XXIV, p. 322.

45. Buffenoir, I, p. 38.

46. As I indicated earlier, Buffenoir maintains that Henriette's version of the correspondence had never been published before his own 1902 edition of that version appeared, but this claim has not yet been substantiated. Given the immense popularity of Rousseau's writings in the decades following his death and the reverence with which they were generally regarded, it seems unlikely that a publisher would have refused a manuscript such as Henriette's that featured several of his unpublished letters.

47. Buffenoir, I, p. 1.

48. See Paul Hoffmann, *La Femme dans la pensée des lumières* (Paris: Eds. Ophrys, 1977), pp. 443–46, and Anna Jaubert, *Etude Stylistique de la Correspondance entre Henriette*** et J.-J. Rousseau. La Subjectivité dans le Discours* (Paris & Geneva: Champion-Slatkine, 1987).

49. Hoffmann, p. 445.

50. Ibid., pp. 445–46. The expression *suppléments de soi-même* alludes to Rousseau's ability to find consolation for many bitter disappointments with friends and lovers through the powers of his imagination. Rousseau's use of this expression to refer to both creative and sexual activities is analyzed in detail by Jean Starobinski in *J.-J. Rousseau, la Transparence et l'Obstacle* (Paris: Gallimard, 1971).

51. Certain letters of Julie de l'Espinasse bear a striking resemblance to those of Henriette, as do the letters of Suzanne Curchod before her marriage to Necker and those of Manon Phlipon before her marriage to Roland. See the discussion of Mme Roland in Chapter 4 and of Mme Necker in Chapter 5.

Chapter 3

1. Voltaire, cited by d'Epinay in *Histoire de Madame de Montbrillant*, ed. Georges Roth (Paris: Gallimard, 1951), v. III, p. 341. (D'Epinay's novel will be referred to hereafter as *Montbrillant*.)

2. Diderot's respect for d'Epinay's editorial skills and judgment is best expressed in two letters in which he asked her to revise his play *Le Joueur*, an adaptation of Edward Moore's *The Gamester*. (Diderot, letters of July 20 and 26, 1760, in *Correspondance*, ed. Georges Roth [Paris: Editions de minuit, 1957], v. III, pp. 38–39.) Similarly, in a letter to d'Epinay accompanying his study on

Horace, Galiani confided: "The style needs some refining, but that's your responsibility. Our arrangment is long-standing on that point: I come up with the ideas, and you find the words to express them." (Letter of 21 June 1777, in Ferdinando Galiani, *Correspondance*, 2 vols., ed. Lucien Perey and Gaston Maugras [Paris: Calmann-Lévy, 1881], v. II, p. 518.) For further discussion of d'Epinay's collaborative literary efforts with Diderot, Galiani, and Grimm, see Ruth Weinreb, *Eagle in a Gauze Cage: Louise d'Epinay, femme de lettres* (New York: AMS Press, 1993), pp. 120–57.

3. *Receveur général des finances* for Metz and Alsace, Francueil was the stepson of Mme Dupin, a well-known salonnière and writer to whom Rousseau served as secretary and research assistant. He was also George Sand's grandfather.

4. According to Roth and Badinter, d'Epinay was the mother of four and possibly five children: Louis-Joseph (born September 25, 1746), Suzanne-Françoise-Thérèse (born August 24, 1747, and deceased June 2, 1748), Angélique-Françoise-Charlotte (the future Mme de Belzunce, born August, 1749, and probably Francueil's daughter, but raised as d'Epinay's child), a son (Jean-Claude Leblanc de Beaulieu, future bishop of Soissons, born May 29, 1753, fathered by Francueil and secretly raised in the country before being placed in a religious order), and possibly a fifth child fathered by Grimm. Details concerning d'Epinay's children by Francueil are provided by his granddaughter George Sand, although Weinreb points out that no document has been discovered to substantiate the birth or death of Leblanc de Beaulieu, d'Epinay's alleged son by Francueil.

For details and speculations concerning Mme d'Epinay's illegitimate children, see Roth, *Histoire de Madame de Montbrillant*, I: 443, n. 2, and II: 465–66, n. 11; Elisabeth Badinter, *Emilie, Emilie. L'Ambition féminine au XVIIIᵉ siècle* (Paris: Flammarion, 1983), pp. 249–50; Weinreb, *Eagle in a Gauze Cage*, p. 16; Lucien Perey and Gaston Maugras, *Une Femme du Monde au XVIIIᵉ siècle: Les Dernières Années de Madame d'Epinay* (Paris: Calmann Lévy, 1883), pp. 4–5; Auguste Rey, *Le Château de la Chevrette et Madame d'Epinay* (Paris: Plon, 1904), pp. 57–59; Henri Valentino, *Une Femme d'Esprit sous Louis XV. Madame d'Epinay* (Paris: Perrin, 1952), pp. 62 and 116; and George Sand, *Histoire de ma vie*, v. I, p. 1064 and p. 1442, n. 1.

5. A note in the author's handwriting found in the manuscript identifies the main characters as follows: "M. et Mme de Montbrillant = d'Epinay; M. et Mme de Lange = d'Houdetot; Dulaurier = Saint-Lambert; Desbarres = Duclos; Rousseau = René; Garnier = Diderot; Volx = Grimm. . . . " Commenting on this list, Roth writes: "For someone who has read the *Confessions* and who is familiar with the events involved, it does not take much time to realize that Mme d'Epinay composed a *roman à clef*, a long autobiographical narrative in which

she presents herself as her heroine, Jean-Jacques as 'René,' . . . and in which all the other characters—parents, friends, and relations—also bear fictitious names. Although the thread of the narrative is based on a story that is partially true, the made-up names assigned to the characters gave the narrator a certain freedom as a novelist—of which she made full use." Roth then asks: "Where does the autobiography leave off and the fiction begin? Quite often, this remains an insoluble question." (Roth, *Montbrillant*, I, pp. xi–xii.)

6. See Roth, *Montbrillant*, I: xii, and Weinreb, *Eagle in a Gauze Cage*, especially Ch. 2, "*Histoire de Madame de Montbrillant*: Life and Art," pp. 49–77 and Ch. 3., "The Hermitage: The Economics of Friendship," pp. 79–97. The tendency to take d'Epinay's novel at face value as authentic memoirs is especially apparent in the biographies by Rey, Valentino, and Badinter cited above. However, Badinter presents a more nuanced analysis of the connections between fiction and reality in the preface to her edition of d'Epinay's novel, *Les Contre-Confessions. Histoire de Madame de Montbrillant* (Paris: Mercure de France, 1988), pp. ix–xxxii.

7. See Zurich, "La première rencontre de Rousseau et Madame d'Epinay," *Annales J.-J. Rousseau* 29 (1941–42).

8. Madame d'Epinay was an active participant in the discussions that took place at the Baron d'Holbach's and not merely a passive spectator, as Alan Kors implies in his study of the famous coterie: "While women were not generally welcome at the gatherings of d'Holbach's circle, they frequently were invited to spend time at Grandval, where d'Holbach's dinners were held during the summer months," writes Kors. "At one time or another, Mme Geoffrin, Mme de Meaux, Mme de Saint-Aubin, Mme Riccoboni, Mme d'Houdetot, Mme d'Epinay, and Mlle d'Ette all dined with the thinkers of d'Holbach's group." (Alan C. Kors, *d'Holbach's Coterie: An Enlightenment in Paris* [Princeton: Princeton Univ. Press, 1976], pp. 106–7.)

In a paper titled "Madame d'Epinay, Personnage Méconnu de la Coterie d'Holbach" (presented at the Annual Meeting of the American Society for Eighteenth-Century Studies in 1986), Léa and Arié Gilon attempted to correct this view of women's role in the d'Holbach circle, insisting on their intellectual equality within the group and their active participation in the discussions. For further discussions of d'Epinay's role among the Encyclopédistes, see Badinter, *Emilie, Emilie*, pp. 354–55, and especially Weinreb, *Eagle in a Gauze Cage*, pp. 99–105 and 116–20.

9. D'Epinay's triumph as a salonnière is perhaps best reflected in the preference shown to her by l'abbé Galiani, the Neapolitan ambassador to France, whose brilliant mind and sparkling wit made him highly sought after in Parisian society. "He was all the rage, especially among the women, who

competed for his attention," notes Badinter. "Madame d'Epinay prevailed. Freer in mind and spirit than Mme Geoffrin, less prudish than Mme Necker, Louise established with him an ongoing intellectual exchange based on a deep mutual affection" (*Emilie, Emilie*, p. 388). After Galiani's return to Naples in 1769, d'Epinay entered into a regular correspondence with him that would continue fourteen years until her death. For an engaging account of d'Epinay's long-standing friendship and correspondence with Galiani, see Francis Steegmuller, *A Woman, a Man, and Two Kingdoms: The Story of Madame d'Epinay and the Abbé Galiani* (New York: Knopf, 1992). Also see Weinreb, *Eagle in a Gauze Cage*, pp. 46–48 and 134–40. A four-volume unabridged edition of the correspondence between d'Epinay and Galiani, edited by Georges Dulac and Daniel Maggetti, is currently being published by Desjonquères in Paris.

10. *Confessions*, in *Œuvres complètes* (Paris: Gallimard, Bibliothèque de la Pléiade, 1969), v. IV, pp. 410–11. (The Pléiade edition of Rousseau's complete works will henceforth be referred to as *OC*.) Rousseau's claim that d'Epinay's motives were self-interested is echoed by her editor Challemel-Lacour: "To amuse herself until the end of the day, she has music and comedies; she has Francueil; and she has philosophical conversations with Duclos, Grimm, Saint-Lambert, . . . and Rousseau, whom she was careful to place within easy reach at l'Ermitage as an additional resource in the summer." (Introduction, *Œuvres de Madame d'Epinay*, ed. M. Challemel-Lacour, 2 vols. [Paris: A. Sauton, 1869], v. I, pp. x–xi. Reprint of original Geneva edition of 1759.)

11. In his *Tablettes*, Diderot enumerates Rousseau's "*scélératesses*" (wicked deeds) toward his former friends, and notably d'Epinay: "He wrote a letter attacking Mme d'Epinay that is monstrously ungrateful. The lady had given him a house at la Chevrette, as well as money for all his basic expenses. . . . He accused her of being the most odious of women during the same period that he threw himself at her feet and begged her pardon for all his wrongs against her. . . . At a time when he owed everything to Mme d'Epinay and was living at her expense, he accused her of trying to take M. de Saint-Lambert away from Mme d'Houdetot, and of trying to win over Mlle Levasseur, so that she would intercept one of the letters that Rousseau wrote to Mme d'Houdetot. . . . This man is truly a monster." (Cited by Roth, *Montbrillant*, III, pp. 585–86.)

12. The most notable of these comparative studies is Frederika MacDonald's two-volume work, *Jean Jacques Rousseau. A New Criticism* (London: Chapman & Hall, 1906), in which she seeks to defend Rousseau against the "conspiracy of lies" allegedly woven against him by d'Epinay and her friends. MacDonald's findings and hypotheses are reiterated by Georges Roth (who translated her book into French as *La Légende de Jean-Jacques Rousseau*, 1909) in his 1951 edition of *Montbrillant*. Support for Rousseau's version of the story is also found in Victor de Musset-Pathay's *Histoire de la vie et des ouvrages de J.-J.*

Rousseau (Paris: J.-L. Brière, 1822) and his *Anecdotes inédites pour servir de suite ou d'éclaircissements aux Mémoires de Madame d'Epinay* (Paris: Baudouin, 1818); Paul Boiteau's introduction to his edition of *Les Mémoires de Madame d'Epinay* (Paris: Charpentier, 1863); G. Streckeisen-Moulton, *J.-J. Rousseau, ses amis et ses ennemis* (Paris: M. Lévy, 1865); Henri Guillemin, "Les affaires de l'Ermitage (1756–57): Examen critique des documents," *Annales J.-J. Rousseau* 29 (1941– 42): 58–275; and in R. A. Leigh's "Note sur *Histoire de Madame de Montbrillant et les Pseudo-Mémoires de Madame d'Epinay*" in his edition of Rousseau's *Correspondance complète* (Geneva: Institut Voltaire, 1966–67), v. III, p. xxviii.

Support for d'Epinay's version of the story is given by Lucien Perey and Gaston Maugras in *Les Dernières Années de Madame d'Epinay*, pp. v–ix; Charles-Augustin Sainte-Beuve in his *Causeries du lundi* (Paris: Garnier, 1851–62), v. II, pp. 187, 207, and v. VII, pp. 287, 328; and Saint-Marc Girardin in *J.-J. Rousseau, sa vie et ses ouvrages* (Paris: Charpentier, 1875).

For a more balanced view of the controversy, see Yvon Belaval's review of Roth's edition of *Montbrillant* in *Critique* 8, 56 (1952): 649–53; Jean Roussel, *Jean-Jacques Rousseau en France après la Révolution, 1795–1830: Lectures et Légende* (Paris: Colin, 1972), pp. 438–67; G. Charlier, "Mme d'Epinay et J.-J. Rousseau," *Revue de Belgique* (1909): 1–18; Weinreb, *Eagle in a Gauze Cage*, pp. 72–97; and the preface to Badinter's edition of d'Epinay's novel, *Les Contre-Confessions. Histoire de Madame de Montbrillant* (Paris: Mercure de France, 1988), pp. ix–xxxii.

13. *Confessions*, I: 461. Rousseau seemed to agree with Diderot's lukewarm appraisal of Books I and II of *Julie*: "I was well aware of these faults myself, but they arose from the feverish state of mind in which I wrote, and I was never able to correct them" (Ibid.). In the two prefaces to *Julie*, he may have been responding to the criticisms of the friends-turned-enemies to whom he had shown the manuscript. In the first preface, he warns: "Whoever decides to read these letters must arm himself with patience regarding the errors of language, the dull, emphatic style, and all the commonplaces expressed in inflated terms. He should remind himself beforehand that the authors of these letters were not French, nor were they intellectuals, academicians, or philosophers" (*Julie*, in *OC*, II: 6). Then, taking the role of devil's advocate in the *préface dialoguée* that follows, he exclaims: "What a stilted epistolary style! . . . What bombast to say such ordinary things! . . . Even if your characters are drawn from nature, you must admit that their style is hardly natural" (II: 13).

14. See Roth, *Montbrillant*, III: 131, n. 4, and Badinter, *Emilie, Emilie*, pp. 268–76.

15. The Sophie referred to here is Sophie de Rambure, the heroine of the novel Emilie is writing and heroine of the novel that d'Epinay herself began

writing before beginning *Montbrillant*. According to Roth, that novel was *L'Histoire de Madame de Rambure*, a purely fictional work that d'Epinay soon abandoned to write *Montbrillant*, a romanticized version of her own life's story. "All that is left of this *Histoire de Madame de Rambure* (which no doubt was never written) is an outline and a list of six characters," notes Roth. "Wife of the president of the Parlement of Aix, the heroine seems to have been a woman of the provincial bourgeoisie with three grown daughters to marry off. Knowing the author's tastes at the time, it's likely that the story took the form of a didactic treatise on conjugal feelings and behavior. . . tied together, of course, by some kind of sentimental plot" (I: xvi).

16. Voltaire, *Lettres à M. de Voltaire sur "La Nouvelle Héloïse" ou Aloisia de Jean-Jacques Rousseau* [January 1761], in Voltaire, *Œuvres complètes* (Paris: Garnier, 1879), v. XXIV, pp. 469, 474.

17. Grimm, "Conversations sur les romans" [February 1763], in *Mémoires historiques, littéraires et anecdotiques* (London, 1814), v. I, p. 183. This same criticism is reiterated in Grimm's two-part review of *La Nouvelle Héloïse* in the *Correspondance littéraire* of January and February 1761. Rousseau himself feared that his novel might bore certain readers: "What I most feared was that, because of its simplicity, my style would be boring and that I would not be able to sustain my readers' interest until the end" (*Confessions*, I: 547). The negative appraisal of the first two books of *Julie* by Rousseau's contemporaries is echoed by a number of twentieth-century critics. Roth, for example, comments: "The first third of the work is by far the least interesting. And yet, it's probably the part that Rousseau wrote with the greatest passion" (*Montbrillant*, III: 100, n. 2).

18. Fréron, *Année littéraire* (April 1761), v. II, p. 307.

19. Sainte-Beuve, "Mémoires et Correspondance de Madame d'Epinay" [article of 10 June 1850], *Causeries du Lundi* (Paris: Garnier, 1851–62), v. II, pp. 187–89.

20. Jules and Edmond Goncourt, *La Femme au XVIIIᵉ siècle* (Paris: Flammarion, 1982), p. 304. Regarding the reception of d'Epinay's novel among succeeding generations of literary critics, see my article "Strategies of Self-Representation: The Influence of Rousseau's *Confessions* and the Woman Autobiographer's Double Bind," *Studies on Voltaire and the Eighteenth Century* 319 (1994): 313–39.

21. See Jochen Schlobach, *Correspondance inédite de Frédéric Melchior Grimm* (Munich: Wilhelm Fink, 1972), pp. 20–23.

22. See Roth, *Montbrillant*, III: 172, n. 2, and Schlobach, p. 23.

23. See in particular Duclos's *Confessions du Comte de* *** (1742) and his *Mémoires pour servir à l'Histoire des Mœurs* (1751), which d'Epinay read and greatly admired. Both works are culminations of the *roman aristocratique et mondain* and of two subgenres often employed in such novels—the *roman de mœurs* and *roman à portraits*—which were to exert considerable influence on the composition of d'Epinay's own novel. For further discussion of Duclos's literary influence on d'Epinay, see Roth's introduction to *Montbrillant*, I: xvi.

24. M. de Montbrillant's apology for marital infidelity is reiterated later by Desbarres [Duclos]: "I do not consider it a crime for a woman to have a lover. Quite to the contrary. Let people suspect her liaison if they wish, so long as she does not call attention to it" (*Montbrillant*, II: 126).

25. See the portrait of Volx (*Montbrillant*, II: 463–65), which reproduces d'Epinay's "Portrait de M. G***" published in *Œuvres de Madame d'Epinay*, v. II. These flattering portraits of Grimm are contradicted, however, by d'Epinay's frequent complaints about him in her letters to Galiani: "Because of his passion for travel and all the celebrities or heads of state vying for his attention, he is either out of town or else in Paris available to everyone, except his friends. I never see him. We live in the same house; but he dines in town every day. . . . The only way I might see him would be if we slept together, but I'm too old to risk proposing it. That might cause him to increase his travels even more" (Letter of 28 August 1775). When Grimm was considering a court position in his native Gotha, d'Epinay confided to Galiani: "My friend, if he left, it would kill me. . . I'm living in the most terrible uncertainty. I've placed my whole existence in him; I can't live without him any more than I can without air" (Letter of 20 September 1772). Grimm's insensitivity toward Mme d'Epinay was noticed as early as 1760 by Diderot, who reported to Sophie Volland: "He organizes his trips so well that he leaves la Chevrette at the very moment I arrive. . . . He sleeps there and that's all. . . . He has almost no time at all for his friends, and I don't know when he has time for love" (Letter of 31 August 1760, in Diderot, *Correspondance*, ed. Georges Roth [Paris: Editions de Minuit, 1955], v. III, p. 44).

26. In their letters, Emilie refers to Volx as "mon père," and he calls her "mon enfant." (See *Montbrillant*, III: 117, 206, 337, 357.) "You are the absolute arbiter of my will," she writes him. "Because of my confidence in your wisdom and fairness, I will always look upon you as my guide in everything. The desire to be worthy of your love and esteem has turned your opinion of me into a second conscience" (III: 330).

27. The individualistic, pragmatic morality defended by Volx in this passage closely resembles the so-called "*morale spéculative*" espoused by Diderot in *Le Supplément au Voyage de Bougainville* and *Le Rêve de d'Alembert*. In a letter accompanying the latter work, Diderot underlines the fact that it presents "a

speculative doctrine that is not intended for the multitude" (Diderot, *Œuvres complètes*, ed. J. Assézat [Paris: Garnier, 1875], IX, p. 252).

28. In her *Souvenirs*, Mme d'Allard (d'Epinay's granddaughter Emilie) notes that in d'Epinay's circle of friends, twelve died of childbed fever before the age of twenty-five. Cited by Roth, I: 286, n. 1.

29. Boiteau, Introduction to *Mémoires de Madame d'Epinay*, v. I, p. 49.

30. See Roth, *Montbrillant*, I: xvi, and Badinter, *Emilie, Emilie*, p. 356.

31. See the discussion in Chapter 1 of Rousseau's correspondence with Mme de Berthier and his campaign for maternal nursing in *Emile*. Also see the works cited there concerning breastfeeding practices and attitudes in eighteenth-century France.

32. Challemel-Lacour, Introduction to *Œuvres de Madame d'Epinay*, v. I, pp. xviii–xix.

33. Auguste Rey, "Le Rôle des Enfants à la Chevrette," in *Le Château de la Chevrette* (Paris: 1904), p. 33.

34. See Badinter, *Emilie, Emilie*, p. 382.

35. Letter from Galiani to Mme d'Epinay, 19 Jan. 1771, in Galiani, *Correspondance*, ed. Perey and Maugras, v. I, p. 342.

36. Letter from Mme d'Epinay to Diderot, Jan. 1772, in Diderot, *Correspondance*, v. XII, pp. 29–30.

37. "Mon Portrait," in *Œuvres de Madame d'Epinay*, v. II, p. 5.

38. See, for example, II: 90–100 and 400–15. "These dinners were called 'du Bout-du-Banc' because of their informal character," explains Roth. "In the middle of the table was placed a writing tablet which each guest used in turn. The guests were copiously served and remained for a long time at the table, where the conversation was free and unconstrained" (*Montbrillant*, II: 89, n. 3). Among the habitual guests at Mlle Quinault's were Marivaux, Diderot, Saint-Lambert, Nivelle de la Chaussée, Destouches, Moncriff, Crébillon fils, Piron, Voisenon, and Duclos.

39. "The salon was really an informal university for women—a place where they could exchange ideas, avail themselves of some of the best minds of their time, receive and give criticism, read their own works and hear the works of others, and, in general, pursue in their own way some form of higher education," writes Bodek. "They illustrate the ingenuity of women, who when excluded from the educational mainstream created an alternate route which satisfied their desire to learn, while at the same time camouflaged their activities behind the acceptable female role of hostess." See Evelyn Gordon Bodek,

"Salonnières and Bluestockings: Educated Obsolescence and Germinating Feminism," *Feminist Studies* 3, 3/4 (Spring-Summer 1976): 185–86.

For the most recent work on the educational function of the salons, see Dena Goodman, "Enlightenment Salons: The Convergence of Female and Philosophic Ambitions," *Eighteenth-Century Studies* 22 (Spring 1989): 329–50; her "Seriousness of Purpose: Salonnières, Philosophes, and the Shaping of the Eighteenth-Century Salon," *Proceedings of the Western Society for French History* 15 (1988): 111–21; and Erica Harth, *Cartesian Women: Versions and Subversions of Rational Discourse in the Old Regime* (Ithaca: Cornell Univ. Press, 1992), pp. 21–25. Also see Carolyn Lougee, *Le Paradis des Femmes: Women, Salons, and Social Stratification in Seventeenth-Century France* (Princeton: Princeton Univ. Press, 1976), pp. 11–30.

40. Letter from d'Epinay to Galiani, 20 Jan. 1771, in Galiani, *Correspondance,* ed. Perey and Maugras, v. I, p. 349.

41. Badinter, *Emilie, Emilie,* p. 445.

42. See d'Epinay, *Les Conversations d'Emilie,* 2 vols. (Paris: Belin, 1783), v. I, pp. viii–ix. (Subsequent references will be to the 1783 Belin edition unless otherwise indicated.)

43. D'Epinay to Galiani, 4 October 1769, in Galiani, *Correspondance,* ed. Perey and Maugras, v. I, pp. 41–42. Despite the marked differences between the pedagogical approaches of Mme d'Epinay and Rousseau, there is a curious parallel between the way d'Epinay takes possession of her granddaughter in infancy ("I'll take her from her mother and take charge of her") in order to shape her according to her own ideals, and the way Emile's tutor takes charge of him: "It makes no difference if he has a father and mother. Since I am responsible for their duties, I assume all their parental rights. . . . He must obey me alone" (*Emile*, in *OC*, IV, p. 267). Both authors seem to be responding to unfulfilled longings as parents, as well as to the inadequacy of the upbringing and education they themselves received.

44. Badinter, *Emilie, Emilie,* p. 391.

45. In the twelve-year period (from 1770 until 1782) during which she worked on *Les Conversations d'Emilie*, d'Epinay was in fact slowly dying of stomach cancer (or of stomach lesions caused by venereal disease), to which she finally succumbed in 1783 at the age of fifty-seven. Only by taking increasingly large doses of opium was she able to calm the pain caused by her illness in order to continue the education of her granddaughter and to complete the second edition of her *Conversations,* published only a few months before her death.

46. *Les Conversations d'Emilie* (Paris: P. Persan, 1822), 2 vols., Conv. 4, v. I, pp. 73–76. Reprint of original edition of 1773. The tale of *La Fille Amazone,*

which appears in the original Persan edition of 1773, disappears in the revised Belin edition of 1783, where it is replaced by a much less daring and highly didactic *conte moral* titled *La Mauvaise Fille*. The latter is also the story of a high-strung girl; however, her ill temper is attributed not to the constraints of a sedentary life and to a poor choice of teaching methods, but rather to defects in her character that need to be corrected through constant supervision and discipline. This second girl is so rebellious that only through strict moral and academic training are her parents able to correct her negative traits. No mention is made in this second tale of the need for physical exercise, although this point is made elsewhere in the 1783 edition (in Conversation 20). In contrast to the androgynous ideal presented in *La Fille Amazone*, *La Mauvaise Fille* presents a model much closer to the traditional "feminine" ideals of modesty, docility, and charm.

47. See Anne-Thérèse de Lambert, *Lettres sur la véritable éducation* (Paris, 1727), and Stéphanie-Felicité de Genlis, *Adèle et Théodore, ou Lettres sur l'éducation*, 4 vols. (Paris: Maradan, 1804). Genlis's views on education are discussed in Chapter 6.

48. See *Considérations sur le gouvernement de Pologne*, in *OC*, III: 966–70. This plan of course contradicts Rousseau's emphasis in *Emile* on private, individualized instruction at home—an emphasis for which he was often criticized by advocates of public education. For further discussion of the contradictions in Rousseau's views on education, see Aubrey Rosenberg, "Rousseau's Emile: The Nature and Purpose of Education," in *The Educational Legacy of Romanticism*, ed. John Willinsky (Waterloo, Ohio: Wilfrid Laurier University Press, 1990), pp. 11–32.

49. See the passages on *Le Misanthrope* in the *Lettre à d'Alembert*, ed. M. Fuchs (Geneva: Droz, 1948), pp. 47–60, and the analysis of these passages by Gagnebin and Raymond in their commentary on the *Confessions*, I: 1516 (n. 1 to p. 496).

50. See *Emile*, in *OC*, IV: 768, and the discussion of this passage in Chapters 1 and 2.

51. Concerning Diderot and Grimm's alleged collaboration on the revision of d'Epinay's novel, particularly the passages attacking Rousseau, see Roth, *Montbrillant*, v. III, p. 151, n. 3; Badinter, *Emilie, Emilie*, pp. 356–57, and the preface to her 1988 edition of d'Epinay's novel, pp. xv–xxv; Weinreb, *Eagle in a Gauze Cage*, pp. 82–88, and the other works cited in note 12 above.

52. According to Joel Cohen, the "other reasons" to which Rousseau obliquely refers here were her affairs with Francueil and Grimm, who were both his friends. See Rousseau, *Confessions*, ed. and trans. by Joel M. Cohen (London: Penguin, 1953), p. 384.

53. Letter from Rousseau to Duclos, *Correspondance Complète de Jean-Jacques Rousseau*, ed. R. A. Leigh (Geneva: Institut Voltaire, 1967), v. XII, p. 221.

54. In the obituary devoted to d'Epinay in the *Correspondance littéraire*, Grimm dismisses d'Epinay's work as incomplete and immature: "She left behind only an unfinished series titled *Les Conversations d'Emilie*, many letters, and the rough draft of a long novel. Her two short works titled *Lettres à mon fils* and *Mes moments heureux* were printed but never published, nor do they seem suited for publication; for they are but the first attempts of an amateur whose writing had not yet attained its full power" (*Correspondance littéraire, philosophique et critique* [Paris: Garnier, 1877–79], ed. Tourneux, v. XIII, p. 394). Grimm's negative appraisal of d'Epinay's work presents a curious contrast to the high praise given it by Volx in *Montbrillant*. Like Rousseau, Grimm portrays her as a dilettante and undermines the seriousness and value of her work. His condescending remarks concerning the writing of the woman who shared his life for thirty years seem particularly ungenerous when one considers d'Epinay's important—and unacknowledged—contributions to the *Correspondance littéraire* documented by Weinreb. See her article "Mme d'Epinay's Contributions to the *Correspondance littéraire*," *Studies in Eighteenth-Century Culture* 18 (1988): 389–403, and the final chapter of her book *Eagle in a Gauze Cage*, pp. 143–57.

55. Originally written in the winter of 1756, d'Epinay's *Lettres à mon fils* were privately printed three years later in a print run of twenty-five copies. The letters were first published by Challemel-Lacour in his 1869 edition of the *Œuvres de Mme d'Epinay*, v. I. See Ruth Weinreb's critical edition of the letters, *Madame d'Epinay's "Lettres à mon fils"* (Concord: Wayside Press, 1989) and her discussion of this work in *An Eagle in a Gauze Cage*, pp. 32–39.

The style and content of the letters remained virtually the same in the 1759 printing as in the original version shown to Rousseau. D'Epinay seems to have largely ignored his criticisms and, as Roth suggests, "she seems to have published these letters in spite of his comments" (II: 532, n. 2). Yet Rousseau's criticisms seem to have been very much in her mind when she wrote *Les Conversations d'Emilie*. In this later work, she carefully avoids a didactic style and an abstract, theoretical approach to education and gears the discussions to her pupil's level and interests, as Rousseau had suggested. Moreover, in the preface to the *Conversations*, she cleverly (and not unjustly) redirects these same criticisms against the leading pedagogical theorists of her day, including the author of *Emile*.

56. D'Epinay, letter to Galiani, 13 September 1773.

57. D'Epinay, letter to Galiani, 9 January 1775.

58. Recalling his early efforts as a writer and composer, Rousseau confides: "It's true that my work, which lacked order and consistency, was at times

sublime and at other times quite dull, as one might expect from someone inspired only by sporadic bursts of genius, without much knowledge or technique to sustain him" (*Confessions*, in *OC*, I: 334). He recognizes that the admiration others expressed for his early work played a crucial role in boosting his self-confidence and in developing his creative potential.

59. Mary Poovey, *The Proper Lady and the Woman Writer: Ideology as Style in the Works of Mary Wollstonecraft, Mary Shelley, and Jane Austen* (Chicago: Univ. of Chicago Press, 1984), p. xv. Although Poovey applies the paradigm of the "Proper Lady" to British women authors of the late eighteenth and early nineteenth centuries (and specifically to the three women mentioned in her title), the ideals of femininity and domesticity that she describes are very similar to the ones elaborated by Rousseau in *Julie* and *Emile*.

60. *Conversations d'Emilie*, Conv. 12, I: 453.

61. Cited by Auguste Rey, in *Le Château de la Chevrette*, p. 188.

62. Marie-Jeanne Roland, *Mémoires de Madame Roland*, ed. Paul de Roux (Paris: Mercure de France, 1966), p. 304. This passage and Mme Roland's view of women writers are discussed in Chapter 4.

63. D'Epinay to Galiani, 26 June 1773, in Galiani, *Correspondance*, ed. Perey and Maugras, II, p. 212.

64. D'Epinay to Galiani, 20 January 1771, in Galiani, *Correspondance*, ed. Perey and Maugras, I, pp. 346–47.

65. See Marie-Jeanne Roland, *Voyage en Suisse* (Neuchâtel: Editions de la Baconnière, 1937), p. 36.

66. Alice Parker, "Louise d'Epinay's Account of Female Epistemology and Sexual Politics, *French Review* 55, 1 (Oct. 1981): 50.

67. In her testament of 1782, d'Epinay left the manuscripts of *Montbrillant* to Grimm, with the following instructions: "If he judges them worthy of publication, I ask him to kindly edit them himself" (cited by Roth, I: xix). This request clearly expresses d'Epinay's hope that her novel would be published after her death and contradicts her declaration to Sedaine cited earlier that "this work will never see the light of day."

68. *Conversations d'Emilie*, "Avertissement," I, pp. i–ii, iv. All further quotations from the "Avertissement" are from the Belin edition, I, pp. i–x.

69. In his brief discussion of women novelists, Fauchery affirms: "Among the women novelists of the period, and particularly among the horde of mediocre ones, we find an annoying tendency to let their fictional creations be invaded by phantoms of their former selves. It seems to be more difficult for women writers than for men to transform their personal experiences into imaginative works of art." Citing *Histoire de Madame de Montbrillant* as a case

in point, he points to the inability of women writers to distance themselves from their personal experiences and frustrations, to go beyond the confines of their familial and social milieu, as a major obstacle to the creation of truly original, imaginative work. (Pierre Fauchery, *La Destinée féminine dans le roman français du dix-huitième siècle* [Paris: A. Colin, 1972], p. 113.) The claim that d'Epinay turned to autobiographical writing for lack of imagination is made more pointedly by Roth. After explaining that the purely fictional novel she originally planned was abandoned and replaced by a novel telling the story of her life, he asks: "Why did she give up writing it? It was because she lacked imagination—a most unfortunate failing in a woman novelist." (Roth, Introduction to *Histoire de Madame de Montbrillant*, I: xvi.) These assessments of d'Epinay's writing are discussed in the Conclusion.

70. Philip Stewart, *Imitation and Illusion in the French Memoir Novel, 1700–1750* (New Haven: Yale Univ. Press, 1969), pp. 121, 302.

71. See, for example, Théophile de Bordeu, *Recherches sur les maladies chroniques* (1774), in Bordeu, *Œuvres complètes* (Paris: Caille et Ravier, 1818), p. 853. Interestingly, Bordeu's explanation of female hysteria is repeated almost word for word in Diderot's *Eléments de physiologie*. See his *Œuvres complètes*, ed. J. Assézat, v. 9, p. 426.

72. For further discussion of the mutilations to which d'Epinay's novel was subjected by its various editors, see my article "Strategies of Self-Representation: The Influence of Rousseau's *Confessions* and the Woman Autobiographer's Double Bind," *Studies on Voltaire and the Eighteenth Century* 319 (1994): 313–39.

73. Three notable exceptions in French literature are Mme de Lafayette's *La Princesse de Clèves* (1678), Mme de Graffigny's *Lettres d'une Péruvienne* (1747), and Mme Riccoboni's *Lettres de Fanni Butlerd* (1757), which had all been published with great success before d'Epinay began her own novel. It is very likely, although not certain, that d'Epinay was influenced by these three women novelists, and particularly by Riccoboni, in her own writing.

74. In her study of Canadian women's fiction, Margaret Atwood provides a useful model for analyzing victim positions and strategies for moving out of them through autobiographical writing. See *Survival* (Toronto: Anansi, 1972), pp. 36–40.

75. Published in January 1772, Thomas's essay examines women's role and condition in various periods and cultures and probes to what extent their character, behavior, and capabilities are derived from nature or nurture. D'Epinay's response to Thomas was presented in a letter to Galiani, dated March 14 of the same year. Diderot's response in his essay *Sur les femmes* appeared a week later in the *Correspondance littéraire*. For further discussion of d'Epinay's and Diderot's responses to Thomas's essay, see my article "Sexual/

Textual Politics in the Enlightenment: Diderot and d'Epinay Respond to Thomas's Essay on Women," *Romanic Review* 84, 2 (March 1994): 98–116. Also see Weinreb, *Eagle in a Gauze Cage*, pp. 46–48 and 137–40.

76. Michèle Duchet, "Du sexe des livres: *Sur les femmes* de Diderot," in *Revue des Sciences Humaines* XLIV, 168 (October-December 1977): 535–36.

77. D'Epinay to Galiani, 14 March 1772, in *La Signora d'Epinay e l'Abate Galiani. Lettere inedite (1769–1772)*, ed. Fausto Nicolini (Bari, Italy: Gius. Laterza & Figli, 1929), pp. 251–55. Subsequent quotations from this letter will be from this edition. (This letter was not included in the Perey-Maugras edition.)

78. D'Alembert contests Rousseau's view that women are by nature inferior to men, insisting that any moral or mental deficiencies displayed by women resulted not from nature, but from the oppressive cultural conditioning to which they had been subjected: "But if, unfortunately, you are right, what would be the sad cause for these weaknesses? They stem from the servitude and degrading condition in which we have placed women, the obstacles we put in the way of their mind and spirit, the trivial and humiliating banter to which we have reduced our interaction with them. . . . Their weaknesses are due above all to the disastrous, almost deadly education we prescribe for them, . . . in which all they learn is to disguise their true selves at all times, to repress their feelings, to hide all their thoughts and opinions." See Jean Le Rond d'Alembert, *Lettre à J.-J. Rousseau sur l'article "Genève"* (1759), reprinted in d'Alembert, *Œuvres complètes de d'Alembert* (Berlin, 1822), v. IV, pp. 450–53.

79. According to Cixous, one of the distinctive characteristics of *l'écriture féminine* is the attempt "to express the inexpressible"—repressed female desires and experiences—through the use of "body language." See Hélène Cixous, "Le Rire de la Méduse," *L'Arc* 6 (1975): 39–54. Translated as "The Laugh of the Medusa" by Keith Cohen and Paula Cohen in *Signs* 1 (Summer 1976): 875–93.

80. The ellipses appear in the original text, which reads as follows: "Ne sachant ni ce que je disais, ni ce que je devais dire, je lui demandai: Aimez-vous quelqu'un? — Hélas! oui, dit-elle en soupirant. — Et qui? . . . Eh bien? . . . Vous ne répondez pas? — Ah! je ne peux pas vous le dire; ne me le demandez pas. . . . — Eh pourquoi? — C'est que . . . je crains . . . , j'ai peur de n'être pas aimée, et j'ai tout autant de peur de l'être. — Ah! sûrement, vous l'êtes! m'écriai-je . . . — Comment? reprit-elle, tout étonnée. Est-ce que vous savez quel est? . . . Ne me le dites pas, ne me le dites pas. Vous ne m'estimez peut-être plus, en mettant les mains sur ses yeux. Parlons d'autre chose. — Je ne vous comprends pas, lui dis-je, croyant la trop entendre, serait-il possible? . . . Elle me ferma la bouche de sa main. — Paix! me dit-elle. Nous gardâmes quelque temps le silence . . . — Eh bien! lui dis-je, ne me dites mot et laissez-moi deviner" (II: 357–58).

Chapter 4

1. "My mother, who no doubt understood that my mind needed a challenge, made no objection to my study of philosophy, even at the risk of exposing me to a bit of atheism," Madame Roland later surmised. "But she no doubt felt that it would be unwise to expose my overly sensitive and passionate nature to Rousseau's writing. Alas, what useless precautions to save me from my destiny!" *Mémoires de Madame Roland*, ed. Paul de Roux (Paris: Mercure de France, 1966), p. 277. (All subsequent references to Roland's memoirs are to this edition unless otherwise indicated.)

2. Ibid. (All translations are mine.)

3. Letter to Sophie Cannet, 21 March 1776, in *Lettres de Madame Roland. Nouvelle série* (1767–76), ed. Claude Perroud (Paris: Imprimerie nationale, 1913), p. 393. To simplify future references to Perroud's four-volume edition of Roland's letters, the volume cited above will be referred to as v. I, the volume containing letters from the years 1776–80 will be referred to as v. II, the volume containing letters from 1780–87 as v. III, and the letters from 1788–90 as v. IV. The first two volumes were published as v. 112, parts 1 and 2 in the series *Collection de documents inédits sur l'histoire de la France*, in 1913 and 1915 respectively; the third and fourth volumes were published earlier in the same series as v. 104, parts 1 and 2, in 1900 and 1902, respectively.

4. "The woman who has read Rousseau without becoming a better person, or at least desiring to become so, has but a soul of clay, an apathetic spirit," insists Roland. "She will never rise above the mediocre" (Ibid.).

5. Ibid.

6. However, discouraged by her daughter's lack of intellectual promise, Roland later abandoned her ambitious educational plans and adopted a far more conservative approach, not unlike that outlined by Rousseau for Sophie.

7. Letter to M. de Fenille, 21 March 1779, in *Lettres*, IV: 48.

8. Letter to Sophie Cannet, 4 Oct. 1777, in *Lettres*, II: 143.

9. See in particular Gita May, "The Revelation of Jean-Jacques Rousseau," in *Madame Roland and the Age of Revolution* (New York: Columbia Univ. Press, 1970), pp. 55–72; and "Voltaire détrôné par Rousseau," in *De Jean-Jacques Rousseau à Madame Roland* (Génève: Droz, 1964), pp. 76–93. Also see May's article "Rousseau's Antifeminism Reconsidered," in Samia Spencer, *French Women and the Age of Enlightenment* (Bloomington: Indiana Univ. Press, 1984), pp. 309–17.
Gita May's work on Roland has been a source of great inspiration to me, but my approach differs from hers in several important respects. May views

Roland's response to Rousseau as a conversion experience that inspired a life-long effort to live up to his idealistic views on women. I, on the other hand, see Roland's initial enthusiasm for Rousseau as a confirmation of the deepest convictions and longings of her youth. This enthusiasm gradually gave way to a questioning and subversion of his narrow ideals under the pressure of external events and in response to her own evolving aspirations—political, literary, and romantic—as a mature woman. It is this gradual evolution in Roland's response to Rousseau, from young militant to married conformist to subverter of his ideals, that I have sought to trace in my study of her.

10. Fragment of journal, 1777, in *Mémoires de Madame Roland*, ed. Claude Perroud (Paris: Plon, 1905), v. II, p. 422. In this passage, Roland negates gender differences at the experiential level, but not at the creative level. She recognizes women's ability to experience the same thoughts and aspirations as men, but underlines the superior ability of male writers (and specifically Rousseau) to express them.

11. *Mémoires*, p. 264. Similarly, recalling the Sunday dances at Soucy (the estate of a wealthy *fermier général* where her great aunt and uncle Besnard had worked as housekeeper and intendant), Roland writes: "I never stayed long. After an hour, escaping from the curiosity of the guests, I withdrew with my parents to continue our walk, the sweet joys of which I would never have sacrificed for the boisterous, but empty pleasures of such appearances in public" (276).

12. "Comment l'éducation des femmes pouvait contribuer à rendre les hommes meilleurs" [1777], in *Mémoires de Madame Roland*, ed. M. P. Faugère (Paris, 1864), v. II, p. 356. The essay was written and sent anonymously as an entry to a literary competition organized by the Académie de Besançon in 1777. Bernardin de Saint-Pierre submitted an essay to the same competition, but neither he nor Manon was awarded the prize.

13. Letter to Bosc, 29 July 1783, in *Lettres*, III: 257.

14. In her *Mémoires*, Roland remarks: "Men who mock women authors are mistaken in only one way, perhaps, and that is to criticize them for faults which they share themselves" (278).

15. Recalling an evening spent with Mme de Puisieux, Roland writes: "At sixty years of age, Mme de Puisieux still put on pretentious airs which would have been unbecoming even in much younger women. I had imagined that a woman author would be a highly respectable person, especially one who had written on education and morals. However, Mme de Puisieux's absurd behavior made me think otherwise. Indeed, her conversation was as lacking in brilliance as her behavior was lacking in judgment" (*Mémoires*, p. 278). A few pages later, she describes in equally scornful terms the mediocre talents and

loose morals of the novelist Mme Benoît (280–81). Yet Mme Roland was as quick to praise talented women writers as she was to criticize mediocre ones. She greatly admired the work of the historian Catherine Macaulay Graham and English women novelists in general, as well as the writings of Mmes de Lafayette and de Sévigné.

16. Letter to Sophie Cannet, 2 Oct. 1776, in *Lettres*, I, p. 492.

17. *Mémoires*, p. 321.

18. Marie-Jeanne Roland, *Un Voyage en Suisse* [1787], ed. G. R. de Beer (Neuchâtel: Editions de la Baconnière, 1937), p. 36.

19. Letter to Sophie Cannet, 29 Feb. 1776, in *Lettres*, I, pp. 384–85. Roland's lack of self-confidence was no doubt aggravated by her perfectionist tendencies, which at times bordered on masochism. This is particularly well illustrated by her comments concerning the essay on women's education cited earlier: "I found my essay defective both in style and content and I amused myself by critiquing it as if it were some other person's work I wished to mock" (*Mémoires*, p. 327).

20. Letter to Sophie Cannet, 2 Oct. 1776, in *Lettres*, I: 492.

21. Letter to Sophie, 27 March 1776, in *Lettres*, I: 396. Similarly, when Manon wrote to Rousseau to try to arrange a meeting with him, she carefully kept her plans secret: "I did not wish to appear any more philosophically inclined to everyone than I already did; enthusiasm for great men always seems ridiculous in the eyes of those who do not share it" (Ibid., p. 383).

22. Letters to Jean-Marie Roland, 22 and 18 Nov. 1787, in *Lettres*, III: 709, 695.

23. Letter to Bosc, 10 June 1783, in *Lettres*, III: 254.

24. *Mémoires*, p. 337.

25. Letter to Bosc, 26 July 1789, in *Lettres*, IV: 53. The shift in Roland's character and tone brought about by the Revolution is clearly reflected in the following passage of her *Mémoires*: "So long as I remained in a peaceful condition in the domestic sphere, my natural sensibility dominated or masked my other qualities. My chief desire was to please and to help others. . . . Since then, however, political storms and other circumstances have shaped my character. Frankness has become my dominant trait. . . . I am not afraid to tell people the blunt truth about themselves, and I do it without showing emotion or anger, whatever the effect may be on my listeners" (202).

26. Letter to Bosc, 26 July 1789, in *Lettres*, IV: 53.

27. In his notes to his edition of Roland's *Mémoires*, de Roux remarks: "Arrested August 4, 1793, Champagneux had to defend himself against the accusation that he had directed this propaganda bureau, whose actual director was probably Madame Roland" (p. 93, n. 1).

28. Recalling her work on her husband's articles as a young bride, she writes: "I worked for him with a humility that makes me laugh when I think of it now and that seems almost incompatible with a mind as independent as mine; but it flowed from my heart. I respected my husband so deeply that it seemed natural that he should see more clearly than I. In any case, he held so strongly to his opinions, and I was so afraid of annoying him, that it was only much later that I gained enough self-confidence to contradict him" (*Mémoires*, p. 333).

29. When Eudora was seven, Roland expressed her discouragement and frustration in a letter to Lavater: "Teach me to control this rebellious, indolent character, upon which gentle caresses have no more effect than severity or punishments. This has become a daily torment for me. Childrearing, that most cherished of tasks for a loving mother, seems to be the hardest trial I have ever had to face" (7 July 1788, in *Lettres*, IV: 22). Four years later in prison, Roland expressed her disenchantment with motherhood with surprising frankness: "My daughter is a pleasant enough girl, but cold and indolent by nature. I nursed and raised her with all the enthusiasm and solicitude a mother could possibly have, but never will her dull mind or lackluster spirit give my heart the sweet pleasures I hoped for" (*Mémoires*, p. 42).

30. Letter to Sophie Cannet, 5 Feb. 1776, in *Lettres*, I: 374–75.

31. "I am distressed that my imagination remains useless, for lack of talent and opportunities to exercise it. . . . To be truly happy, I would need to immerse myself in serious study and have access to all kinds of resources that are denied me. I'll never amount to anything. I'll always feel miserably incomplete, displeasing to those of my kind for failing to resemble them, but lacking the culture necessary to raise myself to the level of others. I am as out of place as one can possibly be" (To Sophie Cannet, 10 Dec. 1776, in *Lettres*, I: 527–28).

32. "Sometimes I'm tempted to put on pants and a cap so that I might have the freedom to seek out the talents of others and to cultivate my own," she confided to her friend. A few months later, in another letter to Sophie, Manon expressed her enthusiasm for d'Holbach's *Système de la nature* and then added: "I can't tell you how much I wish to study physics, astronomy, and other subjects to which I'll probably never have access. What a bore to be a woman! If I were a bit bolder and crazier, I would disguise myself as a man in order to throw off my fetters and I would immerse myself in the pleasure of scholarly pursuits." However, the conclusion of her letter clearly suggests that

Manon did not really feel the need to be a man in order to engage in serious study: "The die is cast, for now that I've begun to reason and to search for answers, I'll never stop. I've set up my own rules and standards to guide my actions, and I'm convinced that happiness depends less on the opinions of others than on one's own character and determination" (Letters to Sophie Cannet, 25 Aug. and 13 Nov. 1776, in *Lettres*, I: 465, 519).

33. Letter to Sophie Cannet, 9 May 1774, in *Lettres*, I: 195.

34. In her self-portrait, Roland underlines her natural sensuousness: "As for my chin, it has all the characteristics that physiognomists generally associate with sensuality. . . . I doubt that anyone was ever better suited for sensual pleasure, yet enjoyed it less" (*Mémoires*, p. 253).

35. Letter to Buzot, 22 June 1793, in *Lettres*, IV: 484.

36. Letter to Buzot, 6 July 1793, in *Lettres*, IV: 498.

37. "Mes Dernières Pensées," [Roland's Last Will and Testament, 8 Oct. 1793], in her *Mémoires*, pp. 342, 346.

38. "No, I am not leaving you; I shall wait for you," writes Julie to Saint-Preux. "The same virtue that separated us on earth will unite us in heaven. . . . I am only too happy to sacrifice my life for the right to love you forever without crime, and to be able to say it to you freely once again" (*Julie*, in *OC*, II: 743).

39. Dorinda Outram, "Words and Flesh: Madame Roland, the Female Body and the Search for Power," in *The Body and the French Revolution. Sex, Class, and Political Culture* (New Haven: Yale Univ. Press, 1989), pp. 138–39. Outram presents her chapter on Roland as a case study to illustrate her central thesis that, during the French Revolution, shifting attitudes toward the body—and specifically the female body—had a determining influence on the unfolding of events. She maintains that, despite the efforts of modern feminists to recapture the female body from male appropriation, "recent women's history of the Revolution has considered its female actors as without embodiment"—as unconscious of their physical specificity and its consequences. She further maintains that modern historiography has failed to show how the effort to exclude women from the public sphere was "inextricably linked to the way that the pre-Revolutionary culture of the eighteenth century had given drama and visibility to women's physicality" (129).

40. May, *Madame Roland and the Age of Revolution*, p. 206.

41. *Analytical Review* 22 (July–Dec. 1795): 145. The reviewer's compliments were however double-edged, since s/he then added: "While her husband continued in office, she assisted him in his political labours, and by her uncommon exertions, rendered herself the centre of a numerous group of enthu-

siastic admirers." The lengthy four-part review was signed "E. D."—initials sometimes used by Mary Wollstonecraft, who was a frequent contributor to the *Analytical Review* at the time Roland's *Mémoires* were published, as well as a passionate observer of the French Revolution. If indeed Wollstonecraft wrote the review, her ambivalence toward Roland's political role—reflected in the repetition of the term "uncommon" and in the sexist phrase "distinguished ornament of her sex"—would strikingly illustrate the power of traditional gender stereotypes over even the most progressive minds of the period.

42. Anecdote recounted in a letter to Sophie Cannet, 29 Feb. 1776, in *Lettres*, I: 384.

43. "It was through genuine devotion to the revolutionary cause rather than to satisfy any personal ambition on her part that Mme Roland came to contradict her restrictive principles concerning women and their proper role in society and politics," writes May. "Extraordinary events in a sense forced her hand. After witnessing the eternal hesitations and waffling of the Girondists and the ineffectiveness of their political program, she could not help but play an increasingly important role in their private deliberations and provide them with support and counsel" (Gita May, *De J.-J. Rousseau à Madame Roland*, p. 187).

44. See, for example, Gerard Walter's note on Mme Roland in his critical edition of Michelet's *Histoire de la Révolution Française* (Bibliothèque de la Pléiade, 1952), v. II, p. 1521; Albert Mathiez, *La Révolution française* (Paris, 1958), v. II, pp. 46–47; v. III, p. 85; and Louis Madelin, *La Révolution française* (Paris: Hachette, 1910).

45. These passages are all cited and discussed in the course of this chapter. See, in particular, Roland's *Lettres*, I, pp. 195, 374–75 and her *Mémoires*, pp. 155, 305, 338–39.

46. Joan Landes, *Women and the Public Sphere in the Age of the French Revolution* (Ithaca: Cornell Univ. Press, 1988), p. 118.

47. Jean-Paul Marat, *Ami du Peuple* 684 (19 Sept. 1792), in *Œuvres de J.-P. Marat*, ed. A. Vermorel (Paris: Décembre-Alonnier, 1869), p. 230.

48. Cited by Guy Chaussinand-Nogaret, *Madame Roland. Une femme en Révolution* (Paris: Seuil, 1985), p. 263.

49. Jacques-René Hébert, *Le Père Duchesne* 202 (20 Dec. 1792).

50. *Père Duchesne* 204 (25 Dec. 1792).

51. *Mémoires*, p. 90.

52. In *The Girondins* (London, 1961), Martin Sydenham argues that Mme Roland had very little real political influence. He maintains that the "myth"

of her negative effect on the Girondist cause was used by her contemporaries (as well as by later historians) to absolve the Girondists of responsibility for their own downfall. According to Sydenham, this myth also had the merit, for the hard-pressed historian, of easily defining just who _were_ the Girondins; by definition, they became the group of politicians known to Mme Roland. Adopting Sydenham's assessment, Outram claims that Mme Roland's political influence was "virtually nil," but that (as in the trials of Marie-Antoinette and Charlotte Corday), her example was used by the Jacobins as a warning to women who sought to play an active role in the public sphere. (See Outram, pp. 127, 130–31, and 151.)

Contrary to both Sydenham and Outram, I would argue that Mme Roland's political influence was very real and that she had an important impact on the turn of events, as I seek to illustrate in this chapter. However, I agree with Sydenham that her influence was at times exaggerated by her political enemies and then used by various historians to absolve the Girondists of responsibility for their downfall.

53. _Père Duchesne_ 243 (20 June 1793).

54. _Père Duchesne_ 205 (1 January 1793).

55. "Projet de défense," in _Mémoires_, pp. 371–73.

56. "Interrogatoire de Madame Roland," in _Mémoires_, p. 95.

57. "Notes sur mon procès et l'interrogatoire qui l'a commencé," in _Mémoires_, p. 367.

58. "My interrogator loaded all his questions with insulting epithets and tried to prevent me from providing any evidence in my defense. Both he and the judge . . . used all possible means to reduce me to silence or to force me to say what they wanted to hear. I was indignant and insisted that, once my case was brought to trial, I would protest this outrageous mode of questioning. I added that I would not let myself be silenced by them and that I acknowledged only the higher authority of reason and nature" (Ibid.).

59. _Le Moniteur universel_ (19 Nov. 1793), cited in Charles-Aimé Dauban, _Etude sur Madame Roland et son temps_ (Paris: Plon, 1864), pp. ccxlviii–ix.

60. Commenting on Roland's execution in _Le Moniteur universel_, Audouin remarks: "True courage does not jest" (9 Nov. 1793). Similarly, in _Le Calendrier républicain_ the same day, Sylvain Maréchal insists: "A truly virtuous woman, a woman who had sacrificed her life to the Republic, would not have behaved in this manner. Not surprisingly, the most insulting commentary on Mme Roland's execution is found in Hébert's _Père Duchesne_: "It's better to kill the devil than to let the devil kill us first. . . . The sans-culottes were wise to call

your bluff, Dame Coco, because if your old cuckold of a husband had not been thrown out of office, you would have become a second Marie-Antoinette" (9 Nov. 1793). French texts cited in Dauban, pp. ccxlviii–ix.

61. *Le Moniteur universel* (19 Nov. 1793), cited in Dauban, p. ccxlix.

62. Cited in *Women in Revolutionary Paris, 1789–1795*, ed. Darline Gay Levy, Harriet Branson Applewhite, and Mary Durham Johnson (Urbana: Univ. of Illinois Press, 1979), p. 220.

63. The negative portrayals of Mme Roland by her enemies form a curious contrast with the glowing description of her shortly before her death by Count Beugnot, a fellow prisoner. Despite his political differences with her and his natural aversion for intellectual, aggressive women, he was rapidly won over by her dignity and charm. He was especially moved when she spoke of her family: "No one defined better than she the duties of a wife and mother and proved more eloquently that a woman knows happiness only in the accomplishment of these sacred duties. The picture of domestic life took on ravishing colors when she painted it; tears fell from her eyes whenever she spoke of her daughter and husband." (*Mémoires du Comte Beugnot*, ed. Robert Lacour-Gayet [Paris: Hachette, 1959], p. 139.)

64. The Rousseauian ideals of motherhood and domesticity were frequently invoked by revolutionary leaders (notably Mirabeau, Robespierre, and Chaumette) to justify the continued subordination of women, as well as the persecution of feminist militants and the suppression of women's revolutionary clubs.

65. See Simon Schama, *Citizens. A Chronicle of the French Revolution* (New York: Knopf, 1989), p. 802.

66. "Without a doubt, Mme Roland's memoirs of the Revolution constitute one of the most energetic and evocative texts of the period," remarks Gita May. "More valuable still are her *Mémoires particuliers*. A chronicle of the private life of the Parisian artisan class between 1760 and 1780, her personal memoirs present us with a splendid inside view of the lifestyle, ideas, sensibility, and tastes of the Parisian middle class at the end of the ancien régime. Moreover, in these memoirs, we discover a writer who is alert and often enchanting" (*De J.-J. Rousseau à Madame Roland*, p. 30). Roland's writing was greatly admired by writers and critics of the Romantic period, including Sainte-Beuve, Lamartine, Brunetière, Stendhal, and the Goncourts.

67. Letter to Jany, Oct. 1793, in *Lettres*, IV: 527–28.

68. Elissa D. Gelfand, "Madame Roland," in *Imagination in Confinement: Women's Writings from French Prisons* (Ithaca: Cornell Univ. Press, 1983), pp. 144–47. Also see her article "A Response to the Void: Madame Roland's

Mémoires particuliers and Her Imprisonment," *Romance Notes* 20, 2 (Fall 1979): 75–80.

69. See *Mémoires*, pp. 217–222, 251–52, and 256. Recalling her wedding night, Roland underlines her lack of sexual knowledge and experience: "After reading the Stoic philosophers of Antiquity, I became convinced that pain was only an illusion, . . . or at least I was determined never to give in to it. My little experiments persuaded me that I could endure the greatest sufferings without flinching. However, my wedding night taught me otherwise. It's true that my surprise had a lot to do with it, since a novice Stoic would naturally be better able to resist suffering for which she is prepared than that which strikes unexpectedly when she is expecting quite the opposite" (256). This passage clearly suggests that her sexual relations with the older and "sexless" Roland did not fulfill her needs or expectations, thereby reinforcing her earlier claim that "I doubt that anyone was ever better suited for sensual pleasure, yet enjoyed it less" (254).

70. Sainte-Beuve, "Madame Roland," in *Portraits de Femmes*, in Sainte-Beuve, *Œuvres*, ed. Maxime Leroy (Paris: Bibliothèque de la Pléiade, 1951), v. II, p. 1156.

71. Sainte-Beuve, "Madame Roland," in *Nouveaux Lundis* (Paris: Calmann-Lévy, 1879), v. VIII, pp. 199–200.

72. Ibid., pp. 200–201.

73. Ibid., p. 264.

74. Ibid., p. 231.

75. Sainte-Beuve, *Portraits de Femmes*, p. 1156.

76. Ibid., p. 1158.

77. Sainte-Beuve, *Nouveaux Lundis*, pp. 217, 221.

Chapter 5

1. Although the two women had several acquaintances in common (most notably Talleyrand and Paine), they do not appear to have ever met or corresponded. This is all the more surprising considering that Wollstonecraft had translated Necker's *De l'importance des opinions religieuses*, a book his daughter cherished. It may be that Wollstonecraft's negative comments on Staël's first published work (her *Lettres sur Rousseau*) had angered the proud baronne and led her to maintain a stony silence toward her English critic. In any case, their paths never seem to have crossed. Wollstonecraft's stay in Paris (December 1792–April 1795) began a few months after Staël's flight to Switzerland, overlapped with her four-month visit to London with Narbonne and Talleyrand

(January–April 1793), and ended shortly before Staël's return to Paris in May 1795. Staël did not return to London until after Wollstonecraft's death in 1797.

2. *Lettres sur les écrits et le caractère de J. J. Rousseau* in *Œuvres complètes de Madame de Staël* (Paris: Firmin Didot, 1838), v. I, p. 1. All future references to the *Lettres sur Rousseau* will be included in parentheses within the text. References to Staël's works, unless otherwise indicated, are to the 1838 edition of her *Œuvres complètes* (hereafter referred to as Staël, *OC*).

3. See Madelyn Gutwirth's article "Madame de Staël, Rousseau, and the Woman Question," *PMLA* 86, 1 (January 1971): 100–9, and her book *Madame de Staël, Novelist. The Emergence of the Artist as Woman* (Urbana: Univ. of Illinois, 1978), pp. 31–52. I am deeply indebited to Gutwirth for her groundbreaking work on Staël. Regarding Staël's literary débuts, also see Simone Balayé, *Madame de Staël: Lumières et liberté* (Paris: Klincksieck, 1979); Charlotte Hogsett, *The Literary Existence of Germaine de Staël* (Carbondale: Southern Illinois Univ. Press, 1987), pp. 28–54; and Gretchen Rous Besser, *Germaine de Staël Revisited* (New York: Twayne Publishers, 1994), pp. 7–35.

4. In the course of her *Lettres*, Staël paints a glowing picture of *le mariage d'amour* and then wistfully asks: "Mustn't one have a strong sense of duty to go through life alone and to die without having been first in the thoughts of another and, without devoting one's thoughts to someone who could be loved without remorse?" (I: 13). As Gutwirth points out, even if Staël claims to be speaking for all women in this passage, it is clear that she is referring above all to herself and appealing to her readers' sympathy and understanding ("Madame de Staël, Rousseau, and the Woman Question," 100).

5. Before her marriage to Necker, Suzanne Curchod had served in her native Switzerland as governess to the children of Pastor Moultou, one of Rousseau's closest friends. It was through Moultou that Suzanne became acquainted with Rousseau, as well as with Voltaire and other literary celebrities.

6. Staël, cited by Gabriel Othenin d'Haussonville, *Le Salon de Madame Necker* (Paris: Calmann-Lévy, 1882), v. II, p. 49.

7. Gutwirth, *Madame de Staël, Novelist. The Emergence of the Artist as Woman*, p. 39.

8. Necker also intrudes, unnamed, into Staël's discussion of Rousseau's First Discourse. After criticizing Rousseau's tendency to sacrifice reason to eloquence, Staël adds: "I know only one man who could combine ardor with moderation, . . . and inspire the same passion for reason that, until now, had only been felt for ideological doctrines" (I: 3). Staël's idolization of her father is well known, for she rarely missed an opportunity of proclaiming it in print. Her *Du Caractère de M. Necker et de sa vie privée* (1804), written after his death, is unashamedly hagiographic.

9. Gutwirth, "Madame de Staël, Rousseau, and the Woman Question," p. 103. On Staël's ambivalent attitude toward both her father and Rousseau, Simone Balayé remarks: "Those two sides of genius—Rousseau and her father, the writer and the statesman—would always remain the two central axes in the thinking of this woman inwardly tormented by the desire to contribute to the happiness of society, yet confined to the role of writer." See Simone Balayé, *Mme de Staël: Lumières et liberté* (Paris: Klincksieck, 1979), p. 32.

10. Staël's false humility is especially apparent in the preface: "Perhaps those indulgent enough to foresee some talent in me will reproach me for hastening to treat a subject beyond even the talents that I could hope eventually to possess. But who knows if the passage of time will not take more away from us than it brings?" (I: 1).

11. Georges Poulet, "La Pensée critique de Mme de Staël," *Preuves* 190 (Dec. 1966): 28. On Staël's approach to literary criticism in general and to Rousseau in particular, also see two articles by Jean Starobinski: "Critique et principe d'autorité (Madame de Staël et Rousseau)," in *Le Préromantisme: Hypothèque ou hypothèse?* [Colloquium organized by the Centre de Recherches Révolutionnaires et Romantiques, Clermont-Ferrand, June 1972], ed. Paul Viallaneix (Paris: Klincksieck, 1975), pp. 326–43, and "The Authority of Feeling and the Origins of Psychological Criticism: Rousseau and Madame de Staël," in *Yearbook of Comparative Criticism 7: Literary Criticism and Psychology*, ed. Joseph Strelka (Philadelphia: Penn State Univ. Press, 1976), pp. 69–87.

12. The French here reads: "Toutes les réflexions des femmes, en ce qui ne tient pas immédiatement à leurs devoirs, doivent tendre à l'étude des hommes ou aux connaissances agréables qui n'ont que le goût pour objet. . . . Quant aux ouvrages de génie, ils passent leur portée" (*Emile*, IV: 736–37).

13. Staël had vehemently rejected her parents' plan to marry her to William Pitt, and resigned herself to marrying the baron de Staël only on condition that she could remain in her beloved Paris.

14. Gutwirth, "Madame de Staël, Rousseau, and the Woman Question," p. 102.

15. Staël's conception of enthusiasm is developed more fully in Chapter X of *De l'Allemagne*, where she writes: "Enthusiasm . . . is love for what is beautiful, an elevation of the soul, and the pleasure derived from devotion united in a single feeling characterized by a calm nobility. The meaning of the word among the Greeks is its noblest definition: *God in us*." (Staël, *OC*, II: 250).

16. Similarly, in Chapter VI of *De l'Allemagne*, Staël describes Rousseau's *Rêveries du promeneur solitaire* as an "eloquent portrait of a person overwhelmed by an imagination stronger than himself." Adopting the role of Rousseau's

father confessor, she then adds: "My son, your rich imagination was needed to write *La Nouvelle Héloïse*; but, to conduct one's affairs here on earth, one needs some common sense" (Staël, *OC*, II: 241).

17. "A Genevan man who was Rousseau's close friend during the last twenty years of his life often described his wife's abominable character to me, how this denatured mother begged him to put her children in the orphanage . . . , and how she filled him with pain and suspicion through her slander and mock fears. It was no doubt utter madness to listen to and love such a woman; but once this first madness is recognized, all the others are believable" (I: 19, n. 1). The class prejudices underlying Staël's scorn for Thérèse are unmistakable, particularly in the allusions to her alleged infidelities, her "vile inclinations for a man of the lowest class" (I: 22). Moreover, Staël's claim that Thérèse was "a denatured mother" is contradicted by Rousseau's own recollections of her grief at being forced by *him* to abandon their children: "moaning with grief, she obeyed" (*Confessions*, I: 345).

18. "My readers will perhaps be surprised to learn that I am convinced that Rousseau committed suicide," writes Staël. She then relays information that Moultou had shared with her: "The morning of his death, Rousseau awoke in perfect health, but declared that he would be seeing the sun for the last time, and then, before going outside, he drank some coffee that he had prepared. . . . Only a few days before, he had noticed his wife's vile inclinations for a man of the lowest standing; he seemed deeply shaken by this discovery" (I: 22, n. 1).

19. Staël's expressions of frustrated love for Rousseau present striking parallels with her feelings for her father. In her diary at age nineteen, she wrote: "Of all the men in the entire world, it is my father whom I would have most wished for as my lover." (Cited by Christopher Herold, *Mistress to an Age: A Life of Madame de Staël* [New York: Bobbs-Merrill, 1958], p. 46). Similarly, after Necker's death in 1804, Staël would write: "I was to lose my protector, my father, my brother, my friend, the one whom I would have chosen as the sole love of my life if fate had not placed me in a different generation from his" (Staël, *Œuvres complètes* [Paris: Treuttel et Würtz, 1820–21], v. VII, p. 105).

20. "They are right to exclude women from politics and government," affirms Staël. "Nothing is more contrary to their natural vocation than any situation leading them to compete with men. For a woman, celebrity leads only to a tragic end of happiness. But if female destiny consists of constant devotion to conjugal love, then the reward for this devotion should be the scrupulous fidelity of the man who is the object of that love. . . . Until there is a radical change in attitudes regarding how men view the fidelity required by their marriage vows, there will always be war between the sexes—a secret and never-ending war full of tricks and perfidy that will undermine the morality

of men and women alike" (*De l'Allemagne*, Ch. XIX ["De l'amour dans le mariage"], in Staël, *OC*, II: 218).

21. "The segregation of the sexes is no doubt preferable in a republic," writes Staël, "but in countries where the power of public opinion alone frees men from the power of their superiors, the applause and approbation of women become an additional source of emulation whose influence it is important to preserve. . . . Moreover, in a monarchy, women maintain perhaps a greater sense of independence and pride than men; the form of government does not affect them; their bondage is the same in all countries, since it is domestic. Consequently, their nature does not become degraded, even in despotic states; but men, who are made for freedom, feel debased when they are deprived of it, and often sink beneath themselves as a result" (I: 4).

22. Staël had five children in all: a daughter Gustavine (who died in infancy), two sons (Auguste and Albert) with Narbonne, a daughter (Albertine) with Constant, and a son (Louis-Alphonse) with John Rocca, who later became her second husband. On the whole, motherhood plays as insignificant a role in Staël's writings as it seems to have played in her life. Unlike most other women authors of her period, Staël left no essays on education—a common genre and preoccupation among eighteenth-century writers of both sexes. In her novels, motherhood is conspicuous by its absence. Delphine remains safely chaste, while Corinne escapes, as if by magic, the inconveniences of pregnancy, despite her many amorous adventures. Both heroines experience a kind of surrogate motherhood—Delphine through her legal adoption of Thérèse's daughter, Corinne through her spiritual adoption of the Nelvils' daughter. However, Staël's heroines are too preoccupied by their love affairs to devote much time or interest to their charges, who are abandoned without regret at their death—not unlike Julie. Indeed, these children, like those in the Wolmar household, are little more than sentimental props in the novels.

23. The health hazards that nursing posed to some women and children are dramatically illustrated in *Delphine* by the death of Léonce's wife and son. Despite her increasingly weak condition and dwindling milk supply, Mathilde ignores both her doctor's orders and Léonce's pleas and stubbornly persists in breastfeeding her baby—at the urging of her father confessor, who insists it is her duty. (See *Delphine*, Part VI, Letters 3–6 [Paris: editions des femmes, 1981], II: 305–15). Like Staël's refusal to nurse, this chapter in *Delphine* contradicts Staël's rather pompous tribute to the Rousseauian ideals of motherhood and maternal breastfeeding in the *Lettres sur Rousseau*.

24. *Delphine*, Part V, Letter 11, II: 312.

25. Albertine Necker de Saussure, "Notice sur le caractère et les écrits de Madame de Staël," in *Œuvres Posthumes de Mme de Staël* (Paris: Firmin Didot, 1838), p. 10.

26. Gutwirth, "Staël, Rousseau, and the Woman Question," p. 100.

27. This passage was published in December 1788, six months before the opening of the Etats Généraux, when Necker was at the height of his popularity as Prime Minister. Staël, like many of her contemporaries, ardently (and naïvely) believed that a constitutional government could be achieved in France through a bloodless revolution, as it had been in England. This passage is of course doubly ironic, given Necker's failed leadership during les Etats Généraux and the bloody events that would follow.

28. David Glass Larg, *La Vie dans l'œuvre* (Paris: Champion, 1924), p. 67.

29. The French here reads: " . . . et ce hasard m'entraîna dans la carrière littéraire." All quotations from the "Seconde Préface" of 1814 to Staël's *Lettres sur Rousseau* are from her *Œuvres complètes* (Paris: Firmin-Didot, 1838), I: 1–2.

30. Gutwirth, "Staël, Rousseau, and the Woman Question," p. 100.

31. Gutwirth attributes Staël's refusal to name Rousseau in the second preface to a recurrence of her old fear of confronting male authority: "Even in the reply she makes, we see evidence of her dread of this battle in her refusal to 'name' Rousseau, to confront him openly. In her superstitious avoidance of his name, her refusal to attribute to him the idea she is combatting, we still see her terror in the face of the masculine disapproval she is about to incur" ("Staël, Rousseau, and the Woman Question," 106). I would argue that Staël's refusal to name Rousseau is, on the contrary, a conscious strategy that allows her to challenge his views on women, without having to disavow her tribute twenty-two years earlier to his important influence on her thinking and writing.

32. This optimistic view of the transcendent power of woman's intellectual and creative gifts contrasts with the narrow, pessimistic view of woman's destiny expressed in *Delphine* by Mme de Ternan. Convinced (like Rousseau) that a woman's sole purpose in life is to please men through her charms, Mme de Ternan felt that her life was over at thirty, when her beauty began to fade (*Delphine*, Part V, Letter 11, II: 212–13).

33. The importance of writing and study in Staël's own life is confirmed by her cousin Albertine: "There was absolutely no affectation or pedantry in her vocation as a writer. For Mme de Staël, writing and study were a necessary resource, a way to calm and renew her agitated spirit and to maintain the true elevation of her mind" (Mme Necker de Saussure, "Notice," in *Œuvres posthumes*, p. 47).

34. The image of the "poupée bien apprise" calls to mind Staël's last comedy, *Le Mannequin* (1811). In this lively farce, a German girl (significantly named Sophie) is promised in marriage by her father to a French count whose traditionalist views on women echo those of Rousseau in *Emile*. "Let my wife read

my letters; that's all the literature that I ask of her," he declares. "A woman is not supposed to shine beside us and to eclipse us by her brilliance. Her role is to sustain us and to console us in the shadows." To mock the count's narrow-minded views, Sophie rigs up a mannequin, whom she introduces as her cousin. The count is enchanted by this attractive creature, who is so demure that she neither speaks nor moves. When he asks for the pretty cousin in marriage, he is crushed to learn that she is only a doll. Sophie savors her little vengeance: "Well, I wanted to show you a woman who was never forward, who never overstepped the rules of social decorum—in short, a true cardboard doll, just like all the live ones we see around us" (*Le Mannequin*, in *Œuvres posthumes*, pp. 489–90). *Le Mannequin* can be read as a parody of Book V of *Emile* and presents strong parallels with the second preface in both tone and viewpoint.

35. Gutwirth, "Madame de Staël, Rousseau, and the Woman Question," p. 107.

36. Staël appears to be responding here to two key passages in *Emile*—first, to the passage in which Rousseau outlines women's "natural" role and duties: "The education of women should revolve entirely around men. To please them and be useful to them, to be loved and honored by them, to raise them when they are young and take care of them when they are grown, to advise and console them, to make life pleasant and pleasurable for them—these are the duties of women throughout the ages" (Rousseau, *OC*, IV: 703). Second, and more pointedly, Staël seems to be responding here to Rousseau's tirade against women writers: "A witty, learned lady is the scourge of her husband, of her children, . . . of everyone. From the sublime elevation of her genius, she disdains all her womanly duties and soon transforms herself into a man. She is always ridiculous and is criticized quite justly. Even if she possessed real talents, any pretensions or affectation on her part would cheapen them. Her dignity and worth lie in remaining unknown: her glory lies in her husband's esteem for her, just as her pleasures are derived from her family's happiness" (Rousseau, *OC*, IV: 768).

37. This passage echoes the attack in *Corinne* on conformism and mediocrity and on the Rousseauian invocation of duty to repress female talents: "Duty, man's noblest aim, can be denatured like any other idea and can become an offensive weapon, which narrow minds . . . use to silence talent and to banish enthusiasm and genius," warns Corinne. "Hearing them, one would think that duty consisted in the sacrifice of whatever special talents one possesses, that intelligence and wit were a crime for which one must atone by leading precisely the same life as those who lack such gifts" (*Corinne*, Part XIV, Letter 1, II: 89–90). These "narrow minds" are epitomized by her stepmother Lady Edgermond, whose strict conformism posed such a threat to talented,

spirited women like herself: "A formidable enemy threatens to discredit me in your eyes," Corinne warns Oswald. "And that is my stepmother's despotic severity, her disdainful mediocrity. Rather than serving to excuse me, my talents are for her my greatest faults. She does not understand their charm, she sees only their dangers. She considers superfluous, even sinful, anything that runs contrary to the destiny she has charted for herself. Indeed, in her view, the poetry of the heart is but an annoying caprice" (*Corinne*, Part XVI, Letter 3, II: 162).

38. The original French here reads: "Enfin, en ne considérant que nos rapports avec nous-mêmes, une plus grande intensité de vie est toujours une augmentation de bonheur. La douleur, il est vrai, entre plus avant dans les âmes d'une certaine énergie; mais, à tout prendre, il n'est personne qui ne doive remercier Dieu de lui avoir donné une faculté de plus" ("Seconde préface," in Staël, *OC*, v. I, p. 2).

39. Germaine de Staël, *De l'Allemagne*, Ch. XIX ("De l'amour dans le mariage"), in Staël, *OC*, v. II, p. 218.

40. "Isn't it in our youth that we owe the most gratitude to Rousseau?" Staël asks. "For this same writer, who was able to transform passion into virtue and to persuade by means of enthusiasm, drew on the positive traits and indeed the faults of young people to become their master and spiritual guide" (Staël, *OC*, v. I, p. 1).

41. After leaving her position as governess to Lord Kingsborough's children in late 1787, Wollstonecraft had resolved to establish herself as a writer in London. She began writing reviews regularly for the *Analytical Review* at the invitation of its editor Joseph Johnson, who had published her *Thoughts on the Education of Daughters* in early 1787 and her translation of Necker's book in 1788. Through Johnson, Wollstonecraft became acquainted with a distinguished circle of avant-garde artists, writers, intellectuals, and Dissenters. It was also through Johnson that she later met her future husband, the political philosopher and novelist William Godwin. Regarding this period in Wollstonecraft's life, see Eleanor Flexner, *Mary Wollstonecraft. A Biography* (New York: Coward, McCann, & Geoghegan, 1972), esp. Chapter 7, "Johnson's Circle," pp. 93–114.

42. *Analytical Review* IV (Aug. 1789): 360.

43. Wollstonecraft's irritation with Staël's pompous tribute to her father can also be attributed to class tensions and personal resentments. Wollstonecraft clearly resented Staël's privileged social and economic position (reflected in her repetition of the title "Baroness" and refusal to name Staël any other way), as well as her effort to capitalize on her father's fame and popularity in her first published work. Wollstonecraft was, by contrast, a self-made woman of

undistinguished middle-class origins, forced to support herself through her writing. She may have secretly envied Staël's close bond with her father, since her relationship with her own father was openly hostile (due in part to his poor management of their family affairs, which forced Mary to assume financial responsibility for her younger siblings at an early age).

44. Wollstonecraft dismisses Necker's book as "a large book [of] various metaphysical shreds of arguments which he had collected from the conversations of men, fond of ingenious subtleties; and the style, excepting some declamatory passages, was as inflated and diffused as the thoughts were far-fetched and unconnected" (*An Historical and Moral View of the French Revolution* [London: Joseph Johnson, 1796], pp. 61–62).

45. *A Vindication of the Rights of Woman with Strictures on Political and Moral Subjects* (New York: Source Book Press, 1971), p. 53. Reprint of first edition by Joseph Johnson, London, 1792. Subsequent references to this work are to this edition and are indicated in parentheses within the text.

46. In her novel *Maria*, Wollstonecraft recalls romping in the fields with her brothers and sisters and describes the haphazard instruction she received at home through books lent her by a cultivated, but often absent uncle. (See *The Wrongs of Woman: or, Maria* [London: Oxford Univ. Press, 1976], pp. 126–28). A similar autobiographical passage is found in her first novel, *Mary*: "She would ramble about the garden, admire the flowers, and play with the dogs. An old house-keeper told her stories, read to her, and, at last, taught her how to read. . . . She perused with avidity every book that came her way. Neglected in every respect, and left to the operations of her own mind, she considered everything that came under her inspection, and learned to think." (*Mary—A Fiction* [London: Oxford Univ. Press, 1976], p. 4). Like a number of well-known women writers of her period (including Roland, Graffigny, Genlis and d'Epinay), Wollstonecraft was almost entirely self-taught. The striking similarities among these women, who developed such strong minds and talents despite their lack of formal instruction, lend support to Wollstonecraft's arguments regarding the inadequacies of traditional female education.

47. *Emile*, IV: 697.

48. "Rousseau respected—almost adored—virtue and yet he allowed himself to love with sensual fondness. His imagination constantly prepared inflammable fewel for his inflammable senses; but, in order to reconcile his respect for self-denial, fortitude, and those heroic virtues, which a mind like his could not coolly admire, he labours to invert the law of nature, and broaches a doctrine pregnant with mischief" (*Rights of Woman*, p. 57).

49. "Their senses are inflamed, and their understanding neglected, consequently they become the prey of their senses, delicately termed sensibility,"

writes Wollstonecraft. "This overstretched sensibility naturally relaxes the other powers of the mind, and prevents intellect from attaining that sovereignty which it ought to attain to render a rational creature useful to others, and content with its own station: for the exercise of the understanding, as life advances, is the only method pointed out by nature to calm the passions. . . . Yet, to their senses, are women slaves, because it is by their sensibility that they obtain present power" (*Rights of Woman*, pp. 79–80).

50. "But if she lent St. Preux, or the demi-god of her fancy, his form, she richly repaid him by the donation of all St. Preux's sentiments and feelings, culled to gratify her own . . . ." (*Maria*, p. 89).

51. Letter to Gilbert Imlay (22 Sept. 1794) in *The Collected Letters of Mary Wollstonecraft*, ed. Ralph M. Wardle (Ithaca: Cornell Univ. Press, 1979), p. 263. This statement occurs at the end of a passage dealing with Mary's daughter by Imlay, Fanny, who was then four months old: "To honour J. J. Rousseau, I intend to give her a sash, the first she has ever had round her—and why not? —for I have always been half in love with him." Wollstonecraft is alluding here to a passage in the *Confessions* where Rousseau recalls the sashes he wove as wedding presents for the young women of his acquaintance to encourage them to breastfeed their children. The context is significant because it shows Wollstonecraft's familiarity with the *Confessions* and suggests that her admiration for Rousseau stemmed in part from his successful efforts to promote maternal nursing.

52. *Analytical Review* XI (1791): 528.

53. Ibid.

54. *Maria*, pp. 89–90.

55. Letter to Everina Wollstonecraft (24 March 1787) in *Collected Letters*, p. 145. To illustrate Rousseau's paradoxes, Wollstonecraft points to the contradiction that lay at the heart of his pedagogical theories: "He chuses (sic) a *common* capacity to educate—and gives as a reason that a genius will educate itself" (Ibid.).

56. Ibid.

57. Letter to William Godwin (17 Aug. 1796) in *Collected Letters*, p. 337.

58. Wollstonecraft's ambivalence toward the Rousseauian ideal of sensibility is expressed most poignantly when she reflects on her year-old daughter's future in one of her letters from Sweden: "I feel more than a mother's fondness and anxiety, when I reflect on the dependent and oppressed state of her sex. I dread lest she should be forced to sacrifice her heart to her principles, or her principles to her heart. With trembling hand I shall cultivate sensibility, lest . . . I sharpen the thorns that will wound the breast I would fain guard —

I dread to unfold her mind, lest it should render her unfit for the world she is to inhabit — Hapless woman! what a fate is thine!" (*A Short Residence in Sweden, Norway, and Denmark*, ed. Richard Holmes [New York: Penguin Books, 1987], p. 97). Mary's fears concerning her daughter's fate strangely foreshadowed Fanny's suicide at the age of twenty over an unhappy love affair.

59. As Mitzi Myers aptly remarks, "Wollstonecraft asserts many claims integral to modern feminism, suing for coeducation, economic independence, legal equality, and freer access to jobs and professions, yet, . . . the core of her manifesto remains middle-class motherhood, a feminist, republicanized adaptation of the female role normative in late eighteenth-century bourgeois notions of the family. . . . Although she does not suggest that woman's only possible place is the home, motherhood provides a pervasive rationale for better education, as well as for civil existence and work. . . . As 'active citizen,' the average woman will advance the common welfare by managing her family, educating her children, and assisting her neighbors, also standing ready for work outside the home to facilitate family maintenance if necessary." See Mitzi Myers, "Reform or Ruin: 'A Revolution in Female Manners,'" *Studies in Eighteenth-Century Culture* 11 (1982): 207.

60. Wollstonecraft's claim that Staël's "eulogium on Rousseau was accidentally put into my hands" is rather mystifying, since she had reviewed the *Lettres sur Rousseau* three years earlier. Perhaps she wished to imply that she would not have read Staël's book if she had not been asked to review it—an indirect way of further deprecating the work and its author.

61. The dangers of female friendship and solidarity are powerfully illustrated in *Delphine* through the perfidy of Mmes de Vernon and de Ternan and the disastrous results of Delphine's kindness to Thérèse and Mathilde. The destructive force of female rivalry is underlined in *Corinne* and numerous other works by Staël.

62. Although Wollstonecraft's two *Vindications* were both written in England, she did in fact write her *History of the French Revolution* during her two-year stay in France in the midst of the Terror. She was, moreover, well aware of the risk she was taking by writing a work highly critical of the revolutionary government. Referring to this work in a letter to her sister Everina, she writes: "I have just sent off the great part of my manuscript which Miss Williams would fain have me burn, following her example—and to tell you the truth—my life would not have been worth much, had it been *found*" (Letter to Everina Wollstonecraft, 10 March 1794, in *Collected Letters*, pp. 250–51).

63. In her dedicatory letter to Talleyrand, Wollstonecraft writes: "Consider, Sir, dispassionately, these observations—for a glimpse of this truth seemed to open before you when you observed 'that to see one half of the human race excluded by the other from all participation of government, was a political

phenomenon that, according to abstract principles, it was impossible to explain.' If so, on what does your constitution rest? ... Consider, I address you as a legislator, whether ... it be not inconsistent and unjust to subjugate women?" In closing, she boldly declares: "I wish, Sir, to set some investigations of this kind afloat in France; and should they lead to a confirmation of my principles, when your constitution is revised the Rights of Woman may be respected, if it be fully proved that reason calls for this respect, and loudly demands JUSTICE for one half of the human race" (*Rights of Woman*, pp. 9, 11). Far from being irritated by this rather impudent letter, Talleyrand thanked Wollstonecraft and even called on her when he was in London the following year—an eloquent testimony to the power of her writing.

64. Hogsett offers two possible explanations for Staël's apparent indifference to the nascent women's rights movement: "If one wishes to attribute her nonparticipation to factors other than masculinism or cowardice, one could argue that her analysis of history caused her to conclude that current initatives for freedom and woman's struggle for rights were not of a piece," writes Hogsett. "Or, less generously, one could maintain that she always saw the status of women as a by-product of or as dependent on other social or political phenomena that were of primary importance to her. Thus, she would not be disposed to ask for women's rights themselves but rather to look for conditions under which they might develop" (Hogsett, p. 140).

65. Wollstonecraft's response to Staël's *Lettres sur Rousseau* has elicited surprisingly little critical commentary, aside from a brief essay by John Cleary, "Madame de Staël, Rousseau, and Mary Wollstonecraft," *Romance Notes* 21, 3 (Spring 1981): 329–33. Cleary focuses on Wollstonecraft's critique of Staël's seemingly blind acceptance of Rousseau's traditionalist view of women and the complicity with the status quo that her *Lettres sur Rousseau* seem to reflect. He does not deal at all with the ambiguities underlying Staël's and Wollstonecraft's responses to Rousseau, nor does he attempt to trace the evolution in their views or to differentiate between Wollstonecraft's initial review of Staël and her more pointed criticisms in the *Rights of Woman*. Moreover, Cleary ignores the striking parallels between the two women reflected in their ambivalent responses to Jean-Jacques. I have sought to explore these questions by taking a closer look at the complex interplay among these three major figures of the revolutionary era, particularly in terms of how they viewed woman's role and destiny in a period fraught with social change.

Chapter 6

1. Olympe de Gouges, "Postambule" to her *Déclaration des droits de la femme*, in *Olympe de Gouges. Œuvres*, ed. Benoîte Groult (Paris: Mercure de France, 1986), p. 109.

2. See Marie-Josephine Diamond's discussion of this paradox in "Olympe de Gouges and the French Revolution: The Construction of Gender as Critique," *Dialectical Anthropology* 15, 2–3 (1990): 96–97. Also see the excellent analyses of Gouges's development as a feminist and revolutionary by Erica Harth in *Cartesian Women: Versions and Subversions of Rational Discourse in the Old Regime* (Ithaca: Cornell Univ. Press, 1992), pp. 213–34, and by Joan Wallach Scott in "French Feminists and the Rights of 'Man': Olympe de Gouges's Declarations," *History Workshop Journal* 28 (Autumn 1989): 1–21.

3. Gouges, *Compte moral* (Paris, 1792), p. 4.

4. Gouges, letter to Bernardin de Saint-Pierre (1792), cited by Olivier Blanc in *Une Femme de Libertés. Olympe de Gouges* (Paris: Editions Syros, 1989), p. 14.

5. Gouges, "Préface pour les dames ou le portrait des femmes" (1791), preface to *Mirabeau aux Champs-Elysées*, in Groult, pp. 115–16.

6. Gouges, *Mirabeau aux Champs-Elysées*, in Groult, pp. 158–59.

7. Gouges, *Molière chez Ninon*, in Groult, p. 28.

8. Interrogation of Olympe de Gouges, cited by A.-J. Fleury, *Mémoires* (Paris, 1844), p. 104.

9. Gouges, letter to her son Pierre Aubry, 3 November 1793; cited by Léopold Lacour, *Les Origines du féminisme contemporain. Trois Femmes de la Révolution: Olympe de Gouges, Théroigne de Méricourt, Rose Lacombe* (Paris: Plon, 1900), p. 422.

10. Stéphanie-Felicité de Genlis, *Mémoires de Mme de Genlis*, ed. François Barrière (Paris: Firmin Didot, 1857), pp. 177–78. Barrière's 450-page one-volume abridged edition is the most widely available edition of Genlis's *Mémoires*.

11. Journal de Caroline de Genlis, Marquise de Lawoestine (1781), cited by Gabriel de Broglie, *Madame de Genlis* (Paris: Librairie Académique Perrin, 1985), pp. 140–41.

12. Broglie cites a number of the attacks on Genlis in the press following her nomination as *gouverneur*. Among the most virulent was an anonymous libel titled *Vie Privée de Mme de Sillery*, which claimed "Elle avait préludé dans un boudoir à l'école de Platon, et ne fit qu'un saut d'un sofa voluptueux au fauteuil pédantesque de gouverneur." [She trained in a boudoir for Plato's school, and then easily jumped from the couch of pleasure to the pedantic chair of head tutor.] (Cited in Broglie, p. 114.)

13. Lemaire (Dean of the Sorbonne Faculté des Lettres), cited by Broglie, pp. 466–67.

14. Conversation with Louis-Philippe in 1847, cited by Victor Hugo in *Choses vues* (Paris, 1887).

15. Stéphanie-Felicité de Genlis, *Adèle et Théodore, ou Lettres sur l'éducation,* 4 vols. (Paris: Maradan, 1804), v. I, p. 46.

16. Genlis, ed., *Emile, ou l'Education, nouvelle édition à l'usage de la jeunesse avec des retranchements, des notes et une préface,* 3 vols. (Paris, 1820), v. I, p. 230. Genlis's expurgated version of *Emile* is discussed later in the chapter.

17. Genlis's two adopted daughters are generally believed to be her own children by the duc de Chartres. According to Broglie, the two girls were sent to England as infants and then brought back to France to serve as English-speaking companions for her pupils. Both received generous dowries from the Duke and married into the upper class. The older adopted daughter Pamela bore a striking resemblance to Genlis and was her avowed favorite, especially after the death in childbirth of her oldest daughter Caroline.

18. Genlis, cited by Broglie, p. 116. Catherine of Russia was a great admirer of Genlis's work and had *Adèle et Théodore* translated into Russian to help improve female education in her country. She and Genlis corresponded regularly for several years.

19. Genlis, ed., *Emile,* I, p. 19.

20. Genlis, *Mémoires,* ed. Barrière, p. 345.

21. Genlis, Preface to *Emile,* I, p. ii.

22. Ibid. For further discussion of Genlis's methods of education and experience as an educator, see Bernard Grosperrin, "Un manuel d'éducation noble: *Adèle et Théodore* de Madame de Genlis," *Cahiers d'Histoire* 19 (1974): 343–52, and Alice M. Laborde, *L'Œuvre de Madame de Genlis* (Paris: Nizet, 1966), especially Ch. 2 "Principes et Méthode d'Education," pp. 60–90.

23. In her *Mémoires,* Genlis is less indulgent toward Rousseau and seems to hold him partly responsible for the misapplications of his methods. Recalling the different educational trends she had witnessed over the previous fifty years, she comments: "At first, children were raised *à la Jean-Jacques* without teachers or lessons. Young children were left to nature, and since nature does not teach spelling, much less Latin, there suddenly appeared in society young people whose ignorance was truly startling. Then educators went to the opposite extreme: children were overloaded with instruction; we wanted to produce child prodigies, especially in the sciences" (*Mémoires,* ed. Barrière, 342).

24. Genlis, *La Religion considérée comme l'unique base de bonheur et de la véritable philosophie* (Paris, 1787), p. 387.

25. Genlis's prudish scorn for Mme de Warens seems rather hypocritical given her own highly publicized affair with the duc de Chartres.

26. Genlis, *La Religion,* p. 388.

27. Ibid., p. 387.

28. Genlis, *Mémoires inédits de Madame la comtesse de Genlis, sur le dix-huitième siècle et la révolution française, depuis 1756 jusqu'à nos jours* (Brussels: P. J. de Mat, 1825–26), 10 vols, v. II, pp. 1–17. (All references to Genlis's *Mémoires* are to this ten-volume edition unless indicated otherwise.) Although the *Mémoires* were not published until 1825, Genlis's account of her friendship with Rousseau was actually written two decades earlier and published by Maradan in the collection of biographical sketches titled *Souvenirs de Félicie* (1804) and *Suite des Souvenirs de Félicie* (1807). Genlis's *Souvenirs* appeared even earlier in serialized form in Maradan's *Bibliothèque Universelle des Romans* beginning in 1801 and in the *Mercure de France* beginning in 1803. The account of her friendship with Rousseau published in the *Mercure de France* on September 8, 1803, is very similar to the version that later appeared in her *Mémoires*.

29. Genlis, letter to Bernardin de Saint-Pierre (15 October 1786), in *Lettres inédites de Mme de Genlis à Bernardin de Saint-Pierre, 1786–1791*, ed. Monique Stern, in *Studies on Voltaire and the Eighteenth Century* 169 (1977): 187–88.

30. See, for example, T. C. Walker, "Madame de Genlis and Rousseau," *Romanic Review* 43 (1952): 95–108. Walker's arguments are discussed below.

31. Victor de Musset-Pathay, *Histoire de la vie et des ouvrages de J.-J. Rousseau* (Paris, 1821). Musset-Pathay cites Genlis's account published in the *Souvenirs de Félicie* (1804) almost *in toto* and contests the dates in a series of footnotes, although he does not question the veracity of her account otherwise.

32. In her *Mémoires*, Genlis claims to have first met Rousseau at the age of eighteen (and hence in 1764) and to have seen him afterward nearly every day for six or seven months. However, since Rousseau was in Môtiers in 1764, these dates are contested by T. C. Walker and by Arnold Rowbotham, who both suggest late 1770 as a more likely date for his first meeting with Genlis and February 1771 as the date their friendship abruptly came to an end. (See Walker, pp. 95–108, and Arnold H. Rowbotham, "Madame de Genlis and Jean-Jacques Rousseau," *Modern Language Quarterly* 3 [1942], p. 364.) This last conjecture is supported by the fact that the opening of Sauvigny's play (date of the falling-out) took place on February 8, 1771. The date of their first meeting is more difficult to determine. November or December of 1770 seems the most likely date, since Genlis herself claims to have met Rousseau six months after his return to Paris (June 24, 1770) and shortly after his first public readings of the *Confessions* (thought to have taken place in November or December 1770). This discrepancy in dates is significant in that Genlis claims to have been eighteen when she became friends with Rousseau and invokes her youth to excuse her childish behavior the night of their first meeting and to explain the fact that she had not yet read his works. If Genlis was actually six years older when she met Rousseau, then her excuses are less convincing and raise ques-

tions about the veracity of her account. Walker maintains that Genlis did not know Rousseau as long or as well as she claimed and perhaps even fabricated much of her story in order to make her memoirs more appealing to the public, always eager for new anecdotes about the eccentric Genevan. In any case, it seems fairly certain that Genlis's friendship with Rousseau lasted only two or three months, instead of six or seven months as she claimed.

33. See Broglie, p. 52.

34. See Rowbotham, p. 367.

35. Genlis, *Discours sur la Suppression des Couvents*, in *Discours Moraux* (Paris, 1791), p. 96.

36. Genlis, *De l'Influence des femmes sur la littérature française comme protectrices des lettres et comme auteurs; ou Précis de l'histoire des femmes françaises les plus célèbres* (Paris: Maradan, 1811), p. 322. Further references, given in parentheses in the text, will be to this edition.

37. Genlis, *Mémoires*, VI, p. 138.

38. Genlis, ed., *Emile, ou l'Education, nouvelle édition à l'usage de la jeunesse avec des retranchements, des notes et une préface*, 3 vols. (Paris, 1820), v. II, p. 8. The volume and page references here are to Genlis's edition.

39. See Broglie, pp. 471–72.

40 Gouges, preface to *L'Homme généreux* (1786), p. vi.

41. Gouges, Letter to the Comédie-Française (1785), in Groult, p. 140. Similarly, in the preface to *Mirabeau*, Gouges confides: "I had no tutor besides nature, and all my reflections, however philosophical, are incapable of effacing the deeply rooted imperfections of my education" (119).

42. Gouges, preface to *Zamore et Mirza* (1788), p. 22.

43. Gouges, preface to *L'Homme généreux*, p. vi.

44. Genlis, letter to John Wilson Croker, 20 November 1821, cited by Broglie, p. 446.

45. Gouges, "Préface sans caractère," preface to *Le Philosophe Corrigé, ou Le Cocu Supposé* (1787), in Groult, p. 136.

46. Ibid., pp. 137, 135.

47. Gouges, "Encore une préface" (1791), preface to the revised edition of *Mirabeau aux Champs-Elysées*, in Groult, p. 151.

48. Gouges, "Mon Dernier Mot à Mes Chers Amis" (1790), in Groult, p. 148.

49. Gouges, *Denkschrift der Madame de Valmont/Mémoire de Madame de Valmont* (1788), ed. Gisela Thiele-Knobloch (Frankfurt: Ulrike Helmer Verlag, 1993), pp. 60–62.

50. Rousseau, *Emile*, in *Œuvres complètes*, IV, p. 768.

51. Gouges, "Encore une préface" (1791), revised edition of *Mirabeau*, in Groult, p. 151.

52. Gouges, undated brochure cited by Groult, p. 23.

53. Cited in Broglie, p. 120. Following the Academie Française's decision, La Harpe remarked: "Against my judgment—and that of the public as well, I believe—Mme d'Epinay won out over Mme de Genlis. It's true that Genlis made the mistake of launching an awkward campaign against the philosophes. But what difference does that make? Let them respond to her criticisms if they wish, and let us give her the award if she deserves it." (Cited in Broglie, p. 120.)

54. Gouges, *Adresse aux représentants de la nation* (1790), p. 24.

55. Fleury, cited by Groult, p. 24.

56. Gouges, preface to *Le Mariage Inattendu de Cherubin* (1786), p. iv.

57. *La Chronique de Paris* (29 December 1789).

58. Gouges's plan for a national women's theater is discussed by Samia Spencer in "Une Remarquable Visionnaire: Olympe de Gouges," *Enlightenment Essays* 9 (1978): 88.

59. Gouges, *Le Bon Sens Français, ou l'Apologie des vrais nobles* (1792), cited by Blanc, p. 55.

60. Gouges, letter to Caron de Beaumarchais, cited by Groult, pp. 28–29.

61. Genlis, cited by Broglie, p. 428.

62. Gouges, preface to *Le Philosophe Corrigé*, in Groult, p. 137.

63. Gouges, *Déclaration des droits de la femme et de la citoyenne* (Paris, 1791), cited in Groult, p. 101. All further quotations from this text are from this edition; page numbers will be indicated in parentheses within the text.

64. Harth, p. 229.

65. Scott, p. 15. Also see Barbara Woshinsky's analysis of Gouges's Declaration in her article "Olympe de Gouges's *Declaration of the Rights of Woman* (1791)," *Mary Wollstonecraft Newsletter* 2 (December 1973): 1–6.

66. Joan Landes, *Women and the Public Sphere in the Age of the French Revolution* (Ithaca: Cornell Univ. Press, 1988), p. 127.

67. Michelet may have confused Gouges's line with Sophie de Condorcet's famous retort to Napoleon. In response to Bonaparte who expressed disdain for women who meddled in politics, Mme de Condorcet is said to have quipped: "In a country where women's heads are chopped off, it is only natural that they want to know why!" (Cited by Groult, p. 39.)

68. Carol Blum, *Rousseau and the Republic of Virtue: The Language of Politics in the French Revolution* (Ithaca: Cornell Univ. Press, 1986), p. 213.

69. *La Feuille du Salut Public* (11 November 1793), cited by Blanc, p. 198.

70. Pierre-Gaspard Chaumette, speech reported in *L'Ancien moniteur* 18 (19 Nov 1793): 450–51. For a provocative analysis of conservative male reactions to Gouges and to other female activists during the French Revolution, see Neil Hertz, "Medusa's Head: Male Hysteria under Political Pressure," *Representations* 4 (Fall 1983): 27–54.

71. Response by Genlis to a hostile article about her published by M. Luzac of Leyde in the anti-Orleanist press in April 1794. There Luzac writes: "Comblée des bienfaits de la cour de France, elle avait fait la Révolution. . . . Enfin, Mme de Sillery respire tranquillement en Suisse!" ["Loaded with gifts and favors from the court of France, she then took part in the Revolution. . . . And now, Mme de Sillery is leading an easy life in Switzerland!"] Cited by Broglie, p. 266.

72. Genlis, *Précis de ma conduite depuis la Révolution* (1796), cited by Broglie, p. 282.

73. For further discussion of Genlis's political opportunism, see Jennifer Birkett's excellent article "Madame de Genlis: The New Men and the Old Eve," *French Studies* 42 (April 1988): 150–64.

74. Gouges, "Le Cri du sage, par une femme" (1789), in Groult, pp. 89–90. This passage recalls Rousseau's rhetoric of contradiction, particularly in the passage where Saint-Preux exclaims: "Women, women! beloved and fatal objects which nature embellished to torture us, . . . whose love and hate are equally pernicious, and whom we can neither seek out nor flee with impunity! . . . abyss of pain and pleasure! . . . unhappy is he who abandons himself to your deceptive calm! It is you who produce the storms that torment the human race" (*Julie*, in *OC*, II: 676).

75. Gouges, "Le Cri du sage, par une femme," in Groult, p. 89.

76. Scott, pp. 9 and 22, n. 38.

77. Gouges, Speech to the Assemblée Législative (20 May 1792), cited by Blanc, p. 191. The pretext for the speech was Gouges's petition to allow women to participate in the Fête de la Loi later that year. Her petition was granted, but not without considerable opposition.

78. Gouges, "Préface pour les dames ou le portrait des femmes," in Groult, pp. 116, 118.

79. Gouges, Preface to *L'Homme Généreux* (1786); cited by Blanc, p. 186.

80. Germaine de Staël, *De l'Allemagne*, Ch. XIX ("De l'amour dans le mariage), in *Œuvres complètes de Mme de Staël* (Paris: Firmin Didot, 1838), v. II, p. 218.

81. See Erica Harth, *Cartesian Women: Versions and Subversions of Rational Discourse in the Old Regime*, pp. 116–17.

82. Genlis, *La Religion*, p. 384.

83. Gouges, *Le Bon Sens français, ou l'apologie des vrais nobles* (April 1792), cited by Blanc, p. 55.

84. See Jean Rabaut, *Histoire des féminismes français* (Paris: Editions Stock, 1977), p. 57.

85. See Carole Pateman,"The Fraternal Social Contract," in *The Disorder of Women: Democracy, Feminism, and Political Theory* (Stanford: Stanford Univ. Press, 1989), pp. 33–57.

86. Georgette Ducrest, *Paris en province et la province à Paris* (1831), v. III, p. 154.

Conclusion

1. Most Charrière scholars agree that Staël's Corinne was patterned after Charrière's Caliste. See Claudine Herrmann's introduction to her edition of Charrière's novel, *Caliste, ou Lettres écrites de Lausanne* (Paris, Editons des femmes, 1979), p. 17.

2. The resistance of these women to the Rousseauian model of gendered spheres of activity and experience supports Lawrence E. Klein's thesis in his recent essay "Gender and the Public/Private Distinction in the Eighteenth Century: Some Questions about Evidence and Analytic Procedure," *Eighteenth-Century Studies* 29, 1 (Fall 1995): 97–109. In his critique of the Habermasian model of women's exclusion from the public sphere, Klein argues convincingly that "the a priori commitment to the publicity of men and the privacy of women is an example of the way in which the concerns of analysts of the nineteenth century are imposed on the eighteenth century. Even granting that the gender dichotomy of public and private spheres is a good description of nineteenth-century ideology and practice (although there are many grounds for suspicion about this claim too), there is no reason for that description to

be accepted as adequate for the eighteenth century" (105). For further discussion of the ongoing debate over the relationship of women to the public sphere, also see Dena Goodman, "Public Sphere and Private Life: Toward a Synthesis of Current Historiographical Approaches to the Old Regime," *History and Theory* 31 (1992): 1–20; Joan DeJean, *Tender Geographies. Women and the Origins of the Novel in France* (New York: Columbia University Press), esp. chap. 1: "Women's Places, Women's Spaces," pp. 17–70; and the forum of articles on "The Public Sphere in the Eighteenth Century" by Sarah Maza, Daniel Gordon, and David Bell in *French Historical Studies* 17, 4 (Fall 1992): 882–956.

3. *Mémoires de Madame Roland*, p. 303.

4. Henriette to Rousseau, 5 February 1765, in *Correspondance Complète de Rousseau*, ed. R. A. Leigh (Geneva: Institut Voltaire, 1967), v. XXIII, p. 298.

5. Madame Necker de Saussure, "Notice," in *Œuvres posthumes de Madame de Staël*, p. 47.

6. Letter to Sophie Cannet, 16 August 1773, in *Lettres de Madame Roland*, I, p. 153.

7. D'Epinay, *Les Conversations d'Emilie* [Conversation 12], I, pp. 466–67, 469.

8. *Adèle et Théodore*, I, p. 45.

9. Henriette to Rousseau, 26 March 1764, in *Correspondance Complète de Rousseau*, v. XIX, p. 244.

10. Written over an eight-year period from 1762 to 1770, the *Confessions* were not actually published until after Rousseau's death (1778). Part I of the *Confessions* (Books 1–6) was first published in Geneva in 1782; Part II (Books 7–12) first appeared in 1789. However, Rousseau's autobiography had already aroused a certain amount of controversy long before their publication through the private readings he made of them to select audiences in late 1770 and early 1771.

11. Philippe Lejeune, *L'Autobiographie en France* (Paris: A. Colin, 1971), p. 82.

12. Rousseau, *Confessions*, Préambule du manuscrit de Neuchâtel (1764), in *Œuvres complètes*, ed. Marcel Raymond and Bernard Gagnebin (Paris: Gallimard, 1959), v. I, pp. 1149, 1153.

13. Letter to Jany, Oct. 1793, in *Lettres de Madame Roland* IV, pp. 527–28.

14. George Sand, *Histoire de ma vie*, in *Œuvres autobiographiques* (Paris: Gallimard, 1970), v. II, p. 13.

15. Sand, letter cited by Béatrice Didier in "Femme/Identité/Ecriture: A Propos de *L'Histoire de ma vie* de George Sand," in *Revue des Sciences Humaines* 168 (1977): 561.

16. Daniel Stern (Marie d'Agoult), letter to Hortense Allard, cited by Jacques Vier, in *La Comtesse d'Agoult et son temps* (Paris: Armand Colin, 1961), v. IV, p. 250.

17. Stern, Preface to *Mes Souvenirs* (Paris: Calmann-Lévy, 1980), pp. vii, ix.

18. Stern, Avant-Propos to *Mémoires* [1833–54] (Paris: Calmann-Lévy, 1927), p. 11.

19. Pierre Fauchery, *La Destinée féminine dans le roman français du dix-huitième siècle: 1713–1807* (Paris: A. Colin, 1972), p. 94.

20. Jean Starobinski, "Suicide et mélancolie chez Madame de Staël," in *Madame de Staël et l'Europe* (Paris: Klincksieck, 1970), pp. 242–52.

21. Colette, *Break of Day*, trans. Enid McLeod (New York: Farrar, Strauss, and Cudahy, 1961), p. 62.

22. Nancy K. Miller, "Writing Fictions: Women's Autobiography in France," in *Life/Lines. Theorizing Women's Autobiography*, ed. Bella Brodzki and Celeste Schenck (Ithaca: Cornell Univ. Press, 1988), p. 49. Because of the cultural diversity of the texts it presents and the excellent foregrounding of the theoretical issues it raises, this is among the best collections of essays on women's autobiography yet to appear. Other noteworthy studies in this rapidly expanding field include Shari Benstock, ed., *The Private Self: Women's Autobiographical Writings* (Chapel Hill: Univ. of North Carolina Press, 1988); Estelle C. Jelinek, *The Tradition of Women's Autobiography: From Antiquity to the Present* (Boston: Twayne, 1986); Jelinek, ed., *Women's Autobiography: Essays in Criticism* (Bloomington: Indiana Univ. Press, 1980); Françoise Lionnet, *Autobiographical Voices: Race, Gender, Self-Portraiture* (Ithaca: Cornell Univ. Press, 1988); Mary G. Mason and Carol Hurd Green, eds., *Journeys: Autobiographical Writings by Women* (Boston: G. K. Hall, 1979); Sidonie Smith, *A Poetics of Women's Autobiography: Marginality and the Fictions of Self-Representation* (Bloomington: Indiana Univ. Press, 1987); and Domna Stanton, *The Female Autograph* (New York: New York Literary Forum, 1984). Also see my article "Strategies of Self-Representation: The Influence of Rousseau's *Confessions* and the Woman Autobiographer's Double Bind," *Studies on Voltaire and the Eighteenth Century* 317 (1994): 313–39.

23. Leading the posthumous campaign against Wollstonecraft, the *Anti-Jacobin Magazine* delivered a general onslaught on the immorality of everything she was supposed to represent, from sexual promiscuity to disrespect for parental authority and the institution of marriage. The attacks culminated in a poem titled "The Vision of Liberty," which the magazine published in 1801: "William hath penn'd a waggon-load of stuff/And Mary's life at last he needs must write,/Thinking her whoredoms were not known enough,/Till fairly printed off in black and white./With wondrous glee and pride, this simple wight/Her brothel feats of wantonness sets down;/Being her spouse, he tells, with huge delight,/How oft she cuckolded the silly clown,/And lent,

O lovely piece!, herself to half the town." Even Wollstonecraft's former friends openly voiced their disapproval of her life as Godwin had presented it. Their position was perhaps best summed up by Harriet Martineau, who observed that "women of the Wollstonecraft order do infinite mischief. For my part, I do not wish to have anything to do with them; she was neither a safe example, nor a successful champion of woman and her rights." Cited by Richard Holmes in his introduction to Godwin's *Memoirs of the Author of The Rights of Woman* (New York: Viking Penguin, 1987), p. 47.

24. See, for example, Challemel-Lacour's comments in the introduction to his edition of *Les Œuvres de Madame d'Epinay* (Paris: A. Sauton, 1869), pp. xviii–xx, and my discussion of his remarks in Chapter 3.

25. Sainte-Beuve, Review of Mme Roland's *Mémoires* in *Revue des Deux Mondes* 92 (15 March 1871): 272. The appraisal of Roland's memoirs by Sainte-Beuve and other nineteenth-century critics is further discussed in Chapter 4.

26. Madelyn Gutwirth, *Madame de Staël, Novelist. The Emergence of the Artist as Woman* (Urbana: Univ. of Illinois Press, 1978), p. 286.

27. Noreen J. Swallow, "The Weapon of Personality: A Review of Sexist Criticism of Madame de Staël," *Atlantis* 8, 1 (Fall 1982): 79.

28. Charlotte Hogsett, *The Literary Existence of Germaine de Staël* (Carbondale: Southern Illinois Univ. Press, 1987), p. 4.

29. See, for example, Genlis's criticism of Julie de l'Espinasse's letters and the novels of Mme de Tencin (especially *Le Siège de Calais*) and Mme Cottin (especially *Claire d'Albe*) in *De l'Influence des femmes sur la littérature*, pp. 284–86, 275–278, and 344–366, respectively. In this same work, Genlis vigorously attacks the immoral character of the private correspondence and posthumous works of the *philosophes* and their circle, citing as many men as women in her critique. "In these works, the authors reveal and prove their own duplicity, viciousness, immorality, unrestrained ambition and vanity, and base envy," she writes. "This is what we find in the letters of La Harpe, Voltaire, d'Alembert, Mme du Châtelet, J.-J. Rousseau, Mlle de l'Espinasse, Mme du Deffant, etc. Henceforth, their greatest enemies . . . will be the editors of their correspondence and of their posthumous works" (pp. 285–86). Not surprisingly, Genlis singles out Rousseau's *Confessions* and Diderot's *La Religieuse* as the most pernicious of these posthumous publications.

30. Mary G. Mason, "The Other Voice," in *Life/Lines. Theorizing Women's Autobiography*, p. 22.

31. One of the earliest articulations of these goals is found in Annette Kolodny's essay "Some Notes on Defining a Feminist Literary Criticism," *Critical Inquiry* 2 (Fall 1975): 78.

32. Sandra Gilbert and Susan Gubar, *The Madwoman in the Attic: The Woman Writer and the Nineteenth-Century Literary Imagination* (New Haven: Yale Univ. Press, 1979), p. 50.

33. Elaine Showalter, "Feminist Criticism in the Wilderness," in *Writing and Sexual Difference*, ed. Elizabeth Abel (Chicago: Univ. of Chicago Press, 1982), p. 34.

34. Ibid., p. 32. Gilbert and Gubar refer to this muted or repressed female tradition as a "palimpsest" within the dominant male tradition. (See *Madwoman*, p. 50.) Nancy Miller also sees "another text" in women's fiction, "more or less muted from novel to novel, but always there to be read." See Nancy K. Miller, "Emphasis Added: Plots and Plausibilities in Women's Fiction," *PMLA* 96 (Jan. 1981): 47.

35. For illuminating perspectives on how conduct books have influenced women's behavior and ideals during different periods of history, including the eighteenth century, see Nancy Armstrong and Leonard Tennenhouse, eds., *The Ideology of Conduct: Essays on Literature and the History of Sexuality* (New York, N.Y.: Methuen, 1987).

36. A fervent disciple of Rousseau's program of maternal nursing, Marie-Jeanne Roland breastfed her daughter faithfully, but only with considerable difficulty. She fell ill, lost her milk, and grew frantic when her baby began to show signs of malnutrition. Eventually, her determination won out. With the help of the *Encyclopédie* and medical manuals, she was able to restore her health through a special diet and to nurse her baby successfully. Her correspondence of the period is filled with detailed accounts of her difficulties. See her correspondence of November 1781 through January 1782, in *Lettres de Madame Roland. Nouvelle série* (1767–76), ed. Claude Perroud (Paris: Imprimerie nationale, 1913), pp. 57–58; 153–55; 164–65; 168–69.

Similarly, the health hazards that nursing posed to some women and children are dramatically illustrated in Staël's novel *Delphine* by the death of Léonce's wife and son. Despite her increasingly weak condition and dwindling milk supply, Mathilde ignores both her doctor's orders and Léonce's pleas and stubbornly persists in breastfeeding her baby—at the urging of her father confessor, who insists it is her duty. (See *Delphine*, Part VI, Letters 3–6 [Paris: editions des femmes, 1981], II: 305–15.) Like Staël's own refusal to nurse, this chapter in *Delphine* contradicts Staël's rather pompous tribute to the Rousseauian ideals of motherhood and maternal breastfeeding in her *Lettres sur les écrits et le caractère de J. J. Rousseau*, in *Œuvres complètes de Madame de Staël* (Paris: Firmin Didot, 1838), I: 12.

37. See Cora Kaplan's discussion of this dual function of women's writing in "The Indefinite Disclosed: Christina Rossetti and Emily Dickinson," in *Women*

Writing and Writing About Women, ed. Mary Jacobus (New York: Barnes & Noble, 1979), p. 64.

38. See Judith K. Gardiner, "On Female Identity and Writing by Women," in *Writing and Sexual Difference*, p. 179: "The maternal metaphor of female authorship clarifies the woman writer's distinctive engagement with her characters and indicates an analogous relationship between woman reader and character." Also see Gardiner's article "The Heroine as Her Author's Daughter," in *Feminist Criticism: Essays on Theory, Poetry, and Prose*, ed. Cheryl L. Brown and Karen Olsen, (Metuchen, N. J.: Scarecrow Press, 1978), pp. 344–53.

39. Hélène Cixous, "The Laugh of the Medusa," in *New French Feminisms*, ed. Elaine Marks and Isabelle de Courtivron (New York: Schocken Books, 1981) p. 249.

Index

References to characters in fictional works are followed by a parenthetical notation of the work in which they appear. Rousseau's works are listed as separate entries. Works by other writers are listed under the author's name. Names containing particles are alphabetized not under *de* or *du*, but under the family name. Fictional characters are generally listed under their first names.